CASES AND MATERIALS

ON

CORPORATIONS

[UNABRIDGED AND CONCISE]

By

WILLIAM L. CARY
Late Dwight Professor of Law,
Columbia University

and

MELVIN ARON EISENBERG
Koret Professor of Law,
University of California at Berkeley

1999 SUPPLEMENT

to

SEVENTH EDITION

By

MELVIN ARON EISENBERG

New York, New York
FOUNDATION PRESS
1999

PREFACE

In the preparation of this edition, the following conventions have been used: Where a portion of the text of an original source (such as a case) has been omitted, the omission is indicated by ellipses (. . .). Material inserted into an original source, for purposes of clarification or style, is enclosed in brackets. The omission of footnotes from original sources is not indicated. For those footnotes that are retained, the original footnote numbers are used.

April 1999

*

ANALYTICAL TABLE OF CONTENTS

TABLE OF CASES

Principal cases are in italic type. Non-principal cases are in roman type. References are to Pages.

1999 Supplement to

CASES AND MATERIALS

ON

CORPORATIONS

*

Chapter I
AGENCY

SECTION 2.   AUTHORITY

Insert the following case at the beginning of this Section, at p. 2 of the Unabridged and Concise Editions, in place of Croisant v. Watrud:

NOTE: CROISANT v. WATRUD SHOULD CONTINUE TO BE USED IN CHAPTER II, SECTION 4 (THE AUTHORITY OF A PARTNER), WHERE IT IS CROSS–REFERENCED AT P. 59 OF THE UNABRIDGED EDITION AND P. 40 OF THE CONCISE EDITION

NOGALES SERVICE CENTER v.
ATLANTIC RICHFIELD CO.
Court of Appeals of Arizona, 1980.
126 Ariz. 133, 613 P.2d 293.

HOWARD, Judge.

The trial below was on Nogales Service Center's (NSC) claim for breach of contract against Atlantic Richfield Company (ARCO). This is an appeal from the judgment entered on a jury verdict in favor of ARCO.   NSC contends the trial court erred in denying certain instructions and in the admission and rejection of evidence.

Prior to June 1969, Albert F. Cafone and Angus McKenzie were produce brokers in Nogales, Arizona.   They decided that profits could be derived from the operation at Nogales of a facility to sell fuel to the great number of trucks which seasonally came to Nogales, loaded with produce to be transported to points in the United States and Canada.   No such enterprise was operating in Nogales at that time.

Before contacting ARCO, Cafone and McKenzie approached Texaco and Shell.   They were looking for a supplier to lend them a large sum of money to be applied towards the construction and equipment of a suitable facility.   They finally contacted ARCO which was itself looking for a truck stop in the area.   Cafone and McKenzie organized a corporation, Nogales Service Center, and entered into an agreement with ARCO for construction of the facility.   The total estimated cost of the facility which was to include an auto/truck service station, coffee shop, motel and brokerage offices, was

1

$508,000. ARCO lent the corporation $300,000 to help finance construction.

Construction of the truck stop began in 1969 and was finished in early 1970. Operations began in April or May of 1970. As originally built, the facility did not include the motel and restaurant, a factor which created a definite problem. The funds which ARCO lent to NSC were not put in escrow and some were spent for a cantaloupe crop which failed, therefore the restaurant was not constructed.

NSC and ARCO also entered into a products agreement on November 4, 1969. It was to be effective for a period of 15 years, subject to termination by mutual agreement after the 10th year, and provided for the sale of fuel at prices to be fixed by ARCO, subject to change by the latter at any time without notice. It called for the purchase of at least 50% of NSC's fuel from ARCO.

NSC's operation was in financial difficulty from the beginning of its operation. Among other things, its price for diesel fuel was not competitive with truck stops in the Tucson area. In May of 1972, Cafone's brother-in-law, William Terpenning, bought out McKenzie and assumed his liability on the $300,000. In July and August, Cafone and Terpenning met in Los Angeles, California with Joe Tucker who was then ARCO's manager of truck stop marketing. The problem of competitive pricing was discussed. It was at these meetings that, according to Terpenning, NSC and ARCO entered into an oral agreement which formed the basis of NSC's claim. Terpenning testified that Tucker told him that the construction of a motel and restaurant at the truck stop was a "must", that if NSC constructed these facilities, which were estimated to cost $400,000, it would lend $100,000; that ARCO would give NSC a 1¢ per gallon across the board discount on all diesel fuel and that it would keep NSC "competitive". In reliance on Tucker's promise, Terpenning bought out Cafone, borrowed money and used his own funds to construct the motel and restaurant. ARCO approved the loan application after the construction was commenced and lent the $100,000 but the 1¢ per gallon discount was disapproved. According to Terpenning, ARCO never made NSC "competitive".

Terpenning and NSC defaulted on the original note and on the $100,000 note. ARCO then brought a foreclosure action and prevailed. This suit involves a counterclaim filed by NSC which was tried after the foreclosure judgment. For convenience in the trial court, NSC, the counterclaimant, was designated the plaintiff and the original plaintiff, ARCO, was designated the defendant.

At trial ARCO contended that Tucker never agreed to make NSC competitive or to give it an across-the-board 1¢ discount; that if such an agreement were made by Tucker it was outside his authority and that the statute of frauds barred any action on the alleged oral contract.

The trial court, without objection, gave the following instructions relating to the authority of an agent:

"An employee-agent has apparent authority to make an agreement binding on his employer-principal, if, but only if, the latter through officers or other agents authorized to do so has held out that employee-agent through [to?] the party dealing with him, has such authority. In this case, in order to find Joe Tucker had apparent authority to make an agreement for ARCO, you must find that ARCO had actually or by necessary implication, represented to the officers of Nogales Service Center that Tucker had such authority; and you must find further that such representations were made by officers or other agents of ARCO having authority from the company to make them.

If you find by a preponderance of all the evidence that such an agreement was made, then you shall consider whether those making it were authorized by their respective companies to do so. An employee-agent can legally bind his employer-principal only when he has actual or apparent authority to do so. Authority of either type, actual or apparent, can be derived only from acts of the employer-principal. An employee-agent cannot confer authority upon himself merely by claiming it for himself. If you find that Joe Tucker had no actual authority to enter into any agreement for ARCO, then he could do so in such a way as to bind ARCO if, but only if, you find that he had apparent authority to make an agreement."

The trial court refused to give the following instruction offered by the appellant:

"Requested Jury Instruction No. 21.

ARCO's employees who dealt with Service Center in the claimed oral agreements made ARCO responsible for any such agreements if they are acts which usually accompany or are incidental to transactions which the agent is authorized to conduct, even if the employees were forbidden to make such agreements, if persons from Nogales Service Center reasonably believed that ARCO's employees were authorized to make them, and has no notice that ARCO's employees were not so authorized."

The trial court also refused appellant's Instruction No. 23, but since we find the essence of that instruction to be covered by Instruction No. 21, we discuss only No. 21.

Appellee contends that No. 21 was covered by the instructions which were given. We do not agree. The instructions given covered only actual or apparent authority. Inherent authority depends upon neither of these concepts since it may make the principal liable because of conduct which he did not desire or direct, to persons who may or may not have known of his existence or who did not rely upon anything which the principal said or did. See, Seavey, Handbook of the Law of Agency, Secs. 58 and 59, at 105–09 (1964).

The Restatement (Second) of Agency Sec. 8A (1957) defines inherent agency power:

"Inherent agency power is a term used in the restatement of this subject to indicate the power of an agent which is derived not from authority, apparent authority or estoppel, but solely from the agency relation and exists for the protection of persons harmed by or dealing with a servant or other agent."

The rationale of inherent agency power is explained in Comment *b* to Sec. 8A:

"The other type of inherent power subjects the principal to contractual liability or to the loss of his property when an agent has acted improperly in entering into contracts or making conveyances. Here the power is based neither upon the consent of the principal nor upon his manifestations. There are three types of situations in which this type of power exists. First is that in which a general agent does something similar to what he is authorized to do, but in violation of orders. In this case the principal may become liable as a party to the transaction, even though he is undisclosed. As to such cases, see Sections 161 and 194. Second is the situation in which an agent acts purely for his own purposes in entering into a transaction which would be authorized if he were actuated by a proper motive. See §§ 165 and 262. The third type is that in which an agent is authorized to dispose of goods and departs from the authorized method of disposal. See §§ 175 and 201.

In many of the cases involving these situations the courts have rested liability upon the ground of 'apparent authority', a phrase which has been used by the courts loosely. If the meaning of the term is restricted, as is done in Section 8, to those situations in which the principal has manifested the existence of authority to third persons, the term does not apply to the above situations. No theory of torts, contract or estoppel is sufficient to allow recovery in the cases. But because agents are fiduciaries acting generally in the principal's interests, and are trusted and controlled by him, it is fairer that the risk of loss caused by disobedience of agents should fall upon the principal rather than upon third persons."

Appellant's offered Instruction No. 21 is a paraphrase of Sec. 161 of the Restatement (Second) of Agency which states:

"A general agent for a disclosed or partially disclosed principal subjects his principal to liability for acts done on his account which usually accompany or are incidental to transactions which the agent is authorized to conduct if, although they are forbidden by the principal, the other party reasonably believes that the agent is authorized to do them and has no notice that he is not so authorized.''

As explained in Comment *b* to Sec. 161, inherent power is to be distinguished from apparent authority:

"The Rule stated in this Section applies to cases in which there is apparent authority, but includes also cases in which there is no apparent authority. Thus, the principal may be liable upon a contract made by a general agent of a kind usually made by such agents, although he had been forbidden to make it and although there had been no manifestation of authority to the person dealing with the agent.''

The rule set forth in Sec. 161 was apparently followed by the court in *Lois Grunow Memorial Clinic v. Davis,* 49 Ariz. 277, 66 P.2d 238 (1937) although the court at times used the term "implied authority'' for inherent authority and confused "apparent authority'' with inherent authority.

Sec. 161 uses the term "general agent''. The Restatement (Second) of Agency defines a "general agent'' as an agent authorized to conduct a series of transactions involving a continuity of service. Restatement (Second) of Agency Sec. 3 (1957). Tucker dealt with the various truck stops accounts in the area of special problems, on matters of investment and discounts. Although the evidence was that he did not have authority to grant the alleged across-the-board discount, he did have authority to grant certain discounts such as volume discounts, gasoline merchandising discounts and dealer temporary aid discounts. On the subject of an agent disobeying the principal it was observed by Judge Learned Hand in the case of *Kidd v. Thomas A. Edison, Inc.,* 239 F. 405 (S.D.N.Y.1917), aff'd, 242 F. 923 (2d Cir.1917) that:

"It makes no difference that the agent may be disregarding his principal's directions, secret or otherwise, so long as he continues in that larger field measured by the general scope of the business intrusted to his care.'' 239 F. at 407.

However, there are two reasons why there was no error in refusing Instructions 21 and 23. First, these instructions conflict with and contradict the instruction given, without objection, which told the jury the agreement was binding only if there was actual or apparent authority. The second reason is the form of objection made to the refusal. It was:

"Plaintiff Nogales Service Center objects to refusal of Instructions 21 and 23 on the grounds that the evidence would support a finding that the agreement sued upon was made within the incidental or ostensible authority of the employees of ARCO who dealt with Service Center. The Instructions are correct statements of the law and are supported by the evidence.''

The first sentence adds nothing to the last sentence. It is a general objection and does not comport with Rule 51(a), Arizona Rules of Civil Procedure, 16 A.R.S. See *Sult v. Bolenbach*, 84 Ariz. 351, 327 P.2d 1023 (1958) . . . .

Affirmed.

RICHMOND, J., and LLOYD FERNANDEZ, Superior Court Judge, concur. . . .

———

Add the following Note at p. 19 of the Unabridged Edition, and p. 15 of the Concise Edition, after the Note on Authority:

NOTE ON DUPUIS v. FEDERAL HOME LOAN MORTGAGE CO.

In Dupuis v. Federal Home Loan Mortgage Corp., 879 F.Supp. 139 (D.Me.1995), Fidelity had made a mortgage loan to Dupuis, and then sold the mortgage loan to the FHLMC, a federal instrumentality. Fidelity contracted with FHLMC to continue servicing the mortgage loan on FHLMC's behalf, pursuant to the terms of FHLMC's Sellers' and Servicers' Guide. Because Dupuis was not notified that the mortgage loan had been sold, FHLMC became the undisclosed principal of Fidelity.

Fidelity took various actions that breached the contract with Dupuis. These actions were prohibited by FHLMC's Sellers' and Servicers' Guide. The issue arose whether FHLMC was responsible for these actions, as Fidelity's principal, despite the fact that Fidelity had neither actual nor apparent authority to take the actions. The court held that the actions could be attributed to FHLMC under the general principles of agency law:

> FHLMC was certainly undisclosed so far as Dupuis was concerned. It is pretty obvious, then, that, if Fidelity was a general agent for FHLMC, FHLMC is liable, as an undisclosed principal, for Dupuis's contract claims. All that *Restatement* section 194 requires in addition is that Fidelity have been authorized to conduct transactions and that Fidelity's actions done on FHLMC's account be ''usual or necessary in such transactions.'' Section 194 makes clear that whether FHLMC authorized or prohibited the specific acts in question is irrelevant. FHLMC hired Fidelity to service loans and mortgages in accordance with the Sellers' and Servicers' Guide, including those of Dupuis. Thus, Fidelity was ''authorized to conduct transactions'' involved in such servicing. Although FHLMC points to provisions of its Guide which, it argues, prohibited Fidelity from treating the Dupuis loan the way it did, Fidelity's acts—done on FHLMC's account—were ''usual or necessary''

acts in a servicing relationship. That is true for the withholding of loan proceeds until the servicer is satisfied that the improvements have been suitably completed; the collection and payment of real estate tax and insurance obligations; the payment of interest on escrowed funds; dealing with a casualty loss on the secured premises and allocation of insurance proceeds for the loss; and negotiating with the borrower to improve the premises in exchange for a further disbursement or a credit against the loan due.

... Plainly, Fidelity serviced this note and mortgage on behalf of FHLMC and in that respect acted as agent. The real issue is whether Fidelity should be treated as a *general* agent. The *Restatement* gives two choices: "general agent," which I have already defined [as "an agent authorized to conduct a series of transactions involving a continuity of services"] (and which produces liability for the undisclosed principal), and "special agent"—"an agent authorized to conduct a single transaction or a series of transactions not involving continuity of service," *Restatement* § 3(2) (and which results in no liability for the undisclosed principal). The commentary states that the distinction between these two categories is "one of degree." Comment a:

> [T]he number of acts to be performed in accomplishing an authorized result, the number of people to be dealt with, and the length of time needed to accomplish the result are the important considerations. Continuity of service rather than the extent of discretion or responsibility is the hall-mark of the general agent. The point at which one becomes a general agent can not be marked with exactitude. One who is an integral part of a business organization and does not require fresh authorization for each transaction is a general agent.

Applying these criteria, I conclude that Fidelity was a general agent for FHLMC with respect to servicing the loans it sold to FHLMC. A huge number of acts must be performed in servicing a loan and mortgage of many years duration. Although only one debtor needs to be dealt with, there are taxing authorities and insurance companies and, in a case like this, potential lienholders who are performing improvements to the property. The length of time is substantial for most home mortgages—here the mortgage term was thirty years. Although FHLMC has argued that its Sellers' and Servicers' Guide posed very severe limitations on what Fidelity could do, the *Restatement* commentary makes clear that "continuity of service" is the key, not the "extent of discretion or responsibility." As servicer, Fidelity became an integral part of FHLMC's administration of its secondary mortgage portfolio. Certainly, fresh authorization was not required for each element of the servicing relationship. Moreover, this was not a one-time event for Fidelity and FHLMC. Fidelity sold 221 loans to FHLMC from 1985 until its bankruptcy and was servicing some 109 loans for FHLMC when it was terminated on October 27, 1992.

I conclude, therefore, that under the *Restatement (Second) of Agency,* Fidelity must be considered a general agent and that FHLMC, as an undisclosed principal, is subject to liability on agency law principles for Fidelity's breaches of contract. I do not profess to understand all the policy reasons for why the *Restatement* drafters reached their liability conclusion for undisclosed principals from common law developments. The commentary unhelpfully states that the rule is an example of "inherent agency power." *Restatement* § 194 cmt. a. *Restatement* § 8A defines "inherent agency power" as a term used to "indicate the power of an agent which is derived not from authority, apparent authority or estoppel, but solely from the agency relation and exists for the protection of persons harmed by or dealing with a servant or other agent." Comment a to section 8A states:

> A principle which will explain [the] cases can be found if it is assumed that a power can exist purely as a product of the agency relation. Because such a power is derived solely from the agency relation and is not based upon principles of contracts or torts, the term inherent agency power is used to distinguish it from other powers of an agent which are sustained upon contract or tort theories.

> Moreover,

> [t]he common law has properly been responsive to the needs of commerce, permitting what older systems of law denied, namely a direct relation between the principal and a third person with whom the agent deals, even when the principal is undisclosed.... It would be unfair for an enterprise to have the benefit of the work of its agents without making it responsible to some extent for their excesses and failures to act carefully.

It seems to be this last factor that justifies the result the *Restatement* principles produce in this case. As a matter of agency law, it would be unfair for FHLMC to have the benefit of Fidelity's servicing of the note and mortgage without also making FHLMC responsible for Fidelity's excesses and failures.

(The court went on to hold that although FHLMC was responsible for Fidelity's actions under the general principles of agency, it was shielded from liability under a federal-law principle that an agent representing a federal instrumentality cannot bind the instrumentality beyond its *actual* authority.)

Chapter II

PARTNERSHIPS

SECTION 10.   LIMITED PARTNERSHIPS

(d) NOTE ON LIMITED PARTNERSHIPS

Add the following cross-reference and Note at the end of Section 10(d), at p. 115 of the Unabridged Edition and p. 72 of the Concise Edition:

INTERNAL REVENUE CODE § 7701 AND REGULATIONS THEREUNDER

[SEE STATUTORY SUPPLEMENT]

NOTE ON THE CHECK–THE–BOX REGULATIONS

Effective 1997, the Internal Revenue Service has swept away the resemblance or characteristics test described in the Note that begins at p. 113 of the Unabridged Edition and p. 70 of the Concise Edition. In place of that test, the IRS has adopted Regulations that, with certain major exceptions, allow partnerships of all kinds, and limited liability companies, to simply elect whether they wish to be treated as partnerships or corporations for federal income tax purposes. Because tax treatment depends on an election, the new Regulations are known as the "check-the-box" Regulations.

Even under the check-the-box Regulations, certain forms of business organizations are locked into corporate-tax status. Among these forms are entities that are organized as corporations under corporate-law statutes, and entities that are taxable as publicly traded partnerships within the meaning of IRC § 7704, which is discussed in the Note that begins at p. 113 of the Unabridged Edition and p. 70 of the Concise Edition.

Chapter III

THE CORPORATE FORM

SECTION 1. DECIDING WHETHER TO INCORPORATE

At pp. 119–20 of the Unabridged Edition and pp. 76–77 of the Concise Edition, the next-last-paragraph of the Note on the Characteristics of the Corporation states five of the conditions for making and maintaining a Subchapter S election. Based on new legislation, change the reference in condition (1) from "thirty-five shareholders" to "seventy-five shareholders" and delete condition (5), concerning nonmembership in affiliated groups.

Insert the following article at p. 124 of the Unabridged Edition, and p. 81 of the Concise Edition, after Keatinge, New Gang in Town:

ROBERT R. KEATINGE, LIMITED LIABILITY COMPANIES AND LIMITED LIABILITY PARTNERSHIPS—A PRÉCIS[1]

History is the progression of revolution becoming orthodoxy. Limited liability companies ("LLCs"), which in the early 1990s were considered an oddity, had, by 1997 become an established alternative business organization.[2] This acceptance has been due in part to significant changes in the federal tax rules dealing with the classification of business organizations for tax purposes (the "Check the Box Regulations") and the adoption of LLC legislation in all fifty states and the District of Columbia. Following closely on LLC, modified

---

1. This section is an update and expansion of Keatinge, New Gang in Town, Limited Liability Companies: An Introduction, 4 Bus. Law Today No. 4 at page 4 (April 1995).

2. According to the Statistics of Income Bulletin, for 1995 tax returns (the most recent period for which statistics are available) there were approximately 1,581,000 partnerships of which approximately 1,167,-000 (with 4,669,000 partners and net in-come of $32.5 billion) were general partnerships, 295,000 (with 10,224,000 partners and net income of $69.4 billion) were limited partnerships, and 119,000 (with 713,000 members and net income of $4.8 billion) were limited liability companies. Timothy D. Wheeler, Partnership Returns, 1995, 17 Statistics of Income Bulletin No. 2 at page 43 (Fall 1997).

forms of general and limited partnerships have also begun to take hold for some businesses. The limited liability partnership ("LLP") and the limited liability limited partnership ("LLLP"), along with the LLC should be considered in any economic endeavor. It is now essential for business organizers to have an understanding of the organization and attributes of these forms of organization. In addition, the first revision since 1914 of the Uniform Partnership Act, law governing general partnerships and certain aspects of limited partnerships, has been adopted by the National Conference of Commissioners on Uniform State Laws ("NCCUSL") and is being adopted or considered in most states.

Limited Liability Companies

Introduction. Over the past five years, the LLC has become universally accepted as a business entity engaged in virtually every type of business from small business ventures to international financial concerns. All states and the District of Columbia now have statutes permitting the organization of LLCs. In addition, many of the federal income tax issues that were of concern to business organizers have been eliminated through the revision of the Treasury Regulations governing the classification of entities.

Definitions. As with any business organization, the LLC has a series of definitions that help in understanding the organization:

> **Limited Liability Company** is an unincorporated organization in which the owners, known as **members**, are not individually liable for the obligations of the organization.

> A **Member** is the owner of an interest in an LLC and a party to the contract (generally known as the **operating agreement**) pursuant to which the LLC is formed.

> The **Operating Agreement** (known, in some states, as "regulations," "limited liability company agreement" or "member control agreement") is the agreement among the members setting forth the rights and duties among the members and between the members and the LLC. Under many statutes, the operating agreement need not be in writing, or need only address certain matters (such as obligations to make contributions and events of dissolution) in writing. Most statutes provide that, with a few exceptions, the operating agreement may establish any rules that the members desire, with the statutes providing "default rules" that govern the LLC where the members have not provided otherwise in the operating agreement. State statutes vary on the matters that must be in writing in an operating agreement. Some require that the entire operating agreement be in writing while most statutes,

following partnership law, permit nonwritten operating agreements to govern all, or all but a few, of the relationships among the members and between the members and the LLC.

The **Articles of Organization** (known in some states as the "certificate of formation") is the document that is filed with the secretary of state of a state at the time of formation of the LLC. The filing of the articles of organization is the action that formally organizes the association as an LLC. The articles of organization contain information on the name and registered agent of the LLC and, under most statutes, contain a statement of whether the LLC will be **member-managed** or **manager-managed.**

Under most statutes, there are two types of LLCs. A **Member–Managed LLC** is an LLC in which members have statutorily granted agency powers, and, except as provided in the operating agreement, authority to participate in management decisions similar to those of partners in a general partnership. Thus, any member in a member-managed LLC has the power to bind the LLC by an action carrying on in the ordinary way the business of the LLC. By contrast, in a **Manager–Managed LLC**, only designated **Managers** (who are not necessarily members) have the authority to bind the LLC, and members, as such, do not have the ability to bind the LLC and often have day to day management authority, with the members having the right to elect managers and approve unusual transactions in a manner similar to that of corporate shareholders.

Contractual Freedom. Unlike many corporation statutes which impose a comparatively strict set of rules on the shareholders, directors, and officers, generally an LLC may be structured in almost any manner that the members select. In fact, some LLC statutes may explicit reference to the legislative intent that operating agreement. This permits the members to select both management structures and financial relationships that accurately reflect their relationships.

The **Single Member LLC.** Most state statutes now permit the single member LLC. A single member LLC is a separate legal entity for state law purposes, but for federal tax purposes will be disregarded as an entity separate from its owner unless it affirmatively elects to be treated as an association taxable as a corporation. As such, the single member LLC provides a powerful tool for segregating liabilities while avoiding having a separate taxable entity.

Partnerships

Introduction. In addition to LLC legislation, the statutes governing other unincorporated business organizations (including partnerships and limited partnerships) has changed dramatically during 1990's. These statutory changes have generally had the effect of enhancing the flexibility and durability of these business organizations and providing more certain statutory rules for the operation of the [business organizations].

Definitions. As with LLCs, there are several definitions that are helpful in understanding the current rules applicable to unincorporated business organizations.

An **Unincorporated Organization** is any association or organization other than a corporation or non-profit corporation. Unincorporated organizations include **general partnerships, limited partnerships, LLPs, LLLPs, and LLCs**. Unlike a corporation which is formed, and then sells shares after incorporation, an unincorporated organization is initially formed by the agreement (the **operating agreement or partnership agreement**) of its owners (or, in the case of a single member LLC, by the will of its sole member) and has owners at the time of organization. Being based on an agreement, the structure of an unincorporated organization is normally more highly dependent on the agreement of the owners than is a corporation, which is normally subject to the comparatively strict rules under state corporation acts.

The **Uniform Partnership Act ("UPA")** was promulgated by NCCUSL in 1914 and had been adopted in every state except Louisiana. In 1994, after several years of work, NCCSL adopted the **Uniform Partnership Act (1994) ("RUPA")** which provided more thorough rules for the operation of general partnerships, has been adopted in several states and is under consideration in most of the others. Both the UPA and RUPA provide rules for the organization, operation, and dissolution and winding up of **general partnerships**. The Revised Uniform Limited Partnership Act ("RULPA"), which was promulgated by NCCUSL in 1979 and significantly revised in 1985, and, to a lesser extent the Uniform Limited Partnership Act, which was promulgated by NCCUSL in 1916, govern the organization, operation and dissolution and winding up of **limited partnerships**, except that the rules governing the rights and duties of general partners in a limited partnership and all matters affecting limited partnerships not expressly addressed by RULPA or the ULPA are governed by the UPA or RUPA as the case may be.

A **General Partnership** is the association of two or more partners to carry on as coowners a business for a profit. The owners of a general partnership known as **general partners** or simply **partners** are each agents of the general partnership for the purposes of taking any action for carrying on in the usual way the business of the partnership and, subject to a contrary provision in the **partnership agreement**, have a right to participate in the management of the partnership. General partners are individually liable to creditors of the partnerships for the debts and obligations of the partnership, and, unless agreed otherwise, have an obligation to the partnership and the other partners to contribute to the losses of the partnership. Partners owe fiduciary duties (which under RUPA are limited to a duty of loyalty and a duty of care) to the partnership and the other partners.

A **Limited Partnership** is a partnership having two partners, including one or more **limited partners** and one or more **general partners**. As noted above, the rights, duties, and liabilities of the general partners in a limited partnership are governed by the UPA or RUPA except to the extent modified by the agreement. A limited partner does not have the right to participate in management to any significant degree under the statute, and, to the extent the limited partner participates in control of management may be liable to third parties who reasonably believe that the limited partner is a general partner as a result of such participation.

The **Partnership Agreement** is the agreement of the partners (including limited partners in the case of a limited partnership) governing the rights and duties of the partners and the relationship among the partners and between the partners and the partnership. Except with respect to certain provisions, such as the obligation to make additional contributions, it need not be in writing. RUPA makes clear that the partnership agreement may modify all but a few of the provisions of the statute governing the relationships of the partners and the operation of the partnership.

A **Limited Liability Partnership** ("LLP") is a general partnership which, by registering with the secretary of state, has modified the individual liability of the partners for the obligations of the partnership. The state statutes vary on the business that may be conducted by LLPs and the degree to which the liability of the general partner is limited. Under some state statutes, general partners remain individually liable for partnership obligations sounding in contract but not in tort. In addition some states limit the use of LLPs to professionals.

Check-the-Box Regulations

Release of final regulations. Final regulations revising the rules for classification of domestic and foreign business entities as corporations or partnerships for federal income tax purposes were released on December 17, 1996.

Prior law. Under prior law, unincorporated entities were classified as partnerships for tax purposes if they lacked at least two of the following four corporate characteristics: centralization of management, continuity of life, free transferability of interests, and limited liability.

Elimination of four factor classification test. In general, Check-the-Box eliminates the four factor classification test and replaces it with an elective test whereby virtually any unincorporated entity may elect to be treated as a partnership or a corporation for federal income tax purposes.

Per se corporations. Under Check-the-Box, certain entities are required to be classified as corporations, and therefore are not eligible to elect to be classified as partnerships. These include entities that are incorporated under state law and an extensive list of foreign entities.

The default rules. Effective January 1, 1997, all newly formed domestic eligible entities having two or more members will be considered partnerships without the need to make an election. Single member domestic eligible organization will be "invisible" for tax purposes (disregarded as an entity separate from its owner). Foreign organization affording limited liability will be considered corporations, while foreign organizations in which a member is liable will be considered partnerships. Except with respect to per se corporations, any eligible entity may elect to be taxed as a corporation or a partnership.

Joint Committee Report (JLS–6–97). In April, 1997, the Joint Committee on Taxation released a report (the "Report") that reviews tax issues relating to entities taxed as partnerships. Among other things, the Report questions "the legal authority for the regulations under the statutory language defining partnerships and corporations, which does not explicitly describe an elective system." The Report suggests that legislation may be necessary to authorize the Check-the-Box Regulations.

Changes in Drafting of Agreements. As a result of Check-the-Box, it may be possible to simplify existing partnership and LLC operating agreements by eliminating provisions that have been included solely for purposes of ensuring that the entity will be treated as a partnership for tax purposes.

Continuity of Life. In many cases, the owners of an unincorporated business might prefer that the business entity have perpetual existence, instead of dissolving upon the occurrence of specified events, such as the death, retirement, resignation, expulsion, bankruptcy or dissolution of a partner or a member. On the other hand, there may be occasions when it remains desirable for an entity to automatically dissolve when the general partner or LLC manager is no longer able to serve, particularly where the replacement general partner or manager may be someone who lacks the approval of the remaining partners or members.

Free Transferability of Interests. There may also be cases where it is appropriate to remove provisions that have been included in the partnership or LLC operating agreement solely to avoid the corporate characteristic of free transferability of interests, such as provisions permitting transfers of only economic interests. On the other hand, in many closely held partnerships or LLCs, it is important that any new partners or members be acceptable to the existing partners or members. Under such circumstances, it may be desirable to retain restrictions on transferability.

Ability to create a pass-through entity with all four corporate characteristics. Under Check-the-Box, it is now possible to create a pass-through entity that possesses all four of the corporate characteristics of limited liability, centralized management, free transferability of interests, and continuity of life. This may be an excellent choice for syndicated businesses in which pass-through tax treatment is important, such as real estate, oil and gas, and start-up businesses. Where such an entity will hold appreciated property, classification of the entity as a partnership is important in order to avoid the corporate tax upon distribution of the appreciated property.

Ability to focus on substantive issues. Check-the-Box will enable practitioners to focus on more substantive issues when drafting agreements, such as the tax impact of partnership allocations and distributions, instead of focusing on the formalities of whether the entity should be classified as a partnership or an association. In addition, Check-the-Box may substantially reduce the expense of drafting a partnership or LLC agreement, especially when the owners of the business desire provisions which in the past may have raised classification issues.

LLCs Soon to Become the Entity of Choice for Family Enterprises. At the time of this writing, many state LLC Acts provide that an LLC will dissolve upon the dissociation of a member unless the business of the LLC is continued by the consent of all or a specified percentage of the members, although several have changed this rule since the adoption of the check the box regulations. Most states allow the members to override such dissolution events by way of express provision in the LLC's operating agreement. For most limited liability companies (and other unincorporated limited liability vehicles) the potential dissolution of the entity upon the dissociation of a member was a necessary evil. Prior to the Check-the-Box regulations, it was tolerated for tax purposes in order to lack the corporate characteristic of continuity of life, but was otherwise disfavored as a threat to the members desire for the LLC to survive a dissociation event. Check-the-Box eliminates the need (at least for federal tax purposes) for state statutes to contain mandatory or default rules which cause a dissolution upon the dissociation event.

As a consequence, many (if not most) states are expected to ᵃnd their statutes to provide that absent a provision in the operating agreement to the contrary, the LLC will not dissolve upon the dissociation of a member. This type of provision combined with a statutory provision which does not give a member the unilateral right to cause the LLC to redeem such member's interest (unless otherwise provided in the operating agreement), should effectively reduce or eliminate concerns that the Internal Revenue Service could use Section 2704(b) [of the estate and gift tax provisions of the Internal Revenue Code] to artificially inflate the value of membership interests for gift and estate tax purposes. LLCs formed pursuant to LLC Acts which contain this type of anti-Section 2704(b) provision will likely be the entity of choice for many family businesses because as compared to an S corporation it is much more flexible. As compared to limited and general partnerships, LLCs provide liability protection to all owners combined with minimal risk of successful challenge from the IRS under Section 2704(b) (if the anti–2704(b) concept is codified).

State Law Considerations. Not all states follow the check-the-box regulations. Accordingly, the State income (and other) tax implications of relying on the check-the-box regulations should be evaluated on a state-by-state basis.

SECTION 4. PREINCORPORATION TRANSACTIONS BY PROMOTERS

(b) Liability of the Corporation

Delete the Note on Clifton & Tomb at p. 148 of the Unabridged Edition and p. 98 of the Concise Edition, and insert the following Note in its place:

ILLINOIS CONTROLS, INC. v. LANGHAM, 70 Ohio St.3d 512, 639 N.E.2d 771 (1994). "The legal relationship between a promoter and the corporate enterprise he seeks to advance is analogous to that between an agent and his principal. Thus, legal principles governing the relationship are derived from the law of agency. ...

"Where an agent purports to act for a principal without the latter's knowledge, the principal may nevertheless be liable on obligations arising from the transaction if the principal later adopts or ratifies the agreement arising from the transaction or receives benefits from the agreement with knowledge of its terms. See 1 Restatement of the Law 2d, Agency (1958), Sections 82 and 98.

This is true even where the principal lacked capacity at the time of the transaction giving rise to the obligation if, after obtaining such capacity, the principal manifests acceptance of the transaction. See id., Sections 104 and 84, Comment d.

"Likewise, a corporation, which is incapable of authorizing an agreement made on its behalf prior to its existence, may nevertheless adopt the agreement after its incorporation. Adoption may be manifested by the corporation's receipt of the contract's benefits with knowledge of its terms. . . .

"A corporation is therefore liable for the breach of an agreement executed on its behalf by its promoters where the corporation expressly adopts the agreement or benefits from it with knowledge of its terms.

. . . It is beyond dispute that the corporation in this case knowingly derived benefits from the agreement executed on its behalf. . . .

"It is axiomatic that the promoters of a corporation are at least initially liable on any contracts they execute in furtherance of the corporate entity prior to its formation. . . . The promoters are released from liability only where the contract provides that performance is to be the obligation of the corporation, . . . the corporation is ultimately formed, . . . and the corporation then formally adopts the contract. . . .

"It is generally recognized that where a pre-incorporation agreement merely indicates that it is undertaken on behalf of a corporation, the corporation will not be exclusively liable in the event of a breach. Under such circumstances the promoters of the corporation remain liable on the contract. See RKO–Stanley Warner Theatres, Inc. v. Graziano (1976), 467 Pa. 220, 355 A.2d 830. . . .

"Formation of the corporation following execution of the contract is a prerequisite to any release of the promoters from liability arising from the pre-incorporation agreement. Inasmuch as the promoter-corporation relationship is based on agency principles, a promoter will not be released from liability if the corporation is never formed, because one may not be an agent for a nonexistent principal. . . .

"Moreover, mere adoption of the contract by the corporation will not relieve promoters from liability in the absence of a subsequent novation. . . . This view is founded upon 'the well-settled principle of the law of contracts that a party to a contract cannot relieve himself from its obligations by the substitution of another person, without the consent of [the] other party.' Ballantine, supra, at 163. See, also, Chapin v. Longworth (1877), 31 Ohio St. 421. Consequently, the promoters of a corporation who execute a contract on its behalf are personally liable for the breach thereof irrespective of the later adoption of the contract by the corporation unless the contract provides that performance thereunder is solely the responsibility of the corporation. . . .

"Under the circumstances presented herein, both the promoters and the corporation are liable under the contract. . . . The corporation is liable because it accepted benefits conferred by the PIA [Pre–Incorporation Agreement] with knowledge of its terms. The promoters are liable because the corporation never formally adopted the PIA, and the PIA does not make the corporation solely responsible for the obligations arising thereunder. . . .

"Inasmuch as both the promoters . . . and the corporation itself are liable, the nature of this shared liability remains to be determined. While our research has failed to discover an Ohio decision which has addressed this specific issue, resort to agency principles is, again, instructive. The relationship between a promoter and a corporation to be formed can be compared to the relationship between an agent and an undisclosed principal. Where a contract is made in furtherance of the interests of an undisclosed principal, both the principal and the agent are liable for breach of its underlying obligations. . . . Under such circumstances, the agent and the undisclosed principal are jointly and severally liable for breach of the agreement. . . .

"We therefore conclude that where a corporation, with knowledge of the agreement's terms, benefits from a pre-incorporation agreement executed on its behalf by its promoters, the corporation and the promoters are jointly and severally liable for breach of the agreement unless the agreement provides that performance is solely the responsibility of the corporation or, subsequent to the formation of the corporate entity, a novation is executed whereby the corporation is substituted for the promoters as a party to the original agreement."

SECTION 6. DISREGARD OF THE CORPORATE ENTITY

Add the following Note at p. 184 of the Unabridged Edition, following the Note on Radaszewski v. Telecom Corp.:

NOTE ON UNITED STATES v. BESTFOODS

In United States v. Bestfoods, 524 U.S. 51, 118 S.Ct. 1876, 141 L.Ed.2d 43 (1998), the Supreme Court analyzed, in an illuminating way, the liability of parent corporations for the actions of their subsidiaries and for their own actions in relation to the conduct the subsidiary's business. The case arose under the Comprehensive Environmental Response, Compensation, and Liability Act of 1980 (CERCLA). Under that Act, the United States may, under certain conditions: (1) use the Hazardous Substance Superfund to finance efforts to clean up pollution from hazardous substances, and then (2) replenish the Fund by bringing suit against "any person who at the time of disposal of any hazardous substance owned or operated any facility" involved in the pollution. The term "owner or operator" is defined, tautologically, as "any person owning or operating" a facility.

Ott Chemical Co.—referred to in the Court's opinion as Ott II—manufactured chemicals at a plant near Muskegon, Michigan, and significantly polluted the soil and ground water by its intentional and unintentional dumping of hazardous materials over a long period of time. From 1956 to 1972, Ott II was a wholly owned subsidiary of CPC International. The United States sued CPC under CERCLA. (Ott II was by this time defunct.) The District Court held CPC liable, but the Sixth Circuit reversed, on the ground that CPC and Ott II maintained separate personalities, and CPC did not utilize the subsidiary's corporate form to perpetuate fraud or subvert justice.

The Supreme Court vacated the Sixth Circuit's opinion, and remanded the case to the District Court for further proceedings pursuant to the Court's opinion. The relevant portions of the Court's opinion follow:

It is a general principle of corporate law deeply "ingrained in our economic and legal systems" that a parent corporation (so-called because of control through ownership of another corporation's stock) is not liable for the acts of its subsidiaries. Douglas & Shanks, Insulation from Liability Through Subsidiary Corporations, 39 *Yale L.J.* 193 (1929) (hereinafter Douglas).... Thus it is hornbook law that "the exercise of the 'control' which stock ownership gives to the stockholders ... will not create liability beyond the assets of the subsidiary. That 'control' includes the election of directors, the making of by-laws ... and the doing of all other acts incident to the legal status of stockholders. Nor will a duplication of some or all of the directors or executive officers be fatal." Douglas 196....

But there is an equally fundamental principle of corporate law, applicable to the parent-subsidiary relationship as well as generally, that the corporate veil may be pierced and the shareholder held liable for the corporation's conduct when, inter alia, the corporate form would otherwise be misused to accomplish certain wrongful purposes, most notably fraud, on the shareholder's behalf.... Nothing in CERCLA purports to rewrite this well-settled rule, either.... [Thus] when (but only 'n) the corporate veil may be pierced, may a parent corporation be charged with derivative CERCLA liability for its subsidiary's actions.

If [CERCLA] rested liability entirely on ownership of a polluting facility, this opinion might end here; but CERCLA liability may turn on operation as well as ownership, and nothing in the statute's terms bars a parent corporation from direct liability for its own actions in operating a facility owned by its subsidiary. As Justice (then-Professor) Douglas noted almost 70 years ago, derivative liability cases are to be distinguished from those in which "the alleged wrong can seemingly be traced to the parent through the conduit of its own personnel and management" and "the parent is directly a participant in the wrong complained of." Douglas 207, 208. In such instances, the parent is directly liable for its own actions. The fact that a corporate subsidiary happens to own a polluting facility operated by its parent does nothing, then, to displace the rule that the parent "corporation is [itself] responsible for the wrongs committed by its agents in the course of its business," *Mine Workers v. Coronado Coal Co.*, 259 U.S. 344, 395, 42 S.Ct. 570, 577, 66 L.Ed. 975 (1922), and whereas the rules of veil-piercing limit derivative liability for the actions of another corporation, CERCLA's "operator" provision is concerned primarily with direct liability for one's own actions.

Under the plain language of the statute, any person who operates a polluting facility is directly liable for the costs of cleaning up the pollution. See 42 U.S.C. § 9607(a)(2). This is so regardless of whether that person is the facility's owner, the owner's parent corporation or business partner, or even a saboteur who sneaks into the facility at night to discharge its poisons out of malice. If any such act of operating a corporate subsidiary's facility is done on behalf of a parent corporation, the existence of the parent-subsidiary relationship under state corporate law is simply irrelevant to the issue of direct liability. . . .

This much is easy to say; the difficulty comes in defining actions sufficient to constitute direct parental "operation." Here of course we may again rue the uselessness of CERCLA's definition of a facility's "operator" as "any person . . . operating" the facility, 42 U.S.C. § 9601(20)(A)(ii), which leaves us to do the best we can to give the term its "ordinary or natural meaning." *Bailey v. United States*, 516 U.S. 137, 145, 116 S.Ct. 501, 506, 133 L.Ed.2d 472 (1995) (internal quotation marks omitted). In a mechanical sense, to "operate" ordinarily means "[t]o control the functioning of; run: operate a sewing machine." *American Heritage Dictionary* 1268 (3d ed. 1992); see also *Webster's New International Dictionary* 1707 (2d ed. 1958) ("to work; as, to operate a machine"). And in the organizational sense more obviously intended by CERCLA, the word ordinarily means "[t]o conduct the affairs of; manage: operate a business." *American Heritage Dictionary, supra*, at 1268; *see also Webster's New International Dictionary, supra*, at 1707 ("to manage"). So, under CERCLA, an operator is simply someone who directs the workings of, manages, or conducts the affairs of a facility. To sharpen the definition for purposes of CERCLA's concern with environmental contamination, an operator must manage, direct, or conduct operations specifically related to pollution, that is, operations having to do with the leakage or disposal of hazardous waste, or decisions about compliance with environmental regulations. . . .

By emphasizing that "CPC is directly liable under section 107(a)(2) as an operator because CPC actively participated in and exerted significant control over Ott II's business and decision-making," 777 F.Supp., at 574, the District Court applied the "actual control" test of whether the parent "actually operated the business of its subsidiary," *id.*, at 573, as several Circuits have employed it. . . .

The well-taken objection to the actual control test, however, is its fusion of direct and indirect liability; the test is administered by asking a question about the relationship between the two corporations (an issue going to indirect liability) instead of a question about the parent's interaction with the subsidiary's facility (the source of any direct liability). If, however, direct liability for the parent's operation of the facility is to be kept distinct from derivative liability for the subsidiary's own operation, the focus of the enquiry must necessarily be different under the two tests. "The question is not whether the parent operates the subsidiary, but rather whether it operates the facility, and that operation is evidenced by participation in the activities of the facility, not the subsidiary. Control of the subsidiary, if extensive enough, gives rise to indirect liability under piercing doctrine, not direct liability under the statutory language." Oswald [, Bifurcation of the Owner and Operator Analysis Under CERCLA, 72 Wash. U.L.Q. 223, 269 (1994)]; *see also Schiavone v. Pearce*, 79 F.3d 248, 254 (C.A.2 1996) ("Any liabilities [the parent] may have as an operator, then, stem directly from its control over the plant"). The District Court was therefore mistaken to rest its analysis on CPC's relationship with Ott II, premising liability on little more than "CPC's 100–percent ownership of Ott II" and "CPC's active participation in, and at times majority control over, Ott II's board of directors." 777 F.Supp., at 575. The analysis should instead have rested on the relationship between CPC and the Muskegon facility itself.

In addition to (and perhaps as a reflection of) the erroneous focus on the relationship between CPC and Ott II, even those findings of the District Court that might be taken to speak to the extent of CPC's activity at the facility itself are flawed, for the District Court wrongly assumed that the actions of the joint officers and directors are necessarily attributable to CPC. The District Court emphasized the facts that CPC placed its own high-level officials on Ott II's board of directors and in key management positions at Ott II, and that those individuals made major policy decisions and conducted day-to-day operations at the facility: "Although Ott II corporate officers set the day-to-day operating policies for the company without any need to obtain formal approval from CPC, CPC actively participated in this decision-making because high-ranking CPC officers served in Ott II management positions." *Id.*, at 559. . . .

In imposing direct liability on these grounds, the District Court failed to recognize that "it is entirely appropriate for directors of a parent corporation to serve as directors of its subsidiary, and that fact alone may not serve to expose the parent corporation to liability for its subsidiary's acts." *American Protein Corp. v. AB Volvo*, 844 F.2d 56, 57(C.A.2), cert. denied, 488 U.S. 852, 109 S.Ct. 136, 102 L.Ed.2d 109 (1988). . . .

This recognition that the corporate personalities remain distinct has its corollary in the "well established principle [of corporate law] that directors and officers holding positions with a parent and its subsidiary can and do 'change hats' to represent the two corporations separately, despite their common ownership." *Lusk v. Foxmeyer Health Corp.*, 129 F.3d 773, 779 (C.A.5 1997); *see also Fisser v. International Bank*, 282 F.2d 231, 238 (C.A.2 1960). Since courts generally presume "that the directors are wearing their 'subsidiary hats' and not their 'parent hats' when acting for the subsidiary," P. Blumberg, *Law of Corporate Groups: Procedural Problems in the Law of Parent and Subsidiary Corporations* S 1.02.1, at 12 (1983), it cannot be enough to establish liability here that dual officers and directors made policy decisions and supervised activities at the facility. The Government would have to show that, despite the general presumption to the contrary, the officers and directors were acting in their capacities as CPC officers and directors, and not as Ott II officers and directors, when they committed those acts.[13] The District Court made no such enquiry here, however, disregarding entirely this time-honored common law rule.

In sum, the District Court's focus on the relationship between parent and subsidiary (rather than parent and facility), combined with its automatic attribution of the actions of dual

---

13. We do not attempt to recite the ways in which the Government could show that dual officers or directors were in fact acting on behalf of the parent. Here, it is prudent to say only that the presumption that an act is taken on behalf of the corporation for whom the officer claims to act is strongest when the act is perfectly consistent with the norms of corporate behavior, but wanes as the distance from those accepted norms approaches the point of action by a dual officer plainly contrary to the interests of the subsidiary yet nonetheless advantageous to the parent.

officers and directors to the corporate parent, erroneously, even if unintentionally, treated CERCLA as though it displaced or fundamentally altered common law standards of limited liability. . . .

We accordingly agree with the Court of Appeals that a participation-and-control test looking to the parent's supervision over the subsidiary, especially one that assumes that dual officers always act on behalf of the parent, cannot be used to identify operation of a facility resulting in direct parental liability. Nonetheless, a return to the ordinary meaning of the word "operate" in the organizational sense will indicate why we think that the Sixth Circuit stopped short when it confined its examples of direct parental operation to exclusive or joint ventures, and declined to find at least the possibility of direct operation by CPC in this case.

In our enquiry into the meaning Congress presumably had in mind when it used the verb "to operate," we recognized that the statute obviously meant something more than mere mechanical activation of pumps and valves, and must be read to contemplate "operation" as including the exercise of direction over the facility's activities. . . . The Court of Appeals recognized this by indicating that a parent can be held directly liable when the parent operates the facility in the stead of its subsidiary or alongside the subsidiary in some sort of a joint venture. *See* 113 F.3d, at 579. We anticipated a further possibility above, however, when we observed that a dual officer or director might depart so far from the norms of parental influence exercised through dual officeholding as to serve the parent, even when ostensibly acting on behalf of the subsidiary in operating the facility. *See* n. 13, *supra.* Yet another possibility, suggested by the facts of this case, is that an agent of the parent with no hat to wear but the parent's hat might manage or direct activities at the facility.

Identifying such an occurrence calls for line drawing yet again, since the acts of direct operation that give rise to parental liability must necessarily be distinguished from the interference that stems from the normal relationship between parent and subsidiary. Again norms of corporate behavior (undisturbed by any CERCLA provision) are crucial reference points. Just as we may look to such norms in identifying the limits of the presumption that a dual officeholder acts in his ostensible capacity, so here we may refer to them in distinguishing a parental officer's oversight of a subsidiary from such an officer's control over the operation of the subsidiary's facility. "[A]ctivities that involve the facility but which are consistent with the parent's investor status, such as monitoring of the subsidiary's performance, supervision of the subsidiary's finance and capital budget decisions, and articulation of general policies and procedures, should not give rise to direct liability." Oswald 282. The critical question is whether, in degree and detail, actions directed to the facility by an agent of the parent alone are eccentric under accepted norms of parental oversight of a subsidiary's facility.

There is, in fact, some evidence that CPC engaged in just this type and degree of activity at the Muskegon plant. The District Court's opinion speaks of an agent of CPC alone who played a conspicuous part in dealing with the toxic risks emanating from the operation of the plant. G.R.D. Williams worked only for CPC; he was not an employee, officer, or director of Ott II, see Tr. of Oral Arg. 7, and thus, his actions were of necessity taken only on behalf of CPC. The District Court found that "CPC became directly involved in environmental and regulatory matters through the work of . . . Williams, CPC's governmental and environmental affairs director. Williams . . . became heavily involved in environmental issues at Ott II." 777 F.Supp., at 561. He "actively participated in and exerted control over a variety of Ott II environmental matters," *ibid.*, and he "issued directives regarding Ott II's responses to regulatory inquiries," *id.*, at 575.

We think that these findings are enough to raise an issue of CPC's operation of the facility through Williams's actions, though we would draw no ultimate conclusion from these findings at this point. Not only would we be deciding in the first instance an issue on which the trial and appellate courts did not focus, but the very fact that the District Court did not see the case as we do suggests that there may be still more to be known about Williams's activities. Indeed, even as the factual findings stand, the trial court offered little in the way of concrete detail for its conclusions about Williams's role in Ott II's environmental affairs, and the parties vigorously dispute the extent of Williams's involvement. Prudence thus counsels us to remand, on the theory of direct operation set out here, for reevaluation of Williams's role, and of the role of any other CPC agent who might be said to have had a part in operating the Muskegon facility.[14]

---

14. There are some passages in the District Court's opinion that might suggest that, without reference to Williams, some of Ott II's actions in operating the facility were in fact dictated by, and thus taken on behalf of, CPC. *See, e.g.,* 777 F.Supp., at 561 ("CPC officials engaged in . . . missions to Ott II in which Ott II officials received instructions on how to improve and change"); *id.*, at 559 ("CPC executives who were not Ott II board members also occa-sionally attended Ott II board meetings"). But nothing in the District Court's findings of fact, as written, even comes close to overcoming the presumption that Ott II officials made their decisions and performed their acts as agents of Ott II. Indeed, the finding that "Ott II corporate officers set the day-to-day operating policies for the company without any need to obtain formal approval from CPC," *ibid.*, indicates just the opposite. Still, the Government is, of course, free on remand to point to any additional evidence, not cited by the District Court, that would tend to establish that Ott II's decisionmakers acted on specific orders from CPC.

Chapter IV

CORPORATE STRUCTURE

SECTION 1. SHAREHOLDERSHIP IN PUBLICLY HELD CORPORATIONS

Add the following Table at p. 253 of the Unabridged Edition and p. 174 of the Concise Edition, after the Note on Shareholdership in Publicly Held Corporations:

NEW YORK STOCK EXCHANGE, SHAREOWNERSHIP 1995, TABLE 12 (1995) [PERCENTAGES OF CORPORATE STOCK HELD BY VARIOUS INVESTOR CATEGORIES IN THE FLOW OF FUNDS ACCOUNTS]

Aggregate Ownership of Corporate Stock, 1952–1994

Year	Households	Bank Personal Trusts	Pensions	Mutual Funds	Foreign	Insurance Companies
1952	89.7%	0.0%	1.1%	3.1%	2.2%	3.4%
1953	88.6	0.0	1.5	3.5	2.2	3.6
1954	89.3	0.0	1.4	3.3	2.2	3.3
1955	88.6	0.0	2.1	3.3	2.2	3.1
1956	88.6	0.0	2.3	3.5	2.2	2.9
1957	87.5	0.0	2.8	3.9	2.2	3.0
1958	87.6	0.0	3.0	4.0	2.1	2.8
1959	86.8	0.0	3.5	4.3	2.2	2.8
1960	85.8	0.0	4.0	4.6	2.2	2.9
1961	85.7	0.0	4.4	4.6	2.2	2.9
1962	84.7	0.0	4.8	4.8	2.2	3.1
1963	84.2	0.0	5.2	4.9	2.2	3.0
1964	84.1	0.0	5.5	4.9	2.1	3.0
1965	83.8	0.0	5.9	5.0	2.0	2.9
1966	83.0	0.0	6.4	5.2	1.9	3.0
1967	81.7	0.0	6.6	5.3	3.1	2.8
1968	81.9	0.0	6.8	5.3	3.0	2.8

Year	Households	Bank Personal Trusts	Pensions	Mutual Funds	Foreign	Insurance Companies
1969	69.1	10.5	8.1	5.5	3.1	3.1
1970	68.0	10.4	9.2	5.2	3.2	3.3
1971	65.9	10.7	10.5	5.5	3.1	3.7
1972	64.1	11.0	11.5	5.1	3.5	4.3
1973	60.4	12.0	12.8	5.1	3.8	5.1
1974	56.1	12.7	15.2	5.4	4.0	5.7
1975	56.7	11.5	16.5	4.9	4.2	5.2
1976	61.8	10.3	14.7	4.1	3.7	4.8
1977	59.0	10.6	16.3	3.9	4.2	5.2
1978	56.9	10.4	18.5	3.7	4.2	5.5
1979	58.7	9.6	18.1	3.4	4.1	5.4
1980	60.9	8.8	17.4	3.1	4.2	5.1
1981	59.0	8.8	18.7	2.9	4.5	5.5
1982	56.1	8.3	21.3	3.3	4.7	5.7
1983	53.5	7.9	22.9	4.1	5.0	5.7
1984	51.4	7.9	24.6	4.6	5.2	5.7
1985	51.3	7.3	24.8	5.0	5.3	5.5
1986	50.6	5.9	25.4	6.1	6.1	5.0
1987	49.8	5.6	25.5	6.9	6.3	5.2
1988	48.8	5.5	26.8	6.5	6.5	5.2
1989	48.0	5.4	27.2	7.0	6.6	5.0
1990	48.6	5.4	27.0	7.1	6.3	5.0
1991	50.8	4.8	26.2	7.7	5.6	4.4
1992	51.4	4.0	25.8	8.7	5.5	4.0
1993	49.7	2.9	25.6	11.5	5.5	4.0
1994	47.7	2.7	25.7	13.6	5.4	4.2

Source: Calculations based on Flow of Funds Accounts, July 1995. Pensions include private and government plans. Mutual funds include closed-end as well as open-end investment companies. Households includes ownership by nonprofit institutions. Insurance companies includes both property/casualty and life insurance companies.

SECTION 2. THE ALLOCATION OF LEGAL POWER BETWEEN MANAGEMENT AND SHAREHOLDERS

Add the following cases at p. 287 of the Unabridged Edition at the end of Chapter IV, Section 2:

WILLIAMS v. GEIER

Supreme Court of Delaware, 1996.
671 A.2d 1368.

JUDGES: Before VEASEY, Chief Justice, WALSH and HART-NETT, Justices, HORSEY, Justice (Retired), and RIDGELY, President Judge, constituting the Court en Banc.　HARTNETT, Justice, and HORSEY, Justice (Retired), dissenting.

This matter was originally heard by a panel of this Court and then was reargued on June 13, 1995 before the Court en Banc, consisting of Veasey, Chief Justice, Walsh, Holland and Hartnett, Justices, and Horsey, Justice (Retired), sitting by designation. . . . Thereafter, Justice Holland recused himself and President Judge Ridgely of the Superior Court was designated to sit. . . .　With the consent of the parties, the matter was submitted for decision on the briefs, without oral argument, on November 28, 1995.　. . .

VEASEY, Chief Justice, for the majority:

In this appeal, we consider whether defendant below-appellee, Cincinnati Milacron ("Milacron"), may validly implement a recapitalization plan (the "Recapitalization") resulting from an amendment to Milacron's certificate of incorporation (the "Amendment").　The Amendment was recommended by resolution of the Milacron Board of Directors (the "Board") and approved by the requisite stockholder vote.　Plaintiff below-appellant, Josephine L. Williams ("Williams"), an individual minority stockholder, brought suit in the Court of Chancery against Milacron and certain members of the Board, challenging the validity of the Amendment and Recapitalization.

The essence of the Recapitalization is to provide for a form of "tenure voting" whereby holders of common stock on the record date would receive ten votes per share.　Upon sale or other transfer, however, each share would revert to one-vote-per-share status until that share is held by its owner for three years.　The Recapitalization applied to every stockholder, whether a stockholder was a minority stockholder or part of the majority bloc.　Williams argues that the Recapitalization disproportionately and invalidly favors stockholders who are part of the majority bloc and disfavors the minority stockholders.　Williams further contends that the sole purpose of the Recapitalization was to entrench Milacron management in office and allow the majority bloc to sell a portion of its holdings while retaining control of the company.

The Court of Chancery granted summary judgment in favor of defendants, holding that Milacron's adoption of the Amendment and Recapitalization was valid.　Specifically, the court held that

Unocal[1] applied, and found that the Board had reasonable grounds to believe that a corporate threat existed and that the Recapitalization was a reasonable response to that threat, there being no improper action or motive. In this appeal, Williams claims that the Court of Chancery erred in analyzing the Recapitalization under *Unocal* rather than *Blasius*.[2] Williams also contends that the trial court incorrectly found that the Board satisfied its burden under *Unocal*. Finally, Williams contends that the stockholder vote approving the Amendment does not validate the Amendment or the Recapitalization.

We AFFIRM the judgment of the Court of Chancery, but on the following grounds: (1) the instant factual situation implicates neither Unocal nor Blasius; (2) the business judgment rule applies to the action of the independent majority of the Board in recommending the advisability of the Amendment to the Milacron stockholders; and (3) since a fully informed majority of the stockholders voted in favor of the Amendment pursuant to the statutory authority of 8 Del.C. § 242 ("Section 242"), the stockholder vote is dispositive.

I. FACTS

Milacron is a Delaware corporation that manufactures machine tools, plastics machinery, computer controls and various other industrial machinery and tools. During the time period relevant to this suit, the Board consisted of ten members—seven independent, disinterested directors[3] who collectively owned less than 1 percent of the common shares outstanding, and three inside directors (deemed not to be independent or disinterested for this purpose) who collectively owned approximately 12.6 percent of the common shares outstanding.[4] With regard to overall share ownership, the Geier family (including the two Geier directors, in-laws and family trusts), together with employee benefit plans owned or controlled in excess of 50 percent of the total voting power of Milacron. We assume, without deciding, therefore, that this group represents a controlling bloc for purposes of this decision.[5] Hence, we will refer

---

1. Unocal Corp. v. Mesa Petroleum Co., Del.Supr., 493 A.2d 946 (1985).

2. Blasius Indus., Inc. v. Atlas Corp., Del.Ch., 564 A.2d 651 (1988).

3. The seven independent, disinterested directors were: Neil A. Armstrong, Chairman of Computer Technologies for Aviation, Inc. and Director of Thiokol Corp., UAL Corp., USX Corp., as well as other companies; Edward W. Asplin, Chairman and CAO of Bemis Co.; Clark Daugherty, retired past Executive Vice President of Dart Indus.; Lyle Everingham, then Chairman and CEO of the Kroger Co.; Donald N. Frey, Chairman and CEO of Bell & Howell Co.; C. Lawson Reed, retired past Chairman of Xomox Corp.; and Joseph A. Steger, President of the University of Cincinnati.

4. The three inside directors were: James A.D. Geier ("Geier") (then Chairman of the Board and CEO of Milacron, as well as a descendant of Milacron's founder), who owned the largest percentage of shares, holding 9.36% of the common stock outstanding; Gilbert Geier McCurdy ("McCurdy") (another descendant of Milacron's founder), who owned 3.06% of the common shares; and Daniel J. Meyer ("Meyer") (then Milacron's Executive Vice President of Finance and Administration), who owned 0.17% of the common shares.

5. But see Shamrock Holdings, Inc. v. Polaroid Corp., Del.Ch., 559 A.2d 278, 290–91 (1989) ("*Polaroid II*") (noting that pension plans do not necessarily vote monolithically).

to the Geier family and the employees and benefit plans collectively as the "Family Group." [6]

Toward the end of 1985, Meyer determined that it would be in Milacron's best interests to develop a recapitalization plan. With that goal in mind, he pursued talks with the First Boston Corporation ("First Boston"). On December 10, 1985, Meyer, along with Geier and several Milacron officers, met with First Boston and Milacron's outside legal counsel, Cravath, Swaine & Moore ("Cravath"), to communicate Milacron's goals and analyze its options. Another meeting followed on January 8, 1986, at which First Boston identified Milacron's objectives as follows:

* Maintain ability to maximize long-term value for shareholders.

* Provide for ability to meet financing needs of corporation without impairing ability of management to maintain focus on long-term values rather than short-term business cycles.

* Protect long-term commitment to continued growth and investment in machine tool business.

* Reduce level of exposure to raiders seeking to capitalize on corporate vulnerability due to short-term business cycles.

* Continue process of diversification away from primary reliance on machine tool business to mix of $\frac{1}{3}$ of revenue and income from machine tools and $\frac{2}{3}$ from other sources.

* Provide Board of Directors with a corporate structure which gives the Board the best opportunity to fairly evaluate and negotiate, in the best interests of all shareholders, any proposal to acquire control of the Company.

In light of these goals, First Boston recommended pursuing a "tenure voting plan," loosely based on the "Smuckers" [7] recapi-

---

6. According to the Proxy Statement for the April 22, 1986 Annual Meeting:

Current and former employees and Directors, employee benefit plans, descendants of the Company's founder, their in-laws and trusts established by them, own or control in excess of 50% of the total voting power of the Company's stock and in excess of two-thirds of the Preferred Stock outstanding. The trustee for the Company's employee benefit plans, which hold approximately 15% of the total voting power of the Company's stock, has informed the Company that, subject to its fiduciary duties, it currently expects to vote shares with respect to which it has not received instructions from employees in favor of the Recapitalization. All officers and directors as a group (21 persons) beneficially own approximately 14% of the total voting power of the Company's stock and are expected to vote in favor of the Recapitalization. Although the Company has not solicited the views of

shareholders, it is also expected that most descendants of the Company's founder and their in-laws will vote shares of the Common Stock and Preferred Stock owned or controlled by them in favor of the Recapitalization. Accordingly, approval of the Recapitalization at the meeting is virtually assured.

Cincinnati Milacron, Inc. Proxy Statement 21 (Mar. 24, 1986) (the "Proxy").

7. The J.M. Smucker Company stockholders adopted a provision whereby existing stockholders would receive ten votes for each share held. These shares would revert to one-vote-per-share status upon transfer and would regain super-voting status only after being held for forty-eight consecutive months. J.M. Smucker Co. Proxy Statement 10–12 (July 25, 1985); see A.A. Sommer, Jr., Two Classes of Common Stock and Other Corporate Governance Issues 1985 (PU Corp. Law & Practice Course Hand-

talization, whereby all shares would be granted multiple votes which would be lost at transfer and then regained by the transferee after holding the shares for a certain period of time.

Pursuant to First Boston's recommendation, Article Fourth of Milacron's Restated Certificate of Incorporation would be amended so that all stockholders owning common stock on the effective date would be entitled to ten votes per share. Upon sale or other transfer of ownership, the voting rights of each share would revert to a single vote per share until such time as the new stockholder held the share for thirty-six consecutive months. If Milacron issued new shares after the effective date, these shares would be treated the same as pre-Recapitalization shares that had been sold or transferred—they would be entitled to only one vote until held for thirty-six consecutive months by the same stockholder. Milacron's officers ultimately decided to pursue the Recapitalization and instructed First Boston to prepare a presentation to be made to the Board.

On January 24, 1986, Milacron management and First Boston presented the Recapitalization to the Board at a special board meeting.[8] First Boston provided the directors with detailed materials focusing on the benefits long-term investors would realize under the Recapitalization, as well as analyses of several other possible recapitalization plans. The Board decided to postpone action concerning the Recapitalization, and agreed to discuss the subject further at its next meeting on February 11, 1986. On March 21, 1986, the Board ultimately adopted a resolution proposing the Amendment and Recapitalization, determining that the Amendment and Recapitalization are "in the best interests of the Company and its shareholders" and recommending a favorable vote by stockholders at the April 22, 1986 Annual Meeting.

Pursuant to 8 Del.C. § 242(b)(1), effectuation of the Amendment required both the Board resolution recommending advisability and approval by the affirmative vote of a majority of the outstanding stock entitled to vote thereon. Accordingly, Milacron sent to stockholders a Notice of Annual Meeting of Shareholders and accompanying Proxy Statement for the April 22, 1986 meeting. The Proxy Statement (the "Proxy") explained that the Board believed the Recapitalization was in the best interests of the stockholders and had the threefold effect of: (1) providing existing and long-term stockholders with a greater voice in the company; (2) permitting issuance of additional shares of common stock with minimal dilution of voting rights; and (3) discouraging hostile takeovers.

book Series No. 498, 1985) (analyzing the policy behind stock exchange voting rules and the interaction of various forms of recapitalization with those rules).

8. All directors attended the meeting except Neil A. Armstrong.

In addition to informing the stockholders of the benefits of the Recapitalization, the Proxy also informed them of possible disadvantages:

(1) if passed, the Recapitalization would "concentrate voting power in the hands of long-term shareholders" including the "descendants of the Company's founder, their in-laws and trusts established by them," Proxy at 16–17; [10]

(2) "the Recapitalization may make [Milacron] a less attractive target for a takeover bid or share accumulation . . ." and, as a result, "approval of the Recapitalization may deprive shareholders of an opportunity to sell their shares at a price higher than that prevailing in the market . . .," Proxy at 15–16;

(3) "if the Recapitalization is approved by the shareholders, the same shareholders who voted to approve the Recapitalization may have insufficient voting power to amend or repeal the Recapitalization at a future date," Proxy at 17; and

(4) if the Recapitalization is approved by less than a 66.7 percent majority, Milacron is likely to be delisted from the New York Stock Exchange ("NYSE"), Proxy at 17–18.

As noted, the Proxy also informed the stockholders that the Family Group owned or controlled in excess of 50 percent of the total voting power, and that, accordingly, "approval of the Recapitalization at the meeting is virtually assured," Proxy at 21.

---

10. Prior to the Recapitalization, the Family Group held over 50% of the outstanding Milacron shares, making it Milacron's controlling stockholder bloc. First Boston prepared an analysis of the relative control the Family Group could expect to exert under the Recapitalization. Assuming 30% of the minority shares were sold, the Family Group would control anywhere from 51.9% if they sold 30% of their own shares, to 59.1% if they held on to all of their shares for a period of three years. Their control would become even greater in the event of a mass minority share sell-off, such as in a hostile tender offer. For example, in a scenario where 70% of the minority shares are sold, the Family Group will control anywhere from 67.3% if they sell 30% of their own holdings, to 73.9% if they do not sell their own shares for a period of three years. Thus, the Recapitalization strengthened the Family Group's "veto" power over any proposed sale of Milacron, and perpetuated the Family Group's control over the election of future directors, even after substantial reduction of Family Group share holdings.

At oral argument, Williams' counsel suggested that the Recapitalization had an immediate dilutive effect upon outside stockholders' voting power. This assertion was based on the fact that all shares held in street name were presumed to be short-term, possessing one vote. Under the terms of the Recapitalization, however, this presumption was rebuttable. By demonstrating that a particular beneficial owner was, in fact, a long-term holder, the shares held in street name would be given full, super-voting power. Thus, any dilution of outside stockholders' voting power came as a result of the inaction of those stockholders. The Family Group did not exercise control over whether the beneficial owners of the shares held in street name would seek to rebut the presumption and attain super-voting status. This was merely an incidental effect, brought about by the logistics of the transaction. Thus, this incidental impact cannot be seen as a non-pro rata or disproportionate benefit accruing to the Family Group. The failure of beneficial owners of shares held in street name to assert their super-voting status increased the relative voting power of all long-term holders, not just the Family Group.

Over 72 percent of the outstanding common stock voted in favor of the Amendment. Assuming all the common stock held by the Family Group voted in favor, of the remaining (presumed unaffiliated) shares present or represented by proxy, approximately 5,858,777 voted in favor and 3,103,608 voted against or abstained. An additional 3,302,759 shares of common stock were not represented at the meeting. This means that there were approximately 6,406,367 presumed unaffiliated common shares that did not vote in person or by proxy or did not vote in favor, compared with approximately 5,858,777 which did vote in favor. Therefore, construing the record most favorably for Williams, the Amendment received less than 50 percent of the votes of all the unaffiliated shares outstanding.

II.   PROCEDURAL HISTORY IN COURT OF CHANCERY

In April 1986, Williams challenged the Recapitalization by bringing suit against Milacron and nine of its directors (collectively, the "Defendants").[13] Williams' complaint purported to state five separate claims as follows: (1) the sole purpose of the Recapitalization was to entrench Milacron management in office and allow the Family Group to liquidate a portion of its holdings while retaining control of the company; (2) the Recapitalization impermissibly creates disparate voting rights within a single class of stock in contravention of established principles of Delaware law; (3) the Recapitalization impermissibly restricts the transferability of Milacron common stock since the transferee may not exercise the full voting power of her shares for a period of three years; (4) the Proxy failed to disclose facts material to a Milacron stockholder's determination of the merits of the Recapitalization; and (5) the Board impermissibly coerced Milacron stockholders into voting for the Recapitalization and thereby breached their fiduciary duties.

Defendants then filed a motion to dismiss the complaint which was granted in part and denied in part. In a Memorandum Opinion dated May 20, 1987, the Court of Chancery permitted Williams to pursue her claim that, in recommending the Recapitalization, Milacron management was motivated solely by a desire to entrench itself in office. The related claim, that the Recapitalization was designed to allow the Family Group to liquidate a portion of its holdings and still retain control of Milacron, was also allowed to proceed. Three of the four remaining claims, including allegations of impermissible creation of disparate voting rights within a single class of stock, improper restrictions on stock transferability and disclosure violations, were dismissed by the court. Williams' remaining claim of substantive coercion was voluntarily dismissed.

After discovery was nearly complete, Williams moved for partial summary judgment as to liability. Defendants cross-moved for

---

13. Williams did not include Donald N. Frey in her suit.

summary judgment.   The Court of Chancery, in an order dated
September 9, 1994, denied Williams' motion, but granted Defendants' cross-motion.   Analyzing the facts under Unocal Corp. v.
Mesa Petroleum, Del.Supr., 493 A.2d 946 (1985), the trial court
found that the Recapitalization was a reasonable defensive measure
in light of the undisputed evidence that the Board carefully considered the Company's long-term needs and its potential vulnerability,
concluding:

> Although plaintiff argues that the real purpose of the recapital-
> ization plan was to allow the Family Group to liquidate some of
> its holdings without losing voting control, the evidence, viewed
> in the light most favorable to plaintiff, does not support this
> claim.   It is true that long-term investors, including the Family
> Group, will be able to maintain their voting power even if they
> sell some of their stock.   However, the fact that a plan has an
> entrenchment effect does not mean that it was so motivated.
> The undisputed evidence establishes that the directors were
> motivated by the good faith belief that long term corporate
> planning would be enhanced by the recapitalization plan.
> Plaintiff's reliance on post-recapitalization stock sales as evi-
> dence of improper motivation, also is misplaced.   The evidence
> establishes that those stock sales were unrelated to the adop-
> tion of the plan.   In particular, Geier stated that tax reasons
> forced the liquidation of a large portion of his deceased par-
> ents' estate including most of its Milacron holdings.

Williams v. Geier, Del.Ch., C.A. No. 8456, at 7 (Sept. 9, 1994)
(order).   . . .

IV.   INAPPLICABILITY OF *UNOCAL* AND *BLASIUS*

Williams begins her attack on the grant of summary judgment
by questioning the trial court's choice of the "more lenient standard
of Unocal" to review the Board's actions, rather than the "heightened standard of scrutiny" used in Blasius Industries v. Atlas Corp.,
Del.Ch., 564 A.2d 651 (1988).   We hold that neither standard is
implicated here because there was no unilateral board action.
Here, there was stockholder approval of the Amendment.   Accordingly, the Board action was not unilateral.   The Board recommended that stockholders vote in favor of the Amendment.   We
must examine, therefore, both the Board action and the validity of
the stockholder approval.   . . .

In *Blasias,* Blasius Industries ("*Blasius* "), the owner of a
substantial block of Atlas Corporation ("Atlas") common stock,
initiated a consent solicitation seeking to amend the Atlas bylaws to
expand the size of the Atlas board from seven to fifteen members.
Blasius, 564 A.2d at 652.   The Atlas board of directors, in an
attempt to preempt the consent solicitation, immediately and unilaterally expanded the size of the board to nine members and filled

the new directorships with its own nominees. Blasius brought an action challenging the validity of Atlas' action. The Court of Chancery held that "when [a board] acts ... for the primary purpose of preventing or impeding an unaffiliated majority of shareholders from expanding the board and electing a new majority," its action "constitute[s] an offense to the relationship between corporate directors and shareholders that has traditionally been protected...." *Blasius,* 564 A.2d at 652. Such disenfranchising actions are not, however, invalid per se. "Rather, ... in such a case, the board bears the heavy burden of demonstrating a compelling justification for such action." *Blasius,* 564 A.2d at 661.[16]

Blasius' burden of demonstrating a "compelling justification" is quite onerous, and is therefore applied rarely. As this Court noted in Stroud v. Grace, Del.Supr., 606 A.2d 75, 92 (1992) ("*Stroud II* "), the application of the "compelling justification" standard set forth in *Blasius* is appropriate only where the " 'primary purpose' of the board's action [is] to interfere with or impede exercise of the shareholder franchise," and the stockholders are not given a "full and fair opportunity to vote."

We can find no evidence to support Williams' claim that the Defendants' primary purpose in adopting the Recapitalization was a desire to impede the Milacron stockholders' vote. The record does not rebut the business judgment rule presumption that the Board acted independently, with due care, in good faith and in the honest belief that its actions were in the stockholders' best interests. See Aronson v. Lewis, Del.Supr., 473 A.2d 805, 812 (1984). According to the Proxy, the directors were motivated by a desire to:

> promote long-term planning and values by enhancement of voting rights of long-term shareholders ... [;] permit the issuance of additional shares of common stock for financing or other purposes with minimal dilution of voting rights of long-term shareholders ... [; and] discourage hostile takeovers and put the Board of Directors in the best position to represent the interests of all shareholders.

Proxy at 14. Plaintiff has submitted no evidence to the contrary.

A *Unocal* analysis should be used only when a board unilaterally (i.e., without stockholder approval) adopts defensive measures in reaction to a perceived threat. *Unocal,* 493 A.2d at 954–55. *Unocal* is a landmark innovation of the dynamic takeover era of the 1980s. It has stood the test of time, and was recently explicated by this Court in Unitrin, Inc. v. American General Corp., Del.Supr., 651 A.2d 1361 (1995). Yet, it is inapplicable here because there was no unilateral board action.

---

16. The Court of Chancery's holding in that case—that a corporate board violates Delaware law when it deliberately acts to frustrate or disenfranchise a stockholder electorate, *Blasius,* 564 A.2d at 661—has been cited with approval by this Court in other contexts. ...

The Court of Chancery did, however, apply a *Unocal* analysis here, finding that a threat to corporate policy and effectiveness existed and that the Recapitalization was a reasonable response to that threat. Specifically, the Court of Chancery found that:

> Milacron's directors were interested in long-term planning and, given the cyclical nature of Milacron's business, they were concerned that the company would be vulnerable during short-term market fluctuations. The reasonableness of the Recapitalization Plan as a defensive measure is established by the fact that the plan achieves Milacron's goals without preventing any stockholder from becoming a long-term stockholder and, thus, obtaining the super voting power.

Williams v. Geier, Del.Ch., C.A. No. 8456, at 6–7 (1994) (order).

The instant case does not involve either unilateral director action in the face of a claimed threat or an act of disenfranchisement. Rather, the instant case implicates the traditional review of disinterested and independent director action in recommending, and the vote of the stockholders in approving, the Amendment and the resulting Recapitalization. Thus, neither *Blasius* nor *Unocal* applies. The Court of Chancery's finding does, however, support the conclusion that the director and stockholder action which effectuated the Recapitalization here "can be attributed to [a] ... rational business purpose." See Sinclair Oil Corp. v. Levien, Del. Supr., 280 A.2d 717, 720 (1971).

V. STANDARD OF JUDICIAL REVIEW OF BOARD ACTION RECOMMENDING THE AMENDMENT TO THE STOCKHOLDERS

The Board's action in recommending the Recapitalization to the stockholders pursuant to Section 242(b)(1) is protected by the presumption of the business judgment rule unless that presumption is rebutted. ...

Williams contends that the action of the Board in recommending the Amendment and Recapitalization to the stockholders constituted either a breach of fiduciary duty or an impermissible effort at entrenchment, both of which are claimed to rebut the business judgment presumption and implicate entire fairness review. We disagree. These contentions are conclusory and have no factual support in this record.

There was on this record: (1) no non-pro rata or disproportionate benefit which accrued to the Family Group on the face of the Recapitalization, although the dynamics of how the Plan would work in practice had the effect of strengthening the Family Group's control;[21] (2) no evidence adduced to show that a majority of the

---

21. See n. 10 supra and the accompanying text for an analysis of the effects of the Recapitalization. In support of its assertion that the Recapitalization disproportionately favors the Family Group, the dissent erroneously suggests that the Recapitaliza-

Board was interested or acted for purposes of entrenching themselves in office; (3) no evidence offered to show that the Board was dominated or controlled by the Family Group;[22] and (4) no violation of fiduciary duty by the Board.

Only by demonstrating that the Board breached its fiduciary duties may the presumption of the business judgment rule be rebutted, thereby shifting the burden to the Board to demonstrate that the transaction complained of was entirely fair to the stockholders. See Cinerama, Inc. v. Technicolor, Inc., Del.Supr., 663 A.2d 1156, 1164 (1995) (*"Technicolor"*); Kahn v. Lynch Communication Systems, Inc., Del.Supr., 638 A.2d 1110, 1115–17 (1994). . . .

Based on the undisputed evidence in this record, we conclude that the Board's action in recommending the Amendment and Recapitalization to the stockholders for approval, pursuant to 8 Del.C. § 242(b)(1), is protected by the business judgment rule. We now turn to the issue of the validity of the stockholder vote.

VI.   THE EFFECT OF THE STOCKHOLDER VOTE

A.   General

The recommendation by a board of directors of the advisability of a charter amendment is merely the first step under the organic, statutory scheme of 8 Del.C. § 242, which authorizes amendments to certificates of incorporation. The second step—the stockholder vote pursuant to which an amendment is approved—must be examined for compliance with the statute, the adequacy of the disclosures advanced to secure the stockholder approval, and compliance with fiduciary duty. In such a situation, "our standard of review is linked to the validity of the shareholder vote." *Stroud II,* 606 A.2d at 83.

Stockholder approval of an organic, statutory change must comply with the statutory procedure and must be based on full and fair disclosure. The burden rests on the party relying on stockholder approval to establish that the approval resulted from a fully

---

tion allows Family Group members to transfer shares among themselves without losing super-voting status. See infra at note 40. As the Proxy reveals, however, no special dispensation is given to Family Group members. Rather, the Recapitalization excludes certain types of transfers from its purview. For example, transfers pursuant to divorce, bequest or gift are deemed not to interrupt the previous owner's tenure, and do not, therefore, cause a diminution in the voting power of the shares transferred. Proxy at 13. The Recapitalization does allow the transfer of shares among Milacron's employee benefit plans without penalty. This is not, however, tantamount to an exclusion of Family Group shares from the effects of the Recapitalization.

22. The mere fact that the Family Group owned a dominant stock interest does not rebut the presumption of the business judgment rule or call the directors' independence into question. See Puma v. Marriott, Del.Ch., 283 A.2d 693 (1971) (where five of nine directors were independent, board approval of transaction with 46% stockholder bloc held governed by the business judgment rule). If domination and control by a majority stockholder is not alleged by particularized facts and supported by evidence, the presumption of independence is intact. See *Aronson,* 473 A.2d at 816–17. That is this case.

informed electorate and that all material facts relevant to the transaction were fully disclosed. . . .

We put to one side those cases, not relevant here, where stockholders are called upon to ratify action which may involve a transaction with an interested director or where the transaction approved by the board may otherwise be voidable.[23] . . .

Our analysis here involves an entirely different application of the Delaware General Corporation Law—namely, the effect of corporate action which, in order to become operative, requires and receives both approval by the board of directors and the stockholders. Three examples are common: amendments to the certificate of incorporation (8 Del.C. § 242); mergers or consolidations of domestic corporations (8 Del.C. § 251); and sales of all or substantially all of a corporation's assets (8 Del.C. § 271, which permits a sequence that may vary from the sequences applicable to amendments or mergers). There are, of course, other examples. . . .

B.　Applicability of Existing Law to this Case

We find that *Stroud II* is applicable here. In *Stroud II*, this Court held that the stockholder vote, being both fully informed and devoid of any fraud, waste, manipulative or other inequitable conduct, effectively implemented the board recommendations adopting amendments to the certificate of incorporation and approving a bylaw change, both of which allegedly benefited the incumbent controlling majority. *Stroud II*, 606 A.2d at 83. The presence of a controlling majority stockholder did not undermine the validity of the stockholder vote.

In the instant case, like *Stroud II*, the Board recommended the advisability of the Amendment to the stockholders who voted in favor of the Amendment. On its face, therefore, the corporate action was authorized and regular. Stockholders (even a controlling stockholder bloc) may properly vote in their own economic interest, and majority stockholders are not to be disenfranchised because they may reap a benefit from corporate action which is regular on its face. As we stated in *Stroud II*:

> The fact that controlling shareholders voted in favor of the transaction is irrelevant as long as they did not breach their fiduciary duties to the minority holders. *Unocal*, 493 A.2d at

---

23. Transactions which are voidable, as distinct from those which are void, may in some circumstances, be ratified.

The key to upholding an interested transaction is the approval of some neutral decision-making body. Under 8 Del.C. § 144, a transaction will be sheltered from shareholder challenge if approved by either a committee of independent directors, the shareholders, or the courts.

Oberly v. Kirby, Del.Supr., 592 A.2d 445, 467 (1991); *Technicolor*, 663 A.2d at 1170; see also In re Wheelabrator Technologies, Inc., Shareholders Litig., Del.Ch., 663 A.2d 1194, 1202 (1995) (noting some such circumstances and concluding that stockholder ratification may not extinguish a "duty of loyalty claim"). . . .

958; Bershad, 535 A.2d at 845; see Ringling Bros.–Barnum & Bailey Combined Shows, Inc. v. Ringling, Del.Supr., 29 Del.Ch. 610, 53 A.2d 441, 447 (1947).

Stroud II, 606 A.2d at 83–84. . . .

Like the statutory scheme relating to mergers under 8 Del.C. § 251, it is significant that two discrete corporate events must occur, in precise sequence, to amend the certificate of incorporation under 8 Del.C. § 242: First, the board of directors must adopt a resolution declaring the advisability of the amendment and calling for a stockholder vote. Second, a majority of the outstanding stock entitled to vote must vote in favor. The stockholders may not act without prior board action. Likewise, the board may not act unilaterally without stockholder approval. Therefore, the stockholders control their own destiny through informed voting. This is the highest and best form of corporate democracy.[28]

C. No "Majority of Minority" Vote Required

In support of her claim that the stockholder vote is ineffective, Williams points to Fliegler v. Lawrence, Del.Supr., 361 A.2d 218 (1976), a case in which this Court held that a stockholder vote to validate an interested director transaction under 8 Del.C. § 144 requires that the approval must come from a majority of the disinterested stockholders. Clearly, Fliegler does not apply here where there was an independent board and no interested director transaction.[29]

There is no requirement under the Delaware General Corporation Law that a majority of the outstanding minority shares must vote in favor of a transaction which benefits the majority. The issue of the role of a "majority of the minority" vote must be clearly understood. Where, as here, there is a controlling stockholder or a controlling bloc, there is no requirement under the Delaware General Corporation Law that the transaction be structured or conditioned so as to require an affirmative vote of a majority of the minority group of outstanding shares. See Rosenblatt v. Getty Oil Co., Del.Supr., 493 A.2d 929, 937 (1985). In those parent-subsidiary situations where the circumstances call for an entire fairness analysis, the burden is normally on the defendants to show entire

---

28. Absent fraud, waste, manipulative or inequitable conduct or other breach of fiduciary duty, a majority stockholder bloc, like the Family Group here, has broad legitimate powers. Of course, the corporate action must have a rational corporate purpose, Sinclair, 280 A.2d at 720, and may not be taken for the sole or primary purpose of entrenchment. Johnson v. Trueblood, 3rd Cir., 629 F.2d 287, 293 (1980). . . .

29. The statutory scheme in *Fliegler* was based upon 8 Del.C. § 144—the inter-

ested director transaction statute. In the case at bar, an entirely different statutory scheme is involved—namely, an amendment to the certificate of incorporation under 8 Del.C. § 242. Those are two statutory frameworks of independent legal significance. See Orzeck v. Englehart, Del. Supr., 41 Del.Ch. 361, 195 A.2d 375, 377 (1963); Heilbrunn v. Sun Chemical Corp., Del.Supr., 38 Del.Ch. 321, 150 A.2d 755, 757–59 (1959).

fairness, but if a majority of the minority votes in favor under certain circumstances, the burden shifts to the plaintiff to show unfairness. Id.; see also *Kahn,* 638 A.2d at 1116–17. The converse does not apply, however—namely, the failure to obtain a majority of the minority does not give rise to any adverse inference of invalidity. Moreover, in a case such as the case at bar where entire fairness is not an issue, the question of whether a majority of the minority was obtained is simply irrelevant. . . .

E.   Whether the Result of the Stockholder Vote was "Fair" to the Minority

Williams contends that the Family Group—due solely to their majority status—benefited from the Amendment and the Recapitalization to a disproportionately greater extent than the minority stockholders. Accordingly, she contends that the Family Group breached its duty of loyalty to the minority, thus requiring that the majority show entire fairness. See *Technicolor,* 663 A.2d at 1162–63. But this argument is misplaced. In Technicolor, the business judgment rule was rebutted by the Chancellor's findings that the board of directors acted without the requisite care. When the presumption of the business judgment rule is rebutted either because the board lacked independence (as in Kahn v. Lynch and Nixon v. Blackwell, for example) or because of lack of due care (as in Technicolor), the burden shifts to the defendants to show entire fairness (fair dealing and fair price). That is not the case here. The Milacron board was independent and acted with the requisite care. There were no disclosure violations. Therefore, the entire fairness inquiry articulated in Technicolor simply has no application here, and plaintiff's reliance thereon is misplaced.

As in *Stroud II,* the stockholder vote in favor of the Amendment "was fully informed, and in the absence of any fraud, waste, manipulative or other inequitable conduct, that should have ended the matter on basic principles of ratification." Stroud II, 606 A.2d at 92. Strict compliance with the statutory scheme laid out in 8 Del.C. § 242(b)(1) will not protect a corporate act if that act involved the excepted misconduct articulated in *Stroud II.* As we stated in Schnell v. Chris–Craft Industries, Inc., Del.Supr., 285 A.2d 437, 439 (1971), for example, "inequitable action does not become permissible simply because it is legally possible." There is no basis for a finding here that the Amendment and Recapitalization involved waste, fraud, or manipulative or other inequitable conduct. Likewise, there is no showing either that the Recapitalization lacked a rational business purpose or that its sole or primary purpose was entrenchment. The burden is on the plaintiff to prove these outer limits on corporate behavior, and plaintiff has not sustained her burden. . . .

Accordingly, the judgment of the Court of Chancery granting summary judgment to defendants is AFFIRMED.

HARTNETT, Justice, and HORSEY, Justice (Retired), dissenting: ...

I.

We believe the action of the Milacron Board in instituting and recommending adoption of the Recapitalization Plan implicates the duty of loyalty and, therefore, must be subject to full judicial scrutiny, not to judicial deference because of the business judgment rule. The Board's stated reason for the Plan is not dispositive, given the Plan's conceded effect: to confer substantial benefits on the majority shareholders, the Geier Family Group, without conferring similar benefits upon the minority shareholders having equally legitimate, but differing, investment objectives.

The shareholders were informed by the Proxy that shareholder approval of the Plan was "virtually assured." (Footnote 6, majority opinion.) We, therefore, do not believe that the Board's submission of the Recapitalization Plan to the shareholders, pursuant to 8 Del.C. § 242, and the approval of it by the same majority shareholders who are the beneficiaries of the Plan lessens judicial scrutiny into the reasonableness of the Plan and its fairness to the minority shareholders.

Even if the shareholder vote was voluntary (which it was not), it would have merely accorded the Plan a presumption of fairness. The Court of Chancery still had a duty to determine whether the power exercised by the Board was oppressive to the minority. See Davis v. Louisville Gas & Electric Co., Del.Ch., 16 Del.Ch. 157, 142 A. 654 (1928); Bailey v. Tubize Rayon Corp., D.Del., 56 F.Supp. 418 (1944).

II.

The majority's reliance on Stroud v. Grace, Del.Supr., 606 A.2d 75 (1992), to preclude or lessen judicial review of the Plan is misplaced. In the present case, the Geier Family Group are the controlling shareholders of a public corporation. The proposed Plan significantly alters shareholder voting rights to the detriment of those minority shareholders who have no interest in preserving the family ownership, or whose investment objectives may have a different time frame from the Family Group. *Stroud* involved a private, closely held corporation that sought to have adopted a "right of first refusal" charter amendment commonly used by such corporations to preclude the transfer of shares to outsiders. Milacron's status as a public corporation does not permit the Court of Chancery to merely defer to the text of the Recapitalization Plan which has the ultimate effect of turning a public corporation into a de facto close corporation.

In *Stroud* this Court relied upon a shareholder vote to cure otherwise suspect board actions involving charter amendments commonly adopted by close corporations. The court found that "in the absence of fraud, a fully informed stockholder vote in favor of even a 'voidable' transaction ratifies board action and places the burden of proof on the challenger." *Stroud,* 606 A.2d at 83.

In the present case, however, the charter amendments worked fundamental changes in the governance of Milacron, as the Proxy concedes. The Recapitalization Plan's ultimate effect will be to confer upon the Geier Family shareholders control not only over the future composition of the Board, but over the strategic long-term planning of the company. A coerced shareholder vote which received the approval of less than 50 percent of the votes of all the unaffiliated [non-Geier Family] shares outstanding cannot be deemed to be a shareholder approval that lessens judicial scrutiny as to the fundamental fairness of the Plan. In our opinion, for there to be a vote that cures a defect . . . the vote must be free from coercion, that is, the shareholder action must be meaningful and voluntary. . . .

Here the minority stockholders were faced with two significant disclosures in the Proxy: (1) the adoption of the Recapitalization Plan was "virtually assured" of approval because of the votes of the Geier Family (the proposers of, and the prime beneficiaries of, the Plan), and (2) the adoption of the proposed Charter Amendment could result in a de-listing of Milacron stock from the New York Stock Exchange unless it was ratified by an affirmative vote of ⅔ of all the shares. The minority stockholders, therefore, had no real choice. Nor did a majority of the minority apparently vote for the Plan.[38] . . . Notwithstanding that the shareholder vote was legally sufficient to meet the requirements of 8 Del.C. § 242, the burden of persuasion to show the unfairness of the Plan was not shifted to the minority shareholders. See Schnell v. Chris–Craft Indus., Inc., Del.Supr., 285 A.2d 437, 439 (1971).

III.

In our opinion, the Board's decision proposing and recommending the adoption of the Recapitalization Plan should be subject to a heightened level of judicial scrutiny, under the rationale of *Unocal,* 493 A.2d 946, or *Blasius,* 564 A.2d 651, or both. When the voting rights of minority stockholders are changed without their consent, there is the omnipresent specter of inherent conflict between a board's duty to all the stockholders and the desires of the block of stockholders holding a majority of the shares. This conflict is similar to the conflict that existed in *Unocal.*

Although an action diminishing a shareholder's vote is not invalid, per se, the right of an individual stockholder to exercise the voting rights of its shares is a fundamental corporate right. Tanzer v. Int'l Gen. Indus., Inc., Del.Supr., 379 A.2d 1121, 1123 (1977);

---

38. If the Charter Amendment had been put to a separate vote of the minority shareholders they would have had an operative choice and, presumably, an affirmative vote would have relieved the Board of its burden of defending the Plan. See Citron v. E.I. Du Pont de Nemours & Co., Del.Ch., 584 A.2d 490, 500 (1990).

Wylain, Inc. v. TRE Corp., Del.Ch., 412 A.2d 338, 344 (1979); Aprahamian v. HBO & Co., Del.Ch., 531 A.2d 1204 (1987); Blasius, 564 A.2d at 659 n. 2 (1988). The right of franchise must not be diluted except where reasonably necessary to accomplish an appropriate corporate business policy. Id.

If the Milacron Board's purpose was to reduce the voting power of the minority shareholders or to increase the voting strength of the Geier Family Group shares, then the Board's action must pass the "compelling justification" standard of scrutiny articulated in *Blasius; Stroud,* 606 A.2d at 92 n. 3. As the majority concedes, the Board's duties were not fulfilled merely by blind compliance with the technical mandates of 8 Del.C. § 242. See *Schnell,* 285 A.2d at 439.

The Court of Chancery's determination that the "compelling justification" standard of *Blasius* was not implicated was apparently based on its conclusory finding that "the recapitalization plan does not interfere with voting rights so as to preclude effective stockholder action." This, however, is contradicted by the Court of Chancery's finding that the Plan has an entrenchment effect. The Court of Chancery's finding of the inevitability of the entrenchment of the Geier Family shareholders in the control of Milacron's future is an indisputable fact fully supported by the record through the Proxy Statement, and acknowledged by the Majority's Opinion at slip op. 11–12 and footnote 20. Hence, the Majority's conclusion to the contrary, at slip op. 24, is not supported by the record. Because the primary issue is shareholder entrenchment, the directors' motivation and good faith are not dispositive. . . .

From a review of the entire record, we are convinced that, notwithstanding the self-serving denials of the proponents of the Plan, its effect on shareholders' voting rights was clearly substantial rather than incidental. The Court of Chancery, in our view, should have held an evidentiary hearing to determine if the Recapitalization Plan has a negative effect on the minority shares and to determine whether the primary purpose of the Plan was to assure the continual control of the corporation by the Geier Family members while permitting them to sell some of their shares.

If the Court of Chancery found these factors existed, it should have reviewed the Plan under the *Blasius* compelling justification standard.

IV.

In *Stroud,* this Court described the relationship between the tests articulated in *Blasius* and *Unocal* and stated that these tests are not mutually exclusive. *Stroud,* 606 A.2d at 92, n.3. Although the Court of Chancery improperly, in our view, rejected the "compelling justification" standard of *Blasius,* unlike the majority, we believe that it correctly found that the action of the Board in adopting the Recapitalization Plan was subject to the heightened judicial scrutiny mandated by *Unocal.* A court must apply the enhanced scrutiny test set forth in *Unocal* whenever the board "adopts any defensive measure taken in response to some threat to corporate policy and effectiveness which touches upon issues of control." Gilbert v. El Paso Co., Del.Supr., 575 A.2d 1131, 1144 (1990).

If the purpose of the Recapitalization Plan was defensive, so as to eliminate challenges to control from hostile acquisition offers or proxy contests, as the Proxy suggests, the *Unocal* standard is triggered, as the Court of Chancery properly found. In conducting its *Unocal* analysis, however, the Court of Chancery failed to recognize that genuine issues of material fact existed that precluded its finding that the Recapitalization was a reasonable response to a perceived corporate threat.

From a review of the entire record, we are convinced that there are several disputed issues of fact that must be resolved before the *Unocal* heightened judicial scrutiny as to the proportionality and reasonableness of the Recapitalization Plan can be completed.[40] Among them are: 1) whether the primary purpose of the Recapitalization Plan was to disenfranchise the non-Geier Family shares; 2) whether the Plan's purpose was to substantially reduce the value and marketability of those shares; and 3) whether the primary purpose of the Plan was to enable the Geier Family members to dispose of a substantial portion of their shares and still retain control of the corporation.

Lastly, we find nothing in the text of 8 Del.C. § 242(b)(1) that precludes the Court of Chancery from exercising judicial oversight over a Recapitalization Plan with such a disproportionate effect on the minority shares. . . .

We believe, therefore, that the case should be remanded to the Court of Chancery for a limited evidentiary hearing to resolve the remaining issues of material fact and for a meaningful review of the Recapitalization Plan in which the proponents of the Plan bear the burden of showing its fairness and reasonableness to the minority shareholders. After resolving the disputed factual issues, the Court of Chancery would be in a position to decide whether the review should be conducted under the enhanced standard of review of *Unocal* or *Blasius.*

---

40. An example of how the Recapitalization Plan was structured to favor the Geier Family shareholders is the Plan's provision that a transfer of shares will cause a reversion of the voting rights from 10 votes per share to a single vote per share for 36 consecutive months after a transfer. This provision will not apply, however, to shares of stock given by members of the Geier family to other family members.

INTERNATIONAL BROTHERHOOD OF TEAMSTERS v. FLEMING COMPANIES, INC.

Supreme Court of Oklahoma, 1999.
___ P.2d ___, 1999 WL 35227.

. . . SIMMS, J.:

The United States Court of Appeals, Tenth Circuit, John C. Porfilio, Presiding Judge, pursuant to 20 O.S. [Oklahoma Statutes] 1991, § 1601, certified to the Oklahoma Supreme Court the following question of law:

Does Oklahoma law [A] restrict the authority to create and implement shareholder rights plans exclusively to the board of directors, or [B] may shareholders propose resolutions requiring that shareholder rights plans be submitted to the shareholders for vote at the succeeding annual meeting?

We answer the first part of the question in the negative and the second part affirmatively. We hold under Oklahoma law there is no exclusive authority granted boards of directors to create and implement shareholder rights plans, where shareholder objection is brought and passed through official channels of corporate governance. We find no Oklahoma law which gives exclusive authority to a corporation's board of directors for the formulation of shareholder rights plans and no authority which precludes shareholders from proposing resolutions or bylaw amendments regarding shareholder rights plans. We hold shareholders may propose bylaws which restrict board implementation of shareholder rights plans, assuming the certificate of incorporation does not provide otherwise.

The International Brotherhood of the Teamsters General Fund [Teamsters] owns sixty-five shares of Fleming Companies, Inc. [Fleming or the company] stock. In 1986, Fleming implemented a shareholder's rights plan with the term of the plan to expire in 1996. The rights plan implemented by Fleming is an anti-takeover mechanism. Such plans give boards of directors authority to adopt and execute discriminatory shareholder rights upon the occurrence of some triggering event, usually when a certain percentage of shares has been amassed by a single shareholder. A board can place "restrictions or conditions on the exercise, transfer or receipt of" shareholder rights which can severely dilute the shareholding power of one seeking control of a company.[1] The defensive plans usually result in entrenching existing management, making a takeover without the approval of incumbent management more difficult. These rights plans can make it far more expensive to effect a takeover. Because the rights plans make the merger of companies more painful for the suitor and assist incumbent management in maintaining control, the plans are often called "poison pill rights plans" or "poison pills."

---

1. John H. Matheson & Brent A. Olson, Shareholder Rights and Legislative Wrongs; Toward Balanced Takeover Legislation, 59 Geo.Wash.L.Rev. 1425, 1450 (1990).

From a target company's perspective, rights plans can often buy valuable time to implement merger strategy or even secure more lucrative offers from other suitors. In this context, a rights plan might serve not only the protectionist objectives of an existing management, but also the company's overall interests in the event of takeover, including the interests of shareholders.

However, rights plans can often stifle mergers, causing some shareholder groups to view them with increasing skepticism, because, company mergers can be financially lucrative for shareholders who own stock in a target company. A poison pill not only makes many mergers cost prohibitive and therefore might prevent a merger altogether, but it can decrease the profits in those mergers which do ultimately occur. As a result, poison pills have the ability to strip shareholders of financial benefit which might normally be associated with a takeover.

The stock market has had a long history of shareholder passivity, but this is likely a thing of the past. The rise of the institutional investor and the increased knowledge of stockholders as a whole is forcing an increased accountability to shareholders for many boards of directors. As a result, the demands of the Teamsters in its case against Fleming is something courts may encounter with increasing frequency in the years to come.

The trial court, which ruled in the Teamsters' (shareholders) favor, expressed concern with Fleming's position, stating that it effectively removed corporate authority regarding share marketability from the shareholders and vested it exclusively in a board of directors, which might view the situation from the most self-interested point of view.

Teamsters were critical of Fleming's rights plan, seeing it as a means of entrenching the current Fleming board of directors in the event Fleming became the target of a takeover. In 1996, the Teamsters organized and introduced a non-binding resolution for the annual shareholders meeting. The 1996 resolution called on the Fleming board to redeem the existing rights plan. The then current rights plan had been in effect since 1986 and was scheduled for renewal. The Teamsters proposal was met with apparent hostility from Fleming's board and the rights plan remained intact, despite a majority shareholder vote in agreement with the Teamsters' resolution to redeem it.

The following year, 1997, Teamsters mounted a more organized effort to change the continued implementation of the rights plan. Teamsters prepared a proxy statement for inclusion in the proxy materials for the 1997 annual shareholder's meeting. With the proxy effort, the Teamsters proposed an amendment to the company's bylaws which would require any rights plan implemented by the board of directors to be put to the shareholders for a majority vote.[3] The proposal was essentially a ratification procedure wherein the shareholders would force the board to formulate a rights plan both the board and shareholders could agree on or do away with such a plan altogether.

Fleming refused to include the resolution in its 1997 proxy statement, declaring the proposal was not a subject for shareholder action under Oklahoma law. Teamsters then brought an action in the Federal District Court for the Western District of Oklahoma. The district court ruled in favor of the Teamsters, the court finding that "shareholders, through the device of bylaws, have a right of review."[4] Fleming appealed to the 10th Circuit Court of Appeals, which submitted the certified question to this Court.

Fleming sought to postpone any shareholder vote on the 1997 proxy issue until after the resolution of this case. But the U.S. District Court and later the 10th Circuit denied Fleming's motion to suspend the injunction. Fleming was then forced to allow its shareholders to vote on the Teamsters' proxy. The Teamsters' resolution passed with approximately 60% of the voted shares.

Fleming's position is that 18 O.S.1991 § 1038 gives the board of directors authority to create and issue shareholder rights plans, subject only to limits which might exist in the corporation's certificate of incorporation; and that shareholders cannot through bylaws restrict the board's powers to implement a rights plan.[5] The Team-

---

3. The 1997 proxy proposal provided:

Resolved, That shareholders hereby exercise their right under 18 O.S.A. Sec. 1013 to amend the bylaws of Fleming Companies, Inc. to add the following Article:

Article X
Poison Pills (Shareholder Rights Plans)

A. The Corporation shall not adopt or maintain a poison pill, shareholder rights plan, rights agreement or any other form of "poison pill" which is designed to or has the effect of making acquisition of large holdings of the Corporation's shares of stock more difficult or expensive (such as the 1986 "Rights Agreement"), unless such plan is first approved by a majority shareholder vote. The Company shall redeem any such rights now in effect. The affirmative vote of a majority of shares voted shall suffice to approve such a plan.

B. This article shall be effective immediately and automatically as of the date it is approved by the affirmative vote of the holders of a majority of the shares, present, in person or by proxy at a regular or special meeting of shareholders.

C. Notwithstanding any other provision of these bylaws, this Article may not be amended, altered, deleted or modified

in any way by the Board of Directors without prior shareholder approval.

4. Transcript of Oral Arguments, District Court's oral ruling, January 14, 1997, p. 31.

5. 18 O.S.1991 § 1038:

Rights and options respecting stock. Subject to any provisions in the certificate of incorporation, every corporation may create and issue, whether or not in connection with the issue and sale of any shares of stock or other securities of the corporation, rights or options entitling the holders thereof to purchase from the corporation any shares of its capital stock of any instrument or instruments as shall be approved by the board of directors. The terms upon which, including the time or times, which may be limited or unlimited in duration, at or within which, and the price or prices at which any such shares may be purchased from the corporation upon the exercise of any such right or option, shall be such as shall be stated in the certificate of incorporation, or in a resolution adopted by the board of directors providing for the creation and issue of such rights or options, and, in every case, shall be set forth or incorporat-

sters' position is that 18 O.S.1991 § 1013 gives shareholders of a publicly traded corporation, such as Fleming, the authority to adopt bylaws addressing a broad range of topics from a corporation's business, corporate affairs, and rights and powers of shareholders and directors.[6] It is this apparent conflict which brings this federal certified question to this Court.

This is a case of first impression in Oklahoma and there is little guidance from other states. Oklahoma and Delaware have substantially similar corporation acts, especially with regard to Title 18, §§ 1013 & 1038 which are of primary concern here. 8 Del.C. § 109(a) & (b); 8 Del.C. § 157. However, a review of Delaware decisions revealed no comparable case from that state.

The 10th Circuit's question is ultimately one of corporate governance and what degree of control shareholders can exact upon the corporations in which they own stock.

In the scheme of corporate governance the role of shareholders has been purposefully indirect. Shareholders' direct authority is limited. State ex rel. Oklahoma Employment Sec. Comm'n v. First Nat'l Bank of Texoma, 197 Okla. 652, 174 P.2d 259 (1946); State ex rel. Oklahoma Employment Sec. Comm'n v. Tulsa Flower Exch., 192 Okla. 293, 135 P.2d 46 (1943); Sumner Coal–Mining Co. v. Pleasant, 127 Okla. 174, 259 P. 1055 (1927); Oberly v. Kirby, 592 A.2d 445, 458 (Del.1991). This is true for obvious reasons. Large corporations with perhaps thousands of stockholders could not function if the daily running of the corporation was subject to the approval of so many relatively attenuated people. However, the authority given a board of directors under the Oklahoma General Corporation Act, 18

ed by reference in the instrument or instruments evidencing such rights or options. In the absence of actual fraud in the transaction, the judgment of the directors as to the consideration for the issuance of such rights or options and the sufficiency thereof shall be conclusive. In case the shares of stock of the corporation to be issued upon the exercise of such rights or options shall be shares having a par value, the price or prices so to be received therefor shall not be less than the par value thereof. In case the shares of stock so to be issued shall be shares of stock without par value, the consideration therefor shall be determined in the manner provided for in Section 34 of this act.

6. 18 O.S.1991 § 1013(A) & (B): Bylaws

A. The original or other bylaws of a corporation may be adopted, amended or repealed by the incorporators, by the initial directors if they were named in the certificate of incorporation, or, before a corporation has received any payment for any of its stock, by its board of directors. After a corporation has received any payment for any of its stock, the power to adopt, amend or repeal bylaws shall be in the shareholders entitled to vote, or, in the case of a nonstock corporation, in its members entitled to vote; provided, however, any corporation, in its certificate of incorporation, may confer the power to adopt, amend or repeal bylaws upon the directors or, in the case of a nonstock corporation, upon its governing body by whatever name designated. The fact that such power has been so conferred upon the directors or governing body, as the case may be, shall not divest the shareholders or members of the power, nor limit their power to adopt, amend or repeal bylaws.

B. The bylaws may contain any provision, not inconsistent with law or with the certificate of incorporation, relating to the business of the corporation, the conduct of its affairs, and its rights or powers or the rights or powers of its shareholders, directors, officers or employees.

O.S.1991 § 1027, is not without shareholder oversight, 18 O.S.1991 § 1013(B).

Fleming's argument relies on this passage, 18 O.S.1991 § 1038 (emphasis added):

> Subject to any provisions in the certificate of incorporation, every corporation may create and issue ... rights or options entitling the holders thereof to purchase from the corporation any shares of its capital stock of any class or classes, such rights or options to be evidenced by or in such instrument or instruments as shall be approved by the board of directors.

In making its argument, Fleming asserts that the word "corporation" is synonymous with "board of directors" as the term is used in 18 § 1038. Therefore, according to Fleming, "every corporation may create and issue ... rights and options[.]", can actually be read to say "[every corporation's board of directors] may create and issue ... rights and options[.]" However, in light of the fact that both terms, "corporation" and "board of directors", are used distinctly throughout the General Corporation Act and within the text of 18 § 1038 itself, this assertion is flawed. Further, the Former Business Corporation Act, 18 § 1.2(1) and (23), defines "corporation" and "director" differently. The statutes indicate our legislature has an understanding of the distinct definitions it assigns to these terms, and we find it unlikely the legislature would interchange them as Fleming contends.

While this Court would agree with Fleming that a corporation may create and issue rights and options within the grant of authority given it in 18 § 1038, it does not automatically translate that the board of directors of that corporation has in itself the same breadth of authority.

A shareholder rights plan is essentially a variety of stock option plan. Its use as an anti-takeover mechanism does not change its essential character. While shareholder ratification of poison pills has not been tested in the courts, the same cannot be said for stock option plans as a whole. There is authority supporting shareholder ratification of stock option plans.

For example, in Michelson v. Duncan, 407 A.2d 211, 218–20 (Del.1979), shareholders ratified a stock option package, curing a voidable act of the corporation's board of directors. Unlike the instant case, Michelson does not focus on whether shareholders have the authority to ratify the stock option plan, but rather explains that shareholder approval can cure the invalidity of an otherwise voidable act of the company's board. Despite this distinction, however, the case does reveal that stock option plans themselves can be subject to shareholder approval. . . .

Further authority for shareholder approval of stock option plans is found in the Internal Revenue Code. 26 U.S.C §§ 422(b)(1) & 423(b)(2) (emphasis added).

422(b) Incentive stock option. . . .

(1) the option is granted pursuant to a plan which includes the aggregate number of shares which may be issued under option and the employees (or class of employees) eligible to receive options, and which is approved by the stockholders of the granting corporation within 12 months before or after the date such plan is adopted[.]

423(b) Employee stock purchase plan. . . .

(2) such plan is approved by the stockholders of the granting corporation within 12 months before or after the date such plan is adopted[.]

Although the option plans referred to in the revenue code are not shareholder rights plans, the revenue code's recognition of shareholder approval of stock options is similar to Michelson, in that it reveals stock option plans are not exempt from shareholder approval or ratification.

We find nothing in the Oklahoma General Corporation Act, 18 O.S.1991 § 1001 et seq., or existing case law which indicates the shareholder rights plan is somehow exempt from shareholder adopted bylaws. Fleming argues that only the certificate of incorporation can limit the board's authority to implement such a plan, relying on § 1038. While this Court might agree that a certificate of incorporation, which somehow precludes bylaw amendments directed at shareholder rights plans, could preclude the Teamsters from seeking the bylaw changes which are proposed in this case, neither party has indicated Fleming's certificate speaks in any way to the board's authority or shareholder constraints regarding shareholder rights plans. We find no authority to support the contention that a certificate of incorporation which is silent with regard to shareholder rights plans precludes shareholder enacted bylaws regarding the implementation of rights plans.

A number of states have taken affirmative steps to ensure their domestic corporations, and in many instances the board of directors itself, are able to implement shareholder rights plans to protect the company from takeover. The legislation is typically called a shareholders rights plan endorsement statute. However, the Oklahoma legislature has not passed such legislation. There are at least twenty-four states with these share rights plan endorsement statutes.

Some examples of shareholders rights plan endorsement statutes which give explicit authority to directors of the corporation read as follows:

Nothing contained in this chapter is intended or shall be construed in any way to limit, modify or restrict an issuing public corporation's authority to take any action which the directors may appropriately determine to be in furtherance of the protection of the interests of the corporation and its shareholders, including without limitation the authority to adopt or enter into plans, arrangements or instruments that deny rights, privileges, power or authority to the holder or holders of at least a specified number of shares or percentage of share ownership or voting power in certain circumstances. Id. St. § 30–1706(1) (emphasis added).

[E]xcept as otherwise provided in the articles of incorporation, a corporation may create and issue, whether or not in connection with the issue and sale of its shares or bonds, rights or options entitling the holders thereof to purchase from the corporation, upon such consideration, terms and conditions as may be fixed by the board, shares of any class or series, whether authorized but unissued shares, treasury shares or shares to be purchased or acquired, notes of the corporation or assets of the corporation. The terms and conditions of such rights or options may include, without limitation, restrictions or conditions that preclude or limit the exercise, transfer or receipt of such rights or options by any person or persons owning or offering to acquire a specified number or percentage of the outstanding common shares or other securities of the corporation, or any transferee or transferees of any such person or persons, or that invalidate or void such rights or options held by any such person or persons or any such transferee or transferees. Il.St. Ch. 805 § 5/6.05(f) (emphasis added). . . .

These examples illustrate how a board of directors can operate with relative autonomy when a rights plan endorsement statute applies. This does not suggest the absence of a share rights plan endorsement statute in Oklahoma precludes the implementation of such a takeover defense. We merely find that without the authority granted in such an endorsement statute, the board may well be subject to the general procedures of corporate governance, including the enactment of bylaws which limit the board's authority to implement shareholder rights plans. . . .

In answering this certified question, we do not suggest all shareholder rights plans are required to submit to shareholder approval, ratification or review; this is not the question presented to us. Instead, we find shareholders may, through the proper channels of corporate governance, restrict the board of directors authority to implement shareholder rights plans.

CERTIFIED QUESTION ANSWERED.

SUMMERS, C.J., HARGRAVE, V.C.J., LAVENDER, OPALA, WILSON, KAUGER, and WATT, JJ., concur.

HODGES, J., no vote.

———

GENERAL DATACOMM INDUSTRIES, INC.
v. WISCONSIN INVESTMENT BOARD

Delaware Chancery Court, 1999.
1999 WL 66533.

I.

In this matter, the plaintiff, General DataComm Industries, Inc., ("GDC"), a Delaware corporation, seeks declaratory and injunctive relief regarding the validity of a bylaw proposed for consideration at GDC's upcoming annual meeting by the defendant, State of Wisconsin Investment Board ("SWIB"). The proposed "Repricing Bylaw" provides as follows:

> Option Repricing. [GDC] shall not reprice any stock options already issued and outstanding to a lower strike price at any time during the term of such option, without the prior approval of the shareholders.

Compl. P 8.

GDC contends that this proposed Repricing Bylaw "restricts unlawfully and in a material way the directors' statutory power and authority, as well as the directors' fiduciary duty, to make decisions on matters of management policy. Because no provision limiting the board's managerial authority is contained in the GDC certificate of incorporation, SWIB's proposed Repricing Bylaw is invalid." Compl. P 15.

Before me now is GDC's motion to expedite proceedings, which was filed on January 28, 1999. GDC's annual meeting is scheduled for February 4, 1999.

According to GDC, "this matter needs prompt resolution so that GDC is not required to suffer a facially invalid bylaw and its directors are not impaired in the management of [GDC's] incentive compensation program for recruitment and retention of key employees due to uncertainty, as long as this dispute remains unresolved, over their authority to act without stockholder approval." P1.'s Mot. P 9.

After a consideration of GDC's motion, I believe that the issues raised in its complaint are not yet ripe for judicial resolution and therefore deny its motion for expedited proceedings. However, in the event that the Repricing Bylaw is adopted by the GDC stockholders, I will promptly, upon renewed application by GDC, consider whether a schedule for expedited proceedings to address the issues raised by its complaint should be put in place.

II.

SWIB first submitted the Repricing Bylaw to GDC for consideration on September 2, 1998. According to GDC, Securities and Exchange Commission ("SEC") rules require GDC to include the Repricing Bylaw proposal in GDC's proxy materials unless an applicable SEC exclusion applies.

Throughout the fall, GDC attempted to obtain SEC approval to exclude the Repricing Bylaw proposal from its proxy materials. In particular, GDC argued that exclusion was proper under SEC Rule 14a–8(i)(1), which enables exclusion if the "proposal is not a proper subject for action by shareholders under the laws of the jurisdiction of the company's organization." Compl. P 11, Ex. B.

SWIB, through the Delaware law firm of Grant & Eisenhofer, disputed this contention. On December 9, 1998, the SEC advised GDC that it could not exclude the Repricing Bylaw from its proxy materials on the basis of Rule 14a–8(i)(1), stating: "Neither counsel for you nor for the proponent has opined as to any compelling state law precedent. In view of the lack of any decided legal authority the Division has determined not to express any view with respect to the application of rule 14a–8(i)(1) to the proposal." Compl. PP 12–13, Ex. D.

On December 14, 1998, GDC sent its stockholders proxy materials setting forth SWIB's proposed Repricing Bylaw, SWIB's supporting statement, and the management response of GDC. Compl. P 14, Ex. E. A particularly pertinent part of the management response provides:

> Requiring the Corporation to submit option repricing to stockholders at the next annual meeting or at a special meeting is both cumbersome and untimely and would effectively eliminate the ability to reprice options for employees who are otherwise leaving their employment. The Corporation has also been advised by its Delaware counsel that in their opinion, the proposal if implemented would violate Delaware law since such restrictions are only permitted in the Certificate of Incorporation. Should the stockholders approve the proposal, the Corporation reserves the right to challenge its validity in appropriate Delaware court proceedings.

ACCORDINGLY, THE BOARD OF DIRECTORS UNANIMOUSLY RECOMMENDS THAT THE STOCKHOLDERS VOTE AGAINST THE PROPOSED BY–LAW ADDITION RESTRICTING OPTION REPRICING.

Compl. P 14, Ex. E at 14.

On January 22, 1999, some three weeks after the Delaware Supreme Court issued its decision in *Quickturn Design Sys., Inc. v. Shapiro, Del. Supr., Nos. 511, 512, 721 A.2d 1281, 1998 WL 954752 (1998),* GDC wrote SWIB asking it to withdraw the Repricing Bylaw on the ground that Quickturn made it clear that the Repricing Bylaw was invalid, or in the alternative, to advise the GDC stockholders that the proposed Repricing Bylaw was invalid. Three days later, GDC wrote to the SEC to advise it of the Quickturn decision and to urge it to reconsider GDC's request to exclude the Repricing Bylaw from its proxy materials. GDC has heard back from neither SWIB nor the SEC.

On January 28, 1999, GDC brought this action seeking declaratory and injunctive relief, to wit: a declaratory judgment that the Repricing Bylaw is invalid; a declaratory judgment that the SWIB proxy discussion of the Repricing Bylaw is false and misleading; an order enjoining SWIB from soliciting votes for the Repricing Bylaw or otherwise seeking adoption of that Bylaw; an order directing that supplemental proxy materials be sent to GDC stockholders advising them of the removal of the Repricing Bylaw from consideration at the annual meeting; and an order permitting GDC to adjourn or postpone the meeting or any vote on the Repricing Bylaw pending the adjudication of its claims in this case. Compl. pp. 8–9, PP A–F.

Earlier today, an office conference was held to consider GDC's motion for expedited proceedings.

III.

GDC seeks to have this court determine the validity of a yet to be adopted bylaw. Therefore, I must weigh the reasons "for not rendering a hypothetical opinion. . . . against the benefits to be derived from the rendering of a declaratory judgment." *Stroud v. Milliken Enter., Inc., Del. Supr., 552 A.2d 476, 480 (1989).* Even in a situation where more substantial corporate interests were at stake, I would be reluctant to grant an advisory opinion in a situation like this. In this matter, where no irreparable harm is threatened, prudence dictates that judicial action regarding whether the Repricing Bylaw is valid should await an affirmative stockholder vote. . . .

. . . [T]he stockholders can cast an informed vote if the proxy materials disclose that there are differing views regarding the validity of the Repricing Bylaw. In fact, the GDC materials already state GDC's view that the Repricing Bylaw is invalid. Compl. P 14, Ex. E at 14.

. . . [A] post-meeting adjudication would not unduly disrupt the corporation's affairs. At most, the Repricing Bylaw will inhibit the GDC board's ability to reprice options in the event that in the board's business judgment such repricing becomes necessary in the period between the Repricing Bylaw's adoption at the annual meeting (if that occurs) and a post-adoption adjudication of its validity by this court. The speculative nature of these eventualities, the availability of prompt injunctive relief, and the fact that this court has committed to consider promptly a request to expedite a post-adoption adjudication eliminates any necessity for a pre-adoption adjudication of the Repricing Bylaw's validity. . . .

This lack of urgency cuts against the need to determine a potentially important issue of Delaware law in haste. It may be that GDC is correct in stating that the Repricing Bylaw is obviously invalid under the teaching of Quickturn. But the question of whether a stockholder-approved bylaw that can potentially be repealed at any time by the GDC board of directors exercising its business judgment, see 8 Del. C. § 109(a)[1], is clearly invalid under the teaching of a case involving a board-approved contractual rights plan precluding, by contract, a new board majority from redeeming the rights under the plan until six months after election seems to me to be a question worthy of careful consideration.[2]

---

1. Under § 109(a) of the Delaware General Corporation Law, the GDC certificate may permissibly vest authority to amend the corporation's bylaws in its board of directors and at oral argument GDC's counsel indicated that the GDC certificate so empowers its board. The question of whether a stockholder-approved bylaw may be repealed by a board of directors with such authority has not clearly been answered by a Delaware Court. However, the Supreme Court's decision in *Centaur Partners, IV v. Nat'l Intergroup, Inc.*, Del. Supr., 582 A.2d 923, 929 (1990) and the views of a learned commentator suggests that the affirmative answer may be the correct one. Lawrence Hamermesh, Corporate Democracy and Stockholder–Adopted By–Laws: Taking Back the Street?, 73 *Tul. L. Rev.* 409, 467–479 (1998). But see 1 R. Franklin Balotti & Jesse A. Finkelstein, The Delaware Law of Corporations & Business Organizations, § 1.11 at 1–16 (1998) (suggesting that the negative answer is correct).

2. At minimum, the question would seem to require consideration of several provisions of the Delaware General Corporation Law, including § 102, § 109, § 141, § 153, and § 157, as well as relevant case law, including Quickturn. A recently published article which addresses the subject of stockholder-adopted bylaws in a sophisticated and comprehensive manner, states well the difficulties this subject generally raises:

> Just as this nascent effort to shift the balance of corporate power from directors to stockholders through the use of stockholder-adopted by-law provisions is gaining momentum, however, it has exposed a critical dearth of precedent. For while stockholders have unquestioned power to adopt by-laws covering a broad range of subjects, it is also well established in corporate law that stockholders may not directly manage the business and affairs of

the corporation, at least without specific authorization either by statute or in the certificate or articles of incorporation. There is an obvious zone of conflict between these precepts: in at least some respects, attempts by stockholders to adopt by-laws limiting or influencing director authority inevitably offend the notion of management by the board of directors. However, neither the courts, the legislators, the SEC, nor legal scholars have clearly articulated the means of resolving this conflict and determining whether a stockholder-adopted by-law provision that constrains director managerial authority is legally effective.

Related to this gap in legal authority is a less substantive but nearly as important area of legal uncertainty. Even if the stockholders could validly initiate and adopt a by-law limiting the authority of the directors, such a by-law amendment would accomplish little or nothing if the board of directors could simply repeal it after the stockholders adopted it. In some jurisdictions, of course, there is no question that such repeal can be prevented. Under many statutory schemes, the board of directors may not repeal a stockholder-adopted by-law if that by-law expressly prohibits such repeal. In other jurisdictions, however, notably Delaware and New York, the corporation statutes allow the board of directors to amend the by-laws if the certificate or articles of incorporation so provide and place no express limits on the application of such director amendment authority to stockholder-adopted by-laws. The second significant legal uncertainty, therefore is whether, in the absence of an explicitly controlling statute, a stockholder-adopted by-law can be made immune from repeal or modification by the board of directors.

As a result, I believe that GDC has not shown a compelling justification sufficient to persuade me to rule on its claims at this time. My reticence to issue a ruling at this time is, I must admit, also influenced by my reluctance to encourage corporations to seek advisory opinions about important issues of Delaware corporation law as a method of shaping their annual meeting proxy materials. *Stroud, 552 A.2d at 479* (Declaratory Judgment Act not to be used as a means of obtaining advisory rulings from Delaware courts). If this option were routinely available, this court could find itself playing a parallel role to the SEC, which is regularly involved, pursuant to its statutory and regulatory authority, in the proxy preparation process. This court's traditional commitment to prompt justice should ordinarily be sufficient to address any legitimate corporate interests threatened by the adoption by stockholders of an invalid bylaw. Absent an imminent threat of irreparable injury, there seems to be no need and much risk for this court to step into the void when the SEC concludes that state law is not clear enough for its Rule 14a–8(i)(1) to exclude a proposal. The SEC's judgment in such a situation would suggest that the issue involved is of a difficult nature and that it deserves careful scrutiny: that is, that the issue is of precisely the sort about which this court should be reluctant to opine until the issue is ripe for judicial resolution. Cf *Stroud, 552 A.2d at 481* (finding that unripe claim raising issues "novel and important ... to Delaware corporate law" should be dismissed).

IV.

For the foregoing reasons, GDC's motion to expedite proceedings is hereby DENIED. IT IS SO ORDERED.

Hamermesh, *73 Tul. L. Rev, at 415–417.* Cf *Int'l Brotherhood of Teamsters Gen. Fund v. Fleming Cos., Inc., P.2d , 1999 OK 3, 1999 Okla. LEXIS 3, 1999 WL* 35227, at *1 (Okla. 1999)....

Chapter V

SHAREHOLDER INFORMATIONAL RIGHTS AND PROXY VOTING

SECTION 1. SHAREHOLDER INFORMATIONAL RIGHTS UNDER STATE LAW

(a) INSPECTION OF BOOKS AND RECORDS

Insert the following case at p. 310 of the Unabridged Edition, and p. 212 of the Concise Edition, in place of Compaq Computer Corp. v. Horton:

SECURITY FIRST CORP. v. U.S. DIE CASTING AND DEVELOPMENT CO.

Supreme Court of Delaware, 1997.
687 A.2d 563.

Before VEASEY, C.J., HOLLAND, HARTNETT and BERGER, JJ., and RIDGELY, President Judge,* constituting the Court en Banc.

VEASEY, Chief Justice.

In this appeal we hold that a stockholder may demonstrate a proper demand for the production of corporate books and records upon a showing, by the preponderance of the evidence, that there exists a credible basis to find probable corporate wrongdoing. The stockholder need not actually prove the wrongdoing itself by a preponderance of the evidence. Therefore, the trial judge's determination of that credible basis after considering the totality of the evidence is entitled to considerable deference.

The Section 220 demand for books and records under the Delaware General Corporation Law serves many salutary goals in the corporate governance landscape, but the burden on the plaintiff is not insubstantial. The statutory remedy is not an invitation to an

---

* Sitting by designation pursuant to Del. Const., Art. IV, §§ 12 and 38, and Supreme Court Rules 2 and 4(a).

indiscriminate fishing expedition. The plaintiff must not only show a credible basis to find probable wrongdoing, but must justify each category of the requested production. Accordingly, the trial court's order must be carefully tailored.

In this case, the judgment of the trial court on the entitlement to books and records is affirmed, but the scope of the judgment is reversed as overly broad on this record. The proceeding is remanded for a determination of a properly tailored order of inspection. In addition, the judgment of the Court of Chancery ordering a stock list is reversed, there being no proper basis on this record for the production of a stock list.

Facts

The following factual background is summarized from the findings set forth in the trial court's opinion.

Defendant Security First Corporation ("Security First") is a Delaware corporation with its principal place of business in Mayfield Heights, Ohio. It serves as a bank holding company for Security First Federal Savings and Loan, an Ohio savings and loan. The stock of Security First is publicly traded on NASDAQ. Charles F. Valentine is the Chairman and Chief Executive Officer of Security First.

Plaintiff U.S. Die Casting and Development Corporation ("U.S. Die") is a closely-held Ohio corporation. It is the record holder of approximately five percent of the common stock of Security First. David Slyman is the President, Chief Executive Officer, and sole stockholder of U.S. Die.

On September 1, 1994, Security First entered into an Agreement and Plan of Merger ("Merger Agreement") with Mid Am, Inc. ("Mid Am"), a much larger regional bank holding company. Mid Am filed documents with the Securities and Exchange Commission by which the value of the merger was fixed at approximately $79 million. After the announcement of the merger, the fair market value of Security First's stock increased significantly.

The Merger Agreement enumerated specific terms by which the parties could terminate the merger. The relevant terms include:

Section 9.01 Termination. This AGREEMENT may be terminated at any time prior to the EFFECTIVE TIME, whether before or after approval by the shareholders of SECURITY and MID AM:

(a) By mutual consent of the Boards of Directors of SECURITY and MID AM;

(b) By the Board of Directors of either SECURITY or MID AM if:

(i) The MERGER shall not have been consummated on or before April 30, 1995 (unless the failure to consummate the MERGER by such date shall be due to the action or failure to act of the party seeking to terminate this AGREEMENT in breach of such party's obligation under this AGREEMENT); or

(ii) Any event occurs which, in the reasonable opinion of either Board, would preclude satisfaction of any of the conditions set forth in Section 7.01 of this AGREEMENT[.]

The Merger Agreement required Security First to pay a termination fee of $2 million, plus third-party expenses not to exceed $250,000, contingent on the occurrence of certain events within one year after termination:

Section 9.05   Termination Fee. In the event of the failure of the SECURITY shareholders to approve the MERGER and this AGREEMENT, provided at the time of the SECURITY shareholders' meeting to vote upon this MERGER either (a) there is outstanding an announced offer by a third-party to acquire SECURITY, by merger[,] consolidation, exchange offer or asset purchase, or a tender offer for at least fifty-one percent (51%) of the outstanding SECURITY common stock in either case providing a per share purchase valued at the time of its announcement of at least $14.79 to the SECURITY shareholders or (b) the Board of Directors of SECURITY fails to favorably recommend approval of the AGREEMENT, then in any such event, SECURITY shall pay Two Million Dollars ($2,000,000) to MID AM as an agreed upon termination fee plus the third-party expenses incurred by MID AM in connection with the transaction contemplated by this AGREEMENT but not to exceed Two Hundred Fifty Thousand Dollars ($250,000) upon the occurrence of any of the following events within one (1) year after termination of this AGREEMENT:

(i) any person or group of persons (other than MID AM and/or its affiliates) shall acquire more than fifty percent (50%) of the outstanding SECURITY common stock at a per share purchase price equal to or greater than $14.79; or

(ii) upon the entry by SECURITY into a definitive agreement with a person or group of persons (other than MID AM and/or its affiliates) for such person or group of persons to acquire, merge, or consolidate with SECURITY or to acquire all or substantially all of SECURITY'S assets and wherein the per share purchase price at the time of the initial public announcement thereof equals or exceeds $14.79.

In December 1994, the merger fell through. Security First alleges that the breakdown resulted from "the realization that Mid Am's management philosophy and direction were fundamentally different from its own."

Without the occurrence of an event specified by Section 9.05 of the Merger Agreement, Security First and Mid Am entered into a Termination Agreement ("Termination Agreement") on December 28, 1994. Pursuant to the Termination Agreement, defendant paid Mid Am $275,000, and agreed to pay an additional $2 million contingent on the occurrence within one and a half years of the Termination Agreement of an event listed in Section 9.05, supra.

After the Termination Agreement was disclosed, the value of defendant's common stock dropped significantly, and has not rebounded. Defendant has increased dividend payments to its stockholders since the termination.

On January 12, 1995, plaintiff submitted a written demand to defendant pursuant to 8 *Del.C.* § 220 ("Section 220")[2] to inspect all of the defendant's and its subsidiaries' books and records related to the Mid Am merger and its termination. Defendant refused to comply.

On February 7, 1995, plaintiff initiated this action in the Court of Chancery. Trial of the matter was held on July 6, 1995. By order dated February 8, 1996, the Court of Chancery granted to plaintiff the relief it sought. From this decision, Security First appeals.

Proper Purpose: U.S. Die's Claim of Mismanagement

Section 220 of the Delaware General Corporation Law permits a stockholder, who shows a specific proper purpose and who complies with the procedural requirements of the statute, to inspect specific books and records of a corporation.[3]

In the case *sub judice*, the Court of Chancery, after a trial which included live witnesses and documentary evidence, found that, "[a]ccording to the *Amended Complaint and Plaintiff's Trial Brief and Plaintiff's Post–Trial Reply Brief*, Plaintiff's purpose for requesting an inspection of Defendant's books and records is to investigate the possibility of corporate mismanagement." It is well established that investigation of mismanagement is a proper purpose for a Section 220 books and records inspection.[5] A stockholder's entitlement to inspection of corporate books and records depends on whether or not a credible basis to find probable wrongdoing on the

---

2. 8 *Del.C.* § 220, Inspection of books and records, provides in pertinent part:

(b) Any stockholder, in person or by attorney or other agent, shall, upon written demand under oath stating the purpose thereof, have the right during the usual hours for business to inspect for any proper purpose the corporation's stock ledger, a list of its stockholders, and its other books and records, and to make copies or extracts therefrom. A proper purpose shall mean a purpose reasonably

related to such person's interest as a stockholder. . . .

3. This Court has encouraged the use of Section 220 as an "information-gathering tool in the derivative context," provided a proper purpose is shown. *Rales v. Blasband*, Del.Supr., 634 A.2d 927, 934–935 n. 10 (1993). *See also Grimes v. Donald*, Del. Supr., 673 A.2d 1207, 1216 (1996).

5. *Thomas & Betts Corp. v. Leviton Manufacturing Co.*, Del.Supr., 681 A.2d 1026, 1031 (1996).

part of corporate mismanagement has been established.[6] At the trial of a summary proceeding under Section 220(d), the plaintiff must show the credible basis by a preponderance of the evidence. The actual wrongdoing itself need not be proved in a Section 220 proceeding, however.

This Court reviews *de novo* the question of a "proper purpose" under Section 220(b).[7] Defendant's first contention is that the Court of Chancery erroneously relied upon plaintiff's "written proffer," *i.e.*, its Amended Complaint, Trial Brief, and Post–Trial Reply Brief. Defendant argues that the trial court should have relied instead on the trial testimony of David Slyman, the President, Chief Executive Officer, and sole stockholder of U.S. Die. Concerning the purpose for the inspection, Slyman testified:

> I would like to make my own decision as to why the merger was not completed. Telling me that it was a difference of philosophies didn't get me to understand why it was not completed. The philosophy was there prior to it. . . .

Defendant argues that the purpose which Slyman articulated at trial was insufficient and that this insufficiency is fatal. This argument must fail. Slyman's testimony does call into question defendant's purported reason for abrogating the Merger Agreement—namely, that "the realization that Mid Am's management philosophy and direction were fundamentally different from its own."[8] The Court of Chancery found defendant's reason suspect. The Court stated that "[a] reasonable stockholder could conclude prudent management would have researched 'fundamental' similarities and dissimilarities of the merging company before entering the Merger Agreement."[9] . . .

Defendant next contends that the Court of Chancery applied an incorrect legal standard, when it stated, "I accept Plaintiff's written proffer [that] this payment alone represents a specific transaction raising the *plausibility* of more than speculative, general mismanagement." This Court recently stated, "In order to meet that burden of proof, a stockholder must present some credible basis from which the court can infer that waste or mismanagement may have occurred,"[13] and cited with approval the following proposition:

> A mere statement of a purpose to investigate possible general mismanagement, without more, will not entitle a shareholder to broad § 220 inspection relief. There must be some evidence of *possible* mismanagement as would warrant further investigation of the matter.[14]

6. *Id. See also Skouras v. Admiralty Enterprises, Inc.*, Del.Ch., 386 A.2d 674, 678 (1978).

7. *Thomas & Betts Corp.*, 681 A.2d at 1030.

8. *U.S. Die*, slip op. at 11.

9. *U.S. Die*, slip op. at 12.

13. *Thomas & Betts Corp.*, 681 A.2d at 1031.

14. *Helmsman Management Servs.*, 525 A.2d at 166 (emphasis added).

The difference between the Vice Chancellor's finding that "a specific transaction rais[ed] the *plausibility* of more than speculative, general mismanagement"[15] and the requirement that "[t]here must be some evidence of possible mismanagement as would warrant further investigation"[16] is merely semantic.

Finally, defendant maintains that plaintiff failed to produce any evidence of mismanagement. This argument misses the point. In a Section 220 action, a stockholder has the burden of proof to demonstrate a proper purpose,[17] but a stockholder is "not required to prove by a preponderance of the evidence that waste and [mis]management are actually occurring."[18] The threshold for a plaintiff in a Section 220 case is not insubstantial. Mere curiosity or a desire for a fishing expedition will not suffice. But the threshold may be satisfied by a credible showing, through documents, logic, testimony or otherwise, that there are legitimate issues of wrongdoing.

As specific instances of misconduct, plaintiff questions defendant's payment of $275,000 to Mid Am "when Defendant never broke the Merger Agreement." Plaintiff also questions defendant's failure to request documentation from Mid Am of its expenses to justify defendant's expenditure of $275,000, which was $25,000 more than the Merger Agreement stipulated for expenses. On their face, these issues raise questions. The effect of the Vice Chancellor's conclusion after trial is that the questions remain.

Defendant also agreed to pay Mid Am $2 million contingent on the certain occurrences within one and a half years of the Termination Agreement. Pursuant to the Merger Agreement, defendant previously had agreed to pay Mid Am $2 million contingent on the same occurrences within one year. As plaintiff's counsel, in a letter dated 1/19/95 to Security First's Chairman and CEO Charles Valentine, stated "This either takes the company 'out of play' or diminishes the amount payable to the stockholders if it is sold. In either event, the agreement seems inappropriate and destructive to stockholder values."

The Court of Chancery also viewed as evidence suggestive of misconduct the fact that, after the Termination Agreement was disclosed, the value of defendant's common stock dropped significantly and has not rebounded. Moreover, defendant has increased dividend payments to its stockholders since the termination. According to the Court of Chancery, "A thoughtful stockholder might look at this dividend increase as an effort to ameliorate dismay about the

15. *U.S. Die*, slip op. at 10.

16. *Helmsman Management Servs.*, 525 A.2d at 166.

17. 8 *Del.C.* § 220(c).

18. *Thomas & Betts Corp.*, 681 A.2d at 1031 ("In order to meet that burden of proof, a stockholder must present some credible basis from which the court can infer that waste or mismanagement may have occurred.").

Board of Directors' abandonment of a seemingly beneficial merger for Security First stockholders."[21]

In the instant case, the Court of Chancery found:

Contrary to Defendant's allegations, the evidentiary hearing produced testimony substantiating Plaintiff's claim. I listened to the trial testimony, observed the demeanor of the witnesses, and assessed their apparent frankness and the fairness of their testimony. I find Plaintiff's stated proper purpose convincing. Plaintiff's proper purpose is tied specifically to the point in time of Defendant's failure to consummate the Merger Agreement. . . .

The trial court's decision turned in part on the Vice Chancellor's determination that defendant's witnesses were not credible.[23] "When the determination of facts turns on a question of credibility and the acceptance or rejection of 'live' testimony by the trial judge, [the trial court's] findings will be approved upon review."[24] We hold that plaintiff has established a proper purpose for its request to inspect some books and records. The scope of that inspection is a separate issue on which plaintiff bears the burden of specific justification.

The Scope of the Books and Records Inspection

Absent any apparent error of law, this Court reviews for abuse of discretion the decision of the trial court regarding the scope of a stockholder's inspection of books and records.[25] The plaintiff bears the burden of proving that each category of books and records is essential to the accomplishment of the stockholder's articulated purpose for the inspection.[26]

Section 220(c) provides that "[t]he Court may, in its discretion, prescribe any limitations or conditions with reference to the inspection." While the trial court has wide latitude in determining the proper scope of inspection, it is the responsibility of the trial court to tailor the inspection to the stockholder's stated purpose. "Undergirding this discretion is a recognition that the interests of the corporation must be harmonized with those of the inspecting stockholder."[27]

In the instant case, the Court of Chancery found that plaintiff's request to inspect books and records was "self-tailored." We disagree.

---

21. *U.S. Die*, slip op. at 11.

23. According to the Court of Chancery, defendant's Chief Executive Officer, Charles Valentine, "delivered patent sophistry from the witness stand. . . ." *U.S. Die*, slip op. at 11. Cf. *Thomas & Betts Corp.*, 681 A.2d at 1032.

24. *Levitt v. Bouvier*, Del.Supr., 287 A.2d 671, 673 (1972); *accord Thomas & Betts Corp.*, 681 A.2d at 1032.

25. 8 *Del.C.* § 220(c); *Thomas & Betts Corp.*, 681 A.2d at 1034–35.

26. *Thomas & Betts Corp.*, 681 A.2d at 1035.

27. *Id.*

Plaintiff sought, and the Court of Chancery granted, inspection of the following:

a.   The agreement by and between Security First and Mid Am reported to have been made on or about September 1, 1994, and any amendments and modifications thereof (hereinafter the "Agreement");

b.   All minutes, notes, records, memoranda, writings, correspondence, telephone messages or the like which in any way directly or indirectly deal with or discuss the Agreement;

c.   All press releases relative to the Agreement;

d.   Any and all documents or records discussing the relationship between the employees of Security First after the completion of the merger contemplated by the Agreement;

e.   Minutes of all proceedings of directors or committees of directors from January 1, 1994;

f.   All minutes, notes, records, memoranda, writings, correspondence, telephone calls or the like which in any way directly or indirectly deal with or discuss the payment of $275,000 to Mid Am and/or a penalty to be paid if Security First and/or its assets are sold to another in the future;

g.   Any and all bank or savings and loan regulatory applications and amendments thereto related to the Agreement;

h.   Any and all correspondence with federal and/or state bank or savings and loan regulatory agencies in connection with the Agreement; and

i.   The most recent list of stockholders.

We find that plaintiff has not met its burden of proof on this record to establish that each category of books and records requested is essential and sufficient to its stated purpose. For example, Paragraph 8(e) of the Amended Complaint requests "Minutes of all proceedings of directors or committees of directors from January 1, 1994." Security First did not enter into discussions with Mid Am until the Spring of 1994. While plaintiff argues that the pre-merger meeting minutes are reasonably related to its purpose, this determination is for the trial court to make.[29]

The scope of the production which the Court of Chancery ordered in this case is more akin to a comprehensive discovery order under Court of Chancery Rule 34 than a Section 220 order. The two procedures are not the same and should not be confused. A Section 220 proceeding should result in an order circumscribed with rifled precision. Rule 34 production orders may often be

---

29. *See Thomas & Betts Corp.*, 681 A.2d at 1035; *Helmsman Management Servs.*,   525 A.2d at 167.

broader in keeping with the scope of discovery under Court of Chancery Rule 26(b).

It may well be that upon remand a record will be developed to justify the breadth of all or a significant portion of the order before us in accordance with this standard. Accordingly, we remand this case to the Court of Chancery to determine whether the stockholder met its burden of showing, by a preponderance of the evidence, a proper purpose entitling the stockholder to an inspection of each category of the documents it seeks.

Inspection of Stockholder List

Under Section 220(c), when a stockholder complies with the statutory requirements governing the form and manner of making a demand to obtain a stockholder list, the corporation bears the burden of proving that the demand is for an improper purpose.[30] This Court reviews *de novo* the question of proper purpose when a stockholder seeks to inspect a stockholder list.[31]

U.S. Die made a written demand for copies of defendant's most recent stockholder list "to communicate with the shareholders of Security with respect to Security's business, particularly the failed merger with Mid Am., Inc." In his deposition and at trial, however, Slyman admitted that he had no idea what he would do with such a list. It is a sufficient defense for a corporation to show that a stockholder list was sought from "idle curiosity."[32] We find that Security First has met its burden of proving that the plaintiff's demand to inspect the stockholder list was not for a proper purpose. Accordingly, we reverse the Court of Chancery's decision to grant plaintiff's request to inspect defendant's stockholder list.

We note, however, that U.S. Die is not precluded from making a new demand and, if necessary, filing a new proceeding to obtain the stockholder list. Neither the doctrine of *res judicata*[33] nor the principle of the law of the case has any application to a subsequent demand by U.S. Die to inspect the stockholder list. If U.S. Die has a *bona fide* purpose to inspect the list and if there has been a material change of circumstances since its February 1995 demand, U.S. Die may be able to establish its entitlement to inspect and copy the list of stockholders of Security First upon reasonable terms and conditions.

Conclusion

Section 220 proceedings are an important part of the corporate governance landscape in Delaware. Stockholders have a right to at

---

30. 8 *Del.C.* § 220(c); *Compaq Computer Corp. v. Horton*, Del.Supr., 631 A.2d 1, 3 (1993).

31. *Western Air Lines, Inc. v. Kerkorian*, Del.Supr., 254 A.2d 240 (1969). *See also Compaq Computer Corp.*, 631 A.2d at 3.

32. *Insuranshares Corporation of Delaware v. Kirchner,* Del.Supr., 5 A.2d 519, 521 (1939).

33. *Hatleigh Corp. v. Lane Bryant, Inc.*, Del.Ch., 428 A.2d 350 (1981).

least a limited inquiry into books and records when they have established some credible basis to believe that there has been wrongdoing. In fact, a Section 220 proceeding may serve a salutary mission as a prelude to a derivative suit.[36] Yet it would invite mischief to open corporate management to indiscriminate fishing expeditions. The trial court must assure that a proper balance is struck.

The judgment of the Court of Chancery granting U.S. Die's entitlement to inspect books and records is **AFFIRMED**. The breadth of the order is **REVERSED** on this record, however. This case is **REMANDED** to the Court of Chancery to open the record and to consider whether the plaintiff has carried its burden of proving that each category of books and records is essential to the accomplishment of the stockholder's articulated purpose for the inspection. The judgment of the Court of Chancery granting U.S. Die's entitlement to inspect the list of Security First's stockholders is **REVERSED**.

Jurisdiction is not retained.

SECTION 5.   THE PROXY RULES (III): SHAREHOLDER PROPOSALS

Add the following SEC No–Action Letter at p. 366 of the Unabridged Edition, after American Telephone & Telegraph Co., and p. 247 of the Concise Edition, after the Note on No–Action Letters Interpreting Rule 14a–8(c)(7):

AON CORPORATION
[SEC NO–ACTION LETTER]
March 6, 1997

[To Aon Corporation:]

The proposal requests that the board initiate a policy mandating no further purchases of tobacco equities and that the Company divest itself of all tobacco stocks by January 1, 1998.

---

36. *Grimes v. Donald*, Del.Supr., 673 A.2d 1207, 1216 n. 11 (1996) (noting that Section 220 may be used in certain cases to secure information to support demand futility); *see also Thomas & Betts Corp.*, 681 A.2d at 1031 n. 3 ("this Court in *Grimes* did not suggest that its reference to a Section 220 demand as one of the 'tools at hand' was intended to eviscerate or modify the need for a stockholder to show a proper purpose under Section 220."). The Court was informed by counsel at oral argument that other litigation between the parties is pending in the Court of Chancery, and that an issue in that litigation is whether or not the claim is derivative for purposes of compliance with Court of Chancery Rule 23.1. We have not considered the existence of that litigation to be relevant for purposes of this Opinion except that we were assured by counsel at oral argument that our decision herein has not thereby been rendered moot.

The Division is unable to concur in your view that the proposal may be omitted from the Company's proxy materials under Rule 14a–8(c)(5). That provision permits the omission of a proposal if it relates to operations which account for less than 5% of the registrant's total assets, net earnings and gross sales, and is not otherwise significantly related to the registrant's business. The staff is of the view that the proposal is "otherwise significantly related" to the Company's business. Accordingly, the Division does not believe the Company may rely on Rule 14a–8(c)(5) as a basis for omitting the proposal from its proxy materials.

The Division is unable to concur in your view that the proposal may be omitted from the Company's proxy materials under Rule 14a–8(c)(7) as a matter relating to ordinary business operations. Accordingly, the Division does not believe that the Company may rely on Rule 14a–8(c)(7) as a basis for omitting the proposal from its proxy materials. . . .

———

Add the following case at p. 373 of the Unabridged Edition, and p. 254 of the Concise Edition, after Roosevelt v. E.I. DuPont de Nemours Co.:

AMALGAMATED CLOTHING AND TEXTILE WORKERS v. WAL–MART STORES

United States Court of Appeals, Second Circuit, 1995.
54 F.3d 69.

Before: NEWMAN, Chief Judge, MINER and CABRANES, Circuit Judges.

Opinion of MINER, Circuit Judge.

Appeal from an order entered on March 14, 1994 in the United States District Court for the Southern District of New York (Wood, J.) awarding attorneys' fees to plaintiffs for services rendered in an action to enjoin the omission of a shareholder proposal from proxy solicitation materials.

Affirmed.

Defendant-appellant Wal–Mart Stores, Inc. appeals from an order entered on March 14, 1994 in the United States District Court for the Southern District of New York (Wood, J.) awarding attorneys' fees to plaintiffs, a group of Wal–Mart shareholders. The fees were awarded for services rendered in the underlying action, in which the court granted summary judgment to plaintiffs enjoining Wal–Mart, in accordance with Rule 14a–8, 17 C.F.R. § 240.14a–8, from omitting a certain shareholder proposal from its proxy materials. For the following reasons, we affirm the order of the district court.

BACKGROUND

In the underlying action, plaintiff shareholders claimed that Wal–Mart violated Securities and Exchange Commission ("SEC") Rule 14a–8 by refusing to include in its proxy solicitation materials a certain shareholder proposal to be voted upon at Wal–Mart's annual meeting. As noted, the district court granted summary judgment for plaintiffs, and familiarity with that decision is assumed. *See Amalgamated Clothing & Textile Workers Union v. Wal–Mart Stores, Inc.,* 821 F.Supp. 877 (S.D.N.Y.1993) (*"Wal–Mart I"*). The pertinent facts are briefly summarized below.

Plaintiffs' proposal required Wal–Mart's directors to prepare and distribute reports about Wal–Mart's equal employment opportunity ("EEO") and affirmative action policies. The reports would include a description of the company's efforts to advise its suppliers of these policies as well as of its efforts to purchase goods and services from minority and female-owned suppliers. Plaintiffs initially sought to include this proposal in the proxy solicitation material for the June 1992 shareholders annual meeting. At that time, Wal–Mart informed plaintiffs that it would not include the proposal because Wal–Mart believed that it concerned a matter relating to the conduct of its ordinary business operations. Wal–Mart relied on SEC Rule 14a–8(c)(7), 17 C.F.R. § 240.14a–8(c)(7), which exempts proposals relating to the conduct of ordinary business operations from inclusion in proxy materials. In accordance with Rule 14a–8(d), Wal–Mart notified the SEC that it had refused to include the proposal. It also requested the SEC to confirm its conclusion that the proposal was not required to be included in its proxy materials. On April 10, 1992, the SEC issued a no-action letter confirming Wal–Mart's position.

After receiving this no-action letter, Wal–Mart mailed its proxy statement without the proposed resolution, and the plaintiffs filed suit. In an amended complaint the plaintiffs alleged that they had resubmitted their proposal for inclusion in Wal–Mart's 1993 proxy materials, and that Wal–Mart again refused to include it. The district court found that the proposal, with some modifications, did not relate to the day-to-day business operations of the company but, rather, that it concerned significant policy issues for the company and thus could not be excluded. *Wal–Mart I,* 821 F.Supp. at 891–92. Wal–Mart did not appeal the district court's decision and included the proposal in its 1993 proxy materials. The proposal was defeated.

Plaintiffs subsequently moved in the district court for an award of attorneys' fees. The court found that, under the common-benefit rule, plaintiffs' action vindicated two substantial interests for all the shareholders of Wal–Mart. First, the proposal "facilitate[d] communication among shareholders and between shareholders and management on a limited range of subjects consistent with the content-based restrictions imposed by Rule 14a–8(c)." Second, the shareholders received "notice of the proposal and management's position on it prior to the meeting" and had "the opportunity to exercise their franchise in voting to approve or reject (or to abstain from voting on) the proposal." Because a substantial benefit was conferred on an "easily identifiable" group and the costs could be shifted to those benefitting, the district court awarded $54,140.00 in attorneys' fees to plaintiffs. This appeal followed.

DISCUSSION

Generally, courts may not award attorneys' fees to a prevailing party absent statutory or contractual authority. *See Alyeska Pipeline Serv. Co. v. Wilderness Soc'y,* 421 U.S. 240, 247–49 (1975). However, courts have carved out certain exceptions to the general rule, one of which is the common-benefit rule. *See, e.g., Mills v. Electric Auto–Lite Co.,* 396 U.S. 375, 392 (1970). The common-benefit rule permits a prevailing party to obtain reimbursement of attorneys' fees "in cases where the litigation has conferred a substantial benefit on the members of an ascertainable class" and where it is possible to spread the costs proportionately among the members of the class. *Id.* at 393–94. This exception is premised on the equitable principle that "persons who obtain the benefit of a lawsuit without contributing to its cost are unjustly enriched at the successful litigant's expense." *Boeing Co. v. Van Gemert,* 444 U.S. 472, 478 (1980). The common-benefit rationale often is applied in suits by a group of shareholders against a corporation to vindicate some substantial right of all the shareholders of the company. *Mills,* 396 U.S. at 396. Although the benefit need not be pecuniary, it "must be something more than technical in its consequence and be one that accomplishes a result which . . . affect[s] the enjoyment or protection of an essential right to the stockholder's interest." *Id.* (internal quotations omitted).

In this case, there is no dispute that the class of persons benefitted is easily identifiable, that the benefits were conferred upon the class, and that the costs of the litigation could be shifted to those benefitting. *See Boeing,* 444 U.S. at 478–79. The issue before us is whether the benefit conferred was so significant as to warrant the award of attorneys' fees and whether such an award was proper under the particular circumstances of this case. We address Wal–Mart's arguments in turn.

A. *Substantial Benefit To Wal–Mart Shareholders*

Wal–Mart claims that, because approximately ninety percent of the voting shares were voted against the proposal, the underlying decision failed to enhance the voting rights of the company's shareholders. We are unpersuaded. The percentage of shares voted against a proposal is insignificant because the right to cast an informed vote, in and of itself, is a substantial interest worthy of vindication.

In the labor context, the Supreme Court has recognized that an action by one union member that helped to preserve union democracy conferred a substantial benefit on all union members and upheld the award of attorneys' fees. *See Hall v. Cole*, 412 U.S. 1, 8–9 (1973). Moreover, the Third Circuit has held that a substantial benefit was conferred on union members for the purpose of awarding fees, where the action "contributed to a fair process in bylaws referenda . . . even though [the proponents'] proposals were defeated." *Pawlak v. Greenawalt*, 713 F.2d 972, 980 (3d Cir.1983), *cert. denied*, 464 U.S. 1042 (1984).

The securities laws address similar concerns regarding corporate suffrage. Section 14(a) of the Securities Exchange Act of 1934 aims to protect shareholders by allowing the SEC to prescribe rules and regulations regarding proxy solicitation materials. *See* 15 U.S.C. § 78n(a). This section "stemmed from the congressional belief that '[f]air corporate suffrage is an important right that should attach to every equity security bought on a public exchange,'" *J.I. Case Co. v. Borak*, 377 U.S. 426, 431 (1964) (quoting H.R.Rep. No. 1383, 73rd Cong., 2d Sess. 13 (1934)), and litigation that enhances suffrage benefits all those eligible to vote. Accordingly, we hold that the promotion of corporate suffrage regarding a significant policy issue confers a substantial benefit regardless of the percentage of votes cast for or against the proposal at issue.

The district court identified the facilitation of communication among shareholders and between shareholders and management as a substantial interest that was vindicated by plaintiffs' action. We agree. In order to exercise the right of corporate suffrage, shareholders must be informed of important issues confronting the corporation. Section 14(a) of the Securities and Exchange Act provides the framework for ensuring that shareholders are properly informed about those issues. *See Roosevelt v. E.I. Du Pont de Nemours & Co.*, 958 F.2d 416, 421–22 (D.C.Cir.1992). Here, plaintiffs sought to inform their fellow shareholders through Wal–Mart's proxy materials. Their attempts were thwarted until they vindicated their right to have their proposal included in the company's proxy materials. The result of this action was to facilitate communications among the shareholders as well as between shareholders and management. Management could not have been aware of the shareholders' views on this subject until the proposal was presented. Thus, the communication of a proposal relating to equal employment opportunity and affirmative action conferred a substantial benefit on the company's shareholders. The benefit is similar to the benefit resulting from a successful claim under Rule 14a–9, prohibiting omission of material facts from proxy statements, and fees are regularly allowed for successful 14a–9 lawsuits. *See Mills*, 396 U.S. at 396–97 . . . .

CONCLUSION

For the foregoing reasons, the order of the district court is AFFIRMED.

————

Chapter VI

THE SPECIAL PROBLEMS OF
CLOSE CORPORATIONS

SECTION 5. FIDUCIARY OBLIGATIONS OF SHAREHOLDERS IN CLOSE CORPORA-TIONS: IMPLIED UNDERSTANDINGS

Insert the following cases and Note at p. 459 of the Unabridged Edition, and p. 321 of the Concise Edition, after Wilkes v. Springside Nursing Homes, Inc.:

MEROLA v. EXERGEN CORP.

Supreme Judicial Court of Massachusetts, 1996.
423 Mass. 461, 668 N.E.2d 351.

Before LIACOS, C.J., and WILKINS, LYNCH, O'CONNOR and GREANEY, JJ.

LYNCH, Justice.

... Exergen was formed in May, 1980, as a corporation in the business of developing and selling infrared heat detection devices. From Exergen's inception to the date of trial, Pompei, the founder, was the majority shareholder in the corporation, as well as its president, owning over sixty per cent of the shares issued. At all relevant times, Pompei actively participated in and controlled the management of Exergen and, as the majority shareholder, had power to elect and change Exergen's board of directors.

The plaintiff began working for Exergen on a part-time basis in late 1980 while he was also employed full-time by Analogic Corporation. In the course of conversations with Pompei in late 1981, and early 1982, the plaintiff was offered full-time employment with Exergen, and he understood that, if he came to work there and invested in Exergen stock, he would have the opportunity to become a major shareholder of Exergen and for continuing employment with Exergen.

As of March 1, 1982, the plaintiff resigned from Analogic and began working full time for Exergen. He also then began purchasing shares in Exergen when the company made periodic offerings to its employees. From March, 1982, through June, 1982, the plaintiff

73

purchased 4,100 shares at $2.25 per share, for a total of $9,225. Exergen announced at the Exergen shareholders meeting in September, 1982, another option program to purchase shares at $5 per share within one year. By late 1983, the plaintiff had exercised his option to purchase an additional 1,200 shares. The plaintiff was not offered additional stock options after late 1983. ...

Principles of employment law permit the termination of employees at will, with or without cause excepting situations within a narrow public policy exception. *King v. Driscoll*, 418 Mass. 576, 581–582, 638 N.E.2d 488 (1994), and cases cited. However, the termination of a minority shareholder's employment may present a situation where the majority interest has breached its fiduciary duty to the minority interest. *Id.* at 586, 638 N.E.2d 488. *Wilkes v. Springside Nursing Home, Inc., supra* at 852–853, 353 N.E.2d 657. There the court concluded that the majority stockholders had attempted unfairly to "freeze out" a minority stockholder by terminating his employment, in part because their policy and practice was to divide the available resources of the corporation equally by way of salaries to the shareholders who all participated in the operation of the enterprise. *Id.* at 846, 353 N.E.2d 657. As the investment became more profitable, the salaries were increased. *Id.* The court recognized that "[t]he minority stockholder typically depends on his salary as the principal return on his investment, since the 'earnings of a close corporation ... are distributed in major part in salaries, bonuses and retirement benefits.'" *Id.* at 850, 353 N.E.2d 657, quoting 1 F.H. O'Neal, Close Corporations § 1.07 (1971). Given those facts, this court concluded that the other shareholders did not show a legitimate business purpose for terminating the minority stockholder and that the other parties acted "in disregard of a longstanding policy of the stockholders that each would be a director of the corporation and that employment with the corporation would go hand in hand with stock ownership." *Id.* at 853, 353 N.E.2d 657.

Here, although the plaintiff invested in the stock of Exergen with the reasonable expectation of continued employment, there was no general policy regarding stock ownership and employment, and there was no evidence that any other stockholders had expectations of continuing employment because they purchased stock. The investment in the stock was an investment in the equity of the corporation which was not tied to employment in any formal way. The plaintiff acknowledged that he could have purchased 5,000 shares of stock while he was working part time before resigning from his position at Analogic Corporation and accepting full-time employment at Exergen. He testified that he was induced to work for Exergen with the promise that he could become a major stockholder. There was no testimony that he was ever required to buy stock as a condition of employment.

Unlike the *Wilkes* case, there was no evidence that the corporation distributed all profits to shareholders in the form of salaries. On the contrary, the perceived value of the stock increased during the time that the plaintiff was employed. The plaintiff first purchased his stock at $2.25 per share and, one year later, he purchased more for $5 per share. This indicated that there was some increase in value to the investment independent of the employment expectation. Neither was the plaintiff a founder of the business, his stock purchases were made after the business was established, and there was no suggestion that he had to purchase stock to keep his job.

The plaintiff testified that, when he sold his stock back to the corporation in 1991, he was paid $17 per share. This was a price that had been paid to other shareholders who sold their shares to the corporation at a previous date, and it is a price which, after consulting with his attorney, he concluded was a fair price. With this payment, the plaintiff realized a significant return on his capital investment independent of the salary he received as an employee.

We conclude that this is not a situation where the majority shareholder breached his fiduciary duty to a minority shareholder. "[T]he controlling group in a close corporation must have some room to maneuver in establishing the business policy of the corporation." *Wilkes v. Springside Nursing Home, Inc., supra* at 851, 353 N.E.2d 657. Although there was no legitimate business purpose for the termination of the plaintiff, neither was the termination for the financial gain of Pompei or contrary to established public policy. Not every discharge of an at-will employee of a close corporation who happens to own stock in the corporation gives rise to a successful breach of fiduciary duty claim. The plaintiff was terminated in accordance with his employment contract and fairly compensated for his stock. He failed to establish a sufficient basis for a breach of fiduciary duty claim under the principles of *Donahue v. Rodd Electrotype Co., supra.* . . .

Judgment reversed.

—————

McCALLUM v. ROSEN'S DIVERSIFIED, INC.

United States Court of Appeals, Eighth Circuit, 1998.
153 F.3d 701.

Before BEAM, ROSS, and MAGILL, Circuit Judges.

BEAM, Circuit Judge.

William B. McCallum, a minority shareholder in Rosen's Diversified, Inc. (RDI), appeals from two adverse grants of summary judgment. McCallum seeks to have his shares in RDI redeemed for fair value pursuant to a court ordered buy-out. The district court held that McCallum failed to present evidence showing that RDI acted unfairly prejudicial toward him. We reverse and remand for a determination of the fair value of McCallum's shares.

I. BACKGROUND

This case involves a contentious dispute between the minority and controlling shareholders of a closely held Minnesota corporation. Two brothers, Elmer and Ludwig Rosen, founded RDI as a livestock trading business in the late 1940's. Today, RDI has grown into a thriving company, primarily engaged in meat packing and other agricultural businesses. In 1992, RDI had more than $400 million in sales. Members of the Rosen family own a majority of RDI's outstanding capital stock.

In January 1984, RDI hired McCallum, who had previously provided legal services to the company, as Executive Vice President and Chief Executive Officer (CEO). He was named a director in 1986. RDI performed well under McCallum's command. Accordingly, RDI rewarded McCallum—and three other key employees—with a bonus of $186,815 in cash and 12,000 shares of common stock in the company.[1] According to RDI, these payments were made because the key employees were almost entirely responsible for the financial success of the corporation, because the compensation package of the employees had been artificially low, and in order to maintain the unswerving loyalty of these employees. The parties did not enter into a shareholder's agreement or provide any mechanism for the transfer of those shares if circumstances changed.

By 1991, the amiable relationship between McCallum and RDI deteriorated, ultimately resulting in McCallum's termination and removal from the board. Subsequently, McCallum proposed that RDI redeem his shares for $5 million. RDI responded with an offer to redeem the shares for $600,000, which was at a small premium over the value determined by the annual valuation for RDI's Employee Stock Ownership Program (ESOP). The parties could not agree on a price and extensive litigation has followed. *See, e.g.,* *McCallum v. Rosen's Diversified, Inc.*, 41 F.3d 1239 (8th Cir.1994). The present case involves McCallum's 12,000 shares of RDI common stock which is not contained in the ESOP.

McCallum alleges that RDI's controlling shareholders have acted unfairly prejudicial toward him because they: (1) undermined his authority as CEO; (2) excluded him from important company decisions; (3) engaged in conduct directed at minimizing the value of the company; (4) terminated his employment; (5) offered to redeem his shares at an artificially low price; (6) denied him access to company books, records, and financial information; (7) engaged in

---

1. During the course of his employment, McCallum also received approximately 3,300 shares of common stock in RDI through an Employee Stock Ownership Program (ESOP). McCallum's total ownership represented nearly 3% of the company's capital stock.

self-dealing, usurped company opportunities, and commingled personal ventures with the affairs of the company.

The district court dismissed many of McCallum's allegations as improperly pleaded derivative claims. The district court dismissed McCallum's request for a buyout of his stock on a subsequent motion for summary judgment. McCallum appeals.

II.　DISCUSSION

Minnesota law governs the substantive issues in this diversity action. See *Vrban v. Deere & Co.*, 129 F.3d 1008, 1009 (8th Cir.1997). We give no deference to the district court's interpretation of Minnesota law. See id. The Supreme Court of Minnesota has not confronted the issue of when a minority shareholder is entitled to a court ordered buy-out. Thus, "we must determine what that court would probably hold were it to decide the issue. In making this determination, we may consider relevant state precedent, analogous decisions, considered dicta, scholarly works and any other reliable data" *Farr v. Farm Bureau Ins. Co.*, 61 F.3d 677, 679 (8th Cir. 1995).

The district court erred in dismissing certain of McCallum's allegations as failing to observe the derivative pleading requirements for shareholder proceedings. McCallum's several assertions were merely examples of unfairly prejudicial conduct on the part of the controlling shareholders, not separate claims in and of themselves. McCallum sought no relief on behalf of the corporation. Cf. *PJ Acquisition Corp. v. Skoglund*, 453 N.W.2d 1, 6 (Minn.1990) (inferring that a shareholder action for equitable relief is not a derivative action). In any event, we find that McCallum is entitled to equitable relief based on the uncontroverted assertions that were not dismissed as derivative claims.

Concerned with the vulnerable position of minority shareholders in closely held corporations, the Minnesota legislature has provided the courts with broad equitable authority to protect the interests of minority shareholders. See Minn.Stat. § 302A.751 (amended 1994) (hereinafter "Section 751"). Section 751 provides for the buy-out of a minority shareholder's interest when "the directors or those in control of the corporation have acted in a manner unfairly prejudicial toward one or more shareholders in their capacities as shareholders or directors ... or as officers or employees of a closely held corporation."

The phrase "unfairly prejudicial" is to be interpreted liberally. See *Pedro v. Pedro*, 463 N.W.2d 285, 288–89 (Minn.Ct.App.1990). One commentator, who helped draft certain revisions to the Minnesota Business Corporation Act and Section 751, stated that:

> The section is remedial in nature and should be liberally construed as an addition to the rights afforded non-controlling shareholders by law and the corporation's governing docu-

ments. The broad scope of Section 751 reflects the Legislature's trust in the ability of the judiciary to achieve equitable results on the facts appearing in individual cases.

See Joseph Edward Olson, Statutory Changes Improve Position of Minority Shareholders in Closely Held Corporations, *The Hennepin Lawyer*, Sept.-Oct.1983, at 11. In deciding whether to order a buy-out, the courts should consider "the reasonable expectations of the shareholders" with respect to each other and the corporation. See Minn.Stat. § 302A.751, subd. 3a (amended 1994). Oftentimes, a shareholder's reasonable expectations include a significant voice in management and an opportunity to work. See Olson at 23.

We find that the uncontested facts demonstrate that McCallum's reasonable expectations were defeated. RDI terminated McCallum's employment as CEO and subsequently offered to purchase his RDI shares at a small premium over the value determined by an annual valuation for RDI's ESOP. McCallum had received these shares as compensation for his outstanding service and as an inducement to remain at RDI, in order to foster its continued growth. Although the employment relationship later deteriorated, our focus is on McCallum's reasonable expectations at the inception of the relationship. See Minn.Stat. § 302A.751, subd. 3a.

On his termination, McCallum was divested of his primary expectations as a minority shareholder in RDI—an active role in the "management of the corporation and input as an employee." Pedro, 463 N.W.2d at 289. This expectation was particularly reasonable since McCallum was CEO of RDI. We need not extend our holding as far as the Minnesota Court of Appeals, which held that controlling shareholders that terminate the employment of a minority shareholder must make a good-faith effort to buy out the shareholder at a fair price. See *Sawyer v. Curt & Co.*, 1991 WL 65320, at *2 (Minn.Ct.App. Feb.12, 1991) (publication order vacated). We simply hold that terminating the CEO—as opposed to an employee that did not have a significant role in management—and then offering to redeem his stock, which was issued partially to lure him to remain at the company, constituted conduct toward McCallum as a shareholder sufficient to invoke the requirements of the Minnesota Act. Accordingly, we remand the matter for a determination of the fair value of his stock.

On remand, the district court shall determine the fair value of McCallum's shares in accordance with Minn.Stat. § 302A.751, subd. 2 (amended 1994) and put an end to this pugnacious litigation. We express no opinion on the fair value of McCallum's shares or whether the ESOP valuation represents fair value.

III.   CONCLUSION

For the foregoing reasons, we reverse the judgment of the district court and remand for further proceedings consistent with this opinion.

SECTION 10. DISSOLUTION FOR OPPRESSION AND MANDATORY BUY–OUT

Add the following case and Notes at p. 538 of the Unabridged Edition, after Balvik v. Sylvester:

BRENNER v. BERKOWITZ

Supreme Court of New Jersey, 1993.
134 N.J. 488, 634 A.2d 1019.

The opinion of the Court was delivered by

GARIBALDI, J.

This appeal concerns the interpretation of two provisions of *N.J.S.A.* 14A:12–7. Specifically, we address the rights and remedies of a minority shareholder in a close corporation who claims fraud, illegality, mismanagement, and oppression by the majority shareholders in violation of *N.J.S.A.* 14A:12–7(1)(c), and the requirements for a court-ordered buy-out of a shareholder's interest in a corporation under *N.J.S.A.* 14A:12–7(8).

I.

In 1973, Irving Resnick invested $144,000 to form Arbee Associates, Inc., (Arbee), a company that sells wholesale furniture to commercial offices. Although Resnick provided the entire start-up capital for Arbee, he retained only ten shares of the company for himself. Resnick distributed the remaining ninety shares as follows: thirty-six shares to his daughter defendant Ruth Berkowitz; thirty-five shares to his daughter plaintiff Judith Brenner; and nineteen shares to Ruth's husband, defendant Howard Berkowitz. (Reference hereafter to Berkowitz is to Howard.)

Resnick entrusted Berkowitz, who had worked for the preceding ten years in Resnick's previous furniture company, with ultimate authority to manage Arbee. The shareholders, at their first meeting, unanimously named Berkowitz president and resolved that "the complete management and supervision of the corporation be ... vested in its president, Howard V. Berkowitz." Further, the shareholders, who had each also been named directors, unanimously resolved that any action taken by the shareholders or directors would require Berkowitz's consent. Berkowitz managed the company between 1981 and 1984 without the benefit of any formal shareholder or board meetings.

Resnick worked with Berkowitz in managing the company until Resnick's death in 1984, whereupon his ten shares were divided equally between his two daughters. Thereafter, the 100 shares of the company were divided as follows: forty shares to plaintiff, Judith Brenner, forty-one shares to defendant Ruth Berkowitz, and nineteen shares to defendant Howard Berkowitz. That share allocation vested a sixty-percent interest in the Berkowitzes.

After Resnick's death, relations between the Brenner family and the Berkowitz family soured. In September 1987, Brenner's future daughter-in-law, Nancy McGrath left the company, and Brenner's son was fired. Plaintiff believed that these incidents demonstrated Berkowitz's attempt to squeeze her family out of active involvement in the company.

Shortly thereafter, on November 14, 1987, Brenner instituted this action against the corporation and the Berkowitzes. The complaint alleged that Ruth and Howard Berkowitz as directors and officers of Arbee had mismanaged the company, abused their authority, and acted illegally, oppressively, and unfairly toward Brenner, a minority shareholder, in violation of *N.J.S.A.* 14A:12–7(1)(c) by (a) failing to have the Board approve Berkowitz's annual salary; (b) denying Brenner's request to have her counsel present at the November 3, 1987, Board of Directors meeting; (c) precluding Brenner from "participating in the decision-making process and operation of Arbee"; and (d) failing "to provide Brenner with any other effective notice of the affairs of Arbee."

In August 1989, the Chancery Division permitted Brenner to amend her original complaint. In her amended claim, plaintiff repeated the allegations contained in her original complaint and asserted additional acts of misconduct that had allegedly jeopardized her interest in Arbee: (a) the misapplication of a supplier's discount to acquire an account; (b) the misrepresentation of union identity for some of Arbee's non-union employees; (c) the failure to pay sales tax on cash sales to employees; (d) the failure to file W–2 and 1099 forms for temporary employees who earn more than $600 in one year; and (e) the misappropriation of cash funds by Berkowitz. Plaintiff hired an accounting firm to inspect Arbee's corporate books, records, ledgers, invoices, and income statements that uncovered most of the acts of misconduct alleged in the amended complaint. Brenner alleged also that the termination of her son and daughter-in-law had been unfair.

Plaintiff sought the following relief: appointment of a custodian, an order for the sale of the Berkowitzes' stock to Brenner, an order for the purchase of plaintiff's stock by Arbee or the Berkowitzes, dissolution of Arbee, . . . and such further relief as the court deemed just.

II.

Evidence adduced at the bench trial established that at the time Arbee was formed, Brenner did not intend to participate in Arbee's management or even to work for Arbee. Brenner's role was solely director and investor.

Brenner received dividends of $17,500 per year from the company until 1985. In that year, Brenner requested an annual salary of $2,000 to $3,000 to establish an Individual Retirement Account. In an arrangement acceptable to Brenner, Arbee began paying Brenner a salary of $26,000 per year in lieu of dividends. Additionally, Brenner received income distributions from real estate holdings connected to Arbee.

Under Berkowitz's management, the company has flourished. Sales have grown from $750,000 in 1973 to $46 million in 1989. A court-appointed expert placed Arbee's value at approximately $4.5 million as of December 31, 1989. In addition, the company has expanded its markets, going beyond New Jersey to open showrooms and warehouses in Washington, D.C. and Maryland. The company has grown from twenty-two employees in 1981 to 155 employees in 1989.

The Chancery Division determined that oppression was required to trigger *N.J.S.A.* 14A:12–7(1)(c). The court held that to demonstrate oppression, the minority shareholder must show that her reasonable expectations had been frustrated, that the majority shareholders had breached their fiduciary duty to her, or that the majority's misconduct had led to a change in the minority's position within the corporate structure. With regard to each of Brenner's allegations, the Chancery Division determined that Brenner had failed to demonstrate oppression sufficient to trigger the statute.

Employment

Brenner testified that she believed that the shareholders intended Arbee to be a "family enterprise." Thus, she sought relief for the departure of her future daughter-in-law, Nancy McGrath, and the firing of her son Andrew from Arbee.

In 1986, McGrath was Arbee's second leading salesperson and by 1987 she was the top salesperson. Nonetheless, McGrath testified that Berkowitz had forced her out of the company to make room in the sales force for his daughter, who was less capable than McGrath. McGrath secured a position in another company after Berkowitz reassigned a particularly lucrative account from McGrath to his own daughter.

Berkowitz fired Brenner's son because Andrew had refused to pay $100 in cash to a company employee for helping him do some work at his home. Apparently, the Brenners and the Berkowitzes had used employees free of charge many times in the past. Brenner's son had refused to pay the cash and instead wrote a check payable to Arbee for $225, the estimated value of the labor and the truck. Berkowitz tore up the check and insisted on the cash payment. When Brenner's son continued to refuse, Berkowitz fired him.

Although Brenner testified that it was her understanding that the company had been formed for "any member of the family, for me or for my children, to take part in, if they so desired . . .," the court found Brenner's family had no reasonable expectation of unconditional employment by the corporation. To trigger the statute, Brenner was required to show that the conditions leading to the departure of McGrath from the company and the firing of Andrew had been "targeted" to oppress her. Because plaintiff had not shown a malicious intent, the court found that the business-judgment rule barred it from second-guessing Arbee's management decisions.

[There was also evidence that Arbee had granted an unauthorized discount of $18,000 on a sale of Steelcase furniture to the U.N.; that Berkowitz, continuing a practice begun by Brenner, the plaintiff's father, had failed to record and collect taxes on sales of office furniture to Arbee employees; that Arbee had improperly failed to issue W–2s or Form 1099s for some temporary employees who made more than $600/year; and that in 1985, Arbee had improperly assigned non-union workers to certain union jobs.]

Berkowitz's Compensation

Brenner also asserted that Berkowitz was receiving a salary in excess of that authorized by his employment agreement. Berkowitz entered into an employment agreement with Arbee in November of 1976 that set his annual salary at $125,000 unless Arbee's board later determined that he should be paid a different amount. Berkowitz received two board-approved salary increases, with the result that in June 1981 he was earning $350,000 per year. Starting in 1983, however, he began to take salaries in excess of the approved sum. By 1989, Berkowitz reported a salary of $474,206.

Although Berkowitz testified that his compensation was clearly reflected in Arbee's financial statements and that the directors of the corporation knew of his compensation through informal discussions, plaintiff had received no official notice of the salary increases. Plaintiff produced evidence that tended to show that Berkowitz's compensation was excessive in comparison to Arbee's pre-tax profits.

The trial court rejected Brenner's allegation that payment of Berkowitz's annual salary was oppressive to her or that her expectations had been frustrated by Berkowitz's salary. It found that Berkowitz's salary was reasonable in light of the company's impressive growth. The court hinted, however, that if Berkowitz's salary continued to grow "at the expense of the corporation and its shareholders," and without corresponding increases of dividends or other benefits to the minority shareholder, Berkowitz's salary might be grounds for "a future claim of oppression."

Brenner's Removal from the Board

Finally, although the removal of plaintiff from the Board of Directors had frustrated her reasonable expectations in the corporation, the court determined that "appointing a receiver or provisional director" as permitted by the statute "would not be feasible given Arbee's consistent growth." Thus, the court ordered that plaintiff be reinstated as a Director. Although the court found that plaintiff had proven the illegal and fraudulent acts of (1) misapplication of discounts, (2) improper assumption of union identity, (3) failure to collect tax on employee sales, and (4) failure to file W–2's and 1099's on behalf of temporary employees, it nonetheless concluded that prior to trial the corporation had taken corrective action to ensure that those acts of misconduct had ceased. Relying on *Balvik v. Sylvester,* 411 *N.W.*2d 383 (N.D.1987), the court determined that for relief to be granted a continuing course of misconduct must be shown. Thus, the court held that "since the above mentioned bases for oppression have ceased, the court [could not] award statutory relief." The court did, however, enjoin Berkowitz from engaging in future misconduct in violation of his fiduciary duties.

More importantly, the court did not believe that considering Arbee's size, the few isolated acts of mismanagement had substantially affected Brenner or put her investment in the corporation at risk. . . .

At the conclusion of the trial, the court granted Brenner an injunction against future misconduct by Arbee and ordered her reinstatement to the Board. In the absence of an appropriate motion, the court believed it had no authority to order a buy-out under the statute. . . .

III.

The Appellate Division reversed the Chancery Division's judgment and remanded the case, holding that a finding of oppression is not necessary to trigger the statute if mismanagement, fraud, or illegality has been shown. *Brenner v. Berkowitz,* 261 *N.J.Super.* 63, 75, 617 *A.*2d 1225 (1992). Further, even if oppression were required, oppression exists whenever a company conducts its business illegally or fraudulently. *Ibid.* The court concluded that proof of "fraud or illegality" establishes a *per se* cause of action under the statute. *Id.* at 75–76, 617 *A.*2d 1225.

In addition, the Appellate Division disagreed with the court's holding that the statute seeks to remedy only "on-going" misconduct, and that because the misconduct had ceased in this case, plaintiff could not prevail under the statute. *Id.* at 77, 617 A.2d 1225.

Based on its conclusion that plaintiff's proofs had triggered the statute, and its finding that a buy-out was a more desirable remedy than dissolution of a thriving company, the Appellate Division remanded the case to the Chancery Division to entertain a buy-out motion from either party. *Id.* at 81, 617 A.2d 1225. ...

We granted defendants' petition for certification, 133 *N.J.* 435, 627 A.2d 1141 (1993)....

V.

N.J.S.A. 14A:12–7(1)(c), which became effective in 1974, provides:

> (1) The Superior Court, in an action brought under this section, may appoint a custodian, appoint a provisional director, order a sale of the corporation's stock as provided below, or enter a judgment dissolving the corporation, upon proof that

* * *

> (c) In the case of a corporation having 25 or less shareholders, the directors or those in control have acted fraudulently or illegally, mismanaged the corporation, or abused their authority as officers or directors or have acted oppressively or unfairly toward one or more minority shareholders in their capacities as shareholders, directors, officers, or employees....

We note that subsection (c) applies only to corporations with twenty-five or fewer shareholders. That requirement recognizes that shareholders in close corporations need special protection because of their unique vulnerability. That special vulnerability exists for three reasons.

First, because the majority has the controlling interest, it has the power to "dictate to the minority the manner in which the corporation is run." *Bostock [v. High Tech Elevator Indus.,],* 260 *N.J.Super.* at 443, 616 A.2d 1314. Second, shareholders in close corporations frequently consist of family members or friends and once the personal relationship is destroyed, the company deteriorates. *Id.* at 444, 616 A.2d 1314. Third, unlike shareholders in larger corporations, minority shareholders in a close corporation cannot readily sell their shares when they become dissatisfied with the management of the corporation. *Ibid.* Indeed, the discord in the corporation makes the minority stock even more difficult to sell. *Ibid.* ...

The limited bases for statutory relief, however, reflect an awareness that minority shareholders know the limitations of their power at the time they make their investment in a close corporation. Mere disagreement or discord between the shareholders is not sufficient for a violation of the close corporation statutory provision.

VI.

Defendants argue that fraudulent and illegal acts alone do not qualify as statutory violations unless the plaintiff also can show that such acts oppress the minority shareholder. That interpretation contradicts the plain language of the statute, which uses "or" rather than "and" in its description of the various bases for recovery. Moreover, as the Appellate Division observed, the legislative history supports a determination that the Legislature drafted the new statute in the disjunctive "to enumerate additional separate causes of action, independent of oppression"; and therefore " 'illegality' and 'fraud' as used in the statute are not meant to be synonymous with 'oppression.' " 261 *N.J.Super.* at 75, 617 *A.*2d 1225.

Oppression has been defined as frustrating a shareholder's reasonable expectations. 2 *O'Neal's Close Corporations* § 9.29 at 132 (Callaghan & Co., 3rd ed. 1988). Illegality and fraud may also frustrate a shareholder's reasonable expectations for a company but nonetheless not qualify as oppression. That is so because oppression is usually directed at a minority shareholder personally, whereas fraudulent or illegal conduct can instead be directed [solely at] the shareholder's investment in the corporation. For example, misappropriation of funds within a corporation may violate a shareholder's reasonable expectations regarding the management of the company but it may not be oppressive because it is not directed specifically at a minority shareholder. Nonetheless, because such fraudulent or illegal conduct would affect the corporation, and hence the shareholder's stock interest in that corporation, such conduct would be actionable under the statute, even in the absence of oppression, because the statute is written in the disjunctive.

Nor must fraudulent or illegal acts be "on-going" at the time of trial for the statute to apply. The statute's plain language provides that a cause of action exists "upon proof that . . . the directors or those in control *have acted* fraudulently or illegally." *N.J.S.A.* 14A:12–7(1)(c) (emphasis added). If the Legislature had intended that the statute apply only to continuing acts, then the use of present tense, *i.e.,* "are acting," would have accomplished that goal. In this statute, the Legislature used a verb form connoting past conduct.

Moreover, as the Appellate Division observed, "A requirement that the fraudulent conduct must be on-going frustrates [the legislative purpose] because it allows the majority to abuse the minority as long as the abuse ceases prior to the date a decision is rendered . . ." 261 *N.J.Super.* at 77, 617 *A.*2d 1225. Requiring that the conduct be continuing would, therefore, work a grave injustice on the minority shareholder by depriving her of a remedy when her reasonable expectations for the corporation are thwarted.

VII.

Although we agree with the Appellate Division on the disjunctive nature of the statute and the rejection of the requirement that the misconduct be continuing, we need to clarify the court's findings about the amount of fraud or illegality that qualifies as a violation of the statute. The language and result of the Appellate Division's opinion might lead to the conclusion that any showing of fraud or illegality qualifies as a *per se* violation of the statute. See 261 *N.J.Super.* at 75–76, 617 A.2d 1225. We disagree. A *per se* rule suggests that a court has no discretion to weigh or to consider the effect, if any, of the misconduct on the minority shareholder or her corporate investment.

We recognize that the statute should be interpreted broadly to provide remedies for the "distinctive problems of close corporations." 2 *O'Neal's Close Corporations, supra,* § 9.29 at 134. However, in addition to demonstrating fraudulent or illegal conduct, mismanagement, or abuse of authority, *or* oppressive or unfair conduct, a plaintiff must also demonstrate a nexus between that misconduct and the minority shareholder or her interest in the corporation. The remedies that a court will apply will logically depend on the harm to the minority shareholder or her interest in the corporation. In enacting the 1972 amendments the Legislature intended that the court "look beyond direct harm to the value of a shareholder's investment and to consider all pertinent factors." *N.J.S.A.* 14A:12–7, Commissioner's Comment—1972 Amendments. Therefore, in determining the nexus between the misconduct and the harm to the shareholder, the court must consider those acts that affect or jeopardize a shareholder's stock interest as well as those acts that may be specifically targeted to the shareholder. The court has discretion to determine which factors are pertinent to its evaluation of the quality and nature of the misconduct, but certain factors apply in most cases.

Because not all violations will cause a minority shareholder ascertainable harm, a court should consider the seriousness of the violation. For example, a corporation's mere failure to abide by a single tax regulation may be insufficient to bring the circumstances within the statute. Similarly, the court should consider whether the misconduct places the minority shareholder's investment at risk. Thus, in the tax violation example, the court should weigh whether the failure to abide by a single tax regulation resulted in a fine that was substantial in relation to the corporation's net earnings, or otherwise threatened the corporation's existence or its ability to function. Focusing on the harm to the minority shareholder reflects a departure from the traditional focus, which was solely on the wrongdoing by those in control, and reflects the current trend of recognizing the special nature of close corporations. *See* Sprat-lin, [*Modern Remedies for Oppression in the Closely Held Corpora-tion,* 60 Miss.L.J. 405, 411 (1990)].

Courts also should consider whether the misconduct thwarts the minority shareholder's reasonable expectations of his or her role in the corporation. The special nature of the close corporation requires that the court go beyond considering merely monetary harm.

> "The special circumstances, arrangements and personal relationships that frequently [underlie] the formation of close corporations generate certain expectations among the share-holders concerning their respective roles in corporate affairs, including management and earnings. These expectations pre-clude the drawing of any conclusions about the impact of a particular course of corporate conduct on a shareholder with-out taking into consideration the role that he is expected to play. Accordingly a court must determine initially the under-standing of the parties in this regard. Armed with this infor-mation, the court can then decide whether the controlling shareholders have acted in a fashion that is contrary to this un-derstanding * * *." [*Exadaktilos v. Cinnaminson Realty Co.,* 167 *N.J.Super.* 141, 154–155, 400 A.2d 554 (Law Div.1979), *aff'd o.b.,* 173 *N.J.Super.* 559, 414 A.2d 994 (App.Div.), *certif. denied,* 85 *N.J.* 112, 425 A.2d 273 (1980).]

In determining whether a shareholder's expectations are rea-sonable and whether the corporation or controlling shareholders or directors unreasonably thwarted them, courts should consider even non-monetary expectations of the shareholder. Indeed, "termi-nation of a shareholder's status as an employee is a much more common means of oppression in a close corporation than is in-fringement of a shareholder's status as a shareholder." 2 *O'Neal's Close Corporations, supra,* § 9.29 at 134. Even the termination of the employment of the shareholder's children in certain situations may constitute oppressive conduct sufficient to constitute a viola-tion under the statute.

Based on the circumstances of a given case, additional factors that may warrant consideration include whether the minority share-holder was aware of the misconduct prior to filing suit but failed to act, and whether the minority shareholder participated in the mis-conduct. A court could reasonably determine that unfairness would result if a minority shareholder were permitted to seek judicial intervention after years of acquiescence or participation in the alleged misconduct. . . .

VIII.

If a minority shareholder has met her burden of demonstrating both misconduct and a nexus between the harm and the minority shareholder's interest in or expectations for the company, the court must then determine what remedy is appropriate to redress the harm.

Subsection (1) provides a list of potential remedies that "may" be imposed when the statute is violated. It states:

> (1) The Superior Court, in an action brought under this section, *may* appoint a custodian, appoint a provisional director, order a sale of the corporation's stock as provided below, or enter a judgment dissolving the corporation * * *. [*N.J.S.A.* 14A:12–7(1) (emphasis added).]

The use of the word "may" indicates that the court has discretion in determining whether any of the enumerated remedies is appropriate to a case. *See, e.g., Harvey v. Board of Chosen Freeholders,* 30 *N.J.* 381, 391, 153 A.2d 10 (1959) (finding that absent legislative intent to the contrary, use of word "may" indicates that provision is permissive, not mandatory). Here, the legislative intent for this statute affirms the plain meaning of the language that the remedies are "discretionary." Comment on 1972 Amendments.

Neither the parties nor the courts in this case have considered dissolution as an appropriate remedy. We agree. Dissolution is an extreme remedy to be imposed with caution after a careful balancing of the interests at stake . . . .

In 1988, the Legislature added subsection (9), which offers guidance for the circumstances under which dissolution is warranted. It states:

> (9) In determining whether to enter a judgment of dissolution in an action brought under this section, the court shall take into consideration whether the corporation is operating profitably and in the best interests of its shareholders, but shall not deny entry of such a judgment solely on that ground. [*N.J.S.A.* 14A:12–7(9).]

The court is thus required to balance the appropriateness of dissolution as a remedy against the loss to society if the corporation is forced to liquidate. Factors to be considered in weighing the loss to society include the shareholders' loss of goodwill because the corporation is not sold as a going concern, the loss of jobs by employees, and the loss of a steady source of income by suppliers. *See* O'Neill, *supra,* 22 *Seton Hall L.Rev.* at 693.

Caution is needed when determining whether dissolution is appropriate, because "the statutory remedy was meant only to protect the minority, not to provide a weapon to enable it to obtain unfair advantage against the majority." Lawrence E. Mitchell, *The Death of Fiduciary Duty in Close Corporations,* 138 *U.Pa.L.Rev.* 1675, 1730 (1990); Pachman, [*Divorce, Corporate Style: Dissolution, Oppression, and Commercial Morality,* 10 *Seton Hall L.Rev.*

315, 331 (1979)]. The statute would become a weapon if dissolution were granted each time a minority shareholder demonstrated some misconduct by the directors or controlling shareholders that falls within the statute's requirements. Then, "[m]inority shareholders [might] use the threat of dissolution to force the majority to accede to their demands or . . . to pay sizeable sums in 'settlement' * * *." Pachman, *supra,* 10 *Seton Hall L.Rev.* at 326.

As an alternative to dissolution the Legislature authorized a court-ordered buy-out. *N.J.S.A.* 14A:12–7(8) provides:

> (8) Upon motion of the corporation or any shareholder who is a party to the proceeding, the court may order the sale of all shares of the corporation's stock held by any other shareholder who is a party to the proceeding to either the corporation or the moving shareholder or shareholders, whichever is specified in the motion, if the court determines in its discretion that such an order would be fair and equitable to all parties under all the circumstances of the case.

Previously, the statute permitted such a motion to be made only by a fifty (50%) percent shareholder. Corporation Law Revision Commission, Comment on 1988 Amendments to *N.J.S.A.* 14A:12–7. The Appellate Division in *Bostock, supra,* properly held that the statute's plain language permits compulsion of the *sale* of a party's stock to either the moving shareholder or the corporation. 260 *N.J.Super.* at 445, 616 A.2d 1314. Defendant argues, however, that the statute does not permit compelling the *purchase* of the minority's stock by either the majority shareholders or the corporation.

Read literally, the statute requires the prospective purchaser—either the corporation or a shareholder in the litigation—to move to compel a purchase of stock held by another shareholder. The requirement that a motion be filed appears to reflect a legislative purpose to authorize specifically only voluntary purchases. Although the Commissioners' Comment suggests that a motion by a shareholder may be sufficient to compel a purchase by the corporation, see Corporation Law Revision Commission, Comment on 1988 Amendments to *N.J.S.A. 14A:12–7,* we are inclined to construe the statute as authorizing specifically only voluntary purchases by either a shareholder or the corporation.

We have no doubt, however, that the enactment of *N.J.S.A.* 14A:12–7 was not intended to supersede the inherent common law power of the Chancery Division to achieve equity. That the court would have the statutory power to order dissolution of a corporation, but not the lesser authority to compel the corporation to use its assets to acquire the stock of an oppressed shareholder, would make no sense. Both dissolution and a corporate purchase of a shareholder's stock involve a distribution of corporate assets. In the case of dissolution, a distribution results in the termination of the corporation's business, with its assets being proportionately distributed to the stockholders. In the case of a buy-out, the corporation may be required to distribute retained as well as prospective earnings, but the corporate enterprise survives.

Accordingly, although the statute authorizes only voluntary purchases of stock, we are persuaded that in appropriate circumstances a court exercising its equitable powers, as an alternative to dissolution, could compel the purchase of a shareholder's stock by the corporation; under exceptional circumstances, the court's equitable power might encompass the power to compel an involuntary buy-out by the other shareholders. In exercising the [remedy] of an involuntary buy-out, however, a court must exercise caution. Because an involuntary purchase of stock is not a statutorily authorized power, its use should be reserved primarily for those instances in which the only practical alternative to an involuntary buy-out would be dissolution. . . .

Although a buy-out may be preferable to dissolution, other remedies may be more appropriate to a buy-out. The statute itself states that a buy-out is warranted only when it would be "fair and equitable to *all* parties." *N.J.S.A.* 14A:12–7(8) (emphasis added). Indeed, the Commission provided that "[e]ach of these remedies is ... not exclusive; accordingly, the court is given the flexibility necessary to handle any particular situation." Corporation Law Revision Commission, Final Report—June 15, 1972, 14A *N.J.S.A.* XVII, XXII (West Supp.1993).

Based on the permissive working of the statute, when a statutory violation occurs, a court retains its discretion to fashion equitable remedies. Such equitable remedies are valuable because they allow relief to be fashioned directly to redress the statutory violations shown. . . .

In many other states, statutes authorize "courts to provide relief other than dissolution, and then [set] out a *nonexclusive* list of what that relief may be." 2 *O'Neal's Close Corporations, supra,* § 9.35 at 169 (emphasis added). Some of the equitable remedies O'Neal lists are:

(1) Cancelling or altering any provision of the articles of incorporation or the bylaws;

(2) Cancelling, altering, or enjoining any resolution or other act of the corporation;

(3) Directing or prohibiting any act of the corporation or of the shareholders, directors, officers, or other persons party to the action;

(4) Providing for the sale of all the property and franchises of the corporation to a single purchaser;

(5) Requiring dissolution at a future date, effective only if the parties do not resolve their differences before that time;

(6) Appointing a receiver or special fiscal agent to continue the operation of the corporation for both majority and minority until differences are resolved or until oppressive conduct ceases;

(7) Retaining jurisdiction for the protection of minority shareholders without the appointment of a custodian, receiver, or similar official;

(8) Ordering an accounting or ordering access to corporate records;

(9) Enjoining continuing acts of oppressive conduct, *e.g.*, by reducing unjustified or excessive salary or bonus payments to controlling shareholders;

(10) Requiring declaration of a dividend;

(11) Permitting the minority to purchase additional shares;

(12) Rescinding a corporate act that is unfair to the minority;

(13) Treating a group of related corporations as a single entity for the purpose of determining appropriate relief. 2 *O'Neal's Close Corporations, supra,* § 9.35 at 170–171; *see also Baker v. Commercial Body Builders, Inc.,* 264 *Or.* 614, 507 *P.*2d 387, 395–96 (1973) (listing ten alternatives to dissolution for resolving minority shareholder's claims against close corporation); Spratlin, *supra,* 60 *Miss. L.J.* at 420–22.

The existence of less harsh remedies has the effect of increasing the willingness of courts to intervene and provide relief to shareholders.

IX.

With regard to *N.J.S.A.* 14A:12–7(1)(c), we hold that (1) the statute is written in the disjunctive and therefore a finding either of fraud or of illegality, without a finding of oppression, may be sufficient to permit a court to conclude that the statute has been violated; (2) the statute does not require that the misconduct be continuing for a violation to be established; and (3) the court must consider the quality of the misconduct to determine whether the minority shareholder has demonstrated a nexus, *i.e.*, that the misconduct caused harm to the minority shareholder or her interest in the corporation.

We reject plaintiff's argument that *any* showing of illegality or fraud qualifies as a *per se* violation of the statute. Instead, the trial court must evaluate the quality of the misconduct or oppression to determine its seriousness. Although we encourage a review of whether the misconduct or oppression is directed at the minority shareholder, even fraudulent acts not directed specifically at the shareholder, but that place the minority shareholder's interest in that corporation at risk, may be sufficient to constitute a violation of the statute.

We hold that the statutory remedies of *N.J.S.A.* 14A:12–7(1) are discretionary. Even when the statute is triggered, the trial court has the discretion to choose the appropriate remedies. Most acts of misconduct or oppression will warrant some type of remedy, but only the most egregious cases will warrant the drastic remedies permitted by the statute. Importantly, courts are not limited to the statutory remedies, but have a wide array of equitable remedies available to them.

Indeed, the statutory remedy of dissolution should be imposed only in the most egregious cases. The buy-out remedy is a preferable alternative to dissolution, but it may not be preferable to equitable remedies also available to the court. In many cases, the court will find that its equitable powers adequately balance the need to redress the statutory violation against society's interest in maintaining functioning corporations.

Cases involving *N.J.S.A.* 14A:12–7(1)(c) are very fact-sensitive, and thus any hard and fast rules are difficult to formulate. The many possible types of relationships in close corporations compel a flexible approach to the problem. The statute intends to protect minority shareholders in the vulnerable setting of a close corporation. Because the Legislature's goal was fairness to all shareholders, however, courts must ensure that minority shareholders are not permitted to use the statute to tyrannize the majority.

Applying the law to the facts of this case, we find that the quantity and substantiality of the acts of misconduct committed by defendants do not warrant any more expansive relief than that granted by the Chancery Division. The record contains substantial proof that Brenner never had any expectations that she was going to manage Arbee. From the inception of the corporation, Brenner was intended to be a minority shareholder and a director. Complete control of the management of the business was given to Berkowitz. None of the isolated incidents recounted above prevented the growth of the corporation or Brenner's investment in the company. Indeed the substantial growth of the business has increased the value of Brenner's investment. Nonetheless, we approve of the Chancery Division's injunction against any future acts of misconduct.

Although Brenner testified that she expected employment benefits from Arbee, she has not demonstrated that the corporation's termination of her son and future daughter-in-law was oppressive to her. In many close corporations, a shareholder herself may expect to be employed with the company from its inception. Here, Brenner instead expected Arbee to employ her children when they became old enough to work. A shareholder's expectation of employment must be balanced against the corporation's ability to run its business efficiently. Even in the more common case of a shareholder's direct employment with a company, the court is hesitant to overturn the corporation's valued exercise of its business judgment. *Exadaktilos, supra,* 167 *N.J.Super.* at 155–56, 400 A.2d 554. Not surprisingly, when the employment of the shareholder's relative is at issue, the shareholder will find it even more difficult to establish that those in control of a corporation acted oppressively. A heightened burden exists particularly in the case of a relative who was not employed at the beginning of the corporate relationship. The Chancery Division properly concluded that it could not second-guess the corporation's exercise of its business-judgment.

Although the corporate founders never intended that Brenner manage Arbee, she was expected to be a director and a substantial shareholder. The Chancery Division properly reinstated Brenner as a director of Arbee. As a director, Brenner is entitled to review the books and records of the company and to participate in the major decision-making processes of Arbee. We expect that she will be a more active director than she has been in the past. Brenner does not challenge the salary and dividends returned on her invest-ment—perhaps because she considered the salary paid to her son an indirect economic benefit. Nevertheless, as a substantial share-holder of Arbee, she is entitled to financial benefits commensurate with her holdings. As did the Chancery Division, we caution the Berkowitzes that any increase in benefits to the majority sharehold-ers without a corresponding benefit to Brenner may provide Bren-ner with a future claim under *N.J.S.A.* 14A:12–7. Moreover, the occurrence of future acts of misconduct may require the court to consider other relief, including the appointment of a provisional director. ...

We conclude that *N.J.S.A.* 14A:12–7(10) does not apply to either plaintiff or defendants.

We reverse the judgment of the Appellate Division and reinstate the judgment of the Chancery Division. No costs.

For Reversal and Reinstatement—Chief Justice WILENTZ, and Justices CLIFFORD, HANDLER, POLLOCK, O'HERN, GARIBALI and STEIN—7.

Opposed—None.

MUELLENBERG v. BIKON CORP., 143 N.J. 168, 669 A.2d 1382 (1996). "... [The trial] court found that at the January 20, 1993 shareholders' meeting, Muellenberg and Passarini [two of the three shareholders in Bikon Corporation (sometimes referred to as BNJ)] had begun efforts to freeze out Burg [the third shareholder, who was Bikon's general manager]. They had declared a $180,000 dividend that they should have known would deprive Bikon of needed cash to operate and thus take away Burg's ability to perform successfully as general manager. In addition, despite the lack of any showing of abuse by Mr. Burg in operating the company, they began to strip Burg of his day-to-day control as general manager by resolving that bank account withdrawals should be made only by plaintiff [Muellenberg] or by joint signatures of plaintiff and defendant Burg. And, finally, the court found that the majority directors, as 'plaintiff's counsel acknowledged ... in summation,' intended to vote Burg out as a director and terminate him as general manager and employee of the company....

"... N.J.S.A. 14A:12–7(1)(c) allows a court to grant relief when controlling shareholders 'have acted fraudulently or illegally, mismanaged the corporation, or abused their authority as officers or directors or have acted oppressively or unfairly' toward a minority shareholder. The trial court did not find any fraud or mismanagement on the part of Muellenberg or Passerini. The question is whether their actions were oppressive. Ordinarily, oppression by shareholders is clearly shown when they have awarded themselves excessive compensation, furnished inadequate dividends, or misapplied and wasted corporate funds. Giannotti v. Hamway, 239 Va. 14, 387 S.E.2d 725 (Va.1990). This did not occur here.

"The remaining measure of oppression in the small corporation is whether the fair expectations of the parties have been met. When personal relations among the participants in a close corporation break down, the 'reasonable expectations' that participants had, for example, the expectation that their employment would be secure or that they would enjoy meaningful participation in the management of the business, become difficult, if not impossible, to fulfill. *Meiselman*, ... 307 S.E.2d 551. A person who buys a minority interest in a close corporation does so, not only in the hope of enjoying an increase in the value of the shareholder's stake in the business, but for the assurance of employment in the business in a managerial position. In addition to the security of long-term employment and the prospect of financial return in the form of salary, the expectation includes a voice in the operation and management of the business and the formulation of its plans for future development. Ingle v. Glamore Motor Sales, 73 N.Y.2d 183, 535 N.E.2d 1311, 1319, 538 N.Y.S.2d 771 (N.Y.1989) (Hancock, J., dissenting). In this case, it is reasonable to conclude that Burg's fair expectations were that should he give up his prior employment with a competitor company and enter this small corporation, he would enjoy an important position in the management affairs of the corporation....

"We agree that it cannot be considered oppression when controlling shareholders seek to rein in management and control the affairs of their corporation. But the expectations of Muellenberg and Passerini that they might exercise majority power conflicted with the expectations of Burg, and were confined by their fiduciary duties to their co-venturer....

"The statute ... plainly allows the minority to seek a court order for the sale of the stock of 'any other shareholder.' In most situations, oppressed minority shareholders will lack the resources to buy out the interests of controlling shareholders. As a result, claims of oppression are typically remedied by arranging for the corporation or the majority shareholders to buy out the interests of the minority shareholder. In this case, the record contained the following evidence in support of Burg: Burg was willing and able to purchase the shares of Muellenberg and Passerini; Burg, who owns the land on which BNJ's offices are located, was most active in operating the company since its inception; Burg is the only shareholder who works full-time for BNJ and the company has been his only source of income for over ten years; Burg was primarily responsible for developing the company's contacts in the United States and Canada and is best situated to maintain the existing operation; and finally, it was Burg who sought to preserve the corporation at a time when Muellenberg and Passerini attempted to dissolve it. See Musto v. Vidas, 281 N.J.Super. 548, 658 A.2d 1305 (App.Div.1995) (reversing minority buy-out of the majority when minority shareholder had not been actively involved in the operation of the company for seven years)....

"Thus, while a minority buy-out of the majority is an uncommon remedy, it was the appropriate one here. The trial court acted within its discretion in ordering Muellenberg and Adda to sell their shares in BNJ to Burg. This remedy is authorized by N.J.S.A. 14A:12–7(8) and is consistent with decisions holding that courts are not limited to statutory remedies, but have a wide variety of equitable remedies also available to them. *Brenner,* ... 134 N.J. at 516; Walensky v. Jonathan Royce Int'l, 264 N.J.Super. 276, 279, 624 A.2d 613 (App.Div.), certif. denied, 134 N.J. 480 (1993)."

NOTE ON EVOLVING EXPECTATIONS

In cases where the contours of fiduciary duties among shareholders in close corporations, or the availability of dissolution for oppression, turn on the shareholders' reasonable expectations, should those expectations be determined as of the time the corporation was formed, or should the court take account of the way in which the shareholders' expectations evolved over time? In A.W. Chesterton Co. v. Chesterton, 128 F.3d 1 (1st Cir.1997), J.W. Chesterton Co. had been a closely held corporation since 1885. In 1985, all the shareholders, including Arthur Chesterton, agreed to change the corporation's tax status under the Internal Revenue Code from a C corporation to an S corporation. In the early 1990s, Arthur Chesterton proposed to transfer some of his stock to two shell corporations that he wholly owned. In order to qualify for S Corporation status, a corporation may not have any shareholders who are themselves corporations. Therefore, Arthur Chesterton's proposed transfer would result in a loss of Chesterton Co.'s favorable tax treatment under subchapter S. Chesterton Co. and its other shareholders sued Arthur Chesterton to enjoin him from making the proposed transfer.

The First Circuit granted the injunction. "Under Massachusetts law, the expectations and understanding of the shareholders are relevant to a breach of fiduciary duty determination ... The existence of the agreement ... sheds light on the Company's and other shareholders' expectations...."

Insert the following Note at p. 552 of the Unabridged Edition, after the Note on Matter of Pace Photographers:

FRIEDMAN v. BEWAY REALTY CORP., 87 N.Y.2d 161, 638 N.Y.S.2d 399, 661 N.E.2d 972 (1995). "[I]n fixing fair value, courts should determine the minority shareholder's proportionate interest in the going concern value of the corporation as a whole, that is, ' "what a willing purchaser, in an arm's length transaction, would offer for the *corporation* as an operating business' " (*Matter of Pace Photographers [Rosen],* 71 N.Y.2d, at 748, *supra,* quoting *Matter of Blake v. Blake Agency,* 107 A.D.2d, at 146, *supra* [emphasis supplied]).

"Consistent with that approach, we have approved a methodology for fixing the fair value of minority shares in a close corporation under which the investment value of the entire enterprise was ascertained through a capitalization of earnings (taking into account the unmarketability of the corporate stock) and then fair value was calculated on the basis of the petitioners' proportionate share of all outstanding corporate stock (*Matter of Seagroatt Floral Co.,* 78 N.Y.2d, at 442, 446, *supra*).

"Imposing a discount for the minority status of the dissenting shares here, as argued by the corporations, would in our view conflict with two central equitable principles of corporate governance we have developed for fair value adjudications of minority shareholder interests under Business Corporation Law §§ 623 and 1118. A minority discount would necessarily deprive minority shareholders of their proportionate interest in a going concern, as guaranteed by our decisions previously discussed. Likewise, imposing a minority discount on the compensation payable to dissenting stockholders for their shares in a proceeding under Business Corporation Law §§ 623 or 1118 would result in minority shares being valued below that of majority shares, thus violating our mandate of equal treatment of all shares of the same class in minority stockholder buyouts.

"A minority discount on the value of dissenters' shares would also significantly undermine one of the major policies behind the appraisal legislation embodied now in Business Corporation Law § 623, the remedial goal of the statute to 'protect[ ] minority shareholders "from being forced to sell at unfair values imposed by those dominating the corporation while allowing the majority to proceed with its desired [corporate action]" ' (*Matter of Cawley v. SCM Corp.*, 72 N.Y.2d, at 471, *supra*, quoting *Alpert v. 28 Williams St. Corp.*, 63 N.Y.2d 557, 567–568). This protective purpose of the statute prevents the shifting of proportionate economic value of the corporation as a going concern from minority to majority stockholders. As stated by the Delaware Supreme Court, 'to fail to accord to a minority shareholder the full proportionate value of his [or her] shares imposes a penalty for lack of control, and unfairly enriches the majority stockholders who may reap a windfall from the appraisal process by cashing out a dissenting shareholder' (*Cavalier Oil Corp. v. Harnett*, 564 A.2d 1137, 1145 [Del.]).

"Furthermore, a mandatory reduction in the fair value of minority shares to reflect their owners' lack of power in the administration of the corporation will inevitably encourage oppressive majority conduct, thereby further driving down the compensation necessary to pay for the value of minority shares. 'Thus, the greater the misconduct by the majority, the less they need to pay for the minority's shares' (Murdock, *The Evolution of Effective Remedies for Minority Shareholders and Its Impact Upon Evaluation of Minority Shares*, 65 Notre Dame L.Rev. 425, 487).

"We also note that a minority discount has been rejected in a substantial majority of other jurisdictions. 'Thus, statistically, minority discounts are almost uniformly viewed with disfavor by State courts' (*id.*, at 481). The imposition of a minority discount in derogation of minority stockholder appraisal remedies has been rejected as well by the American Law Institute in its Principles of Corporate Governance (*see*, 2 ALI, Principles of Corporate Governance § 7.22, at 314–315; comment *e* to § 7.22, at 324 [1994]).
. . .

"We likewise find no basis to disturb the trial court's discretion in failing to assign any additional diminution in value of petitioners' shares here because they were subject to contractual restrictions on voluntary transfer. As we noted in *Matter of Pace Photographers (Rosen) (supra)*, a statutory acquisition of minority shares by a corporation pursuant to the Business Corporation Law is not a voluntary sale of corporate shares as contemplated by a restrictive stockholder agreement and, therefore, 'the express covenant is literally inapplicable' (71 N.Y.2d, at 749). Nor is there any reason to disturb Supreme Court's award of prejudgment interest."

However, the court approved a discount for marketability.

———

Chapter VII

THE DUTY OF CARE AND THE DUTY TO ACT LAWFULLY

SECTION 1. THE DUTY OF CARE

(a) THE BASIC STANDARD OF CARE; THE DUTY TO MONITOR

Insert the following case at p. 584 of the Unabridged Edition, after the excerpt from the Corporate Director's Handbook, and p. 400 of the Concise Edition, after Note on Corporate Criminal Liability, the Sentencing Guidelines, and Compliance Programs:

In Re CAREMARK INTERNATIONAL INC. DERIVATIVE LITIGATION

Delaware Court of Chancery, 1996.
698 A.2d 959.

ALLEN, Chancellor.

Pending is a motion pursuant to Chancery Rule 23.1 to approve as fair and reasonable a proposed settlement of a consolidated derivative action on behalf of Caremark International, Inc. ("Caremark"). The suit involves claims that the members of Caremark's board of directors (the "Board") breached their fiduciary duty of care to Caremark in connection with alleged violations by Caremark employees of federal and state laws and regulations applicable to health care providers. As a result of the alleged violations, Caremark was subject to an extensive four year investigation by the United States Department of Health and Human Services and the Department of Justice. In 1994 Caremark was charged in an indictment with multiple felonies. It thereafter entered into a number of agreements with the Department of Justice and others. Those agreements included a plea agreement in which Caremark pleaded guilty to a single felony of mail fraud and agreed to pay civil and criminal fines. Subsequently, Caremark agreed to make reimbursements to various private and public parties. In all, the payments that Caremark has been required to make total approximately $250 million.

This suit was filed in 1994, purporting to seek on behalf of the company recovery of these losses from the individual defendants who constitute the board of directors of Caremark.[1] The parties now propose that it be settled and, after notice to Caremark shareholders, a hearing on the fairness of the proposal was held on August 16, 1996.

A motion of this type requires the court to assess the strengths and weaknesses of the claims asserted in light of the discovery record and to evaluate the fairness and adequacy of the consideration offered to the corporation in exchange for the release of all claims made or arising from the facts alleged. The ultimate issue then is whether the proposed settlement appears to be fair to the corporation and its absent shareholders. In this effort the court does not determine contested facts, but evaluates the claims and defenses on the discovery record to achieve a sense of the relative strengths of the parties' positions. Polk v. Good, Del.Supr., 507 A.2d 531, 536 (1986). In doing this, in most instances, the court is constrained by the absence of a truly adversarial process, since inevitably both sides support the settlement and legally assisted objectors are rare. Thus, the facts stated hereafter represent the court's effort to understand the context of the motion from the discovery record, but do not deserve the respect that judicial findings after trial are customarily accorded.

Legally, evaluation of the central claim made entails consideration of the legal standard governing a board of directors' obligation to supervise or monitor corporate performance. For the reasons set forth below I conclude, in light of the discovery record, that there is a very low probability that it would be determined that the directors of Caremark breached any duty to appropriately monitor and supervise the enterprise. Indeed the record tends to show an active consideration by Caremark management and its Board of the Caremark structures and programs that ultimately led to the company's indictment and to the large financial losses incurred in the settlement of those claims. It does not tend to show knowing or intentional violation of law. Neither the fact that the Board, although advised by lawyers and accountants, did not accurately predict the severe consequences to the company that would ultimately follow from the deployment by the company of the strategies and practices that ultimately led to this liability, nor the scale of the liability, gives rise to an inference of breach of any duty imposed by corporation law upon the directors of Caremark.

I. BACKGROUND

For these purposes I regard the following facts, suggested by the discovery record, as material. Caremark, a Delaware corpora-

---

1. Thirteen of the Directors have been members of the Board since November 30, 1992. Nancy Brinker joined the Board in October 1993.

tion with its headquarters in Northbrook, Illinois, was created in November 1992 when it was spun-off from Baxter International, Inc. ("Baxter") and became a publicly held company listed on the New York Stock Exchange. The business practices that created the problem pre-dated the spin-off. During the relevant period Caremark was involved in two main health care business segments, providing patient care and managed care services. As part of its patient care business, which accounted for the majority of Caremark's revenues, Caremark provided alternative site health care services, including infusion therapy, growth hormone therapy, HIV/AIDS-related treatments and hemophilia therapy. Caremark's managed care services included prescription drug programs and the operation of multi-specialty group practices.

A. Events Prior to the Government Investigation

A substantial part of the revenues generated by Caremark's businesses is derived from third party payments, insurers, and Medicare and Medicaid reimbursement programs. The latter source of payments are subject to the terms of the Anti–Referral Payments Law ("ARPL") which prohibits health care providers from paying any form of remuneration to induce the referral of Medicare or Medicaid patients. From its inception, Caremark entered into a variety of agreements with hospitals, physicians, and health care providers for advice and services, as well as distribution agreements with drug manufacturers, as had its predecessor prior to 1992. Specifically, Caremark did have a practice of entering into contracts for services (e.g., consultation agreements and research grants) with physicians at least some of whom prescribed or recommended services or products that Caremark provided to Medicare recipients and other patients. Such contracts were not prohibited by the ARPL but they obviously raised a possibility of unlawful "kickbacks."

As early as 1989, Caremark's predecessor issued an internal "Guide to Contractual Relationships" ("Guide") to govern its employees in entering into contracts with physicians and hospitals. The Guide tended to be reviewed annually by lawyers and updated. Each version of the Guide stated as Caremark's and its predecessor's policy that no payments would be made in exchange for or to induce patient referrals. But what one might deem a prohibited quid pro quo was not always clear. Due to a scarcity of court decisions interpreting the ARPL, however, Caremark repeatedly publicly stated that there was uncertainty concerning Caremark's interpretation of the law.

To clarify the scope of the ARPL, the United States Department of Health and Human Services ("HHS") issued "safe harbor" regulations in July 1991 stating conditions under which financial relationships between health care service providers and patient referral sources, such as physicians, would not violate the ARPL. Caremark contends that the narrowly drawn regulations gave limited guidance as to the legality of many of the agreements used by Caremark that did not fall within the safe-harbor. Caremark's predecessor, however, amended many of its standard forms of agreement with health care providers and revised the Guide in an apparent attempt to comply with the new regulations.

B. Government Investigation and Related Litigation

In August 1991, the HHS Office of the Inspector General ("OIG") initiated an investigation of Caremark's predecessor. Caremark's predecessor was served with a subpoena requiring the production of documents, including contracts between Caremark's predecessor and physicians (Quality Service Agreements ("QSAs")). Under the QSAs, Caremark's predecessor appears to have paid physicians fees for monitoring patients under Caremark's predecessor's care, including Medicare and Medicaid recipients. Sometimes apparently those monitoring patients were referring physicians, which raised ARPL concerns.

In March 1992, the Department of Justice ("DOJ") joined the OIG investigation and separate investigations were commenced by several additional federal and state agencies.[2]

C. Caremark's Response to the Investigation

During the relevant period, Caremark had approximately 7,000 employees and ninety branch operations. It had a decentralized management structure. By May 1991, however, Caremark asserts that it had begun making attempts to centralize its management structure in order to increase supervision over its branch operations.

The first action taken by management, as a result of the initiation of the OIG investigation, was an announcement that as of October 1, 1991, Caremark's predecessor would no longer pay management fees to physicians for services to Medicare and Medicaid patients. Despite this decision, Caremark asserts that its management, pursuant to advice, did not believe that such payments were illegal under the existing laws and regulations.

During this period, Caremark's Board took several additional steps consistent with an effort to assure compliance with company policies concerning the ARPL and the contractual forms in the Guide. In April 1992, Caremark published a fourth revised version of its Guide apparently designed to assure that its agreements either complied with the ARPL and regulations or excluded Medicare and Medicaid patients altogether. In addition, in September 1992,

---

2. In addition to investigating whether Caremark's financial relationships with health care providers were intended to induce patient referrals, inquiries were made concerning Caremark's billing practices, activities which might lead to excessive and medically unnecessary treatments for patients, potentially improper waivers of patient co-payment obligations, and the adequacy of records kept at Caremark pharmacies.

Caremark instituted a policy requiring its regional officers, Zone Presidents, to approve each contractual relationship entered into by Caremark with a physician.

Although there is evidence that inside and outside counsel had advised Caremark's directors that their contracts were in accord with the law, Caremark recognized that some uncertainty respecting the correct interpretation of the law existed. In its 1992 annual report, Caremark disclosed the ongoing government investigations, acknowledged that if penalties were imposed on the company they could have a material adverse effect on Caremark's business, and stated that no assurance could be given that its interpretation of the ARPL would prevail if challenged.

Throughout the period of the government investigations, Caremark had an internal audit plan designed to assure compliance with business and ethics policies. In addition, Caremark employed Price Waterhouse as its outside auditor. On February 8, 1993, the [Audit &] Ethics Committee of Caremark's Board received and reviewed an outside auditors report by Price Waterhouse which concluded that there were no material weaknesses in Caremark's control structure.[3] Despite the positive findings of Price Waterhouse, however, on April 20, 1993, the Audit & Ethics Committee adopted a new internal audit charter requiring a comprehensive review of compliance policies and the compilation of an employee ethics handbook concerning such policies.[4]

The Board appears to have been informed about this project and other efforts to assure compliance with the law. For example, Caremark's management reported to the Board that Caremark's sales force was receiving an ongoing education regarding the ARPL and the proper use of Caremark's form contracts which had been approved by in-house counsel. On July 27, 1993, the new ethics manual, expressly prohibiting payments in exchange for referrals and requiring employees to report all illegal conduct to a toll free confidential ethics hotline, was approved and allegedly disseminated.[5] The record suggests that Caremark continued these policies in subsequent years, causing employees to be given revised versions of the ethics manual and requiring them to participate in training sessions concerning compliance with the law.

During 1993, Caremark took several additional steps which appear to have been aimed at increasing management supervision.

---

3. At that time, Price Waterhouse viewed the outcome of the OIG Investigation as uncertain. After further audits, however, on February 7, 1995, Price Waterhouse informed the Audit & Ethics Committee that it had not become aware of any irregularities or illegal acts in relation to the OIG investigation.

4. Price Waterhouse worked in conjunction with the Internal Audit Department.

5. Prior to the distribution of the new ethics manual, on March 12, 1993, Caremark's president had sent a letter to all senior, district, and branch managers restating Caremark's policies that no physician be paid for referrals, that the standard contract forms in the Guide were not to be modified, and that deviation from such policies would result in the immediate termination of employment.

These steps included new policies requiring local branch managers to secure home office approval for all disbursements under agreements with health care providers and to certify compliance with the ethics program. In addition, the chief financial officer was appointed to serve as Caremark's compliance officer. In 1994, a fifth revised Guide was published.

D. Federal Indictments Against Caremark and Officers

On August 4, 1994, a federal grand jury in Minnesota issued a 47 page indictment charging Caremark, two of its officers (not the firm's chief officer), an individual who had been a sales employee of Genentech, Inc., and David R. Brown, a physician practicing in Minneapolis, with violating the ARPL over a lengthy period. According to the indictment, over $1.1 million had been paid to Brown to induce him to distribute Protropin, a human growth hormone drug marketed by Caremark.[6] The substantial payments involved started, according to the allegations of the indictment, in 1986 and continued through 1993. Some payments were "in the guise of research grants", Ind. ¶ 20, and others were "consulting agreements", Ind. ¶ 19. The indictment charged, for example, that Dr. Brown performed virtually none of the consulting functions described in his 1991 agreement with Caremark, but was nevertheless neither required to return the money he had received nor precluded from receiving future funding from Caremark. In addition the indictment charged that Brown received from Caremark payments of staff and office expenses, including telephone answering services and fax rental expenses.

In reaction to the Minnesota Indictment and the subsequent filing of this and other derivative actions in 1994, the Board met and was informed by management that the investigation had resulted in an indictment; Caremark denied any wrongdoing relating to the indictment and believed that the OIG investigation would have a favorable outcome. Management reiterated the grounds for its view that the contracts were in compliance with law.

Subsequently, five stockholder derivative actions were filed in this court and consolidated into this action. The original complaint, dated August 5, 1994, alleged, in relevant part, that Caremark's directors breached their duty of care by failing adequately to supervise the conduct of Caremark employees, or institute corrective measures, thereby exposing Caremark to fines and liability.

On September 21, 1994, a federal grand jury in Columbus, Ohio issued another indictment alleging that an Ohio physician had

---

6. In addition to prescribing Protropin, Dr. Brown had been receiving research grants from Caremark as well as payments for services under a consulting agreement for several years before and after the investigation. According to an undated document from an unknown source, Dr. Brown and six other researchers had been providing patient referrals to Caremark valued at $6.55 for each $1 of research money they received.

defrauded the Medicare program by requesting and receiving $134,-600 in exchange for referrals of patients whose medical costs were in part reimbursed by Medicare in violation of the ARPL. Although unidentified at that time, Caremark was the health care provider who allegedly made such payments. The indictment also charged that the physician, Elliot Neufeld, D.O., was provided with the services of a registered nurse to work in his office at the expense of the infusion company, in addition to free office equipment.

An October 28, 1994 amended complaint in this action added allegations concerning the Ohio indictment as well as new allegations of over billing and inappropriate referral payments in connection with an action brought in Atlanta, *Booth v. Rankin*. Following a newspaper article report that federal investigators were expanding their inquiry to look at Caremark's referral practices in Michigan as well as allegations of fraudulent billing of insurers, a second amended complaint was filed in this action. The third, and final, amended complaint was filed on April 11, 1995, adding allegations that the federal indictments had caused Caremark to incur significant legal fees and forced it to sell its home infusion business at a loss.

After each complaint was filed, defendants filed a motion to dismiss. According to defendants, if a settlement had not been reached in this action, the case would have been dismissed on two grounds. First, they contend that the complaints fail to allege particularized facts sufficient to excuse the demand requirement under Delaware Chancery Court Rule 23.1. Second, defendants assert that plaintiffs had failed to state a cause of action due to the fact that Caremark's charter eliminates directors' personal liability for money damages, to the extent permitted by law.

E.   Settlement Negotiations

In September, following the announcement of the Ohio indictment, Caremark publicly announced that as of January 1, 1995, it would terminate all remaining financial relationships with physicians in its home infusion, hemophilia, and growth hormone lines of business.[9] In addition, Caremark asserts that it extended its restrictive policies to all of its contractual relationships with physicians, rather than just those involving Medicare and Medicaid patients, and terminated its research grant program which had always involved some recipients who referred patients to Caremark.

Caremark began settlement negotiations with federal and state government entities in May 1995. In return for a guilty plea to a single count of mail fraud by the corporation, the payment of a criminal fine, the payment of substantial civil damages, and cooperation with further federal investigations on matters relating to the

---

9. On June 1, 1993, Caremark had stopped entering into new contractual agreements in those business segments.

OIG investigation, the government entities agreed to negotiate a settlement that would permit Caremark to continue participating in Medicare and Medicaid programs. On June 15, 1995, the Board approved a settlement ("Government Settlement Agreement") with the DOJ, OIG, U.S. Veterans Administration, U.S. Federal Employee Health Benefits Program, federal Civilian Health and Medical Program of the Uniformed Services, and related state agencies in all fifty states and the District of Columbia.[10] No senior officers or directors were charged with wrongdoing in the Government Settlement Agreement or in any of the prior indictments. In fact, as part of the sentencing in the Ohio action on June 19, 1995, the United States stipulated that no senior executive of Caremark participated in, condoned, or was willfully ignorant of wrongdoing in connection with the home infusion business practices.

The federal settlement included certain provisions in a "Corporate Integrity Agreement" designed to enhance future compliance with law. The parties have not discussed this agreement, except to say that the negotiated provisions of the settlement of this claim are not redundant of those in that agreement.

Settlement negotiations between the parties in this action commenced in May 1995 as well, based upon a letter proposal of the plaintiffs, dated May 16, 1995. These negotiations resulted in a memorandum of understanding ("MOU"), dated June 7, 1995, and the execution of the Stipulation and Agreement of Compromise and Settlement on June 28, 1995, which is the subject of this action.[13] The MOU, approved by the Board on June 15, 1995, required the Board to adopt several resolutions, discussed below, and to create a new compliance committee. The Compliance and Ethics Committee has been reporting to the Board in accord with its newly specified duties.

After negotiating these settlements, Caremark learned in December 1995 that several private insurance company payors ("Private Payors") believed that Caremark was liable for damages to them for allegedly improper business practices related to those at issue in the OIG investigation. As a result of intensive negotiations with the Private Payors and the Board's extensive consideration of the alternatives for dealing with such claims, the Board approved a $98.5 million settlement agreement with the Private Payors on

---

10. The agreement, covering allegations since 1986, required a Caremark subsidiary to enter a guilty plea to two counts of mail fraud, and required Caremark to pay $29 million in criminal fines, $129.9 million relating to civil claims concerning payment practices, $3.5 million for alleged violations of the Controlled Substances Act, and $2 million, in the form of a donation, to a grant program set up by the Ryan White Comprehensive AIDS Resources Emergency

Act. Caremark also agreed to enter into a compliance agreement with the HHS.

13. Plaintiffs' initial proposal had both a monetary component, requiring Caremark's director-officers to relinquish stock options, and a remedial component, requiring management to adopt and implement several compliance related measures. The monetary component was subsequently eliminated.

March 18, 1996. In its public disclosure statement, Caremark asserted that the settlement did not involve current business practices and contained an express denial of any wrongdoing by Caremark. After further discovery in this action, the plaintiffs decided to continue seeking approval of the proposed settlement agreement.

F.   The Proposed Settlement of this Litigation

In relevant part the terms upon which these claims asserted are proposed to be settled are as follows:

1.   That Caremark undertakes that it and its employees and agents not pay any form of compensation to a third party in exchange for the referral of a patient to a Caremark facility or service or the prescription of drugs marketed or distributed by Caremark for which reimbursement may be sought from Medicare, Medicaid, or a similar state reimbursement program;

2.   That Caremark undertakes for itself and its employees, and agents not to pay to or split fees with physicians, joint ventures, any business combination in which Caremark maintains a direct financial interest, or other health care providers with whom Caremark has a financial relationship or interest, in exchange for the referral of a patient to a Caremark facility or service or the prescription of drugs marketed or distributed by Caremark for which reimbursement may be sought from Medicare, Medicaid, or a similar state reimbursement program;

3.   That the full Board shall discuss all relevant material changes in government health care regulations and their effect on relationships with health care providers on a semi-annual basis;

4.   That Caremark's officers will remove all personnel from health care facilities or hospitals who have been placed in such facility for the purpose of providing remuneration in exchange for a patient referral for which reimbursement may be sought from Medicare, Medicaid, or a similar state reimbursement program;

5.   That every patient will receive written disclosure of any financial relationship between Caremark and the health care professional or provider who made the referral;

6.   That the Board will establish a Compliance and Ethics Committee of four directors, two of which will be non-management directors, to meet at least four times a year to effectuate these policies and monitor business segment compliance with the ARPL, and to report to the Board semi-annually concerning compliance by each business segment; and

7.   That corporate officers responsible for business segments shall serve as compliance officers who must report semi-annually to the Compliance and Ethics Committee and, with

the assistance of outside counsel, review existing contracts and get advance approval of any new contract forms.

II. LEGAL PRINCIPLES

A. Principles Governing Settlements of Derivative Claims

As noted at the outset of this opinion, this Court is now required to exercise an informed judgment whether the proposed settlement is fair and reasonable in the light of all relevant factors. Polk v. Good, Del.Supr., 507 A.2d 531 (1986). On an application of this kind, this Court attempts to protect the best interests of the corporation and its absent shareholders all of whom will be barred from future litigation on these claims if the settlement is approved. The parties proposing the settlement bear the burden of persuading the court that it is in fact fair and reasonable. Fins v. Pearlman, Del.Supr., 424 A.2d 305 (1980).

B. Directors' Duties To Monitor Corporate Operations

The complaint charges the director defendants with breach of their duty of attention or care in connection with the ongoing operation of the corporation's business. The claim is that the directors allowed a situation to develop and continue which exposed the corporation to enormous legal liability and that in so doing they violated a duty to be active monitors of corporate performance. The complaint thus does not charge either director self-dealing or the more difficult loyalty-type problems arising from cases of suspect director motivation, such as entrenchment or sale of control contexts.[14] The theory here advanced is possibly the most difficult theory in corporation law upon which a plaintiff might hope to win a judgment....

1. *Potential liability for directoral decisions:* Director liability for a breach of the duty to exercise appropriate attention may, in theory, arise in two distinct contexts. First, such liability may be said to follow from a board decision that results in a loss because that decision was ill advised or "negligent". Second, liability to the corporation for a loss may be said to arise from an unconsidered failure of the board to act in circumstances in which due attention would, arguably, have prevented the loss. See generally Veasey & Seitz, The Business Judgment Rule in the Revised Model Act ... 63 TEXAS L.REV. 1483 (1985). The first class of cases will typically be subject to review under the director-protective business judgment rule, assuming the decision made was the product of a process that was either deliberately considered in good faith or was otherwise

14. See Weinberger v. UOP, Inc., Del. Supr., 457 A.2d 701, 711 (1983) (entire fairness test when financial conflict of interest involved); Unitrin, Inc. v. American General Corp., Del.Supr., 651 A.2d 1361, 1372 (1995) (intermediate standard of review when "defensive" acts taken); Paramount Communications, Inc. v. QVC Network, Del.Supr., 637 A.2d 34, 45 (1994) (intermediate test when corporate control transferred).

rational.   See Aronson v. Lewis, Del.Supr., 473 A.2d 805 (1984);
Gagliardi v. TriFoods Int'l, Inc., Del.Ch. 683 A.2d 1049 (July 19,
1996)....

2. *Liability for failure to monitor*: The second class of cases
in which director liability for inattention is theoretically possible
entail circumstances in which a loss eventuates not from a decision
but, from unconsidered inaction.   Most of the decisions that a
corporation, acting through its human agents, makes are, of course,
not the subject of director attention.   Legally, the board itself will
be required only to authorize the most significant corporate acts or
transactions: mergers, changes in capital structure, fundamental
changes in business, appointment and compensation of the CEO,
etc.   As the facts of this case graphically demonstrate, ordinary
business decisions that are made by officers and employees deeper
in the interior of the organization can, however, vitally affect the
welfare of the corporation and its ability to achieve its various
strategic and financial goals.   If this case did not prove the point
itself, recent business history would.   Recall for example the dis-
placement of senior management and much of the board of Salomon, Inc.; [18] the replacement of senior management of Kidder,
Peabody following the discovery of large trading losses resulting
from phantom trades by a highly compensated trader; [19] or the
extensive financial loss and reputational injury suffered by Prudential Insurance as a result [of] its junior officers' misrepresentations
in connection with the distribution of limited partnership interests. [20]
Financial and organizational disasters such as these raise the question, what is the board's responsibility with respect to the organization and monitoring of the enterprise to assure that the corporation
functions within the law to achieve its purposes?

Modernly this question has been given special importance by an
increasing tendency, especially under federal law, to employ the
criminal law to assure corporate compliance with external legal
requirements, including environmental, financial, employee and
product safety as well as assorted other health and safety regulations.   In 1991, pursuant to the Sentencing Reform Act of 1984, [21]
the United States Sentencing Commission adopted Organizational
Sentencing Guidelines which impact importantly on the prospective
effect these criminal sanctions might have on business corporations.
The Guidelines set forth a uniform sentencing structure for organizations to be sentenced for violation of federal criminal statutes and

18. See, e.g., Rotten at the Core, the
Economist, August 17, 1991, at 69–70; The
Judgment of Salomon: An Anticlimax, Bus.
Week, June 1, 1992, at 106.

19. See Terence P. Pare, Jack Welch's
Nightmare on Wall Street, Fortune, Sept. 5,
1994, at 40–48.

20. Michael Schroeder and Leah Na-
thans Spiro, Is George Ball's Luck Running

Out?, Bus. Week, November 8, 1993, at 74–
76; Joseph B. Treaster, Prudential To Pay
Policyholders $410 Million, New York
Times, Sept. 25, 1996, (at D–1).

21. See Sentencing Reform Act of 1984,
Pub.L. 98–473, Title II, § 212(a)(2) (1984);
18 U.S.C.A. §§ 3331–4120.

provide for penalties that equal or often massively exceed those previously imposed on corporations.[22] The Guidelines offer powerful incentives for corporations today to have in place compliance programs to detect violations of law, promptly to report violations to appropriate public officials when discovered, and to take prompt, voluntary remedial efforts.

In 1963, the Delaware Supreme Court in Graham v. Allis–Chalmers Mfg. Co.,[23] addressed the question of potential liability of board members for losses experienced by the corporation as a result of the corporation having violated the anti-trust laws of the United States. There was no claim in that case that the directors knew about the behavior of subordinate employees of the corporation that had resulted in the liability. Rather, as in this case, the claim asserted was that the directors ought to have known of it and if they had known they would have been under a duty to bring the corporation into compliance with the law and thus save the corporation from the loss. The Delaware Supreme Court concluded that, under the facts as they appeared, there was no basis to find that the directors had breached a duty to be informed of the ongoing operations of the firm. In notably colorful terms, the court stated that "absent cause for suspicion there is no duty upon the directors to install and operate a corporate system of espionage to ferret out wrongdoing which they have no reason to suspect exists."[24] The Court found that there were no grounds for suspicion in that case and, thus, concluded that the directors were blamelessly unaware of the conduct leading to the corporate liability.[25]

How does one generalize this holding today? Can it be said today that, absent some ground giving rise to suspicion of violation of law, that corporate directors have no duty to assure that a corporate information gathering and reporting system exists which represents a good faith attempt to provide senior management and the Board with information respecting material acts, events or conditions within the corporation, including compliance with applicable statutes and regulations? I certainly do not believe so. I doubt that such a broad generalization of the Graham holding would have been accepted by the Supreme Court in 1963. The case can be more narrowly interpreted as standing for the proposition that, absent grounds to suspect deception, neither corporate boards nor senior officers can be charged with wrongdoing simply for assuming the integrity of employees and the honesty of their dealings on the company's behalf. See 188 A.2d at 130–31.

22. See United States Sentencing Commission, Guidelines Manual, Chapter 8 (U.S. Government Printing Office November 1994).

23. Del.Supr., 188 A.2d 125 (1963).

24. Id. at 130.

25. Recently, the *Graham* standard was applied by the Delaware Chancery in a case involving Baxter. In re Baxter International, Inc. Shareholders Litig., Del.Ch., 654 A.2d 1268, 1270 (1995).

A broader interpretation of *Graham v. Allis Chalmers*—that it means that a corporate board has no responsibility to assure that appropriate information and reporting systems are established by management—would not, in any event, be accepted by the Delaware Supreme Court in 1996, in my opinion. In stating the basis for this view, I start with the recognition that in recent years the Delaware Supreme Court has made it clear—especially in its jurisprudence concerning takeovers, from *Smith v. Van Gorkom* through *Paramount Communications v. QVC* [26]—the seriousness with which the corporation law views the role of the corporate board. Secondly, I note the elementary fact that relevant and timely information is an essential predicate for satisfaction of the board's supervisory and monitoring role under Section 141 of the Delaware General Corporation Law. Thirdly, I note the potential impact of the federal organizational sentencing guidelines on any business organization. Any rational person attempting in good faith to meet an organizational governance responsibility would be bound to take into account this development and the enhanced penalties and the opportunities for reduced sanctions that it offers.

In light of these developments, it would, in my opinion, be a mistake to conclude that our Supreme Court's statement in *Graham* concerning "espionage" means that corporate boards may satisfy their obligation to be reasonably informed concerning the corporation, without assuring themselves that information and reporting systems exist in the organization that are reasonably designed to provide to senior management and to the board itself timely, accurate information sufficient to allow management and the board, each within its scope, to reach informed judgments concerning both the corporation's compliance with law and its business performance.

Obviously the level of detail that is appropriate for such an information system is a question of business judgment. And obviously too, no rationally designed information and reporting system will remove the possibility that the corporation will violate laws or regulations, or that senior officers or directors may nevertheless sometimes be misled or otherwise fail reasonably to detect acts material to the corporation's compliance with the law. But it is important that the board exercise a good faith judgment that the corporation's information and reporting system is in concept and design adequate to assure the board that appropriate information will come to its attention in a timely manner as a matter of ordinary operations, so that it may satisfy its responsibility.

Thus, I am of the view that a director's obligation includes a duty to attempt in good faith to assure that a corporate information and reporting system, which the board concludes is adequate,

---

26. E.g., Smith v. Van Gorkom, Del. Supr., 488 A.2d 858 (1985); Paramount Communications v. QVC Network, Del. Supr., 637 A.2d 34 (1994).

exists, and that failure to do so under some circumstances may, in theory at least, render a director liable for losses caused by non-compliance with applicable legal standards[27]. I now turn to an analysis of the claims asserted with this concept of the directors' duty of care, as a duty satisfied in part by assurance of adequate information flows to the board, in mind.

III. ANALYSIS OF THIRD AMENDED COMPLAINT AND SETTLEMENT

A. The Claims

On balance, after reviewing an extensive record in this case, including numerous documents and three depositions, I conclude that this settlement is fair and reasonable. In light of the fact that the Caremark Board already has a functioning committee charged with overseeing corporate compliance, the changes in corporate practice that are presented as consideration for the settlement do not impress one as very significant. Nonetheless, that consideration appears fully adequate to support dismissal of the derivative claims of director fault asserted, because those claims find no substantial evidentiary support in the record and quite likely were susceptible to a motion to dismiss in all events.[28]

In order to show that the Caremark directors breached their duty of care by failing adequately to control Caremark's employees, plaintiffs would have to show either (1) that the directors knew or (2) should have known that violations of law were occurring and, in either event, (3) that the directors took no steps in a good faith effort to prevent or remedy that situation, and (4) that such failure proximately resulted in the losses complained of, although under Cede & Co. v. Technicolor, Inc., Del.Supr., 636 A.2d 956 (1994) this last element may be thought to constitute an affirmative defense.

1. *Knowing violation of statute*: Concerning the possibility that the Caremark directors knew of violations of law, none of the documents submitted for review, nor any of the deposition transcripts appear to provide evidence of it. Certainly the Board understood that the company had entered into a variety of contracts

---

27. Any action seeking recover for losses would logically entail a judicial determination of proximate cause, since, for reasons that I take to be obvious, it could never be assumed that an adequate information system would be a system that would prevent all losses. I need not touch upon the burden allocation with respect to a proximate cause issue in such a suit. See Cede & Co. v. Technicolor, Inc., Del.Supr., 636 A.2d 956 (1994); Cinerama, Inc. v. Technicolor, Inc., Del.Ch., 663 A.2d 1134 (1994), aff'd., Del.Supr., 663 A.2d 1156 (1995). Moreover, questions of waiver of liability under certificate provisions autho-

rized by 8 Del.C. § 102(b)(7) may also be faced.

28. See In re Baxter International, Inc. Shareholders Litig., Del.Ch., 654 A.2d 1268, 1270 (1995). A claim in some respects similar to that here made was dismissed. The court relied, in part, on the fact that the Baxter certificate of incorporation contained a provision as authorized by Section 102(b)(7) of the Delaware General Corporation Law, waiving director liability for due care violations. Id. at 1270. That fact was thought to require pre-suit demand on the board in that case.

with physicians, researchers, and health care providers and it was understood that some of these contracts were with persons who had prescribed treatments that Caremark participated in providing. The Board was informed that the company's reimbursement for patient care was frequently from government funded sources and that such services were subject to the ARPL. But the Board appears to have been informed by experts that the company's practices, while contestable, were lawful. There is no evidence that reliance on such reports was not reasonable. Thus, this case presents no occasion to apply a principle to the effect that knowingly causing the corporation to violate a criminal statute constitutes a breach of a director's fiduciary duty. See Roth v. Robertson, N.Y.Sup.Ct., 118 N.Y.S. 351 (1909); Miller v. American Tel. & Tel. Co., 507 F.2d 759 (3d Cir.1974). It is not clear that the Board knew the detail found, for example, in the indictments arising from the company's payments. But, of course, the duty to act in good faith to be informed cannot be thought to require directors to possess detailed information about all aspects of the operation of the enterprise. Such a requirement would simply be inconsistent with the scale and scope of efficient organization size in this technological age.

2. *Failure to monitor*: Since it does appears that the Board was to some extent unaware of the activities that led to liability, I turn to a consideration of the other potential avenue to director liability that the pleadings take: director inattention or "negligence". Generally where a claim of directorial liability for corporate loss is predicated upon ignorance of liability creating activities within the corporation, as in Graham or in this case, in my opinion only a sustained or systematic failure of the board to exercise oversight—such as an utter failure to attempt to assure a reasonable information and reporting system exits—will establish the lack of good faith that is a necessary condition to liability. Such a test of liability—lack of good faith as evidenced by sustained or systematic failure of a director to exercise reasonable oversight—is quite high. But, a demanding test of liability in the oversight context is probably beneficial to corporate shareholders as a class, as it is in the board decision context, since it makes board service by qualified persons more likely, while continuing to act as a stimulus to good faith performance of duty by such directors.

Here the record supplies essentially no evidence that the director defendants were guilty of a sustained failure to exercise their oversight function. To the contrary, insofar as I am able to tell on this record, the corporation's information systems appear to have represented a good faith attempt to be informed of relevant facts. If the directors did not know the specifics of the activities that lead to the indictments, they cannot be faulted.

The liability that eventuated in this instance was huge. But the fact that it resulted from a violation of criminal law alone does not create a breach of fiduciary duty by directors. The record at this stage does not support the conclusion that the defendants either lacked good faith in the exercise of their monitoring responsibilities or conscientiously permitted a known violation of law by the corporation to occur. The claims asserted against them must be viewed at this stage as extremely weak.

B. The Consideration For Release of Claim

The proposed settlement provides very modest benefits. Under the settlement agreement, plaintiffs have been given express assurances that Caremark will have a more centralized, active supervisory system in the future. Specifically, the settlement mandates duties to be performed by the newly named Compliance and Ethics Committee on an ongoing basis and increases the responsibility for monitoring compliance with the law at the lower levels of management. In adopting the resolutions required under the settlement, Caremark has further clarified its policies concerning the prohibition of providing remuneration for referrals. These appear to be positive consequences of the settlement of the claims brought by the plaintiffs, even if they are not highly significant. Nonetheless, given the weakness of the plaintiffs' claims the proposed settlement appears to be an adequate, reasonable, and beneficial outcome for all of the parties. Thus, the proposed settlement will be approved.

IV. ATTORNEYS' FEES

The various firms of lawyers involved for plaintiffs seek an award of $1,025,000 in attorneys' fees and reimbursable expenses.[29] In awarding attorneys' fees, this Court considers an array of relevant factors. E.g., In Re Beatrice Companies, Inc. Litigation, Del.Ch., C.A. No. 8248, Allen, C. (Apr. 16, 1986). Such factors include, most importantly, the financial value of the benefit that the lawyers' work produced; the strength of the claims (because substantial settlement value may sometimes be produced even though the litigation added little value—i.e., perhaps any lawyer could have settled this claim for this substantial value or more); the amount of complexity of the legal services; the fee customarily charged for such services; and the contingent nature of the undertaking.

In this case no factor points to a substantial fee, other than the amount and sophistication of the lawyer services required. There is only a modest substantive benefit produced; in the particular circumstances of the government activity there was realistically a very slight contingency faced by the attorneys at the time they expended time. The services rendered required a high degree of sophistication and expertise. I am told that at normal hourly billing rates approximately $710,000 of time was expended by the attorneys.

29. Of the total requested amount, approximately $710,000 is designated as reimbursement for the number of hours spent by the attorneys on the case, calculated at their normal billing rate, and $53,000 for out-of-pocket expenses.

In these circumstances, I conclude that an award of a fee determined by reference to the time expended at normal hourly rates plus a premium of 15% of that amount to reflect the limited degree of real contingency in the undertaking, is fair. Thus I will award a fee of $816,000 plus $53,000 of expenses advanced by counsel.

I am today entering an order consistent with the foregoing.[30]

(c)   The Business Judgment Rule

Add the following passage at p. 631 of the Unabridged Edition, at the end of the Note on Cede v. Technicolor, Inc.:

On appeal, the Delaware Supreme Court upheld the Chancelor's conclusion. Cinerama, Inc. v. Technicolor, Inc., 663 A.2d 1156 (Del.1995).

----

30. The court has been informed by letter of counsel that after the fairness of the proposed settlement had been submitted to the court, Caremark was involved in a merger in which its stock was canceled and the holders of its stock became entitled to shares of stock of the acquiring corporation. No party to this suit, or the surviving corporation, has sought to dismiss this case thereafter on the basis that plaintiffs have lost standing to sue. As plaintiffs continue to have an equity interest in the entity that owns the claims and more especially because no party has moved for any modification of the procedural setting of the matter submitted, I conclude that any merger that may have occurred is without effect on the decision of the motion or the judgment to be entered.

Chapter VIII

THE DUTY OF LOYALTY

SECTION 2. STATUTORY APPROACHES

Add the following material at p. 688 of the Unabridged Edition, at the end of the
Note on the Effect of Approval by Disinterested Directors of Self–Interested
Transactions, and p. 471 of the Concise Edition, after Cookies Food Products
v. Lakes Warehouse:

NOTE ON COOKE v. OOLIE

The most recent pronouncement of the Delaware courts on the interpretation of section 144 of the Delaware statute is *Cooke v. Oolie*, 1997 WL 367034 (Del.Ch.1997). Oolie and Salkind, who were directors and shareholders of The Nostalgia Network (TNN), made two loans to TNN in February 1989 and a third in June 1989. The February loans were negotiated on TNN's behalf by the remaining TNN directors, Janas (the corporation's CEO), Wargo, and Eisman, although Eisman resigned before the final terms were approved. The June loan was apparently negotiated on TNN's behalf by Janas and Wargo. Janas and Wargo approved all three loans in their capacities as TNN directors. Plaintiffs, shareholders in TNN, brought a derivative action claiming that the terms of the loans were unfair to TNN. Defendants contended that under section 144 of the Delaware statute the loans could be reviewed only under the business judgment rule, because they had been approved by disinterested directors. The court rejected this contention:

> The February and June Loans provided by Oolie and Salkind were unanimously approved by TNN's Board. Plaintiffs assert that because two of the four directors stood on both sides of the transactions, the defendants must show that the loans were entirely fair. In support of their argument, they refer to this Court's reasoning in [Rosenberg v. Oolie, Del.Ch.1989] where the Vice Chancellor stated that she assumed, for the purpose of the pending application for a preliminary injunction, "that defendants will lose the burden of proof argument and will be required to establish the intrinsic fairness of [the] loans." Plaintiffs characterize this reasoning as a recognition by the Court that "defendants may not invoke the protection of

the business judgment rule as provided in Section 144 of the DGCL; rather they bear the burden of establishing that there are not triable issues of fact as to the fairness of the loan transactions." Relying on Marciano v. Nakash, defendants assert that compliance with section 144(a)(1) entitles them to the protection of the business judgment rule.

Both parties fail to recognize that the Delaware Supreme Court has, since *Marciano* and *Rosenberg* were decided, more fully developed the standard by which this Court should judge a board's actions when it engages in a transaction with one or more of its own directors. At the time former Vice Chancellor Berger decided *Rosenberg*, our Courts held that an interested board was required to show the entire fairness of a transaction unless the transaction was entitled to a safe harbor in section 144(a)(1) or 144(a)(2), in which case the board would receive the protection of the business judgment rule.

The Court in *Rosenberg* assumed that section 144(a)(1) did not apply. Thus, the Court appropriately assumed in the context of an application for a preliminary injunction that the defendants would be required to bear the burden of showing that the loans were entirely fair. It is now clear that even if a board's action falls within the safe harbor of section 144, the board is not entitled to receive the protection of the business judgment rule. Compliance with section 144 merely shifts the burden to the plaintiffs to demonstrate that the transaction was unfair. . . .

The fact that plaintiffs do not challenge the independence of the approving directors does not automatically entitle the defendants to rely on the safe harbor of section 144 or automatically shift to the plaintiffs the burden of showing that the transaction was unfair. . . . Del.C. § 144(a)(1) provides that a transaction between a corporation and one (or more) of its directors shall not be void solely because that director participated in authorizing the transaction if:

> The material facts as to his relationship or interest and as to the contract or transaction are disclosed or known to the board of directors or the committee, and the board or committee in good faith authorizes the contract or transaction by the affirmative votes of a majority of the disinterested directors, even though the disinterested directors be less than a quorum.

Whether a transaction has been approved under the circumstances described above depends upon the particular facts of the case. There is no question here that the interests of Oolie and Salkind were known to the other Board members. Moreover, the evidence does not suggest (nor do the plaintiffs allege) that the approving Board members were personally interested in the transaction or beholden to Oolie or Salkind. But for me to conclude that the disinterested directors' approval of the transaction shifted the burden of demonstrating the unfairness of the transaction to the plaintiffs, the defendants must demonstrate that they are entitled to rely on section 144(a)(1). That is, they carry the burden of demonstrating that the directors approving the load were "truly independent, fully informed, and had the freedom to negotiate at arm's length." Evidence that the "action taken was as though each of the contending parties had in fact exerted its bargaining power against the other at arm's length is strong evidence that the transaction meets the test of fairness."

The court then found that Janas and Wargo were disinterested directors who had engaged in a process that entitled them to the safe harbor of section 144(a)(1), and that the undisputed material facts showed that the terms of the loans were entirely fair:

> At the time the February Loan was approved, it was clear that TNN was in desperate need of funds and that the directors believed they needed to act quickly to obtain funding in some form. Merrill Lynch [an investment banker] did not believe there was a good chance of raising funds from any source other than a Canadian company and doubted that even that company would make a proposal any time soon. Although Oolie and Salkind proposed the initial loan terms, it is clear that Eisman (before he resigned), Janas and Wargo obtained significant concessions through negotiations with Oolie and Salkind. For example, negotiations resulted in a lower interest rate if the loan were repaid or converted within six months and deferment of interest payments. Moreover, TNN reserved the right to cancel the loans in their entirety if Merrill Lynch, within ten days, could find another lender willing to accept the same loan terms.

> I conclude that the loan terms negotiated by Eisman, Janas and Wargo and approved by Janas and Wargo reflect a true ability to negotiate with Oolie and Salkind. The loan was approved by disinterested directors who engaged in a process entitling them to the safe harbor of section 144(a)(1). Although this does not entitle the defendants to the presumption of the business judgment rule, the burden shifts to the plaintiffs to show that the February Loan transaction was unfair....

> The record does not reveal the existence of any disputed material facts that would preclude the award of summary judgment to the defendants on the issue of entire fairness of the loan transactions.

Add the following new section 2A at p. 689 of the Unabridged Edition, and p. 471 of the Concise Edition, after Chapter VIII, Section 2:

SECTION 2A. THE EFFECT OF SHAREHOLDER RATIFICATION

IN RE WHEELABRATOR TECHNOLOGIES SHAREHOLDERS LITIGATION

Court of Chancery of Delaware, 1995.
663 A.2d 1194.

JACOBS, Vice Chancellor.

This shareholder class action challenges the September 7, 1990 merger (the "merger") of Wheelabrator Technologies, Inc. ("WTI") into a wholly-owned subsidiary of Waste Management, Inc. ("Waste"). The plaintiffs are shareholders of WTI. The named defendants are WTI and the eleven members of WTI's board of directors at the time the merger was negotiated and approved.[1]

The plaintiffs claim that WTI and the director defendants breached their fiduciary obligation to disclose to the class material information concerning the merger. The plaintiffs also claim that in negotiating and approving the merger, the director defendants breached their fiduciary duties of loyalty and care. The defendants deny that they breached any duty of disclosure. They further contend that because the merger was approved by a fully informed shareholder vote, that vote operates as a complete defense to, and extinguishes, the plaintiffs' fiduciary claims.

This is the Opinion of the Court on the defendants' motion for summary judgment. For the reasons elaborated below, the Court concludes that: (1) the plaintiffs have failed to adduce evidence sufficient to defeat summary judgment on their duty of disclosure claim, and that (2) the fully informed shareholder vote approving the merger operated to extinguish the plaintiffs' duty of care claims, but not their duty of loyalty claim. Accordingly, the defendants' summary judgment motion is granted in part and denied in part.

---

1. Three of the eleven individual director defendants, Paul M. Montrone, Rodney C. Gilbert, and Paul M. Meister, were all members of WTI's management. Four directors, Dean L. Buntrock, William P. Hulligan, Phillip B. Rooney, and Donald F. Flynn were officers of Waste Management. The remaining four directors, Michael D. Dingman, Gerald J. Lewis, Thomas P. Stafford, and Edward Montgomery, were outside directors.

I. *PROCEDURAL BACKGROUND*

On April 5, 1990, the plaintiffs commenced these class actions (which were later consolidated) challenging the then-proposed merger with Waste. After expedited discovery, the plaintiffs moved for a preliminary injunction. That motion was denied, *In re Wheelabrator Technologies, Inc. Shareholders Litig.*, Del.Ch., Cons.C.A. No. 11495, Jacobs, V.C., 1990 WL 131351 (Sept. 6, 1990) (*"Wheelabrator I"*), and the merger was approved by WTI's shareholders, specifically, by a majority of WTI's shareholders other than Waste.

On July 22, 1991, the plaintiffs filed a Second Amended Consolidated Class Action Complaint, which the defendants moved to dismiss pursuant to Chancery Court Rule 12(b)(6). That motion was denied in part and granted in part. *In re Wheelabrator Technologies, Inc. Shareholders Litig.*, Del.Ch., Cons.C.A. No. 11495, Jacobs, V.C., 1992 WL 212595 (Sept. 1, 1992). As a result of that ruling, all but three claims alleged in the complaint were dismissed.

The first remaining claim is Count I of the complaint, which alleges that the defendants violated their duty to disclose all material facts related to the merger in the proxy statement issued in connection with the transaction. ...

Count III alleges that the defendants breached their duty of care by failing adequately to investigate alternative transactions, neglecting to consider certain nonpublic information regarding certain of Waste's potential legal liabilities, failing to appoint a committee of independent directors to negotiate the merger, and failing adequately to consider the merger terms.

Count IV alleges that the defendants breached their duty of loyalty, in that a majority of WTI's eleven directors had a conflict of interest that caused them not to seek or obtain the best possible value for the company's shareholders in the merger.

On December 30, 1992, the defendants filed the pending summary judgment motion seeking dismissal of these claims. Following discovery and briefing, that motion was argued on March 3, 1995.

II. *RELEVANT FACTS*

WTI, a publicly held Delaware corporation headquartered in New Hampshire, is engaged in the business of developing and providing refuse-to-energy services. Waste, a Delaware corporation with principal offices in Illinois, provides waste management services to national and international commercial, industrial, and municipal customers.

In August 1988, Waste and WTI entered into a transaction (the "1988 transaction") to take advantage of their complementary business operations. In the 1988 transaction, Waste acquired a 22%

equity interest in WTI in exchange for certain assets that Waste sold to WTI. The two companies also entered into other agreements that concerned WTI's rights to ash disposal, the purchase of real estate for future refuse-to-energy facilities, and other business development opportunities. As a result of the 1988 transaction, Waste became WTI's largest (22%) stockholder and was entitled to nominate four of WTI's eleven directors.

Over the next two years, Waste and WTI periodically discussed other ways to reduce perceived inefficiencies by coordinating their operations. Those discussions intensified in December 1989, when Waste acquired a refuse-to-energy facility in West Germany. That acquisition raised concerns that the four Waste designees to WTI's board of directors might have future conflicts of interest if WTI later decided to enter the West German market.

Prompted by these and other concerns, Waste began, in December 1989, to consider either acquiring a majority equity interest in WTI or, alternatively, divesting all of its WTI stock. After several discussions, both companies agreed that Waste would increase its equity position in WTI. On March 22, 1990, Waste proposed a stock-for-stock, market-to-market (*i.e.* no premium) exchange in which Waste would become WTI's majority stockholder. WTI declined that proposal, and insisted on a transaction in which its shareholders would receive a premium above the current market price of their shares.

The following day, March 23, 1990, representatives of WTI and Waste met in New York City. Accompanying WTI's representatives were members of WTI's investment banking firm, Lazard Frères. At that meeting, Waste's representatives expressed Waste's interest in acquiring an additional 33% of WTI, thereby making Waste the owner of 55% of WTI's outstanding shares. The parties ultimately agreed on that concept. They also agreed to structure the transaction as a stock-for-stock merger that would be conditioned upon the approval of a majority of WTI's disinterested stockholders, *i.e.*, a majority of WTI's stockholders other than Waste. Waste agreed to pay a 10% premium for the additional shares required to reach the 55% equity ownership level. Finally, it was agreed that the merger would involve no "lockup," breakup fees, or other arrangements that would impede WTI from considering alternative transactions.

During the following week, additional face-to-face meetings and telephone conversations took place between the two companies' representatives. Those negotiations resulted in five "ancillary agreements" that give WTI certain funding and business opportunity options, as well as licenses to use certain Waste-owned intellectual property.[2]

2. The ancillary agreements included: (1) $50 million in funding to construct additional WTI refuse-to-energy facilities, (2) an option for WTI to purchase a 15% interest in Waste's international subsidiary at a 15% discount from the market price, (3) an

On March 30, 1990, agreement on the final merger exchange ratio was reached. The parties agreed that WTI shareholders would receive 0.574 shares of WTI stock plus 0.469 shares of Waste stock for each of their premerger WTI shares.

That same day, March 30, 1990, WTI's board of directors held a special meeting to consider the merger agreement. All board members attended except the four Waste designees, who had recused themselves. Also present were WTI's "in-house" and outside counsel, and representatives of Lazard Fréres and Solomon Brothers. The WTI board members reviewed copies of the draft merger agreement and materials furnished by the investment bankers concerning the financial aspects of the transaction. The directors also heard presentations from the investment bankers and from legal counsel, who opined that the transaction was fair. A question and answer session followed.

The seven board members present then voted unanimously to approve the merger and to recommend its approval by WTI's shareholders. After that vote, the four Waste-designated board members joined the meeting, and the full board then voted unanimously to approve and recommend the merger.

On July 30, 1990, WTI and Waste disseminated a joint proxy statement to WTI shareholders, disclosing the recommendation of both boards of directors that their shareholders approve the transaction. At a special shareholders meeting held on September 7, 1990, the merger was approved by a majority of WTI shareholders other than Waste.

III. *THE PARTIES' CONTENTIONS*

The defendants seek the dismissal of plaintiffs' remaining disclosure claim on the ground that it has no evidentiary support. The defendants further contend that the effect of the fully informed shareholder vote approving the merger was to ratify the directors' actions in negotiating and approving the merger, and thereby extinguish the plaintiffs' claims that those actions constituted breaches of fiduciary duty.

The plaintiffs respond that they have raised genuine issues of material fact that preclude the grant of summary judgment on their disclosure claim. They further argue that even if the disclosure claim were dismissed, that would not result in the extinguishment of their breach of loyalty claim.[3] Plaintiffs maintain that the only effect of shareholder ratification would be to impose upon them the

option for WTI to acquire 100% of Waste's medical waste disposal business at a 15% discount from the market price, (4) licenses to WTI for various intellectual property owned by Waste, and (5) a "Master Intercorporate Agreement" providing WTI with options on services ranging from the pre-

sentation of corporate opportunities to cash management and insurance support.

3. The plaintiffs do not dispute that if the shareholder vote was fully informed, that would operate to extinguish their duty of care claim.

burden of proving that the merger was unfair to the corporation, with entire fairness being the applicable standard of judicial review. . . .

IV. *THE DISCLOSURE CLAIM*

[The Court found that the plaintiffs had failed to adduce record evidence sufficient to defeat summary judgment dismissing their claims.]

V. *THE FIDUCIARY DUTY CLAIMS*

In rejecting the disclosure claim, the Court necessarily has determined that the merger was approved by a fully informed vote of a majority of WTI's disinterested stockholders. That determination requires the Court to confront the defendants' argument that that vote constituted shareholder ratification which operated as a complete defense to, and consequently extinguished, the claims that the defendants breached their fiduciary duties of care and loyalty.

The plaintiffs do not dispute that if the WTI shareholder vote was fully informed, it operated to extinguish their due care claim in this case. They avidly insist, however, that that vote could not, as a legal matter, extinguish their duty of loyalty claim. Plaintiffs argue that because the merger was an "interested" transaction subject to the entire fairness standard of review, the sole effect of shareholder ratification was to shift to plaintiffs the burden of proving that the merger was unfair.

I conclude, for the reasons next discussed, that (1) the effect of the informed shareholder vote was to extinguish the plaintiffs' due care claim; (2) that vote did not operate either to extinguish the duty of loyalty claim (as defendants contend), or to shift to the plaintiffs the burden of proving that the merger was unfair (as plaintiffs contend); and (3) the effect of the shareholder vote in this case is to invoke the business judgment standard, which limits review to issues of gift or waste with the burden of proof resting upon the plaintiffs. Because the parties have not yet been heard on the question of how the business judgment standard would apply to these facts, summary judgment with respect to the duty of loyalty claim must be denied.

A. *The Duty of Care Claim.*

As noted, the plaintiffs concede that if the WTI shareholder vote was fully informed, the effect of that informed vote would be to extinguish the claim that the WTI board failed to exercise due care in negotiating and approving the merger. Given the ratification holding of *Smith v. Van Gorkom,* Del.Supr., 488 A.2d 858, 889–90 (1985), that concession is not surprising. In *Van Gorkom,* the defendant directors argued that the shareholder vote approving a challenged merger agreement "had the legal effect of curing any failure of the board to reach an informed business judgment in its approval of the merger." *Id.* at 889. Accepting that legal principle (but not its application to the facts before it), the Supreme Court stated:

> The parties tacitly agree that a discovered failure of the Board to reach an informed business judgment constitutes a voidable, rather than a void, act. Hence, the merger can be sustained, notwithstanding the infirmity of the Board's actions, if its approval by majority vote of the shareholders is found to have been based on an informed electorate.

Id. at 889.

Accordingly, summary judgment dismissing the plaintiffs' due care claim will be granted. That leaves for decision the legal effect of the informed shareholder vote on the duty of loyalty claims alleged in Count IV of the complaint.

B. *The Duty of Loyalty Claim.*

The defendants contend that the informed shareholder approval of the WTI–Waste merger also operated to extinguish the claim that the directors' approval of the merger violated their duty of loyalty to WTI and its stockholders. The plaintiffs counter that a fully informed shareholder vote cannot, as a matter of law, operate to extinguish a duty of loyalty claim. At most, plaintiffs argue, the informed shareholder vote in this case would only shift to the plaintiff the burden of showing that the merger was unfair. Having considered the relevant authorities, and the law on this subject generally, I conclude that neither side's position is correct. . . .

The question of whether or not shareholder ratification should operate to extinguish a duty of loyalty claim cannot be decided in a vacuum, divorced from the broader issue of what generally are the legal consequences of a fully-informed shareholder approval of a challenged transaction. . . .

The basic structure of stockholder ratification law is, at first glance, deceptively simple. Delaware law distinguishes between acts of directors (or management) that are "void" and acts that are "voidable." As the Supreme Court stated in *Michelson v. Duncan,* 407 A.2d 211, 218–19 (1979):

> The essential distinction between voidable and void acts is that the former are those which may be found to have been performed in the interest of the corporation but beyond the authority of management, as distinguished from acts which are *ultra vires,* fraudulent, or waste of corporate assets. The practical distinction, for our purposes, is that voidable acts are susceptible to cure by shareholder approval while void acts are not.

(citations omitted).

One possible reading of *Michelson* is that all "voidable" acts are "susceptible to cure by shareholder approval." Under that reading, shareholder ratification might be thought to constitute a "full defense" (407 A.2d at 219) that would automatically extinguish all claims challenging such acts as a breach of fiduciary duty. Any such reading, however, would be overbroad, because the case law governing the consequences of ratification does not support that view and, in fact, is far more complex.

The Delaware Supreme Court has found shareholder ratification of "voidable" director conduct to result in claim-extinguishment in only two circumstances. The first is where the directors act in good faith, but exceed the board's *de jure* authority. In that circumstance, *Michelson* holds that "a validly accomplished shareholder ratification relates back to cure otherwise unauthorized acts of officers and directors."[5] 407 A.2d at 219. The second circumstance is where the directors fail "to reach an informed business judgment" in approving a transaction. *Van Gorkom*, 488 A.2d at 889.

Except for these two situations, no party has identified any type of board action that the Delaware Supreme Court has deemed "voidable" for claim extinguishment purposes. More specifically, no Supreme Court case has held that shareholder ratification operates automatically to extinguish a duty of loyalty claim. To the contrary, the ratification cases involving duty of loyalty claims have uniformly held that the effect of shareholder ratification is to alter the standard of review, *or* to shift the burden of proof, *or* both. Those cases further frustrate any effort to describe the "ratification" landscape in terms of a simple rule.

The ratification decisions that involve duty of loyalty claims are of two kinds: (a) "interested" transaction cases between a corporation and its directors (or between the corporation and an entity in which the corporation's directors are also directors or have a financial interest), and (b) cases involving a transaction between the corporation and its controlling shareholder.

Regarding the first category, 8 *Del.C.* § 144(a)(2) pertinently provides that an "interested" transaction of this kind will not be voidable if it is approved in good faith by a majority of disinterested stockholders. Approval by fully informed, disinterested shareholders pursuant to § 144(a)(2) invokes "the business judgment rule and limits judicial review to issues of gift or waste with the burden of proof upon the party attacking the transaction." *Marciano v. Nakash*, Del.Supr., 535 A.2d 400, 405 n. 3 (1987). The result is the same in "interested" transaction cases not decided under § 144:

---

5. That holding is fully consistent with conventional agency doctrine and makes sense where the infirmity of the challenged board action is lack of board authority. *See Restatement of Agency (Second)* § 82 and Comment C. In that context, shareholder ratification "cures" that infirmity in a functional sense, because shareholder approval of the board's action supplies the authority that was lacking to begin with.

Where there has been independent shareholder ratification of interested director actions, the objecting stockholder has the burden of showing that no person of ordinary sound business judgment would say that the consideration received for the options was a fair exchange for the options granted.

Michelson, 407 A.2d at 224 (quoting *Kaufman v. Shoenberg*, Del. Ch., 91 A.2d 786, 791 (1952), at 791); *see also Gottlieb v. Heyden Chem. Corp.*, Del.Supr., 91 A.2d 57, 59 (1952); and *Citron v. E.I. Du Pont de Nemours & Co.*, 584 A.2d 490, 501 (citing authorities reaching the same result in mergers involving fiduciaries that were not controlling stockholders).

The second category concerns duty of loyalty cases arising out of transactions between the corporation and its controlling stockholder. Those cases involve primarily parent-subsidiary mergers that were conditioned upon receiving "majority of the minority" stockholder approval. In a parent-subsidiary merger, the standard of review is ordinarily entire fairness, with the directors having the burden of proving that the merger was entirely fair. *Weinberger v. UOP, Inc.*, 457 A.2d 701, 703. But where the merger is conditioned upon approval by a "majority of the minority" stockholder vote, and such approval is granted, the standard of review remains entire fairness, but the burden of demonstrating that the merger was unfair shifts to the plaintiff. *Kahn v. Lynch Communication Sys.*, Del.Supr., 638 A.2d 1110 (1994); *Rosenblatt v. Getty Oil Co.*, 493 A.2d 929, 937–38 (1985); *Weinberger*, at 710; *Citron*, at 502. That burden-shifting effect of ratification has also been held applicable in cases involving mergers with a *de facto* controlling stockholder,[6] and in a case involving a transaction other than a merger. . . .

To repeat: in only two circumstances has the Delaware Supreme Court held that a fully-informed shareholder vote operates to extinguish a claim: (1) where the board of directors takes action that, although not alleged to constitute *ultra vires*, fraud, or waste, is claimed to exceed the board's authority; and (2) where it is claimed that the directors failed to exercise due care to adequately inform themselves before committing the corporation to a transaction. In no case has the Supreme Court held that stockholder ratification automatically extinguishes a claim for breach of the directors' duty of loyalty. Rather, the operative effect of shareholder ratification in duty of loyalty cases has been either to change the standard of review to the business judgment rule, with the burden of proof resting upon the plaintiff, *or* to leave "entire fairness" as the review standard, but shift the burden of proof to the plaintiff. Thus, the Supreme Court ratification decisions do not support the defendants' position.

6. *See Kahn v. Lynch Communication Sys., supra* (merger between corporation and 43.3% stockholder-parent found to have exercised *de facto* control over subsidiary).

That being the present state of the law, the question then becomes whether there exists a policy or doctrinal basis that would justify extending the claim-extinguishing effect of shareholder ratification to cases involving duty of loyalty claims. *Van Gorkom* does not articulate a basis, and the parties have suggested none. ...

In *Kahn v. Lynch Communication Sys., supra,* an "interested" cash out merger between a corporation and its *de facto* controlling stockholder was challenged as a breach of the directors' duty of loyalty. ... The *Kahn* Court disclaimed any suggestion that shareholder ratification obviates further judicial review, by noting that "the unchanging nature of the underlying 'interested' transaction requires careful scrutiny." *Id.* at 1116.

Stroud v. Grace, [606 A.2d 75 (1992)], is similarly instructive. There, as in *Weiss,* the claim was that certain charter amendments proposed by the board whose members were also the corporation's controlling stockholders, were unfair and a breach of the directors' duty of loyalty to the minority stockholders. The charter amendments were found to have been approved by the fully-informed vote of a majority of the minority stockholders. ... [The Court] ruled that the ratifying vote "[shifted] the burden of proof to the [plaintiffs] to prove that the transaction was unfair," 606 A.2d at 90, and then proceeded to consider the plaintiffs' claim that the charter amendments were unfair because (*inter alia*) they were intended to interfere with the shareholder franchise.

From these decisions I conclude that in duty of loyalty cases arising out of transactions with a controlling shareholder, our Supreme Court would reject the proposition that the Delaware courts will have no reviewing function in cases where the challenged transaction is approved by an informed shareholder vote. *Kahn* makes explicit the Supreme Court's concern that even an informed shareholder vote may not afford the minority sufficient protection to obviate the judicial oversight role. Even if the ratified transaction does not involve a controlling stockholder, the result would not be to extinguish a duty of loyalty claim. In such cases the Supreme Court has held that the effect of shareholder ratification is to make business judgment the applicable review standard and shift the burden of proof to the plaintiff stockholder. ... None of these authorities holds that shareholder ratification operates automatically to extinguish a duty of loyalty claim. ...

... Accordingly, the defendants' "claim extinguishment" argument, in the duty of loyalty context, must be rejected.

C. *The Appropriate Review Standard and Burden of Proof*

Having determined what effect shareholder ratification does *not* have, the Court must now determine what effect it does have. The plaintiffs argue that their duty of loyalty claim is governed by the entire fairness standard, with ratification operating only to shift the burden on the fairness issue to the plaintiffs. That is incorrect, because this merger did not involve an interested and controlling stockholder.

In both *Kahn* and *Stroud,* the Supreme Court determined that the effect of a fully informed shareholder vote was to shift the burden of proof within the entire fairness standard of review. *Kahn,* 638 A.2d at 1117; *Stroud,* 606 A.2d at 90. Critical to the result in those cases was that the transaction involved a *de facto* (*Kahn, supra*) or *de jure* (*Stroud, supra*) controlling stockholder. That circumstance brought those cases within the purview of the ratification doctrine articulated in *Rosenblatt, supra, Bershad v. Curtiss–Wright Corp.,* Del.Supr., 535 A.2d 840 (1987), and *Citron v. E.I. Du Pont de Nemours & Co., supra,* all involving mergers between a corporation and its majority stockholder-parent. The participation of the controlling interested stockholder is critical to the application of the entire fairness standard because, as *Kahn* and *Stroud* recognize, the potential for process manipulation by the controlling stockholder, and the concern that the controlling stockholder's continued presence might influence even a fully informed shareholder vote, justify the need for the exacting judicial scrutiny and procedural protection afforded by the entire fairness form of review.

In this case, there is no contention or evidence that Waste, a 22% stockholder of WTI, exercised *de jure* or *de facto* control over WTI. Therefore, neither the holdings of or policy concerns underlying *Kahn* and *Stroud* are implicated here. Accordingly, the review standard applicable to this merger is business judgment, with the plaintiffs having the burden of proof.[8]

The final question concerns the proper application of that review standard to the facts at bar. Because no party has yet been heard on that subject, that issue cannot be determined on this motion. Its resolution must await further proceedings, which counsel may present (if they so choose) on a supplemental motion for summary judgment. ...

For the foregoing reasons, the defendants' motion for summary judgment (1) is granted as to the disclosure claim, (2) is granted as to the duty of care claim, and (3) is denied as to the duty of loyalty

---

8. That result is reached not only by process of elimination but also by application of 8 *Del.C.* § 144(a)(1). That statute provides that when a majority of fully informed, disinterested directors (even if less than a quorum) approve a transaction in which other directors are interested, the transaction will not be void or voidable by reason of the conflict of interest. Under § 144(a)(1), a ratifying disinterested director vote has the same procedural effect as a ratifying disinterested shareholder vote under § 144(a)(2). *See Marciano,* 535 A.2d at 405, n. 3. Here, it is undisputed that the merger was approved by the fully informed vote of WTI's disinterested directors. Those directors were fully aware of both the obvious conflict of the Waste designees and of the conflict of three other directors, created by the prospect of accelerated stock options and of future employment.

claims. Counsel shall submit an appropriate implementing form of order.

SECTION 3. COMPENSATION AND THE DOCTRINE OF WASTE

Insert the following case at p. 689 of the Unabridged Edition, in place of Cohen v. Ayres, and at p. 474 of the Concise Edition, after the Note on the American Tobacco Litigation:

ZUPNICK v. GOIZUETA

Court of Chancery of Delaware, 1997.
698 A.2d 384.

OPINION

JACOBS, Vice Chancellor.

Pending are motions to dismiss this stockholder's derivative action which claims that the directors of The Coca Cola Company ("Coca Cola" or "the corporation") committed corporate waste by granting certain stock options to Coca Cola's Chief Executive Officer, Roberto C. Goizueta ("Goizueta"). The primary thrust of the motion is that the plaintiff failed to make a pre-suit demand upon the corporation's board of directors, as Court of Chancery Rule 23.1 requires.* Defendants also contend that the plaintiffs have failed to state a claim upon which relief may be granted, and that the complaint should also be dismissed under Court of Chancery Rule 12 b(6). For the reasons next discussed, the Court concludes that a demand was required and that the complaint fails to state a cognizable legal claim. Therefore, the motion to dismiss will be granted.

I. FACTS

In 1991, Coca Cola adopted a Stock Option Plan, which was amended in 1995 ("the Plan"). The Plan was adopted by a board of directors, the majority of whom were independent, and it was also approved by Coca Cola's shareholders. Under the Plan, the options are granted at the market price as of the date of the grant, but cannot be exercised for a period of twelve months from the date of

---

* The issue of pre-suit demand is addressed at length in Chapter 10, Section 6, infra. To greatly oversimplify, the general rule is that a shareholder who proposes to bring an action on the corporation's behalf (a derivative action) must make a demand on the board before instituting the action. However, demand may be excused under certain exceptions to the general rule. The exceptions vary somewhat according to the jurisdiction. Vice–Chancellor Jacobs states the Delaware approach in Part II.B of his opinion in this case. (Footnote by ed.).

the grant. Thereafter, the options vest over a three year period. In limited circumstances, however, the options become exercisable immediately, specifically if: (1) the optionee's employment with the corporation is terminated by reason of the employee's death, disability, or retirement, or (2) there is a change of control of the company.

On April 19, 1995, Coca Cola's board of directors, acting through its compensation committee, awarded Goizueta options to purchase one million (1,000,000) shares of the corporation's stock, exercisable through April 19, 2005. The complaint, which relies upon (and quotes) the corporation's 1996 preliminary proxy statement, alleges that the compensation committee based that option award "... on the sustained performance of the Company since [Mr. Goizueta] assumed his current role in March, 1981 and the remarkable increase in market value of the Company during this period (nearly $69 billion)." Compl., ¶ 10. Mr. Goizueta was eligible to retire at the time the option was granted, and had he done so the option would have been exercisable immediately. Goizueta did not retire, however, and has continued to serve as Coca Cola's Chief Executive Officer.

II. STANDARD OF REVIEW AND THE PARTIES' CONTENTIONS

A. The Contentions

The plaintiff does not challenge the legal validity of the Plan or the manner of its adoption by the directors and shareholders. He attacks only the April, 1995 grant to Goizueta of options to purchase 1 million Coca Cola shares. The plaintiff claims that the grant of those options constituted corporate waste because the corporation received no consideration in exchange. He contends that Coca Cola received no consideration because the options were granted for past services that Goizueta was already required to perform and for which he already had been amply compensated.

The defendants respond that they committed no waste because a disinterested board of directors may, in a good faith exercise of its business judgment, award additional retroactive compensation, *i.e.*, a "bonus," to a corporate executive for extraordinary services that substantially benefited the corporation. Moreover, defendants argue, the corporation received other forms of consideration, including Mr. Goizueta's continued performance of his duties and the inducement of other key employees to remain in the corporation's service and to perform at a high level, motivated by the prospect that at a future time they too might be similarly rewarded.

To this the plaintiff responds that (1) the board of directors could not lawfully award compensation retroactively to Goizueta, and (2) that the defendants cannot be heard to argue that consideration for the option grant consisted of inducing Goizueta and other key employees to remain in the company's employ and to perform future services. That is because, plaintiff argues, (a) in the proxy statement the board represented to shareholders that the options were being awarded solely by reason of Goizueta's past services, and (b) the options could not have induced Goizueta to remain in the corporation's employ because the very day he was awarded the options, he could have retired and then immediately exercised them.

The plaintiff concedes that he made no pre-suit demand upon the directors to take corrective action, but claims that in the circumstances he was excused from the demand requirement. The defendants disagree. They contend that as a matter of law the complaint fails to satisfy the stringent pleading standard for a demand to be excused.

B. The Applicable Standard

Under our well developed caselaw in this area, a derivative complaint must be dismissed unless it alleges with particularity facts demonstrating that demand would have been futile. Demand is considered futile, and will be excused, only if the particularized facts alleged in the complaint create a reasonable doubt (*i.e.*, reason to doubt) that (1) the directors upon whom the demand would be made were disinterested and independent or (2) the challenged transaction was otherwise the product of a valid exercise of business judgment. *Aronson v. Lewis,* Del.Supr., 473 A.2d 805, 814 (1984); *Grimes v. Donald*, Del.Supr., 673 A.2d 1207, 1216 (1996). The plaintiff does not claim that the board failed to act in good faith, or that it had a disqualifying self-interest or lacked independence. Rather, he claims that the option grant itself was wasteful and not protected by the business judgment rule. Compl. ¶ 15. That being the claim, the broad issue is whether the complaint alleges, with particularity, facts creating a reasonable doubt that the board's decision to grant the 1995 option was entitled to the protection of the business judgment rule. See Aronson, 473 A.2d at 808.

To answer that question, the Court must also consider what standard is applicable in reviewing the plaintiff's assertion that he has pleaded cognizable claims of waste. Accordingly, the specific standard to be applied to the plaintiff's claim that demand was excused requires an amalgamation of the substantive test for waste and the procedural standard governing motions to dismiss under Rule 23.1. To state a cognizable claim for waste where there is no contention that the directors were interested or that shareholder ratification was improperly obtained, the well-pleaded allegations of the complaint must support the conclusion that "no person of ordinary, sound business judgment would say that the consideration received for the options was a fair exchange for the options granted." *Michelson v. Duncan*, Del.Supr., 407 A.2d 211, 224 (1979); *see also Grobow v. Perot*, 539 A.2d at 189 (plaintiff must allege facts showing that "what the corporation has received is so inadequate in value that no person of ordinary, sound business judgment would deem it worth that which the corporation has paid"). That is "an extreme test, very rarely satisfied by a shareholder plaintiff," because "if under the circumstances any reasonable person might conclude that the deal made sense, then the judicial inquiry ends." *Steiner v. Meyerson*, Del. Ch., C.A. No. 13139, Allen, C. (July 18, 1995), Mem. Op. at 2, 1995 WL 441999. As Chancellor Allen observed in *Steiner*, supra at p. 11:

> [T]he waste theory represents a theoretical exception to the statement very rarely encountered in the world of real transactions. There surely are cases of fraud; of unfair self dealing and, much more rarely negligence. But rarest of all—and indeed like Nessie, possibly non existent—would be the case of disinterested business people making non fraudulent deals (non-negligently) that meet the legal standard of waste!

Because that standard for waste and the procedural Rule 23.1 pleading standard prescribed by *Aronson* and its progeny must both be satisfied, the precise issue becomes whether the particularized factual allegations of the complaint create a reason to doubt that reasonable directors could have expected the corporation to benefit from the grant of the options to Goizueta. For the reasons now discussed, the Court concludes that the complaint fails to satisfy that high standard.

III. ANALYSIS

Any analysis of the waste claim must begin with 8 *Del. C.* § 157. That statute authorizes a Delaware corporation to create and issue (*inter alia*) options to purchase its shares. It also provides that in the absence of actual fraud, "the judgment of the directors as to the consideration for the issuance of such ... options and the sufficiency thereof shall be conclusive." 8 *Del. C.* § 157. That is, so long as there is any consideration for the issuance of shares or options, the sufficiency of the consideration fixed by the directors cannot be challenged in the absence of actual fraud. Only where it is claimed that the issuance of shares or options was entirely without consideration will § 157 not operate as "a legal barrier to any claim for relief as to an illegal gift or waste of corporate assets in the issuance of stock options." *Michelson v. Duncan*, 407 A.2d at 224.

The plaintiff's claim is that Coca Cola received no consideration because the options were issued to compensate Goizueta for his past performance. As the plaintiff alleges, the stock options granted to Goizueta in this case took the form of additional compensation (or a "bonus") for services previously performed. Plaintiff claims that such additional compensation was waste or a gift because Goizueta was already contractually obligated to perform those services and had been compensated for doing so. In these circumstances, that allegation fails to state a cognizable claim for waste.

Normally, stock options issued to employees are made exercisable at some future date after their issuance, in order to motivate the recipient to continue to perform valuable service for the corporation. *See Beard*, 160 A.2d at 736–37; *Kerbs v. California Eastern Airways,* Del.Supr., 90 A.2d 652, 656 (1952). That is, the consideration for stock options is often the reasonable prospect of obtaining the employee's valued future services. But that is not the only permissible form of consideration for a grant of stock options. Under certain limited circumstances, stock options may also be issued as a form of compensation for an employee's past services. In *Blish v. Thompson Automatic Arms Corporation*, Del.Supr., 64 A.2d 581 (1948), the Supreme Court addressed the issue of whether retroactive compensation was proper, and stated:

> The appellant's argument [that the retroactive salary increase was improper] is based upon the general rule that once an officer's salary has been fixed for a given period the Directors cannot at a subsequent meeting raise the [executive's] salary and make their action retroactive. This is so, says the appellant, for the reason that the retroactive feature of the salary ... must be regarded as being without consideration, since the amount of salary to [the executive] had been fixed by previous agreement and the services had been performed.

> Conceding the general rule to be as stated, nevertheless, we find its application subject to two well recognized exceptions: (1) Where an implied contract is shown; (2) Where the amount awarded is not unreasonable in view of the services rendered.

> We conclude from the evidence that the services rendered by [the executive] were unusual in character and extraordinary, from which [the corporation] received great gains and profits; therefore, the retroactive feature of [the executive's] increases in salary ... were proper under the second exception as noted above.

Id., at 606–07 (citations omitted, materials in brackets added); *see also Fletcher Cyc Corp* ¶ 2140 (Perm Ed.). Nor is there any proscription against using options as a form of executive compensation. If a board may properly award a bonus in the form of cash, then *a fortiori* it may award an immediately exercisable option that is the equivalent of cash. *See Steiner v. Meyerson, supra*, at 18–20.

In this case, the pleaded facts establish (for present purposes) that reasonable, disinterested directors could have concluded—and in this instance did conclude—that Goizueta's past services were of that character and that the resulting benefit to the corporation was of that magnitude. *See* Compl., ¶ 10 (option award based " ... on the sustained performance of the Company since [Mr. Goizueta] assumed his current role in March, 1981 and the remarkable increase in market value of the Company during this period (nearly $69 billion)"). This case, therefore, falls within a recognized exception to the common law rule that otherwise generally prohibits retroactive executive compensation. As thus viewed, the fact that the options might have become exercisable immediately had Goizueta chosen to retire is, from a legal standpoint, of no consequence.

For these reasons, the plaintiff's claim that the defendants' grant of stock options to Goizueta constituted waste is insufficient as a matter of law.[6] This Court cannot conclude that a person of ordinary, sound business judgment would be unable to find that the consideration received by the corporation was a fair exchange for the options granted. Nor do the particularized allegations of the complaint create a reasonable doubt in that connection.

IV. CONCLUSION

Because the facts alleged in the complaint establish that a reasonable person could conclude that the grant of the options to Mr. Goizueta made business sense, the complaint fails to state a legally sufficient claim for waste or to establish that a demand would have been futile. For these reasons the complaint will be dismissed under both Rules 12 b(6) and 23.1. IT IS SO ORDERED.

Add the following Note at p. 711 of the Unabridged Edition, at the end of Chapter VIII, Section 3:

NOTE ON THE COMPENSATION OF NONEXECUTIVE DIRECTORS

The compensation of nonexecutive directors has drawn increasing attention within the last few years. The modern theory of the

---

6. *See Steiner v. Meyerson, supra* at 19–20 (holding that "retaining the services of [the] person is not the only legitimate reason" to issue stock options, but rather that the grant of immediately exercisable options is not corporate waste if "there is some rational basis for directors to conclude that the amount and form of compensation is appropriate"); *Haft v. Dart Group Corp.,* 841 F.Supp. 549, 575 (D.Del.1993) (upholding issuance of stock made solely in recognition of recipient's prior service to the corporation); *Fletcher Cyc Corp* ¶ 2140 (Perm. Ed.) ("it has ... been suggested that corporate authority to grant past service benefits in the form of bonuses or pension may often have a favorable effect on the corporation as a whole").

Although plaintiff argues that at this procedural stage, the Court may not look beyond their allegations in the complaint that selectively quote portions of the proxy statement, the Court nonetheless observes that the proxy statement also stated that the Plan was adopted to advance the interests of the corporation, and to attract, retain, and motivate key employees. 1991 Stock Option Plan at 1. In *Beard v. Elster,* the Supreme Court noted that employees' knowledge of a proposed stock option plan "acted as an inducement to those employees to remain in the corporation's service," which constituted consideration. 160 A.2d at 738. Defendants contend that the knowledge of other key employees that they, like Mr. Goizueta, might similarly be rewarded, likewise induced them to remain in the corporation's employ and to maximize their performance on its behalf. Given the basis for the Court's ruling on this motion, it is not necessary to address that contention.

role of the board in publicly held corporations is that the board should monitor the executives' conduct of the business. This monitoring model assumes that directors will be independent of the executives they are to monitor, and will have the proper incentives to play a monitoring role. Directorial independence and incentives, in turn, are affected by the amount and form of directorial compensation.

1. *Amount of Compensation.*   To understand the significance of the amount of a director's compensation, it must be borne in mind that although nominally the executives are selected by the board, in practice the chief executive officer plays a significant and often decisive role in selecting the board. The CEO's role in the selection of directors may be diminishing somewhat but it is still very important. Correspondingly, directors who displease a CEO will often find it difficult to retain their board seats. Accordingly, in most publicly held corporations a director who has material financial incentives to retain his directorship will not be independent of the CEO.

The greater a director's compensation, the greater the director's financial incentives to retain his seat. Thus all other things—such as personal integrity and individual wealth—being equal, the greater the director's compensation, the less the director's independence. To take a simple case, a director who earns, say, $200,000/year, and whose continuation in office is wholly or partly under the control of the CEO, normally could not be deemed independent of the CEO. The trick, therefore, is to compensate directors in an amount that (i) sufficient to give responsible persons an incentive to serve as directors and rewards that service in an appropriate way, but is not so large as to compromise directorial independence.

In the 1980s, directors' fees averaged about $30,000/year. Since the early 1990s, however, directors' compensation has been growing much faster than inflation. In 1994, the average compensation of directors in Fortune 500 corporations (that is, in the country's 500 largest nonfinancial corporations) was $50,000, and compensation of $100,000 was not uncommon. See Report of the National Association of Corporate Directors Blue Ribbon Commission on Director Compensation 29 (1995) ("NACD Report"). Moreover, many directors also provide side services to the corporation in nondirectorial capacities such as consultants, professionals, or the like, which further increases their compensation, and therefore further compromises their independence.

2. *Form of Compensation.*   Directorial independence and incentives may be affected by the *form*, as well as the amount, of a director's compensation.

(a) *Compensation for consulting and other nondirectorial services.*   The effect of the form of a director's compensation is particularly dramatic in the case of side compensation for services that a director renders to the corporation in a nondirectorial capacity. The selection of consultants, professionals, and the like is normally within the sole control of the executives. Therefore even if a director could retain his board seat against the wishes of the CEO, he would stand to lose his side compensation if he falls into the CEO's disfavor.

Side compensation for nondirectorial services can be very large, and may be further augmented by fringe benefits. For example, in 1995 American Express paid Henry Kissinger, a non-executive director, the following compensation: annual consulting fees of $350,000; an annual director's retainer of $64,000; a prospective annual director's pension of $30,000; free director's life insurance; and the right to have American Express make a $500,000 gift to a charity of his choice at the time of his death. Knecht & Lublin, American Express Bars Using Directors as Paid Consultants, Wall St. J. April 12, 1995, at A.3. American Express has now adopted a policy that prohibits outside directors from serving as consultants, but Dr. Kissinger was exempted from the policy. Similarly, until 1995 W.R. Grace paid annual consulting fees totaling $1.5 million to five directors who were longtime friends of Grace's chairman. In that year, the chairman was ousted and Grace adopted a policy that no one with a consulting contract could serve as a director.

(b) *Pensions.* Pensions for directors are a relatively new idea, but lately have become widespread. Like side compensation, directorial pensions present problems of independence and incentives. According to the NACD Report, "The most common director retirement program involves an annual cash retirement fee equal to the board retainer at the time the director retires. The period of time for which a director receives a retirement fee typically is either (1) for the number of years for which the director has served, with some imposing a maximum of 10 years, or (2) for life if the director has served a minimum of 10 years. In some cases, the director's surviving spouse received part of the director's retirement fee upon the director's death—either until a designated number of years have elapsed, or for the spouse's life."

Some pensions are even more generous. Until recently, Warner–Lambert Company paid a lifetime pension of $35,000/year to any director who had served five years and reached age 70. Lublin, More Big Companies Reconsider Lavish Pensions for Directors, Wall St. J., Sept. 7, 1995, at B1, Col. 3. The threat of losing a pension pay-off may be even greater than the threat of losing annual directors' fees, especially as a director approaches retirement age. Moreover, pensions are associated with employment status, and therefore set a poor psychological tone for directorial independence. It is no coincidence that basic directorial compensation has been traditionally called a "fee," or sometimes a "retainer"—not "salary" which, like pensions, connotes employment status.

The NACD Report recommended that directors should be paid only cash and stock, and that pensions and other benefits should not be granted to directors:

> . . . [B]y their very value, generous benefit programs may actually create incentives for directors to oppose actions that could benefit shareholders if such actions would mean challenging management. This is especially true when a term of service is required before the benefits vest. In such cases, prior to vesting, directors have even more to lose in a tussle.

> Most benefit programs are troublesome for yet another reason: They reward directors as though they were employees. Historically in the United States, there have been many norms associated with primary employment, such as the provision of basic health and welfare benefits, retirement plans, and various industry-driven perquisites. Generally speaking, these benefits provide employees with a valuable service or good that they themselves could not easily replicate as individuals, and give employees a strong incentive to stay employed with the company.

> In recent years, there has been a vast proliferation of cash-oriented director retirement plans along with a modest, but noticeable, increase in some health and welfare benefits. . . .

> All of these employee-like benefits pose the risk of dependence. . . . Director retirement programs are particularly insidious in this regard. They suggest that directors have tenure, at the end of which retirement benefits will be paid. Directors, however, do not have tenure. They are elected by shareholders, usually to fixed terms of one or three years, to serve as part-time monitors and guardians of shareholder interests. Almost all directors have other full-time positions as employees of other businesses or organizations, at which they will qualify for and collect retirement benefits (unless they have retired, in which case they already participate in a retirement program provided by their previous employer).

Even before the NACD Report was issued, a number of shareholder resolutions had targeted director-pension plans. Although none of the resolutions was adopted, many received extremely wide support. Partly in reaction to these resolutions, some corporations dropped or modified their director-pension plans. The issuance of the NACD Report is likely to accentuate this movement.

(c) *Payment in stock.* Paying directors in the form of stock, rather than cash, may also matter. Over the years, a director who is paid in stock will find that stock in the corporation represents a significant portion of her wealth, at least if sale of her stock is restricted by its terms. This should tend to align the director's interest more closely with the shareholders, and thereby provide a positive incentive for monitoring. Professor Charles Elson has extensively argued the proposition that paying directors in stock will affect the manner in which directors perform their monitoring role:

> ... [H]ow can we incentivize outside directors in the large public corporation to eschew their traditional passivity? We must make it clear that it is in their own self-interest to do so. They must not become active participants in the oversight process because someone is ordering them to so engage, but must act because they feel that it is in their own self-interest....

> The outside director must be made to consider management activity from the viewpoint of a company stockholder, to whom the director is legally obligated, instead of from the perspective of one beholden to management. Thus, it is crucial that the company's outside directors realign their interests and thinking with those of the shareholders. The most effective way to create such perspective is to appeal directly to these directors' personal pecuniary interests.... If a director's personal capital is potentially affected by inept or corrupt management, that director is much less likely to acquiesce passively to such a group. From a personal standpoint, there is much less incentive to stand watch over what one considers to be someone else's property than over what one considers to be one's own. Interestingly enough, this was the whole point behind the creation of the externally imposed director's duty of care.

> Equity ownership would act to counter the pressures placed on the outside directors as a result of management capture. It is very hard to resist the demands of individuals to whom you owe your position when your involvement in the venture is limited to the fee you receive for your services and the continuance of that fee is subject to the will of management. Possessing an actual stake in the venture itself alters the nature of this relationship considerably....

Elson, The Duty of Care, Compensation, and Stock Ownership, 63 U.Cinn.L.Rev. 649 (1995).

One of the major recommendation of the NACD Report that directors should be paid "solely in the form of equity [common stock] and cash—with equity representing a substantial portion of the total up to 100 percent." Id. at 15. Several corporations had begun paying directors in stock in whole or in part even before the NACD Report. As in the case of directors' pension plans, the issuance of the NACD Report is likely to accentuate the movement in this direction.

———

SECTION 4. THE CORPORATE OPPORTUNITY DOCTRINE

Delete Klinicki v. Lundgren, at p. 716 of the Unabridged Edition and p. 479 of the Concise Edition, and insert the following case and Notes in its place:

NORTHEAST HARBOR GOLF CLUB, INC. v. HARRIS

Supreme Judicial Court of Maine, 1995.
661 A.2d 1146.

Before WATHEN, C.J., and ROBERTS, GLASSMAN, DANA, and LIPEZ, JJ.

ROBERTS, Justice.

Northeast Harbor Golf Club, Inc., appeals from a judgment entered in the Superior Court (Hancock County, *Atwood, J.*) following a nonjury trial. The Club maintains that the trial court erred in finding that Nancy Harris did not breach her fiduciary duty as president of the Club by purchasing and developing property abutting the golf course. Because we today adopt principles different from those applied by the trial court in determining that Harris's activities did not constitute a breach of the corporate opportunity doctrine, we vacate the judgment.

I.

The Facts

Nancy Harris was the president of the Northeast Harbor Golf Club, a Maine corporation, from 1971 until she was asked to resign in 1990. The Club also had a board of directors that was responsible for making or approving significant policy decisions. The Club's only major asset was a golf course in Mount Desert. During Harris's tenure as president, the board occasionally discussed the possibility of developing some of the Club's real estate in order to raise money. Although Harris was generally in favor of tasteful development, the board always "shied away" from that type of activity.

In 1979, Robert Suminsby informed Harris that he was the listing broker for the Gilpin property, which comprised three non-contiguous parcels located among the fairways of the golf course. The property included an unused right-of-way on which the Club's parking lot and clubhouse were located. It was also encumbered by an easement in favor of the Club allowing foot traffic from the green of one hole to the next tee. Suminsby testified that he contacted Harris because she was the president of the Club and he believed that the Club would be interested in buying the property in order to prevent development.

Harris immediately agreed to purchase the Gilpin property in her own name for the asking price of $45,000. She did not disclose her plans to purchase the property to the Club's board prior to the purchase. She informed the board at its annual August meeting that she had purchased the property, that she intended to hold it in her own name, and that the Club would be "protected." The board took no action in response to the Harris purchase. She testified that at the time of the purchase she had no plans to develop the property and that no such plans took shape until 1988.

In 1984, while playing golf with the postmaster of Northeast Harbor, Harris learned that a parcel of land owned by the heirs of the Smallidge family might be available for purchase. The Smallidge parcel was surrounded on three sides by the golf course and on the fourth side by a house lot. It had no access to the road. With the ultimate goal of acquiring the property, Harris instructed her lawyer to locate the Smallidge heirs. Harris testified that she told a number of individual board members about her attempt to acquire the Smallidge parcel. At a board meeting in August 1985, Harris formally disclosed to the board that she had purchased the Smallidge property.[1] The minutes of that meeting show that she told the board she had no present plans to develop the Smallidge parcel. Harris testified that at the time of the purchase of the Smallidge property she nonetheless thought it might be nice to have some houses there. Again, the board took no formal action as a result of Harris's purchase. Harris acquired the Smallidge property from ten heirs, paying a total of $60,000. In 1990, Harris paid $275,000 for the lot and building separating the Smallidge parcel from the road in order to gain access to the otherwise landlocked parcel.

The trial court expressly found that the Club would have been unable to purchase either the Gilpin or Smallidge properties for itself, relying on testimony that the Club continually experienced financial difficulties, operated annually at a deficit, and depended on contributions from the directors to pay its bills. On the other hand, there was evidence that the Club had occasionally engaged in successful fund-raising, including a two-year period shortly after the Gilpin purchase during which the Club raised $115,000. The Club had $90,000 in a capital investment fund at the time of the Smallidge purchase.

In 1987 or 1988, Harris divided the real estate into 41 small lots, 14 on the Smallidge property and 27 on the Gilpin property. Apparently as part of her estate plan, Harris conveyed noncontigu-

---

1. In fact, it appears that Harris did not take title to the property until October 26, 1985. She had only signed a purchase and sale agreement at the time of the August board meeting.

ous lots among the 41 to her children and retained others for herself. In 1991, Harris and her children exchanged deeds to reassemble the small lots into larger parcels. At the time the Club filed this suit, the property was divided into 11 lots, some owned by Harris and others by her children who are also defendants in this case. Harris estimated the value of all the real estate at the time of the trial to be $1,550,000.

In 1988, Harris, who was still president of the Club, and her children began the process of obtaining approval for a five-lot subdivision known as Bushwood on the lower Gilpin property. Even when the board learned of the proposed subdivision, a majority failed to take any action. A group of directors formed a separate organization in order to oppose the subdivision on the basis that it violated the local zoning ordinance. After Harris's resignation as president, the Club also sought unsuccessfully to challenge the subdivision. *See Northeast Harbor Golf Club, Inc. v. Town of Mount Desert*, 618 A.2d 225 (Me.1992). Plans of Harris and her family for development of the other parcels are unclear, but the local zoning ordinance would permit construction of up to 11 houses on the land as currently divided.

After Harris's plans to develop Bushwood became apparent, the board grew increasingly divided concerning the propriety of development near the golf course. At least two directors, Henri Agnese and Nick Ludington, testified that they trusted Harris to act in the best interests of the Club and that they had no problem with the development plans for Bushwood. Other directors disagreed.

In particular, John Schafer, a Washington, D.C., lawyer and long-time member of the board, took issue with Harris's conduct. He testified that he had relied on Harris's representations at the time she acquired the properties that she would not develop them. According to Schafer, matters came to a head in August 1990 when a number of directors concluded that Harris's development plans irreconcilably conflicted with the Club's interests. As a result, Schafer and two other directors asked Harris to resign as president. In April 1991, after a substantial change in the board's membership, the board authorized the instant lawsuit against Harris for the breach of her fiduciary duty to act in the best interests of the corporation. The board simultaneously resolved that the proposed housing development was contrary to the best interests of the corporation.

The Club filed a complaint against Harris, her sons John and Shepard, and her daughter-in-law Melissa Harris. As amended, the complaint alleged that during her term as president Harris breached her fiduciary duty by purchasing the lots without providing notice and an opportunity for the Club to purchase the property and by subdividing the lots for future development. The Club sought an injunction to prevent development and also sought to impose a constructive trust on the property in question for the benefit of the Club.

The trial court found that Harris had not usurped a corporate opportunity because the acquisition of real estate was not in the Club's line of business. Moreover, it found that the corporation lacked the financial ability to purchase the real estate at issue. Finally, the court placed great emphasis on Harris's good faith. It noted her long and dedicated history of service to the Club, her personal oversight of the Club's growth, and her frequent financial contributions to the Club. The court found that her development activities were "generally . . . compatible with the corporation's business." This appeal followed.

II.

The Corporate Opportunity Doctrine

Corporate officers and directors bear a duty of loyalty to the corporations they serve. As Justice Cardozo explained the fiduciary duty in *Meinhard v. Salmon*, 249 N.Y. 458, 164 N.E. 545, 546 (1928):

> A trustee is held to something stricter than the morals of the marketplace. Not honesty alone, but the punctilio of an honor the most sensitive, is then the standard of behavior. As to this there has developed a tradition that is unbending and inveterate.

Maine has embraced this "unbending and inveterate" tradition. Corporate fiduciaries in Maine must discharge their duties in good faith with a view toward furthering the interests of the corporation. They must disclose and not withhold relevant information concerning any potential conflict of interest with the corporation, and they must refrain from using their position, influence, or knowledge of the affairs of the corporation to gain personal advantage. *See Rosenthal v. Rosenthal*, 543 A.2d 348, 352 (Me.1988); 13–A M.R.S.A. § 716 (Supp.1994).

Despite the general acceptance of the proposition that corporate fiduciaries owe a duty of loyalty to their corporations, there has been much confusion about the specific extent of that duty when, as here, it is contended that a fiduciary takes for herself a corporate opportunity. *See, e.g.,* Victor Brudney & Robert C. Clark, *A New Look at Corporate Opportunities*, 94 Harv.L.Rev. 998, 998 (1981) ("Not only are the common formulations vague, but the courts have articulated no theory that would serve as a blueprint for constructing meaningful rules."). This case requires us for the first time to define the scope of the corporate opportunity doctrine in Maine.

Various courts have embraced different versions of the corporate opportunity doctrine. The test applied by the trial court and embraced by Harris is generally known as the "line of business" test. The seminal case applying the line of business test is *Guth v. Loft, Inc.,* 5 A.2d 503 (Del.1939). In *Guth,* the Delaware Supreme Court adopted an intensely factual test stated in general terms as follows:

> [I]f there is presented to a corporate officer or director a business opportunity which the corporation is financially able to undertake, is, from its nature, in the line of the corporation's business and is of practical advantage to it, is one in which the corporation has an interest or a reasonable expectancy, and, by embracing the opportunity, the self-interest of the officer or director will be brought into conflict with that of his corporation, the law will not permit him to seize the opportunity for himself.

Id. at 511. The "real issue" under this test is whether the opportunity "was so closely associated with the existing business activities . . . as to bring the transaction within that class of cases where the acquisition of the property would throw the corporate officer purchasing it into competition with his company." *Id.* at 513. The Delaware court described that inquiry as "a factual question to be decided by reasonable inferences from objective facts." *Id.*

The line of business test suffers from some significant weaknesses. First, the question whether a particular activity is within a corporation's line of business is conceptually difficult to answer. The facts of the instant case demonstrate that difficulty. The Club is in the business of running a golf course. It is not in the business of developing real estate. In the traditional sense, therefore, the trial court correctly observed that the opportunity in this case was not a corporate opportunity within the meaning of the *Guth* test. Nevertheless, the record would support a finding that the Club had made the policy judgment that development of surrounding real estate was detrimental to the best interests of the Club. The acquisition of land adjacent to the golf course for the purpose of preventing future development would have enhanced the ability of the Club to implement that policy. The record also shows that the Club had occasionally considered reversing that policy and expanding its operations to include the development of surrounding real estate. Harris's activities effectively foreclosed the Club from pursuing that option with respect to prime locations adjacent to the golf course.

Second, the *Guth* test includes as an element the financial ability of the corporation to take advantage of the opportunity. The court in this case relied on the Club's supposed financial incapacity as a basis for excusing Harris's conduct. Often, the injection of financial ability into the equation will unduly favor the inside director or executive who has command of the facts relating to the finances of the corporation. Reliance on financial ability will also act as a disincentive to corporate executives to solve corporate financing and other problems. In addition, the Club could have prevented development without spending $275,000 to acquire the property Harris needed to obtain access to the road.

The Massachusetts Supreme Judicial Court adopted a different test in *Durfee v. Durfee & Canning, Inc.*, 323 Mass. 187, 80 N.E.2d 522 (1948). The *Durfee* test has since come to be known as the "fairness test." According to *Durfee*, the

> true basis of governing doctrine rests on the unfairness in the particular circumstances of a director, whose relation to the corporation is fiduciary, taking advantage of an opportunity [for her personal profit] when the interest of the corporation justly call[s] for protection. This calls for application of ethical standards of what is fair and equitable ... in particular sets of facts.

Id. at 529 (quoting *Ballantine on Corporations* 204–05 (rev. ed. 1946)). As with the *Guth* test, the *Durfee* test calls for a broad-ranging, intensely factual inquiry. The *Durfee* test suffers even more than the *Guth* test from a lack of principled content. It provides little or no practical guidance to the corporate officer or director seeking to measure her obligations.

The Minnesota Supreme Court elected "to combine the 'line of business' test with the 'fairness' test." *Miller v. Miller*, 301 Minn. 207, 222 N.W.2d 71, 81 (1974). It engaged in a two-step analysis, first determining whether a particular opportunity was within the corporation's line of business, then scrutinizing "the equitable considerations existing prior to, at the time of, and following the officer's acquisition." *Id.* The *Miller* court hoped by adopting this approach "to ameliorate the often-expressed criticism that the [corporate opportunity] doctrine is vague and subjects today's corporate management to the danger of unpredictable liability." *Id.* In fact, the test adopted in *Miller* merely piles the uncertainty and vagueness of the fairness test on top of the weaknesses in the line of business test.

Despite the weaknesses of each of these approaches to the corporate opportunity doctrine, they nonetheless rest on a single fundamental policy. At bottom, the corporate opportunity doctrine recognizes that a corporate fiduciary should not serve both corporate and personal interests at the same time. As we observed in *Camden Land Co. v. Lewis*, 101 Me. 78, 97, 63 A. 523, 531 (1905), corporate fiduciaries "owe their whole duty to the corporation, and they are not to be permitted to act when duty conflicts with interest. They cannot serve themselves and the corporation at the same time." The various formulations of the test are merely attempts to moderate the potentially harsh consequences of strict adherence to that policy. It is important to preserve some ability for corporate fiduciaries to pursue personal business interests that present no real threat to their duty of loyalty.

III.

The American Law Institute Approach

In an attempt to protect the duty of loyalty while at the same time providing long-needed clarity and guidance for corporate decisionmakers, the American Law Institute has offered the most recently developed version of the corporate opportunity doctrine. PRINCIPLES OF CORPORATE GOVERNANCE § 5.05 (May 13, 1992), provides as follows:

§ 5.05 Taking of Corporate Opportunities by Directors or Senior Executives

(a) *General Rule.* A director [§ 1.13] or senior executive [§ 1.33] may not take advantage of a corporate opportunity unless:

(1) The director or senior executive first offers the corporate opportunity to the corporation and makes disclosure concerning the conflict of interest [§ 1.14(a)] and the corporate opportunity [§ 1.14(b)];

(2) The corporate opportunity is rejected by the corporation; and

(3) Either:

(A) The rejection of the opportunity is fair to the corporation;

(B) The opportunity is rejected in advance, following such disclosure, by disinterested directors [§ 1.15], or, in the case of a senior executive who is not a director, by a disinterested superior, in a manner that satisfies the standards of the business judgment rule [§ 4.01(c)]; or

(C) The rejection is authorized in advance or ratified, following such disclosure, by disinterested shareholders [§ 1.16], and the rejection is not equivalent to a waste of corporate assets [§ 1.42].

(b) *Definition of a Corporate Opportunity.* For purposes of this Section, a corporate opportunity means:

(1) Any opportunity to engage in a business activity of which a director or senior executive becomes aware, either:

(A) In connection with the performance of functions as a director or senior executive, or under circumstances that should reasonably lead the director or senior executive to believe that the person offering the opportunity expects it to be offered to the corporation; or

(B) Through the use of corporate information or property, if the resulting opportunity is one that the director or senior executive should reasonably be expected to believe would be of interest to the corporation; or

(2) Any opportunity to engage in a business activity of which a senior executive becomes aware and knows is closely related to a business in which the corporation is engaged or expects to engage.

(c) *Burden of Proof.* A party who challenges the taking of a corporate opportunity has the burden of proof, except that if such party establishes that the requirements of Subsection (a)(3)(B) or (C) are not met, the director or the senior executive has the burden of proving that the rejection and the taking of the opportunity were fair to the corporation.

(d) *Ratification of Defective Disclosure.* A good faith but defective disclosure of the facts concerning the corporate opportunity may be cured if at any time (but no later than a reasonable time after suit is filed challenging the taking of the corporate opportunity) the original rejection of the corporate opportunity is ratified, following the required disclosure, by the board, the shareholders, or the corporate decisionmaker who initially approved the rejection of the corporate opportunity, or such decisionmaker's successor.

(e) *Special Rule Concerning Delayed Offering of Corporate Opportunities.* Relief based solely on failure to first offer an opportunity to the corporation under Subsection (a)(1) is not available if: (1) such failure resulted from a good faith belief that the business activity did not constitute a corporate opportunity, and (2) not later than a reasonable time after suit is filed challenging the taking of the corporate opportunity, the corporate opportunity is to the extent possible offered to the corporation and rejected in a manner that satisfies the standards of Subsection (a).

The central feature of the ALI test is the strict requirement of full disclosure prior to taking advantage of any corporate opportunity. *Id.,* § 5.05(a)(1). "If the opportunity is not offered to the corporation, the director or senior executive will not have satisfied § 5.05(a)." *Id.,* cmt. to § 5.05(a). The corporation must then formally reject the opportunity. *Id.,* § 505(a)(2). The ALI test is discussed at length and ultimately applied by the Oregon Supreme Court in *Klinicki v. Lundgren,* 298 Or. 662, 695 P.2d 906 (1985). As *Klinicki* describes the test, "full disclosure to the appropriate corporate body is ... an absolute condition precedent to the validity of any forthcoming rejection as well as to the availability to the director or principal senior executive of the defense of fairness." *Id.* at 920. A "good faith but defective disclosure" by the corporate officer may be ratified after the fact only by an affirmative vote of the disinterested directors or shareholders. PRINCIPLES OF CORPORATE GOVERNANCE § 5.05(d).

The ALI test defines "corporate opportunity" broadly. It includes opportunities "closely related to a business in which the corporation is engaged." *Id.,* § 5.05(b). It also encompasses any opportunities that accrue to the fiduciary as a result of her position within the corporation. *Id.* This concept is most clearly illustrated by the testimony of Suminsby, the listing broker for the Gilpin property, which, if believed by the factfinder, would support a finding that the Gilpin property was offered to Harris specifically in her capacity as president of the Club. If the factfinder reached that conclusion, then at least the opportunity to acquire the Gilpin property would be a corporate opportunity. The state of the record concerning the Smallidge purchase precludes us from intimating any opinion whether that too would be a corporate opportunity.

Under the ALI standard, once the Club shows that the opportunity is a corporate opportunity, it must show either that Harris did not offer the opportunity to the Club or that the Club did not reject it properly. If the Club shows that the board did not reject the opportunity by a vote of the disinterested directors after full disclosure, then Harris may defend her actions on the basis that the taking of the opportunity was fair to the corporation. *Id.,* § 5.05(c). If Harris failed to offer the opportunity at all, however, then she may not defend on the basis that the failure to offer the opportunity was fair. *Id.,* cmt. to § 5.05(c).

The *Klinicki* court viewed the ALI test as an opportunity to bring some clarity to a murky area of the law. *Klinicki,* 695 P.2d at 915. We agree, and today we follow the ALI test. The disclosure-oriented approach provides a clear procedure whereby a corporate officer may insulate herself through prompt and complete disclosure from the possibility of a legal challenge. The requirement of disclosure recognizes the paramount importance of the corporate fiduciary's duty of loyalty. At the same time it protects the fiduciary's ability pursuant to the proper procedure to pursue her own business ventures free from the possibility of a lawsuit.

The importance of disclosure is familiar to the law of corporations in Maine. Pursuant to 13–A M.R.S.A. § 717 (1981), a corporate officer or director may enter into a transaction with the corporation in which she has a personal or adverse interest only if she discloses her interest in the transaction and secures ratification by a majority of the disinterested directors or shareholders. Section 717 is part of the Model Business Corporations Act, adopted in Maine in 1971. P.L.1971, ch. 439, § 1. Like the ALI rule, section 717 was designed to "eliminate the inequities and uncertainties caused by the existing rules." MODEL BUSINESS CORP. ACT § 41, ¶ 2, at 844 (1971).

IV.

Conclusion

The question remains how our adoption of the rule affects the result in the instant case. The trial court made a number of factual findings based on an extensive record.[3]   The court made those findings, however, in the light of legal principles that are different from the principles that we today announce.   Similarly, the parties did not have the opportunity to develop the record in this case with knowledge of the applicable legal standard.   In these circumstances, fairness requires that we remand the case for further proceedings. Those further proceedings may include, at the trial court's discretion, the taking of further evidence.

The entry is:

Judgment vacated.

Remanded for further proceedings consistent with the opinion herein.

All concurring.

DEMOULAS v. DEMOULAS SUPER MARKETS, INC., 424 Mass. 501, 677 N.E.2d 159 (1997).

"[O]ther recent formulations of the corporate opportunity doctrine have ... focused on the responsibility of the fiduciary to present these possibilities to the corporation for its consideration. For example, a corporate opportunity has been defined, in part, as '[a]ny opportunity to engage in a business activity of which a director or senior executive becomes aware,' either in connection with performing the functions of those positions, or '[t]hrough the use of corporate information or property, if the resulting opportunity is one that the director or senior executive should reasonably be expected to believe would be of interest to the corporation.' Principles of Corporate Governance § 5.05(b)(1) (1994). See ABA Corporate Director's Guidebook (rev. ed.), 33 Bus. Law. 1591, 1600 (1978) (doctrine applies to any opportunity 'relevant to the enterprise's present or prospective business activities') . . . .

"A director or officer is not entirely barred from pursuing a corporate opportunity, but a person holding either position cannot do so unless the opportunity is first offered to the corporation and rejected by it. In this aspect, the corporate opportunity doctrine may be considered to be a rule of disclosure. *In re Tufts Elecs., Inc.*, 746 F.2d 915, 917 (1st Cir.1984), citing [*Durfee v. Durfee & Canning, Inc.* 323 Mass. 187, 200, 80

----

3. Harris raised the defense of laches and the statute of limitations but the court made no findings on those issues. We do not intimate what result the application of either doctrine would produce in this case. Similarly, it was not necessary for the court to address the issue of remedy in the first trial. The court has broad discretion to fashion an equitable remedy based on the facts and circumstances of the case. We decline to invade its province by commenting prematurely on what remedy, if any, may be appropriate.

N.E.2d 522 (1948)]. To satisfy the principle of fairness to the corporation and to meet his duty of loyalty, the fiduciary must fully disclose to the corporation, all material facts concerning the opportunity. See *Production Mach. Co. v. Howe*, 327 Mass. 372, 375, 99 N.E.2d 32 (1951) (defendant failed to make 'full disclosure which as a fiduciary he owed'); Principles of Corporate Governance, *supra* at § 5.05 comment to § 5.05(a), at 287–288 (director or senior executive must offer opportunity to the corporation before taking it for personal advantage, and should disclose all known material facts). Similarly, to satisfy the duty of loyalty, a fiduciary wishing to engage in a self-dealing transaction must disclose details of the transaction and the conflict of interest to the corporate decisionmakers. See *Puritan Medical Ctr. Inc. v. Cashman*, 413 Mass. 167, 172, 596 N.E.2d 1004 (1992) (self-dealing not ratified in absence of full disclosure); *Dynan v. Fritz*, 400 Mass. 230, 243, 508 N.E.2d 1371 (1987), *S.C., Martin v. F.S. Payne Co.*, 409 Mass. 753, 569 N.E.2d 808 (1991) (good faith requires 'full and honest disclosure of all relevant circumstances'); Principles of Corporate Governance, *supra* at § 5.02(a).

"The disclosure requirement takes from the fiduciary the power to decide whether the opportunity or self-dealing transaction is in the corporation's interest and removes the temptation posed by 'a conflict between self-interest and integrity.' *Durfee, supra* at 198, 80 N.E.2d 522, quoting *Michoud v. Girod*, 45 U.S. (4 How.) 503, 555, 11 L.Ed. 1076 (1846). The conflict may be avoided and fairness to the corporation best ensured if the venture is considered, and a decision made on behalf of the corporation, by disinterested members of the board of directors (or, alternatively, disinterested shareholders). Where the board's decision is made by persons who are subject to the control of the self-interested fiduciary, or who have an interest themselves in the proposed transaction or opportunity, that decision obviously is subject to the same potential for conflict of interest that would exist with a decision made by the fiduciary alone. Therefore, where a corporate opportunity or self-dealing transaction is disclosed to the corporation, but the decision on it is made by self-interested directors, the burden is on those who benefit from the venture to prove that the decision was fair to the corporation.

"The defendants argue that certain ventures at issue, in particular the formation of Seabrook Sales and P & P Foods, were not corporate opportunities for DSM, because the New Hampshire liquor laws then in effect made it legally impossible for DSM to own those companies. We disagree with this argument, which would limit a fiduciary's duty of disclosure to those enterprises judged by the fiduciary to be within the corporation's legal, financial, or institutional capabilities. Establishing such a threshold test for defining a corporate opportunity would contradict the principle just discussed, that a fiduciary who is interested in pursuing an opportunity should not make the decision as to whether the venture is also of interest to the corporation. Instead, to ensure fairness to the corporation, opportunities must be presented to the corporation without regard to possible impediments, and material facts must be fully disclosed, so that the corporation may consider whether and how to address these obstacles. See *Durfee, supra* at 200–202, 80 N.E.2d 522 (corporation's alleged credit weakness does not allow director to exploit opportunity); *Energy Resources Corp. v. Porter*, 14 Mass.App.Ct. 296, 299–302, 438 N.E.2d 391 (1982) (contractor's refusal to deal with corporation not a defense for an officer who formed his own firm to pursue the opportunity without fully disclosing the reasons for the refusal); *Cain v. Cain*, 3 Mass.App.Ct. 467, 476–477, 334 N.E.2d 650 (1975) (officer must disclose customer dissatisfaction to corporation before pursuing opportunity through separate company). See also Principles of Corporate Governance, *supra* at § 5.05 Reporter's Note at 299–300 (corporation is to determine for itself whether obstacles are insuperable). Without such a rule, the fiduciary's self-interest may cloud his judgment or tempt him to overlook his duties. For example, where a third party ostensibly is unwilling to deal with the corporation, '[w]ithout full disclosure it is too difficult to verify the unwillingness to deal and too easy for the executive to induce the unwillingness.' *Porter, supra* at 300–301, 438 N.E.2d 391. In the present case, it was up to DSM, not the defendants, to determine whether any legal obstacles faced by DSM in pursuit of ventures in New Hampshire were insurmountable.

"In short, to meet a fiduciary's duty of loyalty, a director or officer who wishes to take advantage of a corporate opportunity or engage in self-dealing must first disclose material details of the venture to the corporation, and then either receive the assent of disinterested directors or shareholders, or otherwise prove that the decision is fair to the corporation. Otherwise, the officer or director acts in violation of his fiduciary duties, and whatever gain or advantage that he acquires may be held for the benefit of the corporation so as to deny him any benefit or profit. *Durfee, supra* at 198, 80 N.E.2d 522, citing *Guth v. Loft, Inc.*, 23 Del.Ch. 255, 270, 5 A.2d 503 (1939)."

———

OSTROWSKI v. AVERY, 243 Conn. 355, 703 A.2d 117 (1997). "We next address the consequence of the failure of a corporate fiduciary adequately to disclose the possible existence of a corporate opportunity. Courts and commentators have developed three different approaches regarding the effect of such a disclosure or nondisclosure on the liability of such a fiduciary.

1

"One approach, recently espoused in § 5.05 of the American Law Institute's Principles of Corporate Governance: Analysis and Recommendations (1992) (Principles of Corporate Governance), makes disclosure determinative of fiduciary liability. Section 5.05(a) provides, in relevant part, that a director or senior executive may not take advantage of a corporate opportunity unless: '(1) The director or senior executive first offers the corporate opportunity to the corporation and makes disclosure concerning the conflict of interest ... and the corporate opportunity ... (2) The corporate opportunity is rejected by the corporation; and (3) Either: (A) The rejection of the opportunity is fair to the corporation; (B) The opportunity is rejected in advance, following such disclosure, by disinterested directors ... or, in the case of a senior executive who is not a director, by a disinterested superior, in a manner that satisfies the standards of the business judgment rule ... or (C) The rejection is authorized in advance or ratified, following such disclosure, by disinterested shareholders, and the rejection is not equivalent to a waste of corporate assets....' This approach, which unequivocally imposes fiduciary liability in the absence of appropriate disclosure, has been followed by the courts of Maine and Oregon. *Northeast Harbor Golf Club, Inc. v. Harris,* 661 A.2d 1146, 1151–52 (Me.1995); *Klinicki v. Lundgren,* 298 Or. 662, 682–83, 695 P.2d 906 (1985); contra *Broz v. Cellular Information Systems, Inc.,* 673 A.2d 148, 157 (Del.1996).

"The bright line approach taken by the Principles of Corporate Governance has appeal. It promotes efficiency because it provides clear guidance both to corporate officers and directors and to the courts that are called upon to enforce fiduciary obligations. Also, it underscores the importance of timely disclosure in order to ensure timely corporate access to all of the information that the corporation needs to determine what course of action is in the corporation's best interest.

"A one-size-fits-all approach has, however, the drawback of any bright line rule. It offers no opportunity to differentiate among the variety of factual circumstances in which an alleged usurpation of a corporate opportunity may arise. In *Katz Corp.,* we implicitly rejected the claim that the 'defendants should first have presented the opportunity to purchase stock to the corporation by calling a directors' or shareholders' meeting,' because no corporate opportunity existed within the meaning of the avowed business purpose test and the corporation was financially unable to pursue the venture. *Katz Corp. v. T.H. Canty & Co.,* supra, 168 Conn. at 209–10; see also *Bricklin v. Stengol Corp.,* 1 Conn.App. 656, 666, 476 A.2d 584, cert. denied, 194 Conn. 803, 482 A.2d 709 (1984). In a related context, we have refused to apply a bright line rule to determine whether, for res judicata purposes, corporate officers or shareholders are in privity with their corporation. *Joe's Pizza, Inc. v. Aetna Life & Casualty Co.*, 236 Conn. 863, 868, 675 A.2d 441 (1996), citing *Amalgamated Sugar Co. v. NL Industries, Inc.*, 825 F.2d 634, 640 (2d Cir.), cert. denied, 484 U.S. 992, 108 S.Ct. 511, 98 L.Ed.2d 511 (1987). Without denying the significance of timely and full disclosure, we decline to adopt a bright line rule in this area of fiduciary responsibility.

2

"Another case law approach focuses less on adequate disclosure by a corporate fiduciary and more on whether affirmative defenses, such as the corporation's financial inability to avail itself of the corporate opportunity at issue, can be proven by the corporate fiduciary. That was implicitly the position that we took in *Katz Corp. v. T.H. Canty & Co.*, supra, 168 Conn. 201. We reasoned that 'there can be no expectancy in a transaction unless the corporation is financially able to undertake it.' Id. Accordingly, we rejected the plaintiffs' claim for relief in part because the corporation's 'cash on hand and liquid assets were insufficient to enable it to make such a substantial purchase.' Id.

"Courts in other jurisdictions similarly afford the corporate fiduciary the opportunity to prove, as an affirmative defense, that the corporation lacked the financial ability to pursue the opportunity. Some courts permit such a defense in all cases. See, e.g., *Paulman v. Kritzer*, 74 Ill.App.2d 284, 292–296, 219 N.E.2d 541 (1966), aff'd, 38 Ill.2d 101, 230 N.E.2d 262 (1967). Other courts limit the defense of financial inability to cases in which the defendant corporation can be proven to have been insolvent at the relevant time. See, e.g., *Irving Trust Co. v. Deutsch*, 73 F.2d 121, 124 (2d Cir.1934), cert. denied, 294 U.S. 708, 55 S.Ct. 405, 79 L.Ed. 1243 (1935); note, supra, 74 Harv. L. Rev. 773.

"We agree with the perception of those courts that a claim of usurpation of a corporate opportunity should be examined through a wide-angled lens that takes account of a large variety of relevant factors. Nonetheless, we are persuaded by the learned discussion in the Principles of Corporate Governance that a proper multifactor analysis must give special weight to the significance of disclosure or nondisclosure of a possible corporate opportunity to the corporation's board of directors or its shareholders. In our view, without such special weight, a multifactor analysis gives insufficient guidance to the trier of fact.

3

"Adopting yet a third form of analysis, the Delaware Supreme Court, in *Broz v. Cellular Information Systems, Inc.*, supra, 673 A.2d 148, recently enunciated a safe harbor rule. The court concluded that, if a corporate fiduciary made a timely and appropriate disclosure of the opportunity to the corporation's board, the fiduciary would automatically have discharged his or her fiduciary obligation. Id., 157. '[P]resenting the opportunity to the board creates a kind of "safe harbor" for the director, which removes the specter of a post hoc judicial determination that the director or officer has improperly usurped a corporate opportunity.' Id.

"The court in *Broz* declined to hold that [lack of] disclosure, per se, constituted usurpation of a corporate opportunity. Rejecting the contrary view of the Principles of Corporate Governance, the court decided against the adoption of a 'requirement of formal presentation under circumstances where the corporation does not have an interest, expectancy or financial ability.' Id., 157. Instead, relying on principles derived from *Guth v. Loft, Inc.* supra, 23 Del.Ch. 255, and its progeny, the court considered whether: '(1) the corporation [was] financially able to exploit the opportunity; (2) the opportunity [was] within the corporation's line of business; (3) the corporation [had] an interest or expectancy in the opportunity; and (4) by taking the opportunity for his own, the corporate fiduciary [would] thereby be placed in a position inimicable to his duties to the corporation.' *Broz v. Cellular Information Systems, Inc.*, supra, 673 A.2d at 155. Applying that test, the court in *Broz* determined that, in light of the relevant circumstances, the corporate fiduciary in that case had not usurped an opportunity that properly belonged to the corporation.' Id., 157.

"We adopt, for Connecticut, two major propositions of law decided by *Broz*. We agree with the principle that adequate disclosure of a corporate opportunity is an absolute defense to fiduciary liability for alleged usurpation of such a corporate opportunity. A corporate fiduciary who avails himself or herself of such a safe harbor should not be held accountable subsequently for opportunities embraced or forgone. The criteria for adequate disclosure are those that we have discussed earlier in this opinion. [That is, disclosure to disinterested directors.] We also agree that, without prior adequate disclosure, a corporate fiduciary still may prove bona fides by clear and convincing evidence, by establishing that his or her conduct has not harmed the corporation. We add, however, that, in assessing such harm, the trier of fact must give special weight to the effect of nondisclosure on the corporation's entrepreneurial opportunities.

"The Delaware court's decision in *Broz*, moreover, does not make explicit the proper allocation of the burden of proof with regard to these affirmative defenses of corporate fiduciaries. We reiterate, therefore, that, in Connecticut, corporate fiduciaries bear the burden of proving, by clear and convincing evidence, that they have not usurped a corporate opportunity. If they wish to take advantage of a safe harbor, corporate fiduciaries must establish the adequacy of their disclosures to the corporation. In the absence of such disclosures, corporate fiduciaries like the present defendants must prove that, in light of the relevant circumstances outlined in *Broz*, they did not deprive the corporation of an opportunity that the corporation could have pursued. The fact of nondisclosure, although accorded special weight in this determination, is not dispositive. The factual backdrop for these issues in the circumstances of this case will need to be explored further on remand."

———

SECTION 5. DUTIES OF CONTROLLING SHAREHOLDERS

———

Insert the following case and Note at p. 755 of the Unabridged Edition, and p. 501 of the Concise Edition, in place of Kahn v. Lynch Communication Systems:

KAHN v. TREMONT CORP.

Supreme Court of Delaware, 1997.
694 A.2d 422.

Before WALSH, HOLLAND, and BERGER, JJ. and RIDGELY, President Judge* and QUILLEN, Judge,* constituting the Court En Banc.

WALSH, Justice.

This is an appeal by a plaintiff-shareholder, Alan R. Kahn ("Kahn"), from a decision of the Court of Chancery which approved the purchase by Tremont Corporation ("Tremont") of 7.8 million shares of the Common Stock of NL Industries, Inc. ("NL"). The shares, constituting 15% of NL's outstanding stock, were purchased from Valhi, Inc. ("Valhi"), a corporation which was 90 percent owned by a trust for the family of Harold C. Simmons ("Simmons").[1] In turn, Valhi was the owner of a majority of NL's outstanding stock and controlled Tremont through the ownership of 44% of its outstanding shares.

Kahn alleges that Simmons effectively controlled the three related companies and through his influence, structured the purchase of NL shares in a manner which benefited himself at the expense of Tremont. Following a six day trial, the Court of Chancery concluded that due to [Simmons's] status as a controlling shareholder, the transaction must be evaluated under the entire fairness

———

* Appointed pursuant to Art. IV, § 12 of the Delaware Constitution and Supreme Court Rules 2 and 4.

1. The Simmons Trusts did not control Valhi directly, but did so through its 100% ownership of the stock in Contran Corporation ("Contran"), which, in turn, owned 90% of the outstanding stock of Valhi.

standard of review and not the more deferential business judgment rule. Nevertheless, the court found that Tremont's utilization of a Special Committee of disinterested directors was sufficient to shift the burden on the fairness issue to Kahn. With the burden shifted, the court concluded that both the price and the process were fair to Tremont.

Kahn has raised two contentions in this appeal: (i) that the court erred in its burden of proof allocation regarding the entire fairness of the transaction; and (ii) that the circumstances surrounding the purchase of NL shares indicate that the process was tainted and the price unfair to Tremont. After careful review of the record, we conclude that under the circumstances the Special Committee did not operate in an independent or informed manner and therefore, the Court of Chancery erred in shifting the burden of persuasion to Kahn. Accordingly, the judgment of the Court of Chancery is reversed and the matter remanded for a new fairness determination with the burden of proof upon the defendants.

I

The lengthy presentation before the Court of Chancery requires a full exposition of the factual background of the dispute for analysis on appeal. Tremont is a Delaware corporation with its principal executive offices located in Denver, Colorado. Through its subsidiaries, Tremont produces titanium sponge, ingot and mill products. NL is a New Jersey corporation which derives a majority of its earnings from the manufacture and sale of titanium dioxide ("TiO2"), a chemical used to impart whiteness or opacity. NL conducts this business through its European subsidiary Krones, which, accounts for 85% to 90% of NL's total revenue. Valhi is also a Delaware corporation which, through subsidiary stock ownership, is engaged in a variety of businesses, including the production and sale of hardware, forest products, refined sugar, and the fast food restaurant business.

The individual defendants, collectively the board of directors of Tremont, are Susane E. Alderton, Richard J. Boushka, J. Landis Martin, Glenn R. Simmons, Harold C. Simmons, Michael A. Snetzer, Thomas P. Stafford and Avy H. Stein. Aside from their service on the Tremont board, several defendants hold influential positions with other Simmons' controlled entities. Harold Simmons is chairman of the board of Valhi, NL, and Contran, and the CEO of Contran and Valhi. J. Landis Martin is both the president and CEO of NL and Tremont. Susan E. Alderton serves as the vice president and treasurer of Tremont and NL. Glenn R. Simmons is the vice chairman of the board of Valhi as well as the vice chairman of the board and vice president of Contran. Michael A. Snetzer is the president of Valhi and Contran and a director of NL and Contran.

Kahn alleges that the defendants willingly participated in a series of improper transactions, beginning in 1990, which were orchestrated by Simmons for his own benefit. Specifically, he argues that the purchase of NL shares by Tremont was the final step in a series of transactions whereby Simmons was able to shift liquidity from several of his controlled companies to Valhi. Under the theory advanced by Kahn, two preceding transactions, a repurchase program and a "Dutch auction," were initiated in order to artificially inflate the price of NL shares. By increasing NL's per share price, Simmons was able to divest himself, at the expense of Tremont, of the stock in a failing company for above market prices.

In late 1990, NL's board believed that the current market price of NL's stock, then selling between $10 and $11 per share, was significantly undervalued. Accordingly, on October 2, 1990, the board authorized a repurchase program in the open market for up to five million shares. On the prior day NL stock had closed at $10.12 per share. Over the first three months of the program, through January 10, 1991, NL repurchased almost two million shares, at a total cost of over $22 million and an average price of approximately $11 per share.

Satisfied with this response, NL suspended its repurchases from January through May of 1991. From May to July 1991, however, NL resumed buying and purchased 733,700 shares on the open market for a total cost of $10 million or approximately $13.50 a share. The repurchase program was again suspended from August of 1991 to September 11, 1991. Following this brief hiatus, NL once again reinstated its open-market repurchases and continued to repurchase shares into early 1992. All told, NL repurchased over 3 million of its own shares at an average price of $12 per share.

In June of 1991, NL shares were trading at or above $15 per share. At this point NL, as the result of selling a large block of Lockheed stock, was holding approximately $500 million in cash to be used for investment purposes. In August 1991, with the market price of the stock at $16, NL's management decided that it would be advantageous for the company to buy additional NL shares beyond the five million already authorized in the share repurchase program. Accordingly, on August 6, 1991, the NL board voted to approve a Dutch auction self-tender offer for 10 million shares of NL.

Under the Dutch auction mechanism, each shareholder of NL would decide how many, if any, shares to tender and at what price within a designated price range. After the expiration of the auction period, NL would determine the lowest uniform price, within a preset range of $14.50 to $17.50, that would enable it to purchase 10 million shares. All of the shares tendered at or below the sale price would be purchased at the sale price, subject to proration. In the event that more than 10 million shares were tendered at or below the sale price, NL had the option to purchase an additional 1.3 million shares.

On the date the Dutch auction was announced, Valhi owned approximately 68% of the 63.4 million outstanding shares of NL. Valhi tendered all of its shares, at $16, recognizing that with proration it would sell, at most, approximately 10 million shares. At the close of the Dutch auction, $16 per share proved to be the lowest price within the range at which NL could purchase the shares. On September 12, 1991, NL accepted for purchase 11,268,-024 shares, 10,928,750 of which were acquired from Valhi. Shortly following the close of the Dutch auction, NL's stock price fell from $16 to around $13.50.

Upon completion of the Dutch auction, Valhi had sold 10.9 million shares of NL and had reduced its ownership interest in the company from 68% to 62%. If Valhi could sell an additional 7.8 million shares of NL and reduce its ownership interest to below 50%, it would be able to reap two significant benefits. First, it would receive a tax savings of approximately $11.8 million on its proceeds from the Dutch auction, a potential savings of $1.52 per share. Secondly, Valhi would be in a position to deconsolidate NL from its financial statements, thereby improving its access to capital markets. In order to obtain these benefits, however, Valhi needed to sell 7.8 million shares of NL, amounting to 15% of NL's outstanding stock, by the end of calendar year 1991.

To explore the prospect of a further sale of NL shares, Snetzer, Valhi's President, contacted two potential purchasers, RCM Capital and Keystone Inc. Although both maintained significant holdings of NL shares, neither was interested in further purchases. Snetzer also contacted Salomon Brothers and requested an opinion concerning the marketability of the stock. Snetzer was advised by Salomon Brothers that its equity syndicate groups in the U.S. and Europe as well as its private equity people, were in agreement that Valhi would incur an illiquidity discount of 20%, or greater, against NL's then market price in order to sell this unregistered stock in a series of private transactions. Snetzer did not retain Salomon to negotiate a sale because in his view Valhi was unwilling to sell the block of NL shares at that price.

Finding the alternatives unacceptable, Valhi decided to approach Tremont, which had $100 million in excess liquidity and was in the process of searching for a productive investment opportunity.[2] Snetzer was of the opinion that an "all in the family" transaction

2. In October 1990, Tremont's corporate predecessor, Baroid Corp., divided itself into two parts, each to be publicly traded. As part of the spin-off, the new company contributed $100 million of capital to Tremont for acquisition purposes. Tremont had disclosed to its stockholders that the company intended to use this capital to attempt acquisitions, including "participation in the acquisition activities conducted by NL, Valhi and other companies that may be deemed to be controlled by Harold C. Simmons" and "could involve ... the acquisition of securities or other assets from such related

would be more desirable since it had the potential to yield additional benefits for both companies. As a 44% owner of Tremont, Valhi would be more likely to accept an appropriate discount from market because it would still own an indirect 44% interest in the shares. In addition, a lower discount from market might be acceptable to Tremont because its management had access to better information concerning NL's business prospects than any unrelated buyers whom Salomon had considered. As a better informed purchaser, Tremont would be less susceptible to risk than would be a stranger and might be willing to pay a price closer to market. Based on this reasoning, on September 18, 1991, Snetzer wrote to Landis Martin, the President and CEO of Tremont, to propose the sale of 7.8 million shares of NL stock.

After speaking with Snetzer, Martin wrote to Tremont's three outside directors, Richard Boushka, Thomas Stafford, and Avy Stein, asking them to formulate an appropriate response to Valhi's offer. The three men were thereafter designated by the Tremont board as a Special Committee for the purpose of considering the proposal and recommending a course of action. Although the three men were deemed "independent" for purposes of this transaction, all had significant prior business relationships with Simmons or Simmons' controlled companies.

Stein, a lawyer, was affiliated with the law firm which represented Simmons on several of his corporate takeovers and had worked closely with Martin. In 1984 Stein left the law firm to organize and promote various business ventures. Over the next five years, Martin invested in projects which Stein was promoting despite their poor performance. In October of 1988, Stein's business ventures had all but dried up when Martin, then at NL, offered Stein a consulting position at $10,000 a month and bonuses to be paid at Martin's discretion. Stein remained in this position for one year, earning bonuses totaling $325,000, before taking a position with two subsidiaries of Continental Bank, N.A. Stafford was employed by NL in connection with Simmons' proxy contest to acquire control of Lockheed and received $300,000 in fees. Boushka was initially named to Simmons' slate of directors in connection with the Lockheed proxy contest and was paid a fee of $20,000.

Of the three Special Committee members, Stein was the most closely connected to management. Nevertheless, he assumed the role of chairman of the Special Committee and directed its operations. Stafford and Boushka deferred to Stein in the selection of both the financial and legal advisors for the Special Committee. The Court of Chancery noted that Stein's selection of advisors was not reassuring.

parties." Prior to the purchase of the NL shares from Valhi, Tremont's excess capital had been invested temporarily in Treasury bills.

In choosing a financial advisor, the Special Committee considered several banking firms, both national and regional. In the end, at Stein's recommendation, the Special Committee retained Continental Partners ("Continental"), a company with whom Stein was affiliated. Continental is a wholly-owned subsidiary of Continental bank which, in prior years, had earned significant fee income from Simmons related companies. The record also reflects that Martin, not a member of the Special Committee, signed the retainer agreement with Continental Partners. The Special Committee's selection of a legal advisor also took an unusual form. David Garten, General Counsel for both Tremont and NL, recommended C. Neel Lemon of Thompson & Knight as the Special Committee's counsel. In addition, Garten assumed the responsibility for performing the conflicts check. Lemon had previously represented a Special Committee of NL in connection with a proposed merger between NL and Valhi and had also represented an underwriter in connection with a proposed convertible debt offering by Valhi.

On October 8, 1991, Boushka and Stein, along with their advisors, met with representatives of NL to receive a presentation on the business, operating results and prospects of NL. The following day, they met with representatives of Valhi for a presentation of the business purposes behind Valhi's proposal, specifically the tax benefits Valhi hoped to achieve by deconsolidating NL from its balance sheet. In the afternoon following each presentation, a second meeting was held so that the Special Committee members, Continental and the legal advisors could analyze the material presented in the morning sessions.

Stafford, who was in Europe on other business, was unable to attend any of the Special Committee meetings. He kept abreast of events through telephone conferences with the other two members. Boushka attended the morning sessions but did not attend the afternoon sessions. Of the three members of the Special Committee only Stein attended all four meetings and, more importantly, he was the only member who attended the review sessions with the Special Committee's advisors. In addition to the presentations, the Special Committee met twice, later in October, to consider the Valhi proposal prior to the final negotiations.

In considering the NL shares purchase, the Special Committee relied heavily upon the financial analysis performed by NL and its advisor Continental. During the October 8 meeting, NL provided information including its economic projections for the future price of TiO2, estimates of NL's earnings and the assumptions underlying these projections. With respect to the future price of TiO2, NL's projections assumed that an existing slump would end in late 1992 and higher prices and profits would return in the years 1993–1996.

The Special Committee requested Continental independently to assess the reasonableness of NL's projections. In performing a market analysis, Continental utilized five different methodologies to determine the value of the NL stock. These included a comparable company analysis, a comparable transaction analysis, a discounted cash flow analysis, an asset value/replacement cost analysis and a market value analysis. The results of this study were presented at the Special Committee's October 30 meeting. Continental determined that the intrinsic value of the NL shares was between $13 and $20 per share. In addition to this report, Boushka requested that an independent consultant provide a separate analysis concerning future TiO2 prices. Although Boushka did not receive this report prior to the Special Committee's vote on October 30, the consultant appeared to support NL's projections for TiO2 prices.

In hindsight, the price of TiO2 would continue to be much more volatile than either NL's or Continental's predictions. During the late 1980's NL experienced record earnings when TiO2 was in short supply and prices were high. Beginning in 1990, however, prices began to fall as Europe entered into a recession and supply began to catch up with the demand. By year-end 1991, the price of TiO2 had dropped 20% from its high in 1989 and 15% from 1990. As a result, by the end of 1991 NL's profits had turned to losses and it was projected that 1992's operating results would be worse. In fact, in 1992, NL was forced to suspend its dividend as its year-end losses totaled $76.44 million. As of the time of the transaction, it was anticipated that world TiO2 prices would not begin to stabilize until 1995–1997.

Valhi's initial proposal to Tremont, made at the October 9 Special Committee meeting, was $14.50 per share, with no registration rights or other provisions to enhance the liquidity of the shares. On the previous day NL stock had closed at $13 per share. By the October 21 Special Committee meeting, Continental had developed a preliminary estimate of value in the $12.50 to $23 range. Following this meeting, Stein contacted Snetzer and informed him that some provision to afford liquidity to the buyer of the unregistered shares would be necessary. He also attempted to negotiate a per share price below the $14.50 offer. In response, Snetzer suggested Valhi might be willing to lower the asking price below $14 into the high $13 range. On that day NL stock closed slightly over $13 per share.

Stein and Snetzer also met in person to negotiate the non-price terms of the transaction. At the meeting the two discussed solutions to Tremont's liquidity concerns such as registration and co-sale rights, but did not broach the topic of a liquidity discount. Stein also told Snetzer that Tremont would not be willing to consummate a deal near the range suggested by Snetzer—the low to mid $13s. At its October 30 meeting the Special Committee decided to seek a transaction at or below $12 ⅞ per share. Continental indicated that it would be willing to deliver a fairness opinion supporting this price. Stein then met with Snetzer and offered to purchase the stock for $11.25. Eventually it was agreed that the price would be $11.75 per share with Valhi receiving a proration of NL's fourth quarter dividend, amounting to $800,000. In addition Tremont was to receive the registration and co-sale rights as protection for the limited liquidity of the investment. On this date NL stock closed at $12 ¾.

Stein presented the results of his negotiation with Snetzer to the entire Committee which, on October 30, 1991, agreed to recommend the transaction to the entire Tremont board. The Tremont board then met and approved the recommendation of the Special Committee, with the three most interested members of the board (H. Simmons, G. Simmons, and Snetzer) abstaining and the other two members (Martin and Alderton) voting with the Special Committee to provide a quorum.

II

Kahn's attack on both the negotiating process and the resulting price must be evaluated under the standards of Delaware corporate law involving interested transactions by controlling shareholders. In discharging our appellate function, we view the factual findings of the Court of Chancery with considerable deference but exercise *de novo* review concerning the application of legal standards. See *Levitt v. Bouvier*, Del.Supr., 287 A.2d 671 (1972).

Ordinarily, in a challenged transaction involving self-dealing by a controlling shareholder, the substantive legal standard is that of entire fairness, with the burden of persuasion resting upon the defendants.[3] *Weinberger v. UOP, Inc.*, Del.Supr., 457 A.2d 701, 710 (1983); *See Rosenblatt v. Getty Oil Co.*, Del.Supr., 493 A.2d 929, 937 (1985). The burden, however, may be shifted from the defendants to the plaintiff through the use of a well functioning committee of independent directors. *Kahn v. Lynch Communication Sys.*, Del.Supr., 638 A.2d 1110, 1117 (1994). Regardless of where the burden lies, when a controlling shareholder stands on both sides of the transaction the conduct of the parties will be viewed under the more exacting standard of entire fairness as opposed to the more deferential business judgment standard. *Id.* at 1116.

Entire fairness remains applicable even when an independent committee is utilized because the underlying factors which raise the specter of impropriety can never be completely eradicated and still require careful judicial scrutiny. *Weinberger*, 457 A.2d at 710. This policy reflects the reality that in a transaction such as the one considered in this appeal, the controlling shareholder will continue to dominate the company regardless of the outcome of the transaction. *Citron v. E.I. Du Pont de Nemours & Co.*, Del. Ch., 584 A.2d

---

3. The Court of Chancery determined that the sale of NL stock to Tremont was an "all in the family" transaction, with Simmons acting as the controlling shareholder of both the buyer and the seller. This ruling was not challenged by the defendants in this appeal.

490, 502 (1990). The risk is thus created that those who pass upon the propriety of the transaction might perceive that disapproval may result in retaliation by the controlling shareholder. *Id.* Consequently, even when the transaction is negotiated by a special committee of independent directors, "no court could be certain whether the transaction fully approximate [d] what truly independent parties would have achieved in an arm's length negotiation." *Id.* Cognizant of this fact, we have chosen to apply the entire fairness standard to "interested transactions" in order to ensure that all parties to the transaction have fulfilled their fiduciary duties to the corporation and all its shareholders. *Kahn,* 638 A.2d at 1110.

Having established the appropriate legal standard by which the sale of NL stock will be reviewed, we turn to the issue of which party bears the burden of proof. Delaware has long adhered to the principle that the controlling or dominant shareholder is initially allocated the burden of proving the transaction was entirely fair. *Id.* at 1117. In *Rosenblatt,* however, we stated that "approval of a [transaction], as here, by an informed vote of a majority of the minority shareholders, while not a legal prerequisite, shifts the burden of proving the unfairness of the transaction entirely to the plaintiffs." *Rosenblatt,* 493 A.2d at 937. To obtain the benefit of burden shifting, the controlling shareholder must do more than establish a perfunctory special committee of outside directors. *Rabkin v. Olin Corp.,* Del.Ch., C.A. No 7547 (Consolidated), Chandler, V.C., 1990; reprinted in 16 Del.J.Corp.L. 851, 861–62, 1990 WL 47648 (1990), aff'd, Del.Supr., 586 A.2d 1202 (1990). Rather, the committee must function in a manner which indicates that the controlling shareholder did not dictate the terms of the transaction and that the committee exercised real bargaining power "at an arms-length." *Id.*

Here, Tremont, with Valhi's approval, established a Special Committee consisting of three outside directors. In evaluating the composition of Tremont's Special Committee, the Court of Chancery confessed to "having reservations concerning the establishment of the Special Committee and the selection of its advisors." The court's reservations arose from two main concerns. First, Stein was the dominant member of the Special Committee and played a key role in the negotiations. The Chancellor questioned the Special Committee's decision to leave the bulk of the work in the hands of one "who had a long and personally beneficial relationship with Mr. Martin [and Simmons' controlled companies]."

The court's second concern was prompted by its recognition that in complicated financial transactions such as this, professional advisors have the ability to influence directors who are anxious to make the right decision but who are often [*in terra incognita*]. As the Chancellor noted, "the selection of professional advisors for the Special Committee doesn't give comfort; it raises questions." Notably, Tremont's General Counsel suggested the name of an appropriate legal counsel to the Special Committee, and that individual was promptly retained. The Special Committee chose as its financial advisor a bank which had lucrative past dealings with Simmons-related companies and had been affiliated with Stein through his employment with a connected bank.

Despite these reservations and the appearance of conflict, the Chancellor concluded that the Special Committee's advisors satisfied their professional obligations to the Special Committee. The Chancellor further concluded that the Special Committee had discharged its duties in an informed and independent manner. These findings were sufficient, in the Chancellor's view, to shift to the plaintiff the burden of proving that the transaction was unfair.

In our view, the Court of Chancery's determination that the Special Committee of Tremont's outside directors was fully informed, active and appropriately simulated an arms length transaction, is not supported by the record. It is clear that Boushka and Stafford abdicated their responsibility as committee members by permitting Stein, the member whose independence was most suspect, to perform the Special Committee's essential functions. In particular, Stafford's absence from all meetings with advisors or fellow committee members, rendered him ill-suited as a defender of the interests of minority shareholders in the dynamics of fast moving negotiations. Similarly, the circumstances surrounding the retaining of the Special Committee's advisors, as well as the advice given, cast serious doubt on the effectiveness of the Special Committee.

In our view, the Special Committee established to negotiate the purchase of the block of NL stock did not function independently. All three directors had previous affiliations with Simmons or companies which he controlled and, as a result, received significant financial compensation or influential positions on the boards of Simmons' controlled companies. Of the three directors, Stein was arguably the one most beholden to Simmons. In 1988 Stein was paid $10,000 a month as a consultant to NL and received over $325,000 in bonuses. The Special Committee's advisors did little to bolster the independence of the principals. The financial advisor, Continental Partners, was recommended by Stein and quickly retained by the full Special Committee. In the past, an affiliate bank of Continental had derived significant fees from Simmons controlled companies and at the time of the transaction was affiliated with Stein's current employer. In addition to being recommended by the General Counsel for NL and Tremont, the Special Committee's legal advisor had previously been retained by Valhi in connection with a convertible debt offering and by NL with respect to a proposed merger with Valhi.

From its inception, the Special Committee failed to operate in a manner which would create the appearance of objectivity in Tremont's decision to purchase the NL stock. As this Court has previously stated in defining director independence: "[i]t is the care, attention and sense of individual responsibility to the performance of one's duties . . . that generally touches on independence." *Aronson v. Lewis*, Del.Supr., 473 A.2d 805, 816 (1984). The record amply demonstrates that neither Stafford nor Boushka possessed the "care, attention and sense of responsibility" necessary to afford them the status of independent directors. The result was that Stein, arguably the least detached member of the Special Committee, became, de facto, a single member committee—a tenuous role. Stein conducted all negotiations over price and ancillary terms of the proposed purchase with Martin, and did so without the participation of the remaining two directors. "If a single member committee is to be used, the member should, like Caesar's wife, be above reproach." *Lewis v. Fuqua*, Del.Ch., 502 A.2d 962, 967 (1985).

The record is replete with examples of how the lack of the Special Committee's independence fostered an atmosphere in which the directors were permitted to default on their obligation to remain fully informed. Most notable, was the failure of all three directors to attend the informational meetings with the Special Committee's advisors. These meetings were scheduled so that the Special Committee could explore, through the exchange of ideas with its advisors, the validity of the Valhi proposal and what terms the board should demand in order to make the purchase more beneficial to Tremont. Although Boushka had requested an independent analysis with respect to the future of the TiO2 market, and one was ordered, the report was not read prior to the Special Committee's October 30 vote on the purchase of the NL stock.[4] The failure of the individual directors to fully participate in an active process, severely limited the exchange of ideas and prevented the Special Committee as a whole from acquiring critical knowledge of essential aspects of the purchase. In sum, we conclude that the Special Committee did not operate in a manner which entitled the defendants to shift from themselves the burden which encumbers a controlled transaction. *Accord Kahn*, 638 A.2d at 1110.

III

Although our invalidation of the role of the Independent Committee requires a remand for an entire fairness determination with the burden shifted, Kahn has asserted certain claims of "unfair dealing" which we address for the guidance of the parties and the Court of Chancery.

---

4. This report takes on particular significance in light of the fact that Continental in evaluating Valhi's proposal, had relied upon NL's pricing forecast for TiO2. Without the benefit of this independent analysis, the directors, as buyers, relied solely on the projections of NL, the seller. Indeed, Stafford was not aware of the need for a third party analysis because he erroneously thought that Continental had made its own independent forecast.

In *Weinberger* this Court stated that the test of fairness has two aspects: fair price and fair dealing. *Weinberger*, 457 A.2d at 711. *See also Cinerama v. Technicolor, Inc.*, Del.Supr., 663 A.2d 1156 (1995). The element of "fair dealing" focuses upon the conduct of the corporate fiduciaries in effectuating the transaction. These concerns include how the purchase was initiated, negotiated, structured and the manner in which director approval was obtained. *Mills Acquisition Co. v. Macmillan, Inc.*, Del.Supr., 559 A.2d 1261, 1280 (1989). The price element relates to the economic and financial considerations relied upon when valuing the proposed purchase including: assets, market values, future prospects, earnings, and other factors which effect the intrinsic value of the transaction. *Weinberger*, 457 A.2d at 711. This Court and the Court of Chancery have historically applied this heightened standard to ensure that individuals who purport to act as fiduciaries in the face of conflicting loyalties exercise their authority in light of what is best for all entities. *Id*.

Kahn alleges the Court of Chancery erred in several respects in its entire fairness analysis. As to the fair dealing component, Kahn argues that: (1) the initiation and the timing of the purchase were unfair; (2) the Special Committee's performance was deficient to an extent that it compromised the integrity of the negotiation process; and (3) Valhi failed to make material disclosures to Tremont. We address only the initiation and timing claim and the disclosure claim as they may find application in any proceedings on remand.

A.

In evaluating the fair dealing component of the transaction, the Court of Chancery determined that the initiation and timing of the purchase was not prejudicial to Tremont. Although the purchase was initiated and timed by Simmons-controlled Valhi, the court found this to be unimportant when considering the nature of the transaction, i.e., a straightforward purchase of a block of stock. Valhi's decision to offer the stock to Tremont was predicated on its desire to obtain over $11 million in tax benefits. This fact was fully disclosed and explained to the Special Committee which arguably bargained to share in those benefits. The record supports the Chancellor's conclusion that the Committee was afforded adequate time to fully consider Valhi's proposal and to assess its merits. Snetzer, Valhi's president, first proposed the transaction to Tremont in September of 1991 and indicated Valhi's need to conclude the purchase by the end of that calendar year. Although the Tremont board did not take advantage of the entire time period provided, under the terms of Valhi's offer they were afforded sufficient time to consider the proposal.

Initiation by the seller, standing alone, is not incompatible with the concept of fair dealing so long as the controlling shareholder does not gain financial advantage at the expense of the controlled company. *Kahn v. Lynch Communication Sys.*, Del.Supr., 669 A.2d 79, 85 (1995). While Valhi obtained a significant financial advantage in the timing of the purchase, it did not do so at the expense of Tremont. We conclude that there is ample support in the record for the Court of Chancery's finding that the initiation and timing of the transaction was not unfair to Tremont.

B.

With respect to the disclosure issue, Kahn argues that Valhi was required to disclose that two previous companies had rejected an offer to purchase the block of NL stock and that Salomon Brothers had issued an informal opinion which opined that a 20% or greater illiquidity discount from market would be required in order to conclude a sale. In evaluating this claim the Court of Chancery correctly stated that "[a] controlling shareholder ... must disclose fully all material facts and circumstances surrounding the transaction." *Kahn*, 669 A.2d at 88. This standard of disclosure is not unlike that adopted by this Court in defining the level of disclosure necessary where shareholder action is implicated. "[A]n omitted fact is material if there is a substantial likelihood that, the omitted fact would have assumed actual significance in the deliberations of the reasonable shareholder." *Rosenblatt*, 493 A.2d at 944 (quoting *TSC Industries v. Northway*, 426 U.S. 438, 449, 96 S.Ct. 2126, 48 L.Ed.2d 757 (1976)).

Applying the materiality standard, the Court of Chancery determined that the decisions of RCM Capital and Keystone not to purchase the block of NL stock from Valhi were not material. The court noted that their reasons for not wanting to purchase the stock were simply the general concerns that any potential purchaser would have reason to know without specific disclosure; "namely, that the purchaser would own a minority share in a company that it did not control and that the market might react negatively when it learned that a principal stockholder (Valhi) was selling shares." Kahn's argument as to the materiality of this information is further undercut by the fact that Valhi never reached the stage of discussing price or terms with either of the potential buyers. Thus, disinterest of third parties was clearly not the type of information required to be disclosed. We find the Court of Chancery's analysis as to the disclosure of RCM Capitol's and Keystone's decisions not to pursue a purchase with Valhi to be supported by the record.

Kahn's second disclosure argument concerns Salomon Brother's advice to Valhi concerning an appropriate illiquidity discount. Although questioning the significance of this information, the Chancellor, for analysis purposes, assumed that the Salomon opinion would have been material to the Special Committee. The court went on to conclude, however, that, even if material, this information fell within a "narrow residual category of privileged information" which did not need to be disclosed. The Chancellor speculated that if the device of the independent committee is to effectively replicate an arms-length negotiation, this information cannot be required to be disclosed by a seller.

We do not adopt the court's conclusion that the Salomon opinion falls within a category of "privileged" information. We find no authority in Delaware or elsewhere, and counsel for defendants can point to none, which supports the Chancellor's decision to carve out a "privilege" exception to the materiality standard.[5] Under the facts here present, we find Valhi had no duty to disclose information which might be adverse to its interests because the normal standards of arms-length bargaining do not mandate a disclosure of weaknesses. The significance of the illiquidity discount to this transaction lies not in whether Valhi had a duty to disclose it but whether an informed independent committee had a duty to discover it.

IV

Although the Chancellor made extensive findings incident to his fair price analysis he did so in a procedural construct which required Kahn to prove unfairness of price. In resolving issues of valuation the Court of Chancery undertakes a mixed determination of law and fact. *Kahn v. Household Acquisition Corp.*, Del.Supr., 591 A.2d 166, 175 (1991). We recognize the thoroughness of the Chancellor's fair price analysis and the considerable deference due his selection from among the various methodologies offered by competing experts. *Lynch Communication*, 669 A.2d at 87. But here, the process is so intertwined with price that under *Weinberger's* unitary standard a finding that the price negotiated by the Special Committee might have been fair does not save the result. *Cf. Lynch Communication Systems*, 669 A.2d 79.

Arguably, as the Chancellor found, the resulting price might be deemed to be at the lowest level in a broad range of fairness. But this does not satisfy the *Weinberger* test. Although often applied as a bifurcated or disjunctive test, the concept of entire fairness requires the court to examine all aspects of the transaction in an effort to determine whether the deal was entirely fair. *Weinberger*, 457 A.2d at 711. When assigned the burden of persuasion, this test obligates the directors, or their surrogates, to present evidence which demonstrates that the cumulative manner by which it discharged all of its fiduciary duties produced a fair transaction. *Cinerama*, 663 A.2d at 1163.

In our recent decision in *Kahn v. Lynch Communication*, we were confronted with a situation in which the actions of the

---

5. If disclosure is required under the materiality test, information can be withheld only under a recognized claim of privilege. This Court has previously held the relationship between a corporation and its attorney to be such a recognized privilege. *Zirn v. VLI Corp.*, Del.Supr., 621 A.2d 773, 781 (1993) (citing Upjohn Co. v. United States, 449 U.S. 383, 101 S.Ct. 677, 66 L.Ed.2d 584 (1981)).

majority shareholder dominated the negotiation process and stripped the independent committee of its ability to negotiate in an arms-length manner. After concluding that the Court of Chancery erred in shifting the burden of proof with regard to entire fairness to the controlling shareholder, we [remanded] the matter to the Court of Chancery for "a redetermination of the entire fairness . . . with the burden of proof remaining on Alcatel, the dominant and interested shareholder." *Kahn*, 638 A.2d at 1122. A similar course is appropriate here. It is the responsibility of the Court of Chancery to make the requisite factual determinations under the appropriate standards, which underlie the concept of entire fairness. Whether the defendants, shouldering the burden of proof, will be able to demonstrate entire fairness is, in the first instance, a task committed to the Chancellor.

In the event, the Court of Chancery determines that the defendants have not demonstrated the entire fairness of the disputed transaction, we assume that it will grant appropriate relief within its broad equitable authority. *Weinberger*, 457 A.2d at 714. . . .

REVERSED and REMANDED.

QUILLEN, Judge, concurring.

With regard to the burden of proof on the issue of fairness, I concur in the decision reached by Justice Walsh in his excellent opinion. In my opinion, the burden of proof in the case *clearly* should *not* shift from the defendants to the plaintiff on the issue of fairness. Somewhat ironically, in reaching this conclusion, I do not find it necessary to go beyond the basic facts as found by the Chancellor. *See Kahn v. Tremont Corp.*, *et al.*, Del.Ch., C.A. No. 12339, Allen, C., 1996 WL 145452 (Mar. 21, 1996, *revised* Mar. 27, 1996) (herein referred to as *"Op. Below"*). I also concur with Justice Walsh's opinion and decision that the initiation and timing of the purchase were not prejudicial to Tremont Corporation and his further opinion and decisions on the disclosure issues. As to these latter two points, which essentially affirm the Chancellor, I merely note that the Court appears unanimous.

This case is a derivative suit wherein the plaintiff, a stockholder of Tremont Corporation ("Tremont"), alleges that Tremont paid too much for 15% of the stock of NL Industries, Inc. ("NL") in a purchase from Valhi Corporation ("Valhi") through an unfair process. Valhi, controlled by Harold Simmons, itself owned 44.4% of Tremont and 62.5% of NL. The burden of proof on the issue of fairness turns on the independence of Tremont's Special Committee ("Committee") which recommended the purchase. Justice Walsh has ably reviewed the facts and his recitation is more than sufficient context for this modest endeavor.

I accept the Chancellor's statement of the nature of the proceedings and the facts of the case. *Op. Below* 1–15. I also accept the Chancellor's conclusion, in his strongest remark of several, that it is "perfectly appropriate in the circumstances" for Tremont to use its cash reserves to buy stock of NL. *Op. Below* 48–49. It is indeed important the law not "chill" transactions between related companies that can be mutually productive and beneficial to society. *See Op. Below* 3. As noted above, while I join in the reversal, I rely on the Chancellor's findings of basic fact to reach my own conclusion on the burden of proof. Although the same evidence can relate to both the issue of Committee independence and the issue of fairness, the issue of this Committee's independence in this peculiar factual context requires a separate focus from the ultimate issue of entire fairness.

The Chancellor's opinion found: a parent-subsidiary transaction existed, "the context in which the greatest risk of undetectable bias may be present" (*Op. Below* 17–18); Committee member Avy H. Stein, who had prior profitable connections to Harold Simmons and his companies, played the lead Committee role (*Op. Below* 19, including n. 12); Mr. Stein suggested the selection of a financial adviser for the Committee who had prior ties to both Mr. Stein and Mr. Simmons (*Op. Below* 9–10, including n. 5 and n. 6, and 19–20); the suggestion for the Committee's legal advisors came from Tremont's General Counsel (*Op. Below* 9–10, including n. 5 and n. 6, and 19–20); NL, in the thirteen months prior to the subject transaction, repurchased over 20% of its own shares, at least raising an issue of manipulated price inflation (*Op. Below* 5–7); this transaction by Valhi, probably not available in 1991 with a non-Simmons enterprise, was a multi-million dollar one for Valhi from a tax savings standpoint and had to be accomplished in the last quarter of 1991 (Op. Below 7–8); Valhi's chief negotiator knew that an illiquidity discount was appropriate and the block was in fact worth less than market (*Op. Below* 8, 24); in a very short period, NL's stock price fell from over $16 per share in late summer 1991 to $12.75 on the date of the purchase, October 30, 1991, at least raising the question of business viability (*Op. Below* 6–7, 12–24); the Committee relied heavily on regularly prepared projections of NL's management with incomplete help from its own consultant (*Op. Below* 11–12, 31–32); notwithstanding knowledge of the appropriateness of a discount, Valhi's first negotiating suggestion was a premium price and the results of the Committee's negotiations on other issues, splitting the fourth quarter dividend and registration and co-sale rights, are not self-verifying on the independence issue (*Op. Below* 1, 13–14 including n. 8); and the price, as finally negotiated, was found to be "as small a discount as could be accepted as fair," a finding that hardly forecloses questions as to independence (*Op. Below* 33).

In light of the above-enumerated factors, the independence of the Special Committee, integrity in a process sense, was clearly not substantial enough to shift the burden of persuasion to the plaintiff on the issue of fairness. To me, the case cries for Missouri skepticism; the burden should be on the control group to demonstrate entire fairness. While it can be of critical importance to the ultimate result whether or not the burden is shifted, failure to shift the burden is not necessarily outcome determinative. *Compare Nixon v. Blackwell*, Del.Supr., 626 A.2d 1366, 1376, 1381 (1993). Justice Walsh's decision appropriately remands the case to the Court of Chancery for the requisite factual determinations.

As to remedy, if any proves to be appropriate, I join Justice Walsh's opinion that all options are open to the Chancellor's discretion. *Lynch v. Vickers Energy Corp.*, Del.Supr., 429 A.2d 497, 507–08 (1981) (Quillen dissenting); *Weinberger*, 457 A.2d at 703–04.

BERGER, Justice, with whom RIDGELY, President Judge, joins dissenting.

The majority's thorough and well reasoned decision reverses the trial court's equally thorough and well reasoned decision. According to the majority, the Court of Chancery did not err in its legal analysis, but in its evaluation of the facts—particularly with respect to the Special Committee members' independence, level of knowledge and involvement in the negotiations. The trial court recognized these issues and was satisfied, after six days of trial, that the Special Committee members were "informed, active and loyal to the interests of Tremont." That finding is supported by the record and should be accorded deference. I respectfully dissent.

NOTE ON KAHN v. LYNCH COMMUNICATION SYSTEMS

In Kahn v. Lynch Communication Systems, 638 A.2d 1110 (1994), referred to in Kahn v. Tremont, the court said:

> A controlling or dominating shareholder standing on both sides of a transaction, as in a parent-subsidiary context, bears the burden of proving its entire fairness. *Weinberger v. UOP, Inc.*, Del.Supr., 457 A.2d 701, 710 (1983). *See Rosenblatt v. Getty Oil Co.*, Del.Supr., 493 A.2d 929, 937 (1985). The demonstration of fairness that is required was set forth by this Court in *Weinberger*:
>
>> The concept of fairness has two basic aspects: fair dealing and fair price. The former embraces questions of when the transaction was timed, how it was initiated, structured, negotiated, disclosed to the directors, and how the approvals of the directors and the stockholders were obtained. The latter aspect of fairness relates to the economic and financial considerations of the proposed merger, including all relevant factors: assets, market value, earnings, future prospects, and any other elements that affect the intrinsic or inherent value of a company's stock. However, the test for fairness is not a bifurcated one as

between fair dealing and price. All aspects of the issue must be examined as a whole since the question is one of entire fairness.

Weinberger v. UOP, Inc. 457 A.2d at 711 (citations omitted).

The logical question raised by this Court's holding in *Weinberger* was what type of evidence would be reliable to demonstrate entire fairness. That question was not only anticipated but also initially addressed in the *Weinberger* opinion. *Id.* at 709–10 n. 7. This Court suggested that the result "could have been entirely different if UOP had appointed an independent negotiating committee of its outside directors to deal with Signal at arm's length," because "fairness in this context can be equated to conduct by a theoretical, wholly independent, board of directors." *Id.* Accordingly, this Court stated, "a showing that the action taken was as though each of the contending parties had in fact exerted its bargaining power against the other at arm's length is strong *evidence* that the transaction meets the test of fairness." *Id.* (emphasis added).

In this case, the Vice Chancellor noted that the Court of Chancery has expressed "differing views" regarding the effect that an approval of a cash-out merger by a special committee of disinterested directors has upon the controlling or dominating shareholder's burden of demonstrating entire fairness. One view is that such approval shifts to the plaintiff the burden of proving that the transaction was unfair. . . . The other view is that such an approval renders the business judgment rule the applicable standard of judicial review. . . .

"It is often of critical importance whether a particular decision is one to which the business judgment rule applies or the entire fairness rule applies." *Nixon v. Blackwell,* Del.Supr., 626 A.2d 1366, 1376 (1993). The definitive . . . answer with regard to the Court of Chancery's "differing views" is [that] in the context of a . . . proceeding involving a parent-subsidiary merger, . . . the "approval of a merger . . . by an informed vote of a majority of the minority stockholders, while not a legal prerequisite, shifts the burden of proving the unfairness of the merger entirely to the plaintiffs." . . . [Rosenblatt v. Getty Oil Co., 493 A.2d at 937]

Entire fairness remains the proper focus of judicial analysis in examining an interested merger, irrespective of whether the burden of proof remains upon or is shifted away from the controlling or dominating shareholder, because the unchanging nature of the underlying "interested" transaction requires careful scrutiny. *See Weinberger v. UOP, Inc.,* 457 A.2d at 710 (citing *Sterling v. Mayflower Hotel Corp.,* Del.Supr., 93 A.2d 107, 110 (1952)). The policy rationale for the exclusive application of the entire fairness standard to interested merger transactions has been stated as follows:

Parent subsidiary mergers, unlike stock options, are proposed by a party that controls, and will continue to control, the corporation, whether or not the minority stockholders vote to approve or reject the transaction. The controlling stockholder relationship has the potential to influence, however subtly, the vote of [ratifying] minority stockholders in a manner that is not likely to occur in a transaction with a noncontrolling party.

Even where no coercion is intended, shareholders voting on a parent subsidiary merger might perceive that their disapproval could risk retaliation of some kind by the controlling stockholder. For example, the controlling stockholder might decide to stop dividend payments or to effect a subsequent cash out merger at a less favorable price, for which the remedy would be time consuming and costly litigation. At the very least, the potential for that perception, and its possible impact upon a shareholder vote, could never be fully eliminated. Consequently, in a merger between the corporation and its controlling stockholder—even one negotiated by disinterested, independent directors—no court could be certain whether the transaction terms fully approximate what truly independent parties would have achieved in an arm's length negotiation. Given that uncertainty, a court might well conclude that even minority shareholders who have ratified a ... merger need procedural protections beyond those afforded by full disclosure of all material facts. One way to provide such protections would be to adhere to the more stringent entire fairness standard of judicial review.

Citron v. E.I. Du Pont de Nemours & Co., 584 A.2d at 502.

Once again, this Court holds that the exclusive standard of judicial review in examining the propriety of an interested cashout merger transaction by a controlling or dominating shareholder is entire fairness. *Weinberger v. UOP, Inc.,* 457 A.2d at 710–11. The initial burden of establishing entire fairness rests upon the party who stands on both sides of the transaction. *Id.* However, an approval of the transaction by an independent committee of directors or an informed majority of minority shareholders shifts the burden of proof on the issue of fairness from the controlling or dominating shareholder to the challenging shareholder-plaintiff. *See Rosenblatt v. Getty Oil Co.,* 493 A.2d at 937–38. Nevertheless, even when an interested cash-out merger transaction receives the informed approval of a majority of minority stockholders or an independent committee of disinterested directors, an entire fairness analysis is the only proper standard of judicial review. *See id.*

———

Chapter IX

INSIDER TRADING

SECTION 2. SECURITIES EXCHANGE ACT § 10(b) AND RULE 10b–5

Add the following cross-references and Note at p. 860 of the Unabridged Edition, and p. 592 of the Concise Edition, after the Note on Forward–Looking Statements and the "Bespeaks Caution" Doctrine:

SECURITIES ACT § 27A

[See Statutory Supplement]

SECURITIES EXCHANGE ACT § 21E

[See Statutory Supplement]

UNITED STATES v. SMITH, 155 F.3d 1051 (9th Cir.1998). Smith was an officer of PDA Engineering, Inc. He was convicted for trading on inside information that PDA was about to release a negative report about forecasted earnings. Smith appealed on the ground that forecasts of future sales and revenues are "soft," forward-looking information that as a matter of law cannot constitute material information within the meaning of Rule 10b–5. The Ninth Circuit affirmed the conviction:

> In *Basic, Inc. v. Levinson* ... the Supreme Court adopted for § 10(b) and Rule 10b–5 the standard of materiality it had earlier articulated in the context of § 14(a): Materiality "depends on the significance the reasonable investor would place on the withheld or misrepresented information." *Id.* at 240, 108 S.Ct. 978. In other words, in order to be material, "there must be a substantial likelihood that the disclosure of the omitted fact would have been viewed by the reasonable investor as having altered the 'total mix' of information made available." ... Smith does not contend that the information he possessed falls outside the *Basic* definition of materiality—that

a reasonable investor would not have considered it useful or significant. Rather, he argues that "[t]his Circuit has set limits on the type of information that may be considered material as a matter of law." Specifically, Smith says, "this Court has repeatedly held that forecasts of future sales and revenue are too speculative to constitute material facts."

... The decisions Smith cites stand for a more modest proposition, namely, that, in the circumstances presented in those individual cases, the disputed information was not sufficiently certain or significant to be considered material. We have never held—nor even hinted—that forward-looking information or intra-quarter data cannot, as a matter of law, be material. Nor has any other court for that matter, at least to the best of our knowledge. Indeed, both the Supreme Court's landmark decision in *Basic* and preexisting Ninth Circuit authority confirm that so-called "soft" information can, under the proper circumstances, be "material" within the meaning of Rule 10b–5. In *Basic*—the very case that announced the governing standard for Rule 10b–5 materiality—the Supreme Court dealt specifically with preliminary merger negotiations, events it dubbed "contingent or speculative in nature." And although the *Basic* Court acknowledged that its decision did not concern "earnings forecasts or projections" per se, it expressly adopted a "fact-intensive inquiry" to govern the materiality of "contingent or speculative information or events".... It held that, with respect to forward-looking information, materiality "will depend at any given time upon a balancing of both the indicated probability that the event will occur and the anticipated magnitude of the event in light of totality of the company activity." The Court's fact-specific approach fatally undermines Smith's claim that forward-looking information cannot, as a matter of law, be material.

———

Add the following Note at p. 870 of the Unabridged Edition, after the Note on Causation and Reliance:

SEC v. RANA RESEARCH, INC., 8 F.3d 1358 (9th Cir. 1993). The Defendants had issued a press release falsely stating that a firm offer had been made for Superior Industries, a publicly traded firm. The press release appeared on the financial services around 8:00 a.m. on February 9. Immediately thereafter, the American Stock Exchange suspended trading in Superior's stock. No shares were traded on February 9, and at the end of that day a corrective press release was issued. Meanwhile, the Defendants had not purchased or sold any Superior securities. The SEC filed a complaint seeking permanent injunctive relief against the Defendants. The district court entered judgment for the SEC and permanently enjoined Defendants from violating section 10(b) and Rule 10b–5. Affirmed:

Defendants argue that the SEC was required to plead and prove that "at least one investor actually received, read and relied upon the statements contained in the Vista release . . . and, in reasonable reliance thereon . . . actually purchased (or sold) shares of Superior stock as a result. . . ." Appellants' Brief at 40. This circuit has not yet ruled on the issue of whether the SEC must prove reliance to establish a violation of Rule 10b–5 and section 10(b) and the need for injunctive relief.

In approaching this question, we bear in mind that an SEC action to enjoin securities violations is not an action "under" Rule 10b–5, as is the judicially created cause of action for damages implied for private plaintiffs. . . . Rather, it is a "creature[ ] of statute," *SEC v. Management Dynamics, Inc.,* 515 F.2d 801, 808 (2d Cir.1975), legislatively authorized under sections 21(d) and (e) of the Securities Exchange Act. . . .

This distinction is fundamental. The bulk of cases requiring proof of reliance as an element of a Rule 10b–5 violation expressly qualify this holding to actions brought by private plaintiffs seeking damages. Those that do not are nonetheless factually distinguishable on the basis that each involved private plaintiffs claiming damages, rather than the SEC seeking injunctive relief. *See, e.g., Basic Inc. v. Levinson,* 485 U.S. 224, 243, 108 S.Ct. 978, 989, 99 L.Ed.2d 194 (1988) ("We agree that reliance is an element of a Rule 10b–5 cause of action."). . . .

The reliance requirement is not found in Rule 10b–5 itself; it is one of the judicially created elements of and limitations on a private 10b–5 action. These requirements are largely directed toward identifying who has standing to enforce the antifraud laws. . . . But where the SEC is concerned, the matter is settled; Congress designated the SEC as the primary enforcement agency for the securities laws. In adopting the rule that only an actual purchaser or seller may maintain a private action under Rule 10b–5, the Supreme Court took care to state that "the purchaser-seller rule imposes no limitation on the standing of the SEC to bring actions for injunctive relief under § 10(b) and Rule 10b–5." *Blue Chip Stamps,* 421 U.S. at 751 n. 14, 95 S.Ct. at 1933 n. 14.

Judicial decisions defining the conduct necessary to constitute a Rule 10b–5 *violation* do apply to actions by the SEC as well as private parties. Thus, *scienter* is a necessary element of an SEC action to enforce section 10(b) and Rule 10b–5, as well as a private action, because it is required to meet the statutory elements of manipulation and deception. *Aaron v. SEC,* 446 U.S. 680, 690–91, 100 S.Ct. 1945, 1952–53, 64 L.Ed.2d 611 (1980); *SEC v. Murphy,* 626 F.2d at 653–54. The same is true of the "in connection with the purchase or sale of any security" element, discussed above. But restrictions on who may invoke the power of the federal judiciary to enforce the securities laws by collecting damages do not bear on the determination of whether a violation of the securities laws has been committed. . . .

Both the Sixth and Second Circuits hold that reliance is not an element the SEC must prove to enjoin violations of the securities laws. . . .

We agree with the Sixth and Second Circuits. We hold that reliance is not an element of a Rule 10b-5 violation by misrepresentation; rather, it is an element of a private cause of action for damages implied thereunder. The SEC need not prove reliance in its action for injunctive relief on the basis of violations of section 10(b) and Rule 10b-5.

———

Add the following cross-reference at p. 884 of the Unabridged Edition, after the Note on Remedies in Private Actions Under Rule 10b-5, and at p. 599 of the Concise Edition, before Chiarella v. United States:

SECURITIES EXCHANGE ACT § 21D(e)

[See Statutory Supplement]

———

Add the following case at p. 926 of the Unabridged Edition, and p. 625 of the Concise Edition, after the Note on Securities Exchange Act § 20A:

UNITED STATES v. O'HAGAN

United States Supreme Court, 1997.
521 U.S. 642, 117 S.Ct. 2199, 138 L.Ed.2d 724.

JUSTICE GINSBURG delivered the opinion of the Court.

This case concerns the interpretation and enforcement of § 10(b) and § 14(e) of the Securities Exchange Act of 1934, and rules made by the Securities and Exchange Commission pursuant to these provisions, Rule 10b-5 and Rule 14e-3(a). Two prime questions are presented. The first relates to the misappropriation of material, nonpublic information for securities trading; the second concerns fraudulent practices in the tender offer setting. In particular, we address and resolve these issues: (1) Is a person who trades in securities for personal profit, using confidential information misappropriated in breach of a fiduciary duty to the source of the information, guilty of violating § 10(b) and Rule 10b-5? (2) Did the Commission exceed its rulemaking authority by adopting Rule

14e–3(a), which proscribes trading on undisclosed information in the tender offer setting, even in the absence of a duty to disclose? Our answer to the first question is yes, and to the second question, viewed in the context of this case, no.

I

Respondent James Herman O'Hagan was a partner in the law firm of Dorsey & Whitney in Minneapolis, Minnesota. In July 1988, Grand Metropolitan PLC (Grand Met), a company based in London, England, retained Dorsey & Whitney as local counsel to represent Grand Met regarding a potential tender offer for the common stock of the Pillsbury Company, headquartered in Minneapolis. Both Grand Met and Dorsey & Whitney took precautions to protect the confidentiality of Grand Met's tender offer plans. O'Hagan did no work on the Grand Met representation. Dorsey & Whitney withdrew from representing Grand Met on September 9, 1988. Less than a month later, on October 4, 1988, Grand Met publicly announced its tender offer for Pillsbury stock.

On August 18, 1988, while Dorsey & Whitney was still representing Grand Met, O'Hagan began purchasing call options for Pillsbury stock. Each option gave him the right to purchase 100 shares of Pillsbury stock by a specified date in September 1988. Later in August and in September, O'Hagan made additional purchases of Pillsbury call options. By the end of September, he owned 2,500 unexpired Pillsbury options, apparently more than any other individual investor. See App. 85, 148. O'Hagan also purchased, in September 1988, some 5,000 shares of Pillsbury common stock, at a price just under $39 per share. When Grand Met announced its tender offer in October, the price of Pillsbury stock rose to nearly $60 per share. O'Hagan then sold his Pillsbury call options and common stock, making a profit of more than $4.3 million.

The Securities and Exchange Commission (SEC or Commission) initiated an investigation into O'Hagan's transactions, culminating in a 57–count indictment. The indictment alleged that O'Hagan defrauded his law firm and its client, Grand Met, by using for his own trading purposes material, nonpublic information regarding Grand Met's planned tender offer. Id., at 8. According to the indictment, O'Hagan used the profits he gained through this trading to conceal his previous embezzlement and conversion of unrelated client trust funds. Id., at 10.[2] O'Hagan was charged with 20 counts of mail fraud, in violation of 18 U.S.C. § 1341; 17 counts of securities fraud, in violation of § 10(b) of the Securities Exchange Act of 1934 (Exchange Act), 48 Stat. 891, 15 U.S.C. § 78j(b), and SEC Rule 10b–

---

2. O'Hagan was convicted of theft in state court, sentenced to 30 months' imprisonment, and fined. See State v. O'Hagan, 474 N.W.2d 613, 615, 623 (Minn.App.1991). The Supreme Court of Minnesota disbarred O'Hagan from the practice of law. See In re O'Hagan, 450 N.W.2d 571 (Minn.1990).

5, 17 CFR § 240.10b–5 (1996); 17 counts of fraudulent trading in connection with a tender offer, in violation of § 14(e) of the Exchange Act, 15 U.S.C. § 78n(e), and SEC Rule 14e–3(a), 17 CFR § 240.14e–3(a) (1996); and 3 counts of violating federal money laundering statutes, 18 U.S.C. §§ 1956(a)(1)(B)(i), 1957. See App. 13–24. A jury convicted O'Hagan on all 57 counts, and he was sentenced to a 41–month term of imprisonment.

A divided panel of the Court of Appeals for the Eighth Circuit reversed all of O'Hagan's convictions. 92 F.3d 612 (1996). Liability under § 10(b) and Rule 10b–5, the Eighth Circuit held, may not be grounded on the "misappropriation theory" of securities fraud on which the prosecution relied. Id., at 622. The Court of Appeals also held that Rule 14e–3(a)—which prohibits trading while in possession of material, nonpublic information relating to a tender offer—exceeds the SEC's § 14(e) rulemaking authority because the rule contains no breach of fiduciary duty requirement. Id., at 627. The Eighth Circuit further concluded that O'Hagan's mail fraud and money laundering convictions rested on violations of the securities laws, and therefore could not stand once the securities fraud convictions were reversed. Id., at 627–628. Judge Fagg, dissenting, stated that he would recognize and enforce the misappropriation theory, and would hold that the SEC did not exceed its rulemaking authority when it adopted Rule 14e–3(a) without requiring proof of a breach of fiduciary duty. Id., at 628.

Decisions of the Courts of Appeals are in conflict on the propriety of the misappropriation theory under § 10(b) and Rule 10b–5, see infra this page and n. 3, and on the legitimacy of Rule 14e–3(a) under § 14(e), see infra, at 25. We granted certiorari, 519 U.S. ___ (1997), and now reverse the Eighth Circuit's judgment.

II

We address first the Court of Appeals' reversal of O'Hagan's convictions under § 10(b) and Rule 10b–5. Following the Fourth Circuit's lead, see United States v. Bryan, 58 F.3d 933, 943–959 (1995), the Eighth Circuit rejected the misappropriation theory as a basis for § 10(b) liability. We hold, in accord with several other Courts of Appeals,[3] that criminal liability under § 10(b) may be predicated on the misappropriation theory.[4]

---

3. See, e.g., United States v. Chestman, 947 F.2d 551, 566 (C.A.2 1991) (en banc), cert. denied, 503 U.S. 1004 (1992); SEC v. Cherif, 933 F.2d 403, 410 (C.A.7 1991), cert. denied, 502 U.S. 1071 (1992); SEC v. Clark, 915 F.2d 439, 453 (C.A.9 1990).

4. Twice before we have been presented with the question whether criminal liability for violation of § 10(b) may be based on a misappropriation theory. In Chiarella v. United States, 445 U.S. 222, 235–237

(1980), the jury had received no misappropriation theory instructions, so we declined to address the question. See infra, at 17. In Carpenter v. United States, 484 U.S. 19, 24 (1987), the Court divided evenly on whether, under the circumstances of that case, convictions resting on the misappropriation theory should be affirmed. See Aldave, The Misappropriation Theory: Carpenter and Its Aftermath, 49 Ohio St. L.J. 373, 375 (1988) (observing that "Carpenter

A

In pertinent part, § 10(b) of the Exchange Act provides:

"It shall be unlawful for any person, directly or indirectly, by the use of any means or instrumentality of interstate commerce or of the mails, or of any facility of any national securities exchange—

. . . .

"(b) To use or employ, in connection with the purchase or sale of any security registered on a national securities exchange or any security not so registered, any manipulative or deceptive device or contrivance in contravention of such rules and regulations as the [Securities and Exchange] Commission may prescribe as necessary or appropriate in the public interest or for the protection of investors." 15 U.S.C. § 78j(b).

The statute thus proscribes (1) using any deceptive device (2) in connection with the purchase or sale of securities, in contravention of rules prescribed by the Commission. The provision, as written, does not confine its coverage to deception of a purchaser or seller of securities, see United States v. Newman, 664 F.2d 12, 17 (C.A.2 1981); rather, the statute reaches any deceptive device used "in connection with the purchase or sale of any security."

Pursuant to its § 10(b) rulemaking authority, the Commission has adopted Rule 10b–5, which, as relevant here, provides:

"It shall be unlawful for any person, directly or indirectly, by the use of any means or instrumentality of interstate commerce, or of the mails or of any facility of any national securities exchange,

"(a) To employ any device, scheme, or artifice to defraud, [or]

. . . .

"(c) To engage in any act, practice, or course of business which operates or would operate as a fraud or deceit upon any person,

"in connection with the purchase or sale of any security." 17 CFR § 240.10b–5 (1996).

Liability under Rule 10b–5, our precedent indicates, does not extend beyond conduct encompassed by § 10(b)'s prohibition. See Ernst & Ernst v. Hochfelder, 425 U.S. 185, 214 (1976) (scope of Rule 10b–5 cannot exceed power Congress granted Commission under § 10(b)); see also Central Bank of Denver, N.A. v. First Interstate Bank of Denver, N.A., 511 U.S. 164, 173 (1994) ("We have refused to allow [private] 10b–5 challenges to conduct not prohibited by the text of the statute.").

was, by any reckoning, an unusual case," for the information there misappropriated belonged not to a company preparing to engage in securities transactions, e.g., a bidder in a corporate acquisition, but to the Wall Street Journal).

Under the "traditional" or "classical theory" of insider trading liability, § 10(b) and Rule 10b–5 are violated when a corporate insider trades in the securities of his corporation on the basis of material, nonpublic information.   Trading on such information qualifies as a "deceptive device" under § 10(b), we have affirmed, because "a relationship of trust and confidence [exists] between the shareholders of a corporation and those insiders who have obtained confidential information by reason of their position with that corporation."   Chiarella v. United States, 445 U.S. 222, 228 (1980).   That relationship, we recognized, "gives rise to a duty to disclose [or to abstain from trading] because of the 'necessity of preventing a corporate insider from . . . taking unfair advantage of . . . uninformed . . . stockholders.' "   Id., at 228–229 (citation omitted). The classical theory applies not only to officers, directors, and other permanent insiders of a corporation, but also to attorneys, accountants, consultants, and others who temporarily become fiduciaries of a corporation.   See Dirks v. SEC, 463 U.S. 646, 655, n. 14 (1983).

The "misappropriation theory" holds that a person commits fraud "in connection with" a securities transaction, and thereby violates § 10(b) and Rule 10b–5, when he misappropriates confidential information for securities trading purposes, in breach of a duty owed to the source of the information.   See Brief for United States 14.   Under this theory, a fiduciary's undisclosed, self-serving use of a principal's information to purchase or sell securities, in breach of a duty of loyalty and confidentiality, defrauds the principal of the exclusive use of that information.   In lieu of premising liability on a fiduciary relationship between company insider and purchaser or seller of the company's stock, the misappropriation theory premises liability on a fiduciary-turned-trader's deception of those who entrusted him with access to confidential information.

The two theories are complementary, each addressing efforts to capitalize on nonpublic information through the purchase or sale of securities.   The classical theory targets a corporate insider's breach of duty to shareholders with whom the insider transacts;   the misappropriation theory outlaws trading on the basis of nonpublic information by a corporate "outsider" in breach of a duty owed not to a trading party, but to the source of the information.   The misappropriation theory is thus designed to "protect the integrity of the securities markets against abuses by 'outsiders' to a corporation who have access to confidential information that will affect the corporation's security price when revealed, but who owe no fiduciary or other duty to that corporation's shareholders."   Ibid.

In this case, the indictment alleged that O'Hagan, in breach of a duty of trust and confidence he owed to his law firm, Dorsey & Whitney, and to its client, Grand Met, traded on the basis of nonpublic information regarding Grand Met's planned tender offer for Pillsbury common stock.   App. 16.   This conduct, the Government charged, constituted a fraudulent device in connection with the purchase and sale of securities.[5]

B

We agree with the Government that misappropriation, as just defined, satisfies § 10(b)'s requirement that chargeable conduct involve a "deceptive device or contrivance" used "in connection with" the purchase or sale of securities. We observe, first, that misappropriators, as the Government describes them, deal in deception. A fiduciary who "[pretends] loyalty to the principal while secretly converting the principal's information for personal gain," Brief for United States 17, "dupes" or defrauds the principal. See Aldave, Misappropriation: A General Theory of Liability for Trading on Nonpublic Information, 13 Hofstra L.Rev. 101, 119 (1984).

We addressed fraud of the same species in Carpenter v. United States, 484 U.S. 19 (1987), which involved the mail fraud statute's proscription of "any scheme or artifice to defraud," 18 U.S.C. § 1341. Affirming convictions under that statute, we said in Carpenter that an employee's undertaking not to reveal his employer's confidential information "became a sham" when the employee provided the information to his co-conspirators in a scheme to obtain trading profits. 484 U.S. at 27. A company's confidential information, we recognized in Carpenter, qualifies as property to which the company has a right of exclusive use. Id., at 25–27. The undisclosed misappropriation of such information, in violation of a fiduciary duty, the Court said in Carpenter, constitutes fraud akin to embezzlement—" 'the fraudulent appropriation to one's own use of the money or goods entrusted to one's care by another.' " Id., at 27 (quoting Grin v. Shine, 187 U.S. 181, 189 (1902)); see Aldave, 13 Hofstra L.Rev., at 119. Carpenter's discussion of the fraudulent misuse of confidential information, the Government notes, "is a particularly apt source of guidance here, because [the mail fraud statute] (like Section 10(b)) has long been held to require deception, not merely the breach of a fiduciary duty." Brief for United States 18, n. 9 (citation omitted).

Deception through nondisclosure is central to the theory of liability for which the Government seeks recognition. As counsel for the Government stated in explanation of the theory at oral argument: "To satisfy the common law rule that a trustee may not use the property that [has] been entrusted [to] him, there would have to be consent. To satisfy the requirement of the Securities Act

---

5. The Government could not have prosecuted O'Hagan under the classical theory, for O'Hagan was not an "insider" of Pillsbury, the corporation in whose stock he traded. Although an "outsider" with respect to Pillsbury, O'Hagan had an intimate association with, and was found to have traded on confidential information from Dorsey & Whitney, counsel to tender offeror Grand Met. Under the misappropriation theory, O'Hagan's securities trading does not escape Exchange Act sanction, as it would under the dissent's reasoning, simply because he was associated with, and gained nonpublic information from, the bidder, rather than the target.

that there be no deception, there would only have to be disclosure." Tr. of Oral Arg. 12; see generally Restatement (Second) of Agency §§ 390, 395 (1958) (agent's disclosure obligation regarding use of confidential information).[6]

The misappropriation theory advanced by the Government is consistent with Santa Fe Industries, Inc. v. Green, 430 U.S. 462 (1977), a decision underscoring that § 10(b) is not an all-purpose breach of fiduciary duty ban; rather, it trains on conduct involving manipulation or deception. See id., at 473–476. In contrast to the Government's allegations in this case, in Santa Fe Industries, all pertinent facts were disclosed by the persons charged with violating § 10(b) and Rule 10b–5, see id., at 474; therefore, there was no deception through nondisclosure to which liability under those provisions could attach, see id., at 476. Similarly, full disclosure forecloses liability under the misappropriation theory: Because the deception essential to the misappropriation theory involves feigning fidelity to the source of information, if the fiduciary discloses to the source that he plans to trade on the nonpublic information, there is no "deceptive device" and thus no § 10(b) violation—although the fiduciary-turned-trader may remain liable under state law for breach of a duty of loyalty.[7]

We turn next to the § 10(b) requirement that the misappropriator's deceptive use of information be "in connection with the purchase or sale of [a] security." This element is satisfied because the fiduciary's fraud is consummated, not when the fiduciary gains the confidential information, but when, without disclosure to his principal, he uses the information to purchase or sell securities. The securities transaction and the breach of duty thus coincide. This is so even though the person or entity defrauded is not the other party to the trade, but is, instead, the source of the nonpublic information. See Aldave, 13 Hofstra L.Rev., at 120 ("a fraud or deceit can be practiced on one person, with resultant harm to another person or group of persons"). A misappropriator who trades on the basis of material, nonpublic information, in short, gains his advantageous market position through deception; he deceives the source of the information and simultaneously harms members of the investing public. See id., at 120–121, and n. 107.

---

6. Under the misappropriation theory urged in this case, the disclosure obligation runs to the source of the information, here, Dorsey & Whitney and Grand Met. Chief Justice Burger, dissenting in Chiarella, advanced a broader reading of § 10(b) and Rule 10b–5; the disclosure obligation, as he envisioned it, ran to those with whom the misappropriator trades. 445 U.S., at 240 ("a person who has misappropriated nonpublic information has an absolute duty to disclose that information or to refrain from trading"); see also id., at 243, n. 4. The Government does not propose that we adopt a misappropriation theory of that breadth.

7. Where, however, a person trading on the basis of material, nonpublic information owes a duty of loyalty and confidentiality to two entities or persons—for example, a law firm and its client—but makes disclosure to only one, the trader may still be liable under the misappropriation theory.

The misappropriation theory targets information of a sort that misappropriators ordinarily capitalize upon to gain no-risk profits through the purchase or sale of securities. Should a misappropriator put such information to other use, the statute's prohibition would not be implicated. The theory does not catch all conceivable forms of fraud involving confidential information; rather, it catches fraudulent means of capitalizing on such information through securities transactions.

The Government notes another limitation on the forms of fraud § 10(b) reaches: "The misappropriation theory would not ... apply to a case in which a person defrauded a bank into giving him a loan or embezzled cash from another, and then used the proceeds of the misdeed to purchase securities." Brief for United States 24, n. 13. In such a case, the Government states, "the proceeds would have value to the malefactor apart from their use in a securities transaction, and the fraud would be complete as soon as the money was obtained." Ibid. In other words, money can buy, if not anything, then at least many things; its misappropriation may thus be viewed as sufficiently detached from a subsequent securities transaction that § 10(b)'s "in connection with" requirement would not be met. Ibid.

The dissent's charge that the misappropriation theory is incoherent because information, like funds, can be put to multiple uses, misses the point. The Exchange Act was enacted in part "to insure the maintenance of fair and honest markets," 15 U.S.C. § 78b, and there is no question that fraudulent uses of confidential information fall within § 10(b)'s prohibition if the fraud is "in connection with" a securities transaction. It is hardly remarkable that a rule suitably applied to the fraudulent uses of certain kinds of information would be stretched beyond reason were it applied to the fraudulent use of money.

The dissent does catch the Government in overstatement. Observing that money can be used for all manner of purposes and purchases, the Government urges that confidential information of the kind at issue derives its value only from its utility in securities trading. See Brief for United States 10, 21: post, at 4–6 (several times emphasizing the word "only"). Substitute "ordinarily" for "only," and the Government is on the mark.[8]

---

8. The dissent's evident struggle to invent other uses to which O'Hagan plausibly might have put the nonpublic information, ... is telling. It is imaginative to suggest that a trade journal would have paid O'Hagan dollars in the millions to publish his information. See Tr. of Oral Arg. 36–37. Counsel of O'Hagan hypothesized, as a nontrading use, that O'Hagan could have "misappropriated this information of [his] law firm and its client, delivered it to [Pillsbury], and suggested that [Pillsbury] in the future ... might find it very desirable to use [O'Hagan] for legal work." Id., at 37. But Pillsbury might well have had large doubts about engaging for its legal work a lawyer who so stunningly displayed his readiness to betray a client's confidence. Nor is the Commission's theory "incoherent" or "inconsistent," ... for failing to inhibit use of confidential information for "personal amusement ... in a fantasy stock trading game," ....

Our recognition that the Government's "only" is an overstatement has provoked the dissent to cry "new theory." . . . But the very case on which the dissent relies, Motor Vehicle Mfrs. Assn. of United States, Inc. v. State Farm Mut. Automobile Ins. Co., 463 U.S. 29 (1983), shows the extremity of that charge. In State Farm, we reviewed an agency's rescission of a rule under the same "arbitrary and capricious" standard by which the promulgation of a rule under the relevant statute was to be judged, see id., at 41–42; in our decision concluding that the agency had not adequately explained its regulatory action, see id., at 57, we cautioned that a "reviewing court should not attempt itself to make up for such deficiencies," id., at 43. Here, by contrast, Rule 10b–5's promulgation has not been challenged; we consider only the Government's charge that O'Hagan's alleged fraudulent conduct falls within the prohibitions of the rule and § 10(b). In this context, we acknowledge simply that, in defending the Government's interpretation of the rule and statute in this Court, the Government's lawyers have pressed a solid point too far, something lawyers, occasionally even judges, are wont to do.

The misappropriation theory comports with § 10(b)'s language, which requires deception "in connection with the purchase or sale of any security," not deception of an identifiable purchaser or seller. The theory is also well-tuned to an animating purpose of the Exchange Act: to insure honest securities markets and thereby promote investor confidence. See 45 Fed.Reg. 60412 (1980) (trading on misappropriated information "undermines the integrity of, and investor confidence in, the securities markets"). Although informational disparity is inevitable in the securities markets, investors likely would hesitate to venture their capital in a market where trading based on misappropriated nonpublic information is unchecked by law. An investor's informational disadvantage vis-a-vis a misappropriator with material, nonpublic information stems from contrivance, not luck; it is a disadvantage that cannot be overcome with research or skill. See Brudney, Insiders, Outsiders, and Informational Advantages Under the Federal Securities Laws, 93 Harv. L.Rev. 322, 356 (1979) ("If the market is thought to be systematically populated with . . . transactors [trading on the basis of misappropriated information] some investors will refrain from dealing altogether, and others will incur costs to avoid dealing with such transactors or corruptly to overcome their unerodable informational advantages."); Aldave, 13 Hofstra L.Rev., at 122–123.

In sum, considering the inhibiting impact on market participation of trading on misappropriated information, and the congressional purposes underlying § 10(b), it makes scant sense to hold a lawyer like O'Hagan a § 10(b) violator if he works for a law firm representing the target of a tender offer, but not if he works for a law firm representing the bidder. The text of the statute requires no such result.[9] The misappropriation at issue here was properly made the subject of a § 10(b) charge because it meets the statutory requirement that there be "deceptive" conduct "in connection with" securities transactions.

C

The Court of Appeals rejected the misappropriation theory primarily on two grounds. First, as the Eighth Circuit comprehended the theory, it requires neither misrepresentation nor nondisclosure. See 92 F.3d, at 618. As we just explained, however, see supra, at 8–10, deceptive nondisclosure is essential to the § 10(b) liability at issue. Concretely, in this case, "it [was O'Hagan's] failure to disclose his personal trading to Grand Met and Dorsey in breach of his duty to do so, that made his conduct 'deceptive' within the meaning of [§]10(b)." Reply Brief 7.

Second and "more obvious," the Court of Appeals said, the misappropriation theory is not moored to § 10(b)'s requirement that "the fraud be 'in connection with the purchase or sale of any security.'" See 92 F.3d, at 618 (quoting 15 U.S.C. § 78j(b)). According to the Eighth Circuit, three of our decisions reveal that § 10(b) liability cannot be predicated on a duty owed to the source of nonpublic information: Chiarella v. United States, 445 U.S. 222 (1980); Dirks v. SEC, 463 U.S. 646 (1983); and Central Bank of Denver, N.A. v. First Interstate Bank of Denver, N.A., 511 U.S. 164 (1994). "Only a breach of a duty to parties to the securities transaction," the Court of Appeals concluded, "or, at the most, to other market participants such as investors, will be sufficient to give rise to § 10(b) liability." 92 F.3d, at 618. We read the statute and our precedent differently, and note again that § 10(b) refers to "the purchase or sale of any security," not to identifiable purchasers or sellers of securities.

Chiarella involved securities trades by a printer employed at a shop that printed documents announcing corporate takeover bids. See 445 U.S., at 224. Deducing the names of target companies from documents he handled, the printer bought shares of the targets before takeover bids were announced, expecting (correctly) that the share prices would rise upon announcement. In these transactions, the printer did not disclose to the sellers of the

9. As noted earlier, however, see supra, at 9–10, the textual requirement of deception precludes § 10(b) liability when a person trading on the basis of nonpublic information has disclosed his trading plans to, or obtained authorization from, the principal—even though such conduct may affect the securities markets in the same manner as the conduct reached by the misappropriation theory. Contrary to the dissent's suggestion, see post, at 11–13, the fact that § 10(b) is only a partial antidote to the problems it was designed to alleviate does not call into question its prohibition of conduct that falls within its textual proscription. Moreover, once a disloyal agent discloses his imminent breach of duty, his principal may seek appropriate equitable relief under state law. Furthermore, in the context of a tender offer, the principal who authorizes an agent's trading on confidential information may, in the Commission's view, incur liability for an Exchange Act violation under Rule 14e–3(a).

securities (the target companies' shareholders) the nonpublic information on which he traded. See ibid. For that trading, the printer was convicted of violating § 10(b) and Rule 10b–5. We reversed the Court of Appeals judgment that had affirmed the conviction. See id., at 225.

The jury in Chiarella had been instructed that it could convict the defendant if he willfully failed to inform sellers of target company securities that he knew of a takeover bid that would increase the value of their shares. See id., at 226. Emphasizing that the printer had no agency or other fiduciary relationship with the sellers, we held that liability could not be imposed on so broad a theory. See id., at 235. There is under § 10(b), we explained, no "general duty between all participants in market transactions to forgo actions based on material, nonpublic information." Id., at 233. Under established doctrine, we said, a duty to disclose or abstain from trading "arises from a specific relationship between two parties." Ibid.

The Court did not hold in Chiarella that the only relationship prompting liability for trading on undisclosed information is the relationship between a corporation's insiders and shareholders. That is evident from our response to the Government's argument before this Court that the printer's misappropriation of information from his employer for purposes of securities trading—in violation of a duty of confidentiality owed to the acquiring companies—constituted fraud in connection with the purchase or sale of a security, and thereby satisfied the terms of § 10(b). Id., at 235–236. The Court declined to reach that potential basis for the printer's liability, because the theory had not been submitted to the jury. See id., at 236–237. But four Justices found merit in it. See id., at 239 (Brennan, J., concurring in judgment); id., at 240–243 (Burger, C.J., dissenting); id., at 245 (Blackmun, J., joined by Marshall, J., dissenting). And a fifth Justice stated that the Court "wisely left the resolution of this issue for another day." Id., at 238 (STEVENS, J., concurring).

Chiarella thus expressly left open the misappropriation theory before us today. Certain statements in Chiarella, however, led the Eighth Circuit in the instant case to conclude that § 10(b) liability hinges exclusively on a breach of duty owed to a purchaser or seller of securities. See 92 F.3d, at 618. The Court said in Chiarella that § 10(b) liability "is premised upon a duty to disclose arising from a relationship of trust and confidence between parties to a transaction," 445 U.S., at 230 ..., and observed that the printshop employee defendant in that case "was not a person in whom the sellers had placed their trust and confidence," see id., at 232. These statements rejected the notion that § 10(b) stretches so far as to impose "a general duty between all participants in market transactions to forgo actions based on material, nonpublic information," id., at 233, and we confine them to that context. The statements highlighted by the Eighth Circuit, in short, appear in an opinion carefully leaving for future resolution the validity of the misappropriation theory, and therefore cannot be read to foreclose that theory.

Dirks, too, left room for application of the misappropriation theory in cases like the one we confront.[10]   Dirks involved an investment analyst who had received information from a former insider of a corporation with which the analyst had no connection. See 463 U.S., at 648–649.   The information indicated that the corporation had engaged in a massive fraud.   The analyst investigated the fraud, obtaining corroborating information from employees of the corporation.   During his investigation, the analyst discussed his findings with clients and investors, some of whom sold their holdings in the company the analyst suspected of gross wrongdoing. See id., at 649.

The SEC censured the analyst for, inter alia, aiding and abetting § 10(b) and Rule 10b–5 violations by clients and investors who sold their holdings based on the nonpublic information the analyst passed on.   See id., at 650–652.   In the SEC's view, the analyst, as a "tippee" of corporation insiders, had a duty under § 10(b) and Rule 10b–5 to refrain from communicating the nonpublic information to persons likely to trade on the basis of it.   See id., at 651, 655–656.   This Court found no such obligation, see id., at 665–667, and repeated the key point made in Chiarella: There is no " 'general duty between all participants in market transactions to forgo actions based on material, nonpublic information.' "   Id., at 655 (quoting Chiarella, 445 U.S., at 233); see Aldave, 13 Hofstra L.Rev., at 122 (misappropriation theory bars only "trading on the basis of information that the wrongdoer converted to his own use in violation of some fiduciary, contractual, or similar obligation to the owner or rightful possessor of the information").

No showing had been made in Dirks that the "tippers" had violated any duty by disclosing to the analyst nonpublic information about their former employer.   The insiders had acted not for personal profit, but to expose a massive fraud within the corporation.   See Dirks, 463 U.S., at 666–667.   Absent any violation by the tippers, there could be no derivative liability for the tippee.   See id., at 667.   Most important for purposes of the instant case, the Court observed in Dirks: "There was no expectation by [the analyst's] sources that he would keep their information in confidence.   Nor did [the analyst] misappropriate or illegally obtain the information. . . ."   Id., at 665.   Dirks thus presents no suggestion that a person who gains nonpublic information through misappropriation

---

10. The Eighth Circuit's conclusion to the contrary was based in large part on Dirks's reiteration of the Chiarella language quoted and discussed above. See 92 F.3d 612, 618–619 (1996).

in breach of a fiduciary duty escapes § 10(b) liability when, without alerting the source, he trades on the information.

Last of the three cases the Eighth Circuit regarded as warranting disapproval of the misappropriation theory, Central Bank held that "a private plaintiff may not maintain an aiding and abetting suit under § 10(b)." 511 U.S., at 191. We immediately cautioned in Central Bank that secondary actors in the securities markets may sometimes be chargeable under the securities Acts: "Any person or entity, including a lawyer, accountant, or bank, who employs a manipulative device or makes a material misstatement (or omission) on which a purchaser or seller of securities relies may be liable as a primary violator under 10b–5, assuming . . . the requirements for primary liability under Rule 10b–5 are met." Ibid. (emphasis added). The Eighth Circuit isolated the statement just quoted and drew from it the conclusion that § 10(b) covers only deceptive statements or omissions on which purchasers and sellers, and perhaps other market participants, rely. See 92 F.3d, at 619. It is evident from the question presented in Central Bank, however, that this Court, in the quoted passage, sought only to clarify that secondary actors, although not subject to aiding and abetting liability, remain subject to primary liability under § 10(b) and Rule 10b–5 for certain conduct.

Furthermore, Central Bank's discussion concerned only private civil litigation under § 10(b) and Rule 10b–5, not criminal liability. Central Bank's reference to purchasers or sellers of securities must be read in light of a longstanding limitation on private § 10(b) suits. In Blue Chip Stamps v. Manor Drug Stores, 421 U.S. 723 (1975), we held that only actual purchasers or sellers of securities may maintain a private civil action under § 10(b) and Rule 10b–5. We so confined the § 10(b) private right of action because of "policy considerations." Id., at 737. In particular, Blue Chip Stamps recognized the abuse potential and proof problems inherent in suits by investors who neither bought nor sold, but asserted they would have traded absent fraudulent conduct by others. See id., at 739–747; see also Holmes v. Securities Investor Protection Corporation, 503 U.S. 258, 285 (1992) (O'CONNOR, J., concurring in part and concurring in judgment): id., at 289–290 (SCALIA, J., concurring in judgment). Criminal prosecutions do not present the dangers the Court addressed in Blue Chip Stamps, so that decision is "inapplicable" to indictments for violations of § 10(b) and Rule 10b–5. United States v. Naftalin, 441 U.S. 768, 774, n. 6 (1979); see also Holmes, 503 U.S., at 281 (O'CONNOR, J., concurring in part and concurring in judgment) ("The purchaser/seller standing requirement for private civil actions under § 10(b) and Rule 10b–5 is of no import in criminal prosecutions for willful violations of those provisions.").

In sum, the misappropriation theory, as we have examined and explained it in this opinion, is both consistent with the statute and with our precedent.[11] Vital to our decision that criminal liability may be sustained under the misappropriation theory, we emphasize, are two sturdy safeguards Congress has provided regarding scienter. To establish a criminal violation of Rule 10b–5, the Government must prove that a person "willfully" violated the provision. See 15 U.S.C. § 78ff(a).[12] Furthermore, a defendant may not be imprisoned for violating Rule 10b–5 if he proves that he had no knowledge of the rule. See ibid.[13] O'Hagan's charge that the misappropriation theory is too indefinite to permit the imposition of criminal liability, see Brief for Respondent 30–33, thus fails not only because the theory is limited to those who breach a recognized duty. In addition, the statute's "requirement of the presence of culpable intent as a necessary element of the offense does much to destroy any force in the argument that application of the [statute]" in circumstances such as O'Hagan's is unjust. *Boyce Motor Lines, Inc. v. United States*, 342 U.S. 337, 342 (1952).

The Eighth Circuit erred in holding that the misappropriation theory is inconsistent with § 10(b). The Court of Appeals may address on remand O'Hagan's other challenges to his convictions under § 10(b) and Rule 10b–5.

III

We consider next the ground on which the Court of Appeals reversed O'Hagan's convictions for fraudulent trading in connection with a tender offer, in violation of § 14(e) of the Exchange Act and SEC Rule 14e–3(a). A sole question is before us as to these convictions: Did the Commission, as the Court of Appeals held, exceed its rulemaking authority under § 14(e) when it adopted Rule

---

11. The United States additionally argues that Congress confirmed the validity of the misappropriation theory in the Insider Trading and Securities Fraud Enforcement Act of 1988 (ITSFEA), § 2(1), 102 Stat. 4677, note following 15 U.S.C. § 78u–1. See Brief for United States 32–35. ITSFEA declares that "the rules and regulations of the Securities and Exchange Commission under the Securities Exchange Act of 1934 . . . governing trading while in possession of material, nonpublic information are, as required by such Act, necessary and appropriate in the public interest and for the protection of investors." Note following 15 U.S.C. § 78u–1. ITSFEA also includes a new § 20A(a) of the Exchange Act expressly providing a private cause of action against persons who violate the Exchange Act "by purchasing or selling a security while in possession of material, nonpublic information", such an action may be brought by "any person who, contemporaneously with the purchase or sale of securities that is the subject of such violation, has purchased . . .

or sold . . . securities of the same class." 15 U.S.C. § 78r–1(a). Because we uphold the misappropriation theory on the basis of § 10(b) itself, we do not address ITSFEA's significance for cases of this genre.

12. In relevant part, § 32 of the Exchange Act, as set forth in 15 U.S.C. § 78ff(a), provides:

"Any person who willfully violates any provision of this chapter . . . or any rule or regulation thereunder the violation of which is made unlawful or the observance of which is required under the terms of this chapter . . . shall upon conviction be fined not more than $1,000,000, or imprisoned not more than 10 years, or both . . .; but no person shall be subject to imprisonment under this section for the violation of any rule or regulation if he proves that he had no knowledge of such rule or regulation."

13. The statute provides no such defense to imposition of monetary fines. See ibid.

14e–3(a) without requiring a showing that the trading at issue entailed a breach of fiduciary duty? We hold that the Commission, in this regard and to the extent relevant to this case, did not exceed its authority.

The governing statutory provision, § 14(e) of the Exchange Act, reads in relevant part:

"It shall be unlawful for any person ... to engage in any fraudulent, deceptive, or manipulative acts or practices, in connection with any tender offer.... The [SEC] shall, for the purposes of this subsection, by rules and regulations define, and prescribe means reasonably designed to prevent, such acts and practices as are fraudulent, deceptive, or manipulative." 15 U.S.C. § 78n(e).

Section 14(e)'s first sentence prohibits fraudulent acts in connection with a tender offer. This self-operating proscription was one of several provisions added to the Exchange Act in 1968 by the Williams Act, 82 Stat. 454. The section's second sentence delegates definitional and prophylactic rulemaking authority to the Commission. Congress added this rulemaking delegation to § 14(e) in 1970 amendments to the Williams Act. See § 5, 84 Stat. 1497.

Through § 14(e) and other provisions on disclosure in the Williams Act, Congress sought to ensure that shareholders "confronted by a cash tender offer for their stock [would] not be required to respond without adequate information." Rondeau v. Mosinee Paper Corp., 422 U.S. 49, 58 (1975); see Lewis v. McGraw, 619 F.2d 192, 195 (C.A.2 1980) (per curiam) ("very purpose" of Williams Act was "informed decisionmaking by shareholders"). As we recognized in Schreiber v. Burlington Northern, Inc., 472 U.S. 1 (1985), Congress designed the Williams Act to make "disclosure, rather than court-imposed principles of 'fairness' or 'artificiality,' ... the preferred method of market regulation." Id., at 9, n. 8. Section 14(e), we explained, "supplements the more precise disclosure provisions found elsewhere in the Williams Act, while requiring disclosure more explicitly addressed to the tender offer context than that required by § 10(b)." Id., at 10–11.

Relying on § 14(e)'s rulemaking authorization, the Commission, in 1980, promulgated Rule 14e–3(a). That measure provides:

"(a) If any person has taken a substantial step or steps to commence, or has commenced, a tender offer (the 'offering person'), it shall constitute a fraudulent, deceptive or manipulative act or practice within the meaning of section 14(e) of the [Exchange] Act for any other person who is in possession of material information relating to such tender offer which information he knows or has reason to know is nonpublic and which he knows or has reason to know has been acquired directly or indirectly from:

"(1) The offering person,

"(2) The issuer of the securities sought or to be sought by such tender offer, or

"(3) Any officer, director, partner or employee or any other person acting on behalf of the offering person or such issuer, to purchase or sell or cause to be purchased or sold any of such securities or any securities convertible into or exchangeable for any such securities or any option or right to obtain or to dispose of any of the foregoing securities, unless within a reasonable time prior to any purchase or sale such information and its source are publicly disclosed by press release or otherwise."   17 CFR § 240.14e–3(a) (1996).

As characterized by the Commission, Rule 14e–3(a) is a "disclose or abstain from trading" requirement.   45 Fed. Reg. 60410 (1980).[15]   The Second Circuit concisely described the rule's thrust:

"One violates Rule 14e–3(a) if he trades on the basis of material nonpublic information concerning a pending tender offer that he knows or has reason to know has been acquired 'directly or indirectly' from an insider of the offeror or issuer, or someone working on their behalf.   Rule 14e–3(a) is a disclosure provision.   It creates a duty in those traders who fall within its ambit to abstain or disclose, without regard to whether the trader owes a pre-existing fiduciary duty to respect the confidentiality of the information."   United States v. Chestman, 947 F.2d 551, 557 (1991) (en banc) (emphasis added), cert. denied, 503 U.S. 1004 (1992).

See also SEC v. Maio, 51 F.3d 623, 635 (C.A.7 1995) ("Rule 14e–3 creates a duty to disclose material nonpublic information, or abstain from trading in stocks implicated by an impending tender offer, regardless of whether such information was obtained through a breach of fiduciary duty.") (emphasis added); SEC v. Peters, 978 F.2d 1162, 1165 (C.A.10 1992) (as written, Rule 14e–3(a) has no fiduciary duty requirement).

In the Eighth Circuit's view, because Rule 14e–3(a) applies whether or not the trading in question breaches a fiduciary duty, the regulation exceeds the SEC's § 14(e) rulemaking authority.   See 92 F.3d, at 624, 627.   Contra, Maio, 51 F.3d, at 634–635 (CA7); Peters, 978 F.2d, at 1165–1167 (CA10);   Chestman, 947 F.2d, at 556–563 (CA2) (all holding Rule 14e–3(a) a proper exercise of SEC's statutory authority).   In support of its holding, the Eighth Circuit relied on the text of § 14(e) and our decisions in Schreiber and Chiarella.   See 92 F.3d, at 624–627.

---

15. The rule thus adopts for the tender offer context a requirement resembling the one Chief Justice Burger would have adopted in Chiarella for misappropriators under § 10(b). See supra, at 10, n. 6.

The Eighth Circuit homed in on the essence of § 14(e)'s rulemaking authorization: "The statute empowers the SEC to 'define' and 'prescribe means reasonably designed to prevent' 'acts and practices' which are 'fraudulent.'" Id., at 624. All that means, the Eighth Circuit found plain, is that the SEC may "identify and regulate," in the tender offer context, "acts and practices" the law already defines as "fraudulent"; but, the Eighth Circuit maintained, the SEC may not "create its own definition of fraud." Ibid. (internal quotation marks omitted).

This Court, the Eighth Circuit pointed out, held in Schreiber that the word "manipulative" in the § 14(e) phrase "fraudulent, deceptive, or manipulative acts or practices" means just what the word means in § 10(b): Absent misrepresentation or nondisclosure, an act cannot be indicted as manipulative. See 92 F.3d, at 625 (citing Schreiber, 472 U.S., at 7–8, and n. 6). Section 10(b) interpretations guide construction of § 14(e), the Eighth Circuit added, see 92 F.3d, at 625, citing this Court's acknowledgment in Schreiber that § 14(e)'s " 'broad antifraud prohibition' ... [is] modeled on the antifraud provisions of § 10(b) ... and Rule 10b–5," 472 U.S., at 10 (citation omitted); see id., at 10–11, n. 10.

For the meaning of "fraudulent" under § 10(b), the Eighth Circuit looked to Chiarella. See 92 F.3d, at 625. In that case, the Eighth Circuit recounted, this Court held that a failure to disclose information could be "fraudulent" under § 10(b) only when there was a duty to speak arising out of " 'a fiduciary or other similar relationship of trust and confidence.' " Chiarella, 445 U.S., at 228 (quoting Restatement (Second) of Torts § 551(2)(a) (1976)). Just as § 10(b) demands a showing of a breach of fiduciary duty, so such a breach is necessary to make out a § 14(e) violation, the Eighth Circuit concluded.

As to the Commission's § 14(e) authority to "prescribe means reasonably designed to prevent" fraudulent acts, the Eighth Circuit stated: "Properly read, this provision means simply that the SEC has broad regulatory powers in the field of tender offers, but the statutory terms have a fixed meaning which the SEC cannot alter by way of an administrative rule." 92 F.3d, at 627.

The United States urges that the Eighth Circuit's reading of § 14(e) misapprehends both the Commission's authority to define fraudulent acts and the Commission's power to prevent them. "The 'defining' power," the United States submits, "would be a virtual nullity were the SEC not permitted to go beyond common law fraud (which is separately prohibited in the first [self-operative] sentence of Section 14(e))." Brief for United States 11; see id., at 37.

In maintaining that the Commission's power to define fraudulent acts under § 14(e) is broader than its rulemaking power under § 10(b), the United States questions the Court of Appeals' reading of Schreiber. See id., at 38–40. Parenthetically, the United States notes that the word before the Schreiber Court was "manipulative"; unlike "fraudulent," the United States observes, " 'manipulative' . . . is 'virtually a term of art when used in connection with the securities markets.' " Id., at 38, n. 20 (quoting Schreiber, 472 U.S., at 6). Most tellingly, the United States submits, Schreiber involved acts alleged to violate the self-operative provision in § 14(e)'s first sentence, a sentence containing language similar to § 10(b). But § 14(e)'s second sentence, containing the rulemaking authorization, the United States points out, does not track § 10(b), which simply authorizes the SEC to proscribe "manipulative or deceptive devices or contrivances." Brief for United States 38. Instead, § 14(e)'s rulemaking prescription tracks § 15(c)(2)(D) of the Exchange Act, 15 U.S.C. § 78o(c)(2)(D), which concerns the conduct of broker-dealers in over-the-counter markets. See Brief for United States 38–39. Since 1938, see 52 Stat. 1075, § 15(c)(2) has given the Commission authority to "define, and prescribe means reasonably designed to prevent, such [broker-dealer] acts and practices as are fraudulent, deceptive, or manipulative." 15 U.S.C. § 78o(c)(2)(D). When Congress added this same rulemaking language to § 14(e) in 1970, the Government states, the Commission had already used its § 15(c)(2) authority to reach beyond common law fraud. See Brief for United States 39, n. 22.[16]

We need not resolve in this case whether the Commission's authority under § 14(e) to "define . . . such acts and practices as are fraudulent" is broader than the Commission's fraud-defining authority under § 10(b), for we agree with the United States that Rule 14e–3(a), as applied to cases of this genre, qualifies under § 14(e) as a "means reasonably designed to prevent" fraudulent trading on material, nonpublic information in the tender offer context.[17] A prophylactic measure, because its mission is to pre-

---

16. The Government draws our attention to the following measures: 17 CFR § 240.15c2–1 (1970) (prohibiting a broker-dealer's hypothecation of a customer's securities if hypothecated securities would be commingled with the securities of another customer, absent written consent); § 240.15c2–3 (1970) (prohibiting transactions by broker-dealers in unvalidated German securities); § 240.15c2–4 (1970) (prohibiting broker-dealers from accepting any part of the sale price of a security being distributed unless the money received is promptly transmitted to the persons entitled to it); § 240.15c2–5 (1970) (requiring broker-dealers to provide written disclosure of credit terms and commissions in connection with securities sales in which broker-dealers extend credit, or participate in arranging for loans, to the purchasers). See Brief for United States 39, n. 22.

17. We leave for another day, when the issue requires decision, the legitimacy of Rule 14e–3(a) as applied to "warehousing," which the Government describes as "the practice by which bidders leak advance information of a tender offer to allies and encourage them to purchase the target company's stock before the bid is announced." Reply Brief 17. As we observed in Chiarella, one of the Commission's purposes in proposing Rule 14e–3(a) was "to bar warehousing under its authority to regulate tender offers." 445 U.S., at 234. The Government acknowledges that trading authorized by a principal breaches no fiduciary duty. See Reply Brief 17. The instant case, however, does not involve trading authorized by a principal; therefore, we need not here decide whether the Commission's proscription of warehousing falls within its § 14(e) authority to define or prevent fraud.

vent, typically encompasses more than the core activity prohibited. As we noted in Schreiber, § 14(e)'s rulemaking authorization gives the Commission "latitude," even in the context of a term of art like "manipulative," "to regulate nondeceptive activities as a 'reasonably designed' means of preventing manipulative acts, without suggesting any change in the meaning of the term 'manipulative' itself." 472 U.S., at 11, n. 11. We hold, accordingly, that under § 14(e), the Commission may prohibit acts, not themselves fraudulent under the common law or § 10(b), if the prohibition is "reasonably designed to prevent ... acts and practices [that] are fraudulent." 15 U.S.C. § 78n(c).[18]

Because Congress has authorized the Commission, in § 14(e), to prescribe legislative rules, we owe the Commission's judgment "more than mere deference or weight." Batterton v. Francis, 432 U.S. 416, 424–426 (1977). Therefore, in determining whether Rule 14e–3(a)'s "disclose or abstain from trading" requirement is reasonably designed to prevent fraudulent acts, we must accord the Commission's assessment "controlling weight unless [it is] arbitrary, capricious, or manifestly contrary to the statute." Chevron U.S.A. Inc. v. Natural Resources Defense Council, Inc., 467 U.S. 837, 844 (1984). In this case, we conclude, the Commission's assessment is none of these.[19]

In adopting the "disclose or abstain" rule, the SEC explained:

"The Commission has previously expressed and continues to have serious concerns about trading by persons in possession of material, nonpublic information relating to a tender offer. This practice results in unfair disparities in market information and market disruption. Security holders who purchase from or sell to such persons are effectively denied the benefits of disclosure and the substantive protections of the Williams Act. If furnished with the information, these security holders would be able to make an informed investment decision, which could involve deferring the purchase or sale of the securities until the material information had been disseminated or until the tender offer has been commenced or terminated." 45 Fed.Reg. 60412 (1980) (footnotes omitted).

The Commission thus justified Rule 14e–3(a) as a means necessary and proper to assure the efficacy of Williams Act protections.

---

18. The Commission's power under § 10(b) is more limited. See supra, at 6 (Rule 10b–5 may proscribe only conduct that § 10(b) prohibits).

19. The dissent urges that the Commission must be precise about the authority it is exercising—that it must say whether it is acting to "define" or to "prevent" fraud—and that in this instance it has purported only to define, not to prevent. See post, at 18–19. The dissent sees this precision in Rule 14e–3(a)'s words: "it shall constitute a fraudulent ... act ... within the meaning of section 14(e)...." We do not find the Commission's rule vulnerable for failure to recite as a regulatory preamble: We hereby exercise our authority to "define, and prescribe means reasonably designed to prevent, ... [fraudulent] acts." Sensibly read, the rule is an exercise of the Commission's full authority. Logically and practically, such a rule may be conceived and defended, alternatively, as definitional or preventive.

The United States emphasizes that Rule 14e–3(a) reaches trading in which "a breach of duty is likely but difficult to prove." Reply Brief 16. "Particularly in the context of a tender offer," as the Tenth Circuit recognized, "there is a fairly wide circle of people with confidential information," Peters, 978 F.2d, at 1167, notably, the attorneys, investment bankers, and accountants involved in structuring the transaction. The availability of that information may lead to abuse, for "even a hint of an upcoming tender offer may send the price of the target company's stock soaring." SEC v. Materia, 745 F.2d 197, 199 (C.A.2 1984). Individuals entrusted with nonpublic information, particularly if they have no long-term loyalty to the issuer, may find the temptation to trade on that information hard to resist in view of "the very large short-term profits potentially available [to them]." Peters, 978 F.2d, at 1167.

"It may be possible to prove circumstantially that a person [traded on the basis of material, nonpublic information], but almost impossible to prove that the trader obtained such information in breach of a fiduciary duty owed either by the trader or by the ultimate insider source of the information." Ibid. The example of a "tippee" who trades on information received from an insider illustrates the problem. Under Rule 10b–5, "a tippee assumes a fiduciary duty to the shareholders of a corporation not to trade on material nonpublic information only when the insider has breached his fiduciary duty to the shareholders by disclosing the information to the tippee and the tippee knows or should know that there has been a breach." Dirks, 463 U.S., at 660. To show that a tippee who traded on nonpublic information about a tender offer had breached a fiduciary duty would require proof not only that the insider source breached a fiduciary duty, but that the tippee knew or should have known of that breach. "Yet, in most cases, the only parties to the [information transfer] will be the insider and the alleged tippee." Peters, 978 F.2d, at 1167.[20]

In sum, it is a fair assumption that trading on the basis of material, nonpublic information will often involve a breach of a duty of confidentiality to the bidder or target company or their representatives. The SEC, cognizant of the proof problem that could enable sophisticated traders to escape responsibility, placed in Rule 14e–3(a) a "disclose or abstain from trading" command that does not require specific proof of a breach of fiduciary duty. That prescription, we are satisfied, applied to this case, is a "means reasonably

---

20. The dissent opines that there is no reason to anticipate difficulties in proving breach of duty in "misappropriation" cases. "Once the source of the [purloined] information has been identified," the dissent asserts, "it should be a simple task to obtain proof of any breach of duty." Post, at 20. To test that assertion, assume a misappropriating partner at Dorsey & Whitney told his daughter or son and a wealthy friend that a tender for Pillsbury was in the offing, and each tippee promptly purchased Pillsbury stock, the child borrowing the purchase price from the wealthy friend. The dissent's confidence, post, at 20, n. 12, that "there is no reason to suspect that the tipper would gratuitously protect the tippee," seems misplaced.

designed to prevent" fraudulent trading on material, nonpublic information in the tender offer context. See Chestman, 947 F.2d, at 560 ("While dispensing with the subtle problems of proof associated with demonstrating fiduciary breach in the problematic area of tender offer insider trading, [Rule 14e–3(a)] retains a close nexus between the prohibited conduct and the statutory aims."); accord, Maio, 51 F.3d, at 635, and n. 14; Peters, 978 F.2d, at 1167.[21] Therefore, insofar as it serves to prevent the type of misappropriation charged against O'Hagan, Rule 14e–3(a) is a proper exercise of the Commission's prophylactic power under § 14(e).[22]

As an alternate ground for affirming the Eighth Circuit's judgment, O'Hagan urges that Rule 14e–3(a) is invalid because it prohibits trading in advance of a tender offer—when "a substantial step . . . to commence" such an offer has been taken—while § 14(e) prohibits fraudulent acts "in connection with any tender offer." See Brief for Respondent 41–42. O'Hagan further contends that, by covering pre-offer conduct, Rule 14e–3(a) "fails to comport with due process on two levels": The rule does not "give fair notice as to when, in advance of a tender offer, a violation of § 14(e) occurs," id., at 42; and it "disposes of any scienter requirement," id., at 43. The Court of Appeals did not address these arguments, and O'Hagan did not raise the due process points in his briefs before that court. We decline to consider these contentions in the first instance.[23] The Court of Appeals may address on remand any arguments O'Hagan has preserved.

IV

Based on its dispositions of the securities fraud convictions, the Court of Appeals also reversed O'Hagan's convictions, under 18 U.S.C. § 1341, for mail fraud. See 92 F.3d, at 627–628. Reversal of the securities convictions, the Court of Appeals recognized, "did not as a matter of law require that the mail fraud convictions likewise be reversed." Id., at 627 (citing Carpenter, 484 U.S., at 24, in which this Court unanimously affirmed mail and wire fraud convictions based on the same conduct that evenly divided the Court on the defendants' securities fraud convictions). But in this case, the Court of Appeals said, the indictment was so structured that the mail fraud charges could not be disassociated from the securities

---

21. The dissent insists that even if the misappropriation of information from the bidder about a tender offer is fraud, the Commission has not explained why such fraud is "in connection with" a tender offer. Post, at 19. What else, one can only wonder, might such fraud be "in connection with"?

22. Repeating the argument it made concerning the misappropriation theory, see supra, at 21, n. 11, the United States urges that Congress confirmed Rule 14e–3(a)'s validity in ITSFEA, 15 U.S.C. § 78u–I. See

Brief for United States 44–45. We uphold Rule 14e–3(a) on the basis of § 14(e) itself and need not address ITSFEA's relevance to this case.

23. As to O'Hagan's scienter argument, we reiterate that 15 U.S.C. § 78ff(a) requires the Government to prove "willful violation" of the securities laws, and that lack of knowledge of the relevant rule is an affirmative defense to a sentence of imprisonment. See supra, at 21–22.

fraud charges, and absent any securities fraud, "there was no fraud upon which to base the mail fraud charges." 92 F.3d, at 627–628.[24]

The United States urges that the Court of Appeals' position is irreconcilable with Carpenter: Just as in Carpenter, so here, the "mail fraud charges are independent of [the] securities fraud charges, even [though] both rest on the same set of facts." Brief for United States 46–47. We need not linger over this matter, for our rulings on the securities fraud issues require that we reverse the Court of Appeals judgment on the mail fraud counts as well.[25]

O'Hagan, we note, attacked the mail fraud convictions in the Court of Appeals on alternate grounds; his other arguments, not yet addressed by the Eighth Circuit, remain open for consideration on remand.

    * * *

The judgment of the Court of Appeals for the Eighth Circuit is reversed, and the case is remanded for further proceedings consistent with this opinion.

It is so ordered.

DISSENT: JUSTICE SCALIA, concurring in part and dissenting in part.

I join Parts I, III, and IV of the Court's opinion. I do not agree, however, with Part II of the Court's opinion, containing its analysis of respondent's convictions under § 10(b) and Rule 10b–5.

I do not entirely agree with JUSTICE THOMAS'S analysis of those convictions either, principally because it seems to me irrelevant whether the Government's theory of why respondent's acts were covered is "coherent and consistent," post, at 13. It is true that with respect to matters over which an agency has been accorded adjudicative authority or policymaking discretion, the agency's action must be supported by the reasons that the agency sets forth, SEC v. Chenery Corp., 318 U.S. 80, 94 (1943); see also SEC v. Chenery Corp., 332 U.S. 194, 196 (1947), but I do not think an agency's unadorned application of the law need be, at least where (as here) no Chevron deference is being given to the agency's

---

24. The Court of Appeals reversed respondent's money laundering convictions on similar reasoning. See 92 F.3d, at 628. Because the United States did not seek review of that ruling, we leave undisturbed that portion of the Court of Appeals' judgment.

25. The dissent finds O'Hagan's convictions on the mail fraud counts, but not on the securities fraud counts, sustainable. Post, at 23–24. Under the dissent's view, securities traders like O'Hagan would escape SEC civil actions and federal prosecutions under legislation targeting securities

fraud, only to be caught for their trading activities in the broad mail fraud net. If misappropriation theory cases could proceed only under the federal mail and wire fraud statutes, practical consequences for individual defendants might not be large, see Aldave, 49 Ohio St. L.J., at 381, and n. 60; however, "proportionally more persons accused of insider trading [might] be pursued by a U.S. Attorney, and proportionally fewer by the SEC," id., at 382. Our decision, of course, does not rest on such enforcement policy considerations.

interpretation. In point of fact, respondent's actions either violated § 10(b) and Rule 10b–5, or they did not—regardless of the reasons the Government gave. And it is for us to decide.

While the Court's explanation of the scope of § 10(b) and Rule 10b–5 would be entirely reasonable in some other context, it does not seem to accord with the principle of lenity we apply to criminal statutes (which cannot be mitigated here by the Rule, which is no less ambiguous than the statute). See Reno v. Koray, 515 U.S. 50, 64–65 (1995) (explaining circumstances in which rule of lenity applies); United States v. Bass, 404 U.S. 336, 347–348 (1971) (discussing policies underlying rule of lenity). In light of that principle, it seems to me that the unelaborated statutory language: "to use or employ in connection with the purchase or sale of any security . . . any manipulative or deceptive device or contrivance," § 10(b), must be construed to require the manipulation or deception of a party to a securities transaction.

[The opinion of Justice Thomas, concurring with the majority on the Mail Fraud Act issue, but dissenting on the Rule 10b–5 and Rule 14e–3(a) issues, is omitted. Chief Justice Rehnquist concurred in this opinion.]

———

Add the following sentence at the end of the Note on Rule 14e–3 at p. 896 of the Unabridged Edition and p. 608 of the Concise Edition:

See United States v. O'Hagan, supra this supplement.

———

Add the following Note at p. 929 of the Unabridged Edition, following the Note on Blue Chip Stamps v. Manor Drug Stores and the "In Connection With" Requirement:

IN RE CARTER–WALLACE SECURITIES LITIGATION, 150 F.3d 153 (2d Cir.1998). In August 1993, Carter–Wallace began selling Felbatol, which it hailed as the first major anti-epileptic drug to be introduced in the United States in over fifteen years. To promote Felbatol, Carter–Wallace ran a sixteen-page advertisement in the January 1994 issue of *Neurology*. The advertisement recited Felbatol's safety record and stated that "no life-threatening liver toxicities or blood dyscrasias have been attributed to Felbatol monotherapy." An identical advertisement appeared in the January 1994 issue of *Archives of Neurology*. Five-page advertisements containing the same statement appeared in the February, March, April, May, June, and July 1994 issues of *Neurology* and *Archives of Neurology*.

During the period in which the advertisements were running, Carter–Wallace received information indicating that in some patients

Felbatol caused a fatal form of acquired bone-marrow failure known as aplastic anemia. Carter–Wallace received the first report of Felbatol-related aplastic anemia death in January 1994. A report of another such death was received in March, and reports of two more deaths were received in each of April and May. Four additional deaths were reported in July. On August 1, 1994, Carter–Wallace and the FDA issued a "Dear Doctors" letter, recommending that most patients be withdrawn from Felbatol treatment.

Plaintiffs purchased shares of Carter–Wallace stock in June and July 1994. They brought suit against Carter–Wallace under Rule 10b–5, alleging that the advertisements in the medical journals were false, misled the market, and distorted the price of Carter–Wallace stock.

The district court dismissed the complaint. It found that the advertisements were false in stating that no reports of life-threatening effect had been received. However, it held that the advertisements were not actionable under Section 10(b) because as a matter of law drug advertisements in medical journals "[a]re not made in connection with the purchase or sale of securities, but [a]re directed at a technical audience intimately familiar with the potential adverse side effects of new drugs." The Second Circuit reversed:

> We have broadly construed the phrase "in connection with," holding that Congress, in using the phrase "intended only that the device employed, whatever it might be, be of a sort that would cause reasonable investors to rely thereon, and, in connection therewith, so relying, cause them to purchase or sell a corporation's securities," *SEC v. Texas Gulf Sulphur Co.*, 401 F.2d 833, 860 (2d Cir.1968) (en banc) ("TGS"); *see also In re Ames Dep't Stores Inc. Stock Litig.*, 991 F.2d 953, 965 (2d Cir.1993). Moreover, when, as here, a claim is based on the fraud-on-the-market theory, a "straightforward cause and effect" test is applied, *In re Ames*, 991 F.2d at 967, under which it is sufficient that "statements which manipulate the market are connected to resultant stock trading." *Id.* at 966.

> Under the "cause and effect" test, we cannot say that, as a matter of law, detailed drug advertisements using technical jargon and published in sophisticated medical journals can never constitute statements made "in connection with" a securities transaction. As the Supreme Court has noted, "market professional generally consider most publicly announced material statements about companies, thereby affecting stock market prices." *Basic Inc. v. Levinson*, 485 U.S. 224, 247 n. 24, 108 S.Ct. 978, 99 L.Ed.2d 194 (1988). Technical advertisements in sophisticated medical journals detailing the attributes of a new drug could be highly relevant to analysts evaluating the stock of the company marketing the drug. *See In re Time Warner*, 9 F.3d at 265 (discussing analysts' use of information).

That the market can absorb technical medical information is neither novel nor surprising. *See Wielgos v. Commonwealth Edison Co.*, 892 F.2d 509, 514–15 (7th Cir.1989) (finding generally that market absorbs complex scientific data). Technical information about the medical efficacy of new drugs, whether found in advertisements or elsewhere, has an obvious bearing on the financial future of a drug company. In an economy that produces highly sophisticated products, technical information is of enormous importance to financial analysts, whether such companies are producing drugs, as here, or nuclear power plants, as in *Wielgos*. The fact that such information is found in a specialized medical journal, as here, rather than in a statement addressed to participants in financial markets, as in TGS, seems to us irrelevant, so long as the journals are used by analysts studying the prospects of drug companies. In fact, an analyst might consider such an advertisement more informative than a non-technical but corresponding statement to financial market professionals. . . .

We hold, therefore, that false advertisements in technical journals may be "in connection with" a securities transaction if the proof at trial establishes that the advertisements were used by market professionals in evaluating the stock of the company. We leave it to the district court on remand to decide whether the appellants' complaint with respect to the advertisements sufficiently alleges the other elements of a Section 10(b) claim.

———

Add the following Note at p. 933 of the Unabridged Edition, following the Note on the Scienter Requirement:

NOTE ON THE USE TEST UNDER RULE 10b–5

In 1998, the Ninth and Eleventh Circuits held that Rule 10b–5 is not violated unless the defendant not only *possessed* material inside information when she traded, but actually *used* the information in deciding to buy or sell. These decisions were rested on the theory that having inside information in one's possession when trading does not wrongfully cause harm; only using such information wrongfully causes harm. SEC v. Adler, 137 F.3d 1325 (11th Cir. 1998); United States v. Smith, 155 F.3d 1051 (9th Cir.1998).

This esoteric distinction between possession and use of inside information had been rejected by the Second Circuit in 1993, in United States v. Teicher, 987 F.2d 112. There the court said:

A number of factors weigh in favor of a "knowing possession" standard. First, as the government points out, both § 10(b) and Rule 10b–5 require only that a deceptive practice be conducted "in connection with the purchase or sale of a security." We have previously stated that the "in connection with" clause must be "construed . . . flexibly to include deceptive practices 'touching' the sale of securities, a relationship which has been described as 'very tenuous indeed.' " *United States v. Newman*, 664 F.2d 12, 18 (2d Cir.1981), cert. denied, 464 U.S. 863, 104 S.Ct. 193, 78 L.Ed.2d 170 (1983). . . .

In addition, a "knowing possession" standard comports with the oft-quoted maxim that one with a fiduciary or similar duty to hold material nonpublic information in confidence must either "disclose or abstain" with regard to trading. See Chiarella v. United States, 445 U.S. 222, 227, 100 S.Ct. 1108, 1114, 63 L.Ed.2d 348 (1980). . . .

Finally, a "knowing possession" standard has the attribute of simplicity. It recognizes that one who trades while knowingly possessing material inside information has an informational advantage over other traders. Because the advantage is in the form of information, it exists in the mind of the trader. Unlike a loaded weapon which may stand ready but unused, material information can not lay idle in the human brain. The individual with such information may decide to trade upon that information, to alter a previously decided-upon transaction, to continue with a previously planned transaction even though publicly available information would now suggest otherwise, or simply to do nothing. In our increasingly sophisticated securities markets, where subtle shifts in strategy can produce dramatic results, it would be a mistake to think of such decisions as merely binary choices—to buy or to sell.

As a matter of policy then, a requirement of a causal connection between the information and the trade could frustrate attempts to distinguish between legitimate trades and those conducted in connection with inside information. See 7 L. Loss & J. Seligman, Securities Regulation 3505 (3d ed. 1991) ("The very difficulty of establishing actual use of inside information points to possession as the test.").

In SEC. v. Adler, supra, the Eleventh Circuit rejected this reasoning and adopted a use test. The court said:

> We believe that the use test best comports with precedent and Congressional intent, and that mere knowing possession— i.e., proof that an insider traded while in possession of material nonpublic information—is not a per se violation. However, when an insider trades while in possession of material nonpublic information, a strong inference arises that such information was used by the insider in trading. The insider can attempt to

rebut the inference by adducing evidence that there was no causal connection between the information and the trade—i.e., that the information was not used. The factfinder would then weigh all of the evidence and make a finding of fact as to whether the inside information was used.

We adopt this test for the following reasons. First, of the several arguments in support of the knowing possession test, the strongest is the fact that it often would be difficult for the SEC to prove that an alleged violator actually used the material nonpublic information; the motivations for the trader's decision to trade are difficult to prove and peculiarly within the trader's knowledge. However, we believe that the inference of use, which arises from the fact that the insider traded while in knowing possession of material nonpublic information, alleviates the SEC's problem. The inference allows the SEC to make out its prima facie case without having to prove the causal connection with more direct evidence.

In United States v. Smith, supra, the Ninth Circuit also adopted a use test. In fact, the Ninth Circuit in *Smith* went further than the Eleventh Circuit had in *Adler*, because *Smith* didn't adopt the *Adler* presumption—although in part because *Smith* was a criminal case. The Ninth Circuit based its adoption of the use test in part on the theory that causation had to be proved in 10b–5 cases, and in part by gleaning stray dicta from earlier Supreme Court decisions on other issues.

It's hard to resist the conclusion that the courts in *Adler* and *Smith* were operating under highly questionable assumptions about human psychology. If A has inside information that's relevant to an action she takes, the information must be a cause in fact of her action, because every action a person takes is based on all the information she then has that is relevant to the action. Even the trader can't really know if she would have traded in the absence of the information, unless she was contractually committed to trade before she obtained the information.

———

Add the following cross-reference at p. 938 of the Unabridged Edition, and p. 625 of the Concise Edition, after the Note on Aiding and Abetting Liability under Rule 10b–5:

SECURITIES EXCHANGE ACT § 20(f)

[See Statutory Supplement]

SECTION 4. THE COMMON LAW REVISITED

Add the following case at the end of p. 995 of the Unabridged Edition, and the end of p. 652 of the Concise Edition, following Diamond v. Oreamuno:

MALONE v. BRINCAT
Supreme Court of Delaware, 1998.
722 A.2d 5.

Before VEASEY, Chief Justice, WALSH, HOLLAND, HARTNETT and BERGER, Justices (constituting the Court en Banc).

HOLLAND, Justice:

Doran Malone, Joseph P. Danielle, and Adrienne M. Danielle, the plaintiffs-appellants, filed this individual and class action in the Court of Chancery. The complaint alleged that the directors of Mercury Finance Company ("Mercury"), a Delaware corporation, breached their fiduciary duty of disclosure. The individual defendant-appellee directors are John N. Brincat, Dennis H. Chookaszian, William C. Croft, Clifford R. Johnson, Andrew McNally, IV, Bruce I. McPhee, Fred G. Steingraber, and Phillip J. Wicklander. The complaint also alleged that the defendant-appellee, KPMG Peat Marwick LLP ("KPMG") aided and abetted the Mercury directors' breaches of fiduciary duty. The Court of Chancery dismissed the complaint with prejudice pursuant to Chancery Rule 12(b)(6) for failure to state a claim upon which relief may be granted.

The complaint alleged that the director defendants intentionally overstated the financial condition of Mercury on repeated occasions throughout a four-year period in disclosures to Mercury's shareholders. Plaintiffs contend that the complaint states a claim upon which relief can be granted for a breach of the fiduciary duty of disclosure. Plaintiffs also contend that, because the director defendants breached their fiduciary duty of disclosure to the Mercury shareholders, the Court of Chancery erroneously dismissed the aiding and abetting claim against KPMG.

This Court has concluded that the Court of Chancery properly granted the defendants' motions to dismiss the complaint. That dismissal, however, should have been without prejudice. Plaintiffs are entitled to file an amended complaint. Therefore, the judgment of the Court of Chancery is affirmed in part, reversed in part, and remanded for further proceedings consistent with this opinion.

Facts

Mercury is a publicly-traded company engaged primarily in purchasing installment sales contracts from automobile dealers and providing short-term installment loans directly to consumers. This action was filed on behalf of the named plaintiffs and all persons (excluding defendants) who owned common stock of Mercury from 1993 through the present and their successors in interest, heirs and assigns (the "putative class"). The complaint alleged that the directors "knowingly and intentionally breached their fiduciary duty of disclosure because the SEC filings made by the directors and every communication from the company to the shareholders since 1994 was materially false" and that "as a direct result of the false disclosures . . . the Company has lost all or virtually all of its value (about $2 billion)." The complaint also alleged that KPMG knowingly participated in the directors' breaches of their fiduciary duty of disclosure.

According to plaintiffs, since 1994, the director defendants caused Mercury to disseminate information containing overstatements of Mercury's earnings, financial performance and shareholders' equity. Mercury's earnings for 1996 were actually only $56.7 million, or $.33 a share, rather than the $120.7 million, or $.70 a share, as reported by the director defendants. Mercury's earnings in 1995 were actually $76.9 million, or $.44 a share, rather than $98.9 million, or $.57 a share, as reported by the director defendants. Mercury's earnings for 1994 were $83 million, or $.47 a share, rather than $86.5 million, or $.49 a share, as reported by the director defendants. Mercury's earnings for 1993 were $64.2 million, rather than $64.9 million, as reported by the director defendants. Shareholders' equity on December 31, 1996 was disclosed by the director defendants as $353 million, but was only $263 million or less. The complaint alleged that all of the foregoing inaccurate information was included or referenced in virtually every filing Mercury made with the SEC and every communication Mercury's directors made to the shareholders during this period of time.

Having alleged these violations of fiduciary duty, which (if true) are egregious, plaintiffs alleged that as "a direct result of [these] false disclosures . . . the company has lost all or virtually all its value (about $2 billion)," and seeks class action status to pursue damages against the directors and KPMG for the individual plaintiffs and common stockholders. The individual director defendants filed a motion to dismiss, contending that they owed no fiduciary duty of disclosure under the circumstances alleged in the complaint. KPMG also filed a motion to dismiss the aiding and abetting claim asserted against it.

After briefing and oral argument, the Court of Chancery granted both of the motions to dismiss with prejudice. The Court of Chancery held that directors have no fiduciary duty of disclosure under Delaware law in the absence of a request for shareholder action. In so holding, the Court stated:

> The federal securities laws ensure the timely release of accurate information into the marketplace. The federal power to regulate should not be duplicated or impliedly usurped by Delaware. When a shareholder is damaged merely as a result of the release of inaccurate information into the marketplace, uncon-

nected with any Delaware corporate governance issue, that shareholder must seek a remedy under federal law.

We disagree, and although we hold that the Complaint as drafted should have been dismissed, our rationale is different.

Standard of Review

A motion to dismiss a complaint presents the trial court with a question of law and is subject to de novo review by this Court on appeal. This Court and the trial court must accept all well-pleaded allegations of fact as true. A complaint should be dismissed for failure to state a claim only when it appears "with a reasonable certainty that a plaintiff would not be entitled to the relief sought under any set of facts which could be proven to support the action."

Issue On Appeal

This Court has held that a board of directors is under a fiduciary duty to disclose material information when seeking shareholder action:

> It is well-established that the duty of disclosure "represents nothing more than the well-recognized proposition that directors of Delaware corporations are under a fiduciary duty to disclose fully and fairly all material information within the board's control when it seeks shareholder action."[6]

The majority of opinions from the Court of Chancery have held that there may be a cause of action for disclosure violations only where directors seek shareholder action.[7] The present appeal requires this Court to decide whether a director's fiduciary duty arising out of misdisclosure is implicated in the absence of a request for shareholder action. We hold that directors who knowingly disseminate false information that results in corporate injury or damage to an individual stockholder violate their fiduciary duty, and may be held accountable in a manner appropriate to the circumstances.

Fiduciary Duty
Delaware Corporate Directors

An underlying premise for the imposition of fiduciary duties is a separation of legal control from beneficial ownership. Equitable principles act in those circumstances to protect the beneficiaries who are not in a position to protect themselves. One of the fundamental tenets of Delaware corporate law provides for a separation of control and ownership. The board of directors has the legal

---

6. *Zirn v. VLI Corp.*, Del.Supr., 681 A.2d 1050, 1056 (1996) quoting Stroud v. Grace, 606 A.2d at 84 (emphasis added).

7. *Kahn v. Roberts*, Del.Supr., 679 A.2d 460, 467 (1996) (collecting cases). *Cf. Ciro, Inc. v. Gold*, D. Del., 816 F.Supp. 253, 267 (1993).

responsibility to manage the business of a corporation for the benefit of its shareholder owners. Accordingly, fiduciary duties are imposed on the directors of Delaware corporations to regulate their conduct when they discharge that function.

The directors of Delaware corporations stand in a fiduciary relationship not only to the stockholders but also to the corporations upon whose boards they serve.[12] The director's fiduciary duty to both the corporation and its shareholders has been characterized by this Court as a triad: due care, good faith, and loyalty.[13] That triparte fiduciary duty does not operate intermittently but is the constant compass by which all director actions for the corporation and interactions with its shareholders must be guided.

Although the fiduciary duty of a Delaware director is unremitting, the exact course of conduct that must be charted to properly discharge that responsibility will change in the specific context of the action the director is taking with regard to either the corporation or its shareholders. This Court has endeavored to provide the directors with clear signal beacons and brightly lined-channel markers as they navigate with due care, good faith, and loyalty on behalf of a Delaware corporation and its shareholders. This Court has also endeavored to mark the safe harbors clearly.

Director Communications
Shareholder Reliance Justified

The shareholder constituents of a Delaware corporation are entitled to rely upon their elected directors to discharge their fiduciary duties at all times. Whenever directors communicate publicly or directly with shareholders about the corporation's affairs, with or without a request for shareholder action, directors have a fiduciary duty to shareholders to exercise due care, good faith and loyalty. It follows a fortiori that when directors communicate publicly or directly with shareholders about corporate matters the sine qua non of directors' fiduciary duty to shareholders is honesty.[17]

According to the appellants, the focus of the fiduciary duty of disclosure is to protect shareholders as the "beneficiaries" of all material information disseminated by the directors. The duty of disclosure is, and always has been, a specific application of the general fiduciary duty owed by directors. The duty of disclosure obligates directors to provide the stockholders with accurate and

---

12. *Guth v. Loft*, Del.Supr., 5 A.2d 503, 510 (1939). *See David A. Drexler et al.,* Delaware Corporation Law § 15.02 (Matthew Bender 1988).

13. *Cede & Co. v. Technicolor, Inc.*, Del. Supr., 634 A.2d 345, 361 (1993).

17. *Marhart, Inc. v. Calmat Co.*, Del. Ch., CA. No. 11820, Berger, V.C., 1992 WL 212587 (Apr. 22, 1992), slip op. at 6 (reported in 18 Del. J. Corp. L. 330 (1992)) ("Delaware directors are fiduciaries and are held to a high standard of conduct.... It is entirely consistent with this settled principle of law that fiduciaries who undertake the responsibility of informing shareholders about corporate affairs, be required to do so honestly.").

complete information material to a transaction or other corporate event that is being presented to them for action.

The issue in this case is not whether Mercury's directors breached their duty of disclosure. It is whether they breached their more general fiduciary duty of loyalty and good faith by knowingly disseminating to the stockholders false information about the financial condition of the company. The directors' fiduciary duties include the duty to deal with their stockholders honestly.

Shareholders are entitled to rely upon the truthfulness of all information disseminated to them by the directors they elect to manage the corporate enterprise. Delaware directors disseminate information in at least three contexts: public statements made to the market, including shareholders; statements informing shareholders about the affairs of the corporation without a request for shareholder action; and, statements to shareholders in conjunction with a request for shareholder action. Inaccurate information in these contexts may be the result of violation of the fiduciary duties of care, loyalty or good faith. We will examine the remedies that are available to shareholders for misrepresentations in each of these three contexts by the directors of a Delaware corporation.

State Fiduciary Disclosure Duty
Shareholder Remedy In Action Requested Context

In the absence of a request for stockholder action, the Delaware General Corporation Law does not require directors to provide shareholders with information concerning the finances or affairs of the corporation. Even when shareholder action is sought, the provisions in the General Corporation Law requiring notice to the shareholders of the proposed action do not require the directors to convey substantive information beyond a statutory minimum.[20] Consequently, in the context of a request for shareholder action, the protection afforded by Delaware law is a judicially recognized equitable cause of action by shareholders against directors.

The fiduciary duty of directors in connection with disclosure violations in Delaware jurisprudence was restated in *Lynch v. Vickers Energy Corp.*, Del.Supr., 383 A.2d 278 (1977). In *Lynch*, this Court held that, in making a tender offer to acquire the stock of the minority stockholders, a majority stockholder "owed a fiduciary duty ... which required 'complete candor' in disclosing fully 'all the facts and circumstances surrounding the' tender offer."[21] In

---

20. See *Stroud v. Grace*, 606 A.2d at 85 (discussing 8 Del. C. § 222(a) and 242(b)(1)).

21. *Lynch v. Vickers Energy Corp.*, Del. Supr., 383 A.2d 278, 279 (1977) quoting *Lynch v. Vickers Energy Corp.*, Del. Ch., 351 A.2d 570, 573 (1976); *accord Shell Petroleum, Inc. v. Smith*, Del.Supr., 606 A.2d 112,

114–15 (1992) (majority stockholder bears burden of showing full disclosure of all facts within its knowledge that are material to stockholder action). The fiduciary duty of disclosure is also applicable to directors of a Delaware corporation, *In re Anderson, Clayton Shareholders Litig.*, Del. Ch., 519 A.2d 680, 688–90 (1986); *Smith v. Van Gorkom*,

Stroud v. Grace, we noted that the language of our jurisprudence should be clarified to the extent that "candor" requires no more than the duty to disclose all material facts when seeking stockholder action.[22] An article by Professor Lawrence Hamermesh[23] includes an excellent historical summary of the content, context, and parameters of the law of disclosure, as it has been developed in a series of decisions during the last two decades.

The duty of directors to observe proper disclosure requirements derives from the combination of the fiduciary duties of care, loyalty and good faith.[25] The plaintiffs contend that, because directors fiduciary responsibilities are not "intermittent duties," there is no reason why the duty of disclosure should not be implicated in every public communication by a corporate board of directors. The directors of a Delaware corporation are required to disclose fully and fairly all material information within the board's control when it seeks shareholder action. When the directors disseminate information to stockholders when no stockholder action is sought, the fiduciary duties of care, loyalty and good faith apply. Dissemination of false information could violate one or more of those duties.

An action for a breach of fiduciary duty arising out of disclosure violations in connection with a request for stockholder action does not include the elements of reliance, causation and actual quantifiable monetary damages.[27] Instead, such actions require the challenged disclosure to have a connection to the request for shareholder action. The essential inquiry in such an action is whether the alleged omission or misrepresentation is material. Materiality is determined with respect to the shareholder action being sought.

The directors' duty to disclose all available material information in connection with a request for shareholder action must be balanced against its concomitant duty to protect the corporate enterprise, in particular, by keeping certain financial information confidential. Directors are required to provide shareholders with all information that is material to the action being requested and to provide a balanced, truthful account of all matters disclosed in the communications with shareholders.[31] Accordingly, directors have

Del. Supr ., 488 A.2d 858, 890 (1985) and to less-than-majority shareholders who control or affirmatively attempt to mandate the destiny of the corporation. *In re Tri–Star Pictures, Inc. Litig.*, 634 A.2d at 328–29.

22. *Stroud v. Grace*, 606 A.2d at 84.

23. Lawrence A. Hamermesh, Calling Off the Lynch Mob: A Corporate Director's Fiduciary Disclosure Duty, 49 *Vand. L.Rev.* 1087, 1174 n. 394 (1996).

25. *See Cinerama, Inc. v. Technicolor, Inc.*, Del. Supr, 663 A.2d 1156, 1160 (1995); *Zirn v. VLI Corp.*, 621 A.2d at 778.

27. *See Cinerama, Inc. v. Technicolor, Inc.*, 663 A.2d at 1163; *In re Tri–Star Pic-*

tures, Inc. Litig., 634 A.2d at 327 n. 10 and 333. *Loudon v. Archer–Daniels–Midland Co.*, 700 A.2d at 142 ("where directors have breached their disclosure duties in a corporate transaction ... there must at least be an award of nominal damages.").

31. *Zirn v. VLI Corp.*, 681 A.2d at 1056. In *Zirn II*, this Court held, "in addition to the traditional duty to disclose all facts material to the proffered transaction, directors are under a fiduciary obligation to avoid misleading partial disclosures. The law of partial disclosure is likewise clear: Once defendants travel down the road of partial disclosure they have an obligation to

definitive guidance in discharging their fiduciary duty by an analysis of the factual circumstances relating to the specific shareholder action being requested and an inquiry into the potential for deception or misinformation.[32]

Fraud On Market Regulated by Federal Law

When corporate directors impart information they must comport with the obligations imposed by both the Delaware law and the federal statutes and regulations of the United States Securities and Exchange Commission ("SEC"). Historically, federal law has regulated disclosures by corporate directors into the general interstate market. This Court has noted that "in observing its congressional mandate the SEC has adopted a 'basic philosophy of disclosure.' "[35] Accordingly, this Court has held that there is "no legitimate basis to create a new cause of action which would replicate, by state decisional law, the provisions of . . . the 1934 Act."[36] In deference to the panoply of federal protections that are available to investors in connection with the purchase or sale of securities of Delaware corporations, this Court has decided not to recognize a state common law cause of action against the directors of Delaware corporations for "fraud on the market."[37] Here, it is to be noted, the claim appears to be made by those who did not sell and, therefore, would not implicate federal securities laws which relate to the purchase or sale of securities.

The historic roles played by state and federal law in regulating corporate disclosures have been not only compatible but complementary.[38] That symbiotic relationship has been perpetuated by the recently enacted federal Securities Litigation Uniform Standards Act of 1998.[39] Although that statute by its terms does not apply to this case, the new statute will require securities class actions involving the purchase or sale of nationally traded securities, based upon false or misleading statements, to be brought exclusively in federal court

provide the stockholders with an accurate, full and fair characterization of those historic events." (internal quotations omitted).

32. See Zirn v. VLI Corp., 681 A.2d at 1062 ("a good faith erroneous judgment as to the proper scope or content of required disclosure implicates the duty of care rather than the duty of loyalty."); Arnold v. Society for Savings Bancorp, 650 A.2d at 1287–88 & n. 36.

35. Stroud v. Grace, Del.Supr., 606 A.2d 75, 86 (1992). See, e.g., Randall S. Thomas & Catherine T. Dixon, Aranow & Einhorn on Proxy Contests for Corporation Control, § 21.02 (3d ed.1998).

36. Arnold v. Society for Savings Bancorp, Inc., Del.Supr., 678 A.2d 533, 539 (1996).

37. Gaffin v. Teledyne, Inc., Del.Supr., 611 A.2d 467, 472 (1992). See Basic Incorporated v. Levinson, 485 U.S. 224, 241–42, 108 S.Ct. 978, 99 L.Ed.2d 194 (1988) (discussing the theory of fraud on the market).

38. See Santa Fe Industries, Inc. v. Green, 430 U.S. 462, 474–80, 97 S.Ct. 1292, 51 L.Ed.2d 480 (1977) (discussing state corporation law and the purpose of disclosure in federal securities law). Cf. Roberta Romano, Empowering Investors: A Market Approach to Securities Regulation 107 Yale L.J. 2359 (1998) ("advocating fundamental reform of the current strategy toward securities regulation by implementing a regulatory approach of competitive federalism.").

39. Securities Litigation Uniform Standards Act of 1998, Pub.L. No. 105–353, 112 Stat. 3227 (1998).

under federal law. The 1998 Act, however, contains two important exceptions:[40] the first provides that an "exclusively derivative action brought by one or more shareholders on behalf of a corporation" is not preempted; the second preserves the availability of state court class actions, where state law already provides that corporate directors have fiduciary disclosure obligations to shareholders.[41] These exceptions have become known as the "Delaware carve-outs."[42]

We need not decide at this time, however, whether this new Act will have any effect on this litigation if plaintiffs elect to replead. See Section (c) of the Act:

> (c) Applicability.—The amendments made by this section shall not affect or apply to any action commenced before and pending on the date of enactment of this Act.

State Common Law Shareholder Remedy In Nonaction Context

Delaware law also protects shareholders who receive false communications from directors even in the absence of a request for shareholder action. When the directors are not seeking shareholder action, but are deliberately misinforming shareholders about the business of the corporation, either directly or by a public statement, there is a violation of fiduciary duty. That violation may result in a

---

40. Section 16(d) of the Act provides:

(d) Preservation of Certain Actions.—

(1) Actions under state law of state of incorporation.—

(A) Actions preserved.—Notwithstanding subsection (b) or (c), a covered class action described in subparagraph (B) of this paragraph that is based upon the statutory or common law of the State in which the issuer is incorporated (in the case of a corporation) or organized (in the case of any other entity) may be maintained in a State or Federal court by a private party.

(B) Permissible actions.—A covered class action is described in this subparagraph if it involves—

(i) the purchase or sale of securities by the issuer or an affiliate of the issuer exclusively from or to holders of equity securities of the issuer; or

(ii) any recommendation, position, or other communication with respect to the sale of securities of the issuer that—

(I) is made by or on behalf of the issuer or an affiliate of the issuer to holders of equity securities of the issuer; and

(II) concerns decisions of those equity holders with respect to voting their securities, acting in response to a tender or exchange offer, or exercising dissenters' or appraisal rights.

Securities Litigation Uniform Standards Act of 1998, Pub.L. No. 105–353, § 16(d) 112 Stat. 3227 (1998).

41. See, e.g., Zirn v. VLI Corp., 621 A.2d 773; Zirn v. VLI Corp., 681 A.2d at 1060–61. See also Michael A. Perino, Fraud and Federalism: Preempting Private State Securities Fraud Causes of Action, 50 Stan. L.Rev. 273 (1998).

42. The Senate Committee Report on the Act is instructive. It states, in part:

The Committee is keenly aware of the importance of state corporate law, specifically those states that have laws that establish a fiduciary duty of disclosure. It is not the intent of the Committee in adopting this legislation to interfere with state law regarding the duties and performance of an issuer's directors or officers in connection with a purchase or sale of securities by the issuer or an affiliate from current shareholders or communicating with existing shareholders with respect to voting their shares, acting in response to a tender or exchange offer, or exercising dissenters' or appraisal rights.

S. Rep. No. 105–182, at 11–12 (May 4, 1998).

derivative claim on behalf of the corporation or a cause of action for damages. There may also be a basis for equitable relief to remedy the violation.

Complaint Properly Dismissed No Shareholder Action Requested

Here the complaint alleges (if true) an egregious violation of fiduciary duty by the directors in knowingly disseminating materially false information. Then it alleges that the corporation lost about $2 billion in value as a result. Then it merely claims that the action is brought on behalf of the named plaintiffs and the putative class. It is a non sequitur rather than a syllogism.

The allegation in paragraph 3 that the false disclosures resulted in the corporation losing virtually all its equity seems obliquely to claim an injury to the corporation. The plaintiffs, however, never expressly assert a derivative claim on behalf of the corporation or allege compliance with Court of Chancery Rule 23.1, which requires pre-suit demand or cognizable and particularized allegations that demand is excused.[44] If the plaintiffs intend to assert a derivative claim,[45] they should be permitted to replead to assert such a claim and any damage or equitable remedy sought on behalf of the corporation.[46] Likewise, the plaintiffs should have the opportunity to replead to assert any individual cause of action and articulate a remedy that is appropriate on behalf of the named plaintiffs individually, or a properly recognizable class consistent with Court of Chancery Rule 23, and our decision in *Gaffin*.[47]

The Court of Chancery properly dismissed the complaint before it against the individual director defendants, in the absence of well-pleaded allegations stating a derivative, class or individual cause of action and properly assertable remedy. Without a well-pleaded allegation in the complaint for a breach of fiduciary duty, there can be no claim for aiding and abetting such a breach. Accordingly, the plaintiffs' aiding and abetting claim against KPMG was also properly dismissed.

---

44. It seems that plaintiffs have attempted to allege the basis for demand excusal by the very nature of the central claim that the directors knowingly misstated the company's financial condition, thus seemingly taking this case out of the business judgment rule because all the directors are alleged to be implicated in the wrongdoing.

45. This will require an articulation of the classic "direct v. derivative" theory. *See Grimes v. Donald*, Del.Supr., 673 A.2d 1207 (1996) (distinguishing individual and derivative actions).

46. We express no opinion whether equitable remedies such as injunctive relief, judicial removal of directors or disqualification from directorship could be asserted here. No such equitable relief has been sought in the current complaint. *See* Randall S. Thomas & Catherine T. Dixon, Aranow & Einhorn on *Proxy Contests for Corporate Control*, § 19.01 (3d ed.1998).

47. *Gaffin v. Teledyne, Inc.*, 611 A.2d 467, 474 (1992) ("A class action may not be maintained in a purely common law or equitable fraud case since individual questions of law or fact, particularly as to the element of justifiable reliance, will inevitably predominate over common questions of law or fact.") . . . .

Nevertheless, we disagree with the Court of Chancery's holding that such a claim cannot be articulated on these facts. The plaintiffs should have been permitted to amend their complaint, if possible, to state a properly cognizable cause of action against the individual defendants and KPMG. Consequently, the Court of Chancery should have dismissed the complaint without prejudice.

Conclusion

The judgment of the Court of Chancery to dismiss the complaint is affirmed. The judgment to dismiss the complaint with prejudice is reversed. This matter is remanded for further proceedings in accordance with this opinion.

———

Chapter X

SHAREHOLDER SUITS

SECTION 2. THE NATURE OF THE DERIVATIVE ACTION

Add the following material at p. 1016 of the Unabridged Edition, and p. 664 of the Concise Edition, at the end of Chapter X, Section 2:

GRIMES v. DONALD, 673 A.2d 1207 (Del.1996). DSC Communications Corp. entered into an Employment Agreement with James Donald, its CEO. Under the Agreement, Donald was entitled to very substantial severance payments if in his good faith judgment there was "substantial interference . . . by the Board . . . in [Donald's] carrying out" the general management and affairs of DSC. Grimes, a shareholder in DSC, brought an action seeking a declaration that the Agreement was invalid on the ground that the board had breached its fiduciary duties by abdicating its authority to Grimes. Held, the action was direct, not derivative:

> As the Court of Chancery has noted: "Although the tests have been articulated many times, it is often difficult to distinguish between a derivative and an individual action." In re Rexene Corp. Shareholders Litig., Del.Ch., 17 Del.J.Corp.L. 342, 348 (1991); see also Abelow v. Symonds, 38 Del.Ch. 572, 156 A.2d 416, 420 (1959) ("line of distinction . . . is often a narrow one . . ."). The distinction depends upon " 'the nature of the wrong alleged' and the relief, if any, which could result if plaintiff were to prevail." Kramer v. Western Pacific, 546 A.2d at 352 (quoting Elster v. American Airlines, Inc., 34 Del.Ch. 94, 100 A.2d 219, 221–223 (1953)). To pursue a direct action, the stockholder-plaintiff "must allege more than an injury resulting from a wrong to the corporation." Id. at 351. The plaintiff must state a claim for " 'an injury which is separate and distinct from that suffered by other shareholders,' . . . or a wrong involving a contractual right of a shareholder . . . which exists independently of any right of the corporation." Moran v. Household Int'l, Inc., 490 A.2d 1059, 1070, aff'd, Del.Supr., 500 A.2d 1346 (1985) (quoting 12B Fletcher Cyclopedia Corps., § 5291 (Perm.Ed.1984)).

212

The American Law Institute ("ALI") Principles of Corporate Governance: Analysis and Recommendations (1992) ("Principles") is helpful in this instance. Section 7.01 of the Principles undertakes to state the common law with respect to the distinction between direct and derivative actions. Id. § 7.01, cmt. a. The Comment also discusses a situation relevant to the case sub judice:

> In some instances, actions that essentially involve the structural relationship of the shareholder to the corporation . . . may also give rise to a derivative action when the corporation suffers or is threatened with a loss. One example would be a case in which a corporate official knowingly acts in a manner that the certificate of incorporation [or the Delaware General Corporation Law] denied the official authority to do, thereby violating both specific restraints imposed by the shareholders [or the GCL] and the official's duty of care.

Id., cmt. c. The Comment further notes that, "courts have been more prepared to permit the plaintiff to characterize the action as direct when the plaintiff is seeking only injunctive or prospective relief." Id., cmt. d.

With respect to the abdication claim, Grimes seeks only a declaration of the invalidity of the Agreements. Monetary recovery will not accrue to the corporation as a result. Chancellor Seitz illustrated this distinction in *Bennett*. The Court of Chancery there allowed the plaintiff-stockholder to proceed individually on his claim that stock was issued for an improper purpose and entrenchment; he proceeded derivatively on his claim that the stock was issued for an insufficient price. 99 A.2d at 241. . . .

Since the abdication claim is direct, not derivative, a motion to dismiss such a claim pursuant to Chancery Rule 12(b)(6) implicates the pleading standard of Chancery Rule 8(a). Solomon v. Pathe Communications Corp., 672 A.2d 35 (Del. Supr.1996), slip op. at 9, Hartnett, J. (Jan. 4, 1996). Neither the pleading standard of Chancery Rule 9(b) ("circumstances constituting fraud or mistake shall be stated with particularity") nor that of Chancery Rule 23.1 which requires, with respect to derivative claims, that a plaintiff plead "with particularity the efforts, if any . . . to obtain the action the plaintiff desires . . . and the reasons for the . . . failure to obtain the action or for not making the effort," is implicated. . . .

———

BARTH v. BARTH

Supreme Court of Indiana, 1995.
659 N.E.2d 559.

JUDGES: SULLIVAN, Justice, SHEPARD, C.J., and DeBRULER, DICK-SON and SELBY, JJ., concur.

SULLIVAN, Justice.

Background

This lawsuit was brought against defendants Barth Electric Co., Inc., and its president and majority shareholder Michael G. Barth, Jr., by plaintiff minority shareholder Robert Barth individually (rather than derivatively on behalf of the corporation).[1] Plaintiff Robert Barth alleged that defendant Michael Barth had taken certain actions which had the effect of "substantially reducing the value of Plaintiff's shares of common stock" in the corporation. Specifically, plaintiff contended that defendant Michael Barth had: (1) paid excessive salaries to himself and to members of his immediate family; (2) used corporate employees to perform services on his and his son's homes without compensating the corporation; (3) dramatically lowered dividend payments; and (4) appropriated corporate funds for personal investments. *Barth v. Barth* (Ind.App. 1995), 651 N.E.2d 291. Michael Barth and the corporation moved to dismiss Robert Barth's complaint for the failure to state a claim upon which relief can be granted, Ind. Trial Rule 12(B)(6), arguing that a derivative action was required to redress claims of this nature. The trial court granted the motion to dismiss. The Court of Appeals acknowledged that the "well-established general rule" prohibits a shareholder from maintaining an action in the shareholder's own name but found that requiring a derivative action here would "exalt form over substance" since Robert Barth could have satisfied the requirements for bringing a derivative action and that none of the reasons underlying the general derivative action requirement were present. *Barth v. Barth*, 651 N.E.2d at 293. The Court of Appeals reversed the trial court; the corporation and Michael Barth seek transfer.

Discussion

As the Court of Appeals made clear, the well-established general rule is that shareholders of a corporation may not maintain actions at law in their own names to redress an injury to the corporation even if the value of their stock is impaired as a result of the injury. *Moll v. South Central Solar Systems, Inc.* (Ind.App.1981), 419 N.E.2d 154, 161 . . . . In *Moll*, Judge Ratliff discussed the purpose of the rule in the following terms:

---

1. Michael Barth owns 51% of the shares of the corporation. Robert Barth owns 29.8%. A third individual owns the remaining shares.

The rationale supporting this rule is based on sound public policy considerations. It is recognized that authorization of shareholder actions in such cases would constitute authorization of multitudinous litigation and disregard for the corporate entity. ... Sound policy considerations have been said to require that a single action be brought rather than to permit separate suits by each shareholder even when the corporation and the shareholder are the same. ...

Moll, 419 N.E.2d at 161. In W & W Equipment Co., Inc. v. Mink (1991), Ind.App., 568 N.E.2d 564, Judge Baker set forth additional reasons for this rule: the protection of corporate creditors by putting the proceeds of the recovery back in the corporation; the protection of the interests of all the shareholders rather than allowing one shareholder to prejudice the interests of other shareholders; and the adequate compensation of the injured shareholder by increasing the value of the shares when recovery is put back into the corporation. *Id.,* 568 N.E.2d at 571 (citing *Caswell v. Jordan* (1987), 184 Ga.App. 755, 362 S.E.2d 769, cert. denied).

While we affirm the general rule requiring a shareholder to bring a derivative rather than direct action when seeking redress for injury to the corporation, we nevertheless observe two reasons why this rule will not always apply in the case of closely-held corporations.[5] First, shareholders in a close corporation stand in a fiduciary relationship to each other, and as such, must deal fairly, honestly, and openly with the corporation and with their fellow shareholders. *W & W Equipment Co.,* 568 N.E.2d at 570; *Krukemeier v. Krukemeier Machine and Tool Co., Inc.* (Ind.App.1990), 551 N.E.2d 885; *Garbe v. Excel Mold, Inc.* (Ind.App.1979), 397 N.E.2d 296.[6] Second, shareholder litigation in the closely-held corporation context will often not implicate the policies that mandate requiring derivative litigation when more widely-held corporations are involved. W & W Equipment Co., Inc. v. Mink is a leading case in this regard. There our Court of Appeals was faced with a lawsuit filed by one of two 50% shareholders of a corporation after the other shareholder joined with nonshareholder directors to fire the plaintiff shareholder and arrange for the payment of certain corporate assets to the other shareholder. The court concluded that no useful purpose would be served by forcing the plaintiff to proceed derivatively where the policies favoring derivative actions were not implicated—

5. A closely-held corporation is one which typically has relatively few shareholders and whose shares are not generally traded in the securities market. *W & W Equipment Co., Inc. v. Mink* (Ind.App.1991), 568 N.E.2d 564, 570 (citing F. Hodge O'Neal & Robert B. Thompson, O'Neal's Close Corporations § 1.02 (3d ed.)). Accord, American Law Institute, Principles of Corporate Governance: Analysis and Recommendations § 1.06 (1994).

6. This principle of Indiana corporate law mirrors that reached by the Supreme Judicial Court of Massachusetts in .... *Donahue v. Rodd Electrotype Co. of New England, Inc.,* 367 Mass. 578, 328 N.E.2d 505, 515 (Mass.1975) ....

direct corporate recovery was not necessary to protect absent shareholders or creditors as none existed. *Id.,* 568 N.E.2d at 571.

Because shareholders of closely-held corporations have very direct obligations to one another and because shareholder litigation in the closely-held corporation context will often not implicate the principles which gave rise to the rule requiring derivative litigation, courts in many cases are permitting direct suits by shareholders of closely-held corporations where the complaint is one that in a public corporation would have to be brought as a derivative action. See F. Hodge O'Neal & Robert B. Thompson, O'Neal's Close Corporations § 8.16 n. 32 (3d ed. & 1995 Cum.Supp.) (collecting cases); American Law Institute, Principles of Corporate Governance: Analysis and Recommendations § 7.01, reporter's n. 4 (1994) (collecting cases). However, it is important to keep in mind that the principles which gave rise to the rule requiring derivative actions will sometimes be present even in litigation involving closely-held corporations. For example, because a corporate recovery in a derivative action will benefit creditors while a direct recovery by a shareholder will not, the protection of creditors principle could well be implicated in a shareholder suit against a closely-held corporation with debt. ...

In its recently-completed corporate governance project, the American Law Institute proposed the following rule for determining when a shareholder of a closely-held corporation may proceed by direct or derivative action:

> In the case of a closely held corporation, the court in its discretion may treat an action raising derivative claims as a direct action, exempt it from those restrictions and defenses applicable only to derivative actions, and order an individual recovery, if it finds that to do so will not (i) unfairly expose the corporation or the defendants to a multiplicity of actions, (ii) materially prejudice the interests of creditors of the corporation, or (iii) interfere with a fair distribution of the recovery among all interested persons.

A.L.I., Principles of Corporate Governance § 7.01(d). We have studied this rule and find that it is consistent with the approach taken by our Court of Appeals and by most other jurisdictions in similar cases and that it represents a fair and workable approach for balancing the relative interests in closely-held corporation shareholder litigation.

In determining that a trial court has discretion to decide whether a plaintiff must proceed by direct or by derivative action, we make the following observations, drawn largely from the Comment to § 7.01(d). First, permitting such litigation to proceed as a direct action will exempt the plaintiff from the requirements of Ind.Code § 23–1–32–1 et seq., including the provisions that permit a special committee of the board of directors to recommend dismissal of the lawsuit. Ind.Code § 23–1–32–4. As such, the court in making its decision should consider whether the corporation has a disinterested board that should be permitted to consider the lawsuit's impact on the corporation. A.L.I., Corporate Governance Project § 7.01 comment e. Second, in some situations it may actually be to the benefit of the corporation to permit the plaintiff to proceed by direct action. This will permit the defendant to file a counterclaim against the plaintiff, whereas counterclaims are generally prohibited in derivative actions. Also, in a direct action each side will normally be responsible for its own legal expenses; the plaintiff, even if successful, cannot ordinarily look to the corporation for attorney's fees. Id.

Conclusion

We grant transfer, vacate the opinion of the Court of Appeals, and remand this cause to the trial court for reconsideration of its order of dismissal in light of the rule adopted in this opinion.

SHEPARD, C.J., and DeBRULER, DICKSON and SELBY, JJ., concur.

SECTION 6. DEMAND ON THE BOARD AND TERMINATION OF DERIVATIVE ACTIONS ON THE RECOMMENDATION OF THE BOARD OR A COMMITTEE

Delete Barr v. Wackman, at p. 1034 of the Unabridged Edition and p. 679 of the Concise Edition, and insert the following case in its place:

MARX v. AKERS

New York Court of Appeals, 1996.
88 N.Y.2d 189, 644 N.Y.S.2d 121, 666 N.E.2d 1034.

JUDGES: Opinion by Judge SMITH. Chief Judge KAYE and Judges SIMONS, TITONE, LEVINE and CIPARICK concur. Judge BELLACOSA took no part.

SMITH, J.:

Plaintiff commenced this shareholder derivative action against International Business Machines Corporation (IBM) and IBM's board of directors without first demanding that the board initiate a lawsuit. The amended complaint (complaint) alleges that the board wasted corporate assets by awarding excessive compensation to IBM's executives and outside directors. The issues raised on this appeal are whether the Appellate Division abused its discretion by dismissing plaintiff's complaint for failure to make a demand and whether plaintiff's complaint fails to state a cause of action. We affirm the order of the Appellate Division because we conclude that plaintiff was not excused from making a demand with respect to the executive compensation claim and that plaintiff has failed to state a cause of action for corporate waste in connection with the allegations concerning payments to IBM's outside directors.

Facts and Procedural History

The complaint alleges that during a period of declining profitability at IBM the director defendants engaged in self-dealing by awarding excessive compensation to the 15 outside directors on the 18–member board. Although the complaint identifies only one of the three inside directors as an IBM executive (defendant Akers is identified as a former chief executive officer of IBM),[1] plaintiff also appears to allege that the director defendants violated their fiduciary duties to IBM by voting for unreasonably high compensation for IBM executives.[2]

Defendants moved to dismiss the complaint for (1) failure to state a cause of action, and (2) failure to serve a demand on IBM's board to initiate a lawsuit based on the complaint's allegations. The Supreme Court dismissed, holding that plaintiff failed to establish the futility of a demand. Supreme Court concluded that excusing a demand here would render Business Corporation Law § 626(c) "virtually meaningless in any shareholders' derivative action in which all members of a corporate board are named as defendants." Having decided the demand issue in favor of defendants, the court did not reach the issue of whether plaintiff's complaint stated a cause of action. The Appellate Division affirmed the dismissal, concluding that the complaint did not contain any details from which the futility of a demand could be inferred. The Appellate Division found that plaintiff's objections to the level of compensation were not stated with sufficient particularity in light of statutory authority permitting directors to set their own compensation.

Background

A shareholder's derivative action is an action "brought in the right of a domestic or foreign corporation to procure a judgment in its favor, by a holder of shares or of voting trust certificates of the corporation or of a beneficial interest in such shares or certificates"

---

1. The other inside directors, although identified as Employee Directors, are never explicitly identified as executive officers in the complaint. However, the names of these directors appear on a chart disclosing "payments to certain executives."

2. Executives at IBM are compensated through a fixed salary and performance incentives. Payouts on the performance incentives are based on IBM's earnings per share, return on equity and cash flow. Plaintiff's complaint criticizes only the performance incentive component of executive compensation as excessive because of certain accounting practices which plaintiff alleges artificially inflate earnings, return on equity and cash flow.

(Business Corporation Law § 626[a]). "Derivative claims against corporate directors belong to the corporation itself" (Auerbach v. Bennett, 47 N.Y. 2d 619, 631).

> "The remedy sought is for wrong done to the corporation; the primary cause of action belongs to the corporation; recovery must enure to the benefit of the corporation. The stockholder brings the action, in behalf of others similarly situated, to vindicate the corporate rights and a judgment on the merits is a binding adjudication of these rights (citations omitted)" (Isaac v. Marcus, 258 N.Y. 257, 264).

Business Corporation Law § 626(c) provides that in any shareholders' derivative action, "the complaint shall set forth with particularity the efforts of the plaintiff to secure the initiation of such action by the board or the reasons for not making such effort." Enacted in 1961 (L 1961, ch 855), section 626(c) codified a rule of equity developed in early shareholder derivative actions requiring plaintiffs to demand that the corporation initiate an action, unless such demand was futile, before commencing an action on the corporation's behalf (Barr v. Wackman, 36 N.Y. 2d 371, 377).[3] The purposes of the demand requirement are to (1) relieve courts from deciding matters of internal corporate governance by providing corporate directors with opportunities to correct alleged abuses, (2) provide corporate boards with reasonable protection from harassment by litigation on matters clearly within the discretion of directors, and (3) discourage "strike suits" commenced by shareholders for personal gain rather than for the benefit of the corporation (Barr, 36 NY2d at 378). "The demand is generally designed to weed out unnecessary or illegitimate shareholder derivative suits" (id.).

By their very nature, shareholder derivative actions infringe upon the managerial discretion of corporate boards. "As with other questions of corporate policy and management, the decision whether and to what extent to explore and prosecute such [derivative] claims lies within the judgment and control of the corporation's board of directors" (Auerbach, supra, 47 NY2d at 631). Consequently, we have historically been reluctant to permit shareholder derivative suits, noting that the power of courts to direct the management of a corporation's affairs should be "exercised with restraint" (Gordon v. Elliman, 306 N.Y. 456, 462).

In permitting a shareholder derivative action to proceed because a demand on the corporation's directors would be futile,

> "the object is for the court to chart the course for the corporation which the directors should have selected, and which it is presumed that they would have chosen if they had not been

---

3. Section 626(c) was also partially based on former rule 23(b) (now rule 23.1) of the Federal Rules of Civil Procedure (see, Legislative Studies and Reports, McKinney's Cons Laws of NY, Book 6, Business Corporation Law § 626 at 351).

actuated by fraud or bad faith. Due to their misconduct, the court substitutes its judgment ad hoc for that of the directors in the conduct of its business" (id. at 462).

Achieving a balance between preserving the discretion of directors to manage a corporation without undue interference, through the demand requirement, and permitting shareholders to bring claims on behalf of the corporation when it is evident that directors will wrongfully refuse to bring such claims, through the demand futility exception, has been accomplished by various jurisdictions in different ways. One widely cited approach to demand futility which attempts to balance these competing concerns has been developed by Delaware courts and applies a two-pronged test to each case to determine whether a failure to serve a demand is justified. At the other end of the spectrum is a universal demand requirement which would abandon particularized determinations in favor of requiring a demand in every case before a shareholder derivative suit may be filed.

The Delaware Approach

Delaware's demand requirement, codified in Delaware Chancery Court Rule 23.1, provides, in relevant part,

> "In a derivative action brought by 1 or more shareholders or members to enforce a right of a corporation * * * [the complaint shall allege] with particularity the efforts, if any, made by the plaintiff to obtain the action the plaintiff desires from the directors or comparable authority and the reasons for the plaintiff's failure to obtain the action or for not making the effort."

Interpreting Rule 23.1, the Delaware Supreme Court in Aronson v. Lewis (473 A.2d 805) developed a two-prong test for determining the futility of a demand. Plaintiffs must allege particularized facts which create a reasonable doubt that,

> "(1) the directors are disinterested and independent and (2) the challenged transaction was otherwise the product of a valid exercise of business judgment. Hence, the Court of Chancery must make two inquiries, one into the independence and disinterestedness of the directors and the other into the substantive nature of the challenged transaction and the board's approval thereof" (473 A2d at 814).

The two branches of the *Aronson* test are disjunctive (see, Levine v. Smith, 591 A.2d 194, 205). Once director interest has been established, the business judgment rule becomes inapplicable and the demand excused without further inquiry (*Aronson*, 473 A2d at 814). Similarly, a director whose independence is compromised by undue influence exerted by an interested party cannot properly exercise business judgment and the loss of independence also justifies the excusal of a demand without further inquiry (see,

Levine, supra, 591 A2d at 205–206). Whether a board has validly exercised its business judgment must be evaluated by determining whether the directors exercised procedural (informed decision) and substantive (terms of the transaction) due care (Grobow v. Perot, 539 A.2d 180, 189).

The reasonable doubt threshold of Delaware's two-fold approach to demand futility has been criticized. The use of a standard of proof which is the heart of a jury's determination in a criminal case has raised questions concerning its applicability in the corporate context (see, Starrels v. First Natl. Bank, 870 F.2d 1168, 1175 (7th Cir.)) [Easterbrook, J, concurring]. The reasonable doubt standard has also been criticized as overly subjective, thereby permitting a wide variance in the application of Delaware law to similar facts (2 American Law Institute, Principles of Corporate Governance: Analysis and Recommendations § 7.03, Comment d at 57 [1992]).

Universal Demand

A universal demand requirement would dispense with the necessity of making case-specific determinations and impose an easily applied bright line rule. The Business Law Section of the American Bar Association has proposed requiring a demand in all cases, without exception, and permits the commencement of a derivative proceeding within 90 days of the demand unless the demand is rejected earlier (Model Business Corporation Act § 7.42[1] [1995 Supplement]). However, plaintiffs may file suit before the expiration of 90 days, even if their demand has not been rejected, if the corporation would suffer irreparable injury as a result (Model Business Corporation Act § 7.42[2]).

The American Law Institute (ALI) has also proposed a "universal" demand. Section 7.03 of ALI's Principles of Corporate Governance would require shareholder derivative action plaintiffs to serve a written demand on the corporation unless a demand is excused because "the plaintiff makes a specific showing that irreparable injury to the corporation would otherwise result" (2 American Law Institute, Principles of Corporate Governance: Analysis and Recommendations, § 7.03[b] at 53–54, [1992]). Once a demand has been made and rejected, however, the ALI would subject the board's decision to "an elaborate set of standards that calibrates the deference afforded the decision of the directors to the character of the claim being asserted" (Kamen v. Kemper Financial Services, Inc., 500 U.S. 90, 104).

At least 11 states have adopted, by statute, the universal demand requirement proposed in the Model Business Corporation Act. Georgia, Michigan, Wisconsin, Montana, Virginia, New Hampshire, Mississippi, Connecticut, Nebraska and North Carolina require shareholders to wait 90 days after serving a demand before filing a derivative suit unless the demand is rejected before the expiration of the 90 days, or irreparable injury to the corporation would result (see, Ga Code Ann § 14–2–742 [enacted 1988]; Mich Comp Laws § 450.1493a [enacted 1989]; Wis Stat § 180.0742 [enacted 1991]; Mont Code Ann § 35–1–543 [enacted 1991]; Va Code Ann § 13.1–672.1 [enacted 1992]; NH Rev Stat Ann § 293–A:7.42 [enacted 1992]; Miss Code Ann § 79–4–7.42 [enacted 1993]; Conn Gen Stat § 33–722 [enacted 1994, effective Jan. 1, 1997]; Neb Rev Stat § 21–2072 [enacted 1995]; NC Gen Stat § 55–742 [enacted 1995]). Arizona additionally permits shareholders to file suit before the expiration of 90 days if the statute of limitations would expire during the 90 day period (Ariz Rev Stat Ann § 10–742 [enacted 1994]). Florida also appears to have adopted a universal demand requirement, although the statutory language does not track the Model Business Corporation Act. Florida's statute provides, "A complaint in a proceeding brought in the right of a corporation must be verified and allege with particularity the demand made to obtain action by the board of directors and that the demand was refused or ignored (emphasis added)" (Fla Stat Ann § 607.07401[2]).

New York State has also considered and continues to consider implementing a universal demand requirement. However, even though bills to adopt a universal demand have been presented over three legislative sessions, the Legislature has yet to enact a universal demand requirement [4] (see, e.g., S6395/A8897 [1991/92 Legislative Session] ["An act to amend the business corporation law, in relation to shareholder derivative suits"]; S1018 ["An act to amend the business corporation law and the civil practice law and rules, in relation to shareholder derivative suits"] and S6222 ["An act to amend the business corporation law and the civil practice law and rules, in relation to shareholder derivative suits and providing for the repeal of certain provisions upon expiration thereof"] [1993/94 Legislative Session]; S1117/A1629 [1995/96 Legislative Session] ["An act to amend the business corporation law and the civil practice law and rules, in relation to shareholder derivative suits and providing for the repeal of certain provisions upon expiration thereof"]).

New York's Approach to Demand Futility

Although instructive, neither the universal demand requirement nor the Delaware approach to demand futility is adopted here.

---

4. The most recent bill (S1117/A1629), which is currently pending in the 1995/96 Legislative Session, proposes the following requirement:

"(C) Demand. No shareholder may commence a derivative proceeding until:

(1) a written demand has been made on the corporation to take suitable action; and

(2) ninety days have expired from the date the demand was made, unless the shareholder has earlier been notified that the demand has been rejected by the corporation or unless irreparable injury to the corporation or extinguishment of the claim would result by waiting for the expiration of the ninety day period."

Since New York's demand requirement is codified in Business Corporation Law § 626(c), a universal demand can only be adopted by the Legislature. Delaware's approach, which resembles New York law in some respects, incorporates a "reasonable doubt" standard which, as we have already pointed out, has provoked criticism as confusing and overly subjective. An analysis of the *Barr* decision compels the conclusion that in New York, a demand would be futile if a complaint alleges with particularity that (1) a majority of the directors are interested in the transaction, or (2) the directors failed to inform themselves to a degree reasonably necessary about the transaction, or (3) the directors failed to exercise their business judgment in approving the transaction.

In Barr v. Wackman (36 N.Y. 2d 371, supra), we considered whether the plaintiff was excused from making a demand where the board of Talcott National Corporation (Talcott), consisting of 13 outside directors, a director affiliated with a related company and four interested inside directors, rejected a merger proposal involving Gulf & Western Industries (Gulf & Western) in favor of another proposal on allegedly less favorable terms for Talcott and its shareholders. The merger proposal, memorialized in a board-approved "agreement in principle," proposed exchanging one share of Talcott common stock for approximately $24.00 consisting of $17.00 in cash and 0.6 of a warrant to purchase Gulf & Western stock, worth approximately $7.00. This proposal was abandoned in favor of a cash tender offer for Talcott shares by Associated First Capital Corporation (a Gulf & Western subsidiary) at $20.00 per share— four dollars less than proposed for the merger.

The plaintiff in *Barr* alleged that Talcott's board discarded the merger proposal after the four "controlling" inside directors received pecuniary and personal benefits from Gulf & Western in exchange for ceding control of Talcott on terms less favorable to Talcott's shareholders. As alleged in the complaint, these benefits included new and favorable employment contracts for nine Talcott officers, including five-year employment contracts for three of the controlling directors. In addition to his annual salary of $125,000 with Talcott, defendant Silverman (a controlling director) would allegedly receive $60,000 a year under a five year employment contract with Associated First Capital, and an aggregate of $275,000 for the next five years in an arrangement with Associated First Capital to serve as a consultant. This additional compensation would be awarded to Silverman after control of Talcott passed to Associated First Capital and Gulf & Western. Plaintiff also alleged that Gulf & Western and Associated First Capital paid an excessive "finder's fee" of $340,000 to a company where Silverman's son was an executive vice president. In addition to alleging that the controlling defendants obtained personal benefits, the complaint also alleged that Talcott's board agreed to sell a Talcott subsidiary at a net loss of $6,100,000 solely to accommodate Gulf & Western.

In *Barr,* we held that insofar as the complaint attacked the controlling directors' acts in causing the corporation to enter into a transaction for their own financial benefit, demand was excused because of the self-dealing, or self-interest of those directors in the challenged transaction.   Specifically, we pointed to the allegation that the controlling directors "breached their fiduciary obligations to Talcott in return for personal benefits" (id., at 376).

We also held in *Barr,* however, that as to the disinterested outside directors, demand could be excused even in the absence of their receiving any financial benefit from the transaction.   That was because the complaint alleged that, by approving the terms of the less advantageous offer, those directors were guilty of a "breach of their duties of due care and diligence to the corporation" (id., at 380).   Their performance of the duty of care would have "put them on notice of the claimed self-dealing of the affiliated directors" (id.).   The complaint charged that the outside directors failed "to do more than passively rubber stamp the decisions of the active managers" (id., at 381) resulting in corporate detriment.   These allegations, the *Barr* Court concluded, also excused demand as to the charges against the disinterested directors.

Barr also makes clear that "it is not sufficient * * * merely to name a majority of the directors as parties defendant with the conclusory allegation of wrongdoing or control by wrongdoers" (id., at 379) to justify failure to make a demand.   Thus, *Barr* reflects the statutory requirement that the complaint "must set forth with particularity the * * * reasons for not making such effort" (Business Corporation Law § 626[c]).

Unfortunately, various courts have overlooked the explicit warning that conclusory allegations of wrongdoing against each member of the board are not sufficient to excuse demand and have misinterpreted *Barr* as excusing demand whenever a majority of the board members who approved the transaction are named as defendants (see, Miller v. Schreyer, 200 A.D. 2d 492; Curreri v. Verni, 156 A.D. 2d 420; MacKay v. Pierce, 86 A.D. 2d 655; Joseph v. Amrep Corp., 59 A.D. 2d 841; see also, Allison Publ. Inc. v. Mutual Benefit Life Ins., 197 A.D. 2d 463).   As stated most recently, "the rule is clear in this State that no demand is necessary 'if the complaint alleges acts for which a majority of the directors may be liable and plaintiff reasonably concluded that the board would not be responsive to a demand' " (Miller v Schreyer, supra, at 494 [quoting from *Barr,* supra, 36 N.Y.2d at 371]; but see, Lewis v. Welch, 126 A.D. 2d 519, 521).   The problem with such an approach is that it permits plaintiffs to frame their complaint in such a way as to automatically excuse demand, thereby allowing the exception to swallow the rule.

We thus deem it necessary to offer the following elaboration of *Barr's* demand/futility standard.   (1) Demand is excused because of futility when a complaint alleges with particularity that a majority of the board of directors is interested in the challenged transaction. Director interest may either be self-interest in the transaction at issue (see, Barr v Wackman, supra, at 376 [receipt of "personal benefits"]), or a loss of independence because a director with no direct interest in a transaction is "controlled" by a self-interested director. (2) Demand is excused because of futility when a complaint alleges with particularity that the board of directors did not fully inform themselves about the challenged transaction to the extent reasonably appropriate under the circumstances (see, *Barr,* supra, at 380). The "long-standing rule" is that a director "does not exempt himself from liability by failing to do more than passively rubber-stamp the decisions of the active managers" (id., at 381). (3) Demand is excused because of futility when a complaint alleges with particularity that the challenged transaction was so egregious on its face that it could not have been the product of sound business judgment of the directors.[5]

The Current Appeal

Plaintiff argues that the demand requirement was excused both because the outside directors awarded themselves generous compensation packages and because of the acquiescence of the disinterested directors in the executive compensation schemes. The complaint states:

"Plaintiff has made no demand upon the directors of IBM to institute this lawsuit because such demand would be futile. As set forth above, each of the directors authorized, approved, participated and/or acquiesced in the acts and transactions complained of herein and are liable therefor. Further, each of the Non–Employee [outside] Directors has received and retained the benefit of his excessive compensation and each of the other directors has received and retained the benefit of the incentive compensation described above. The defendants cannot be expected to vote to prosecute an action against themselves. Demand upon the company to bring action (sic) to redress the wrongs herein is therefore unnecessary."

Defendants argue that neither the Supreme Court nor the Appellate Division abused its discretion in holding that plaintiff's complaint did not set forth the futility of a demand with particularity.

As in *Barr,* we look to the complaint here to determine whether the allegations are sufficient and establish with particularity that demand would have been futile. Here, the plaintiff alleges that

---

5. "A director shall perform his duties as a director * * * in good faith and with that degree of care which an ordinarily prudent person in a like position would use under similar circumstances" (Business Corporation Law § 717; see also, *Auerbach,* 47 NY2d at 629 [observing that the business judgment doctrine "bars judicial inquiry into actions of corporate directors taken in good faith and in the exercise of honest judgment in the lawful and legitimate furtherance of corporate purposes"]).

the compensation awarded to IBM's outside directors and certain IBM executives was excessive.

Defendant's motion to dismiss for failure to make a demand as to the allegations concerning the compensation paid to IBM's executive officers was properly granted. A board is not interested "in voting compensation for one of its members as an executive or in some other nondirectorial capacity, such as a consultant to the corporation," although "so-called 'back-scratching' arrangements, pursuant to which all directors vote to approve each other's compensation as officers or employees, do not constitute disinterested directors' action" (1 ALI, supra, at 250). Since only three directors are alleged to have received the benefit of the executive compensation scheme, plaintiff has failed to allege that a majority of the board was interested in setting executive compensation. Nor do the allegations that the board used faulty accounting procedures to calculate executive compensation levels move beyond "conclusory allegations of wrongdoing" (Barr v Wackman, supra, at 379) which are insufficient to excuse demand. The complaint does not allege particular facts in contending that the board failed to deliberate or exercise its business judgment in setting those levels. Consequently, the failure to make a demand regarding the fixing of executive compensation was fatal to [the] portion of the complaint challenging that transaction.

However, a review of the complaint indicates that plaintiff also alleged that a majority of the board was self-interested in setting the compensation of outside directors because the outside directors comprised a majority of the board.

Directors are self-interested in a challenged transaction where they will receive a direct financial benefit from the transaction which is different from the benefit to shareholders generally (see, Rales v. Blasband, 634 A.2d 927, 936 [Del Sup Ct]; Bergstein v. Texas Intern. Co., 453 A.2d 467, 472–473 [Del Ch]; ALI, Principles of Corporate Governance § 1.23, at 25; 13 Fletcher, Cyclopedia Corporations § 5965, at 138). A director who votes him or herself a raise in directors' compensation is always "interested" because that person will receive a personal financial benefit from the transaction not shared in by stockholders (see, 1 ALI Principles of Corporate Governance § 5.03, comment g, at 250 ["if the board votes directorial compensation for itself, the board is interested"]; see also, Steiner v. Meyerson, [1995 Transfer Binder] , Fed. Sec. L. Rep. P 98857 [Del Ch], 1995 WL 441999, at 12 ["As the outside directors comprise a majority of the Telxon board and are personally interested in their compensation levels, demand upon them to challenge or decrease their own compensation is excused"]). Consequently, a demand was excused as to plaintiff's allegations that the compensation set for outside directors was excessive.

Corporate Waste

Our conclusion that demand should have been excused as to the part of the complaint challenging the fixing of directors' compensation does not end our inquiry, however. We must also determine whether plaintiff has stated a cause of action regarding that transaction, i.e., some wrong to the corporation. We conclude that plaintiff has not, and thus dismiss the complaint in its entirety.

Historically, directors did not receive any compensation for their work as directors (see, Fletcher, Cyclopedia Corporations, § 2109). Thus, a bare allegation that corporate directors voted themselves excessive compensation was sufficient to state a cause of action (e.g., Walsh v. Van Ameringen-Haebler, Inc., 257 N.Y. 478, 480; Jacobson v. Brooklyn Lumber Co., 184 N.Y. 152, 162). Many jurisdictions, including New York, have since changed the common law rule by statute providing that a corporation's board of directors has the authority to fix director compensation unless the corporation's charter or bylaws provides otherwise. Thus, the allegation that directors have voted themselves compensation is clearly no longer an allegation which gives rise to a cause of action, as the directors are statutorily entitled to set those levels. Nor does a conclusory allegation that the compensation directors have set for themselves is excessive give rise to a cause of action.

> The courts will not undertake to review the fairness of the official salaries, at the suit of a shareholder attacking them as excessive, unless wrongdoing and oppression or possible abuse of a fiduciary position are shown. However, the courts will take a hand in the matter at the instance of the corporation or of shareholders in extreme cases. A case of fraud is presented where directors increase their collective salaries so as to use up nearly the entire earnings of a company; where directors or officers appropriate the income so as to deprive shareholders of reasonable dividends, or perhaps so reduce to assets as to threaten the corporation with insolvency * * * (Fletcher, Cyclopedia Corporations, § 2122, at 46–47).

Thus, a complaint challenging the excessiveness of director compensation must—to survive a dismissal motion—allege compensation rates excessive on their face or other facts which call into question whether the compensation was fair to the corporation when approved, the good faith of the directors setting those rates, or that the decision to set the compensation could not have been a product of valid business judgment.[6]

6. There is general agreement that the allocation of the burden of proof differs depending on whether the compensation was approved by disinterested directors or shareholders, or by interested directors. Plaintiffs must prove wrongdoing or waste as to compensation arrangements regarding disinterested directors or shareholders, but directors who approve their own compensation bear the burden of proving that the transaction was fair to the corporation (see, Block, et al, The Business Judgment Rule, at 149 [4th ed.]; Fletcher, supra, § 514.1, 632; ALI, supra, § 5.03). However, at the

Applying the foregoing principles to plaintiff's complaint, it is clear that it must be dismissed. The complaint alleges that the directors increased their compensation rates from a base of $20,000 plus $500 for each meeting attended to a retainer of $55,000 plus 100 shares of IBM stock over a five-year period. The complaint also alleges that "this compensation bears little relation to the part-time services rendered by the Non–Employee Directors or to the profitability of IBM. The board's responsibilities have not increased, its performance, measured by the company's earnings and stock price, has been poor yet its compensation has increased far in excess of the cost of living."

These conclusory allegations do not state a cause of action. There are no factually-based allegations of wrongdoing or waste which would, if true, sustain a verdict in plaintiff's favor. Plaintiff's bare allegations that the compensation set lacked a relationship to duties performed or to the cost of living are insufficient as a matter of law to state a cause of action.

Accordingly, the order of the Appellate Division should be affirmed, with costs.

———

Add the following case at p. 1069 of the Unabridged Edition, and p. 710 of the Concise Edition, at the end of Section 6:

CUKER v. MIKALAUSKAS

Supreme Court of Pennsylvania, 1997.
547 Pa. 600, 692 A.2d 1042.

OPINION OF THE COURT

FLAHERTY, Chief Justice.

PECO Energy Company filed a motion for summary judgment seeking termination of minority shareholder derivative actions. When the motion was denied by the court of common pleas, PECO sought extraordinary relief in this court pursuant to Pa.R.A.P. 3309. We granted the petition, limited to the issue of "whether the 'business judgment rule' permits the board of directors of a Pennsylvania corporation to terminate derivative lawsuits brought by minority shareholders."

PECO is a publicly regulated utility incorporated in Pennsylvania which sells electricity and gas to residential, commercial, and industrial customers in Philadelphia and four surrounding counties. PECO is required to conform to PUC regulations which govern the provision of service to residential customers, including opening, billing, and terminating accounts. PECO is required to report regu-

pleading stage we are not concerned with burdens of proof.

larly to the PUC on a wide variety of statistical and performance information regarding its compliance with the regulations as interpreted by the PUC. Like other utilities, PECO is required to undergo a comprehensive management audit at the direction of the PUC approximately every ten years. The most recent audit was conducted by Ernst & Young. The report issued in 1991 recommended changes in twenty-two areas, including criticisms and recommendations regarding PECO's credit and collection function.

Two trustees, on behalf of a group of minority shareholders, made a demand on PECO, alleging wrongdoing by some PECO directors and officers. This Katzman demand, made in May, 1993, asserted that the delinquent officers had damaged PECO by mismanaging the credit and collection function, particularly as to the collection of overdue accounts. The shareholders demanded that PECO authorize litigation against the wrongdoers to recover monetary damages sustained by PECO. At its meeting of June 28, 1993, PECO's board responded by creating a special litigation committee to investigate the Katzman allegations.

Less than a month later, a second group of minority shareholders filed a complaint against PECO officers and directors. *Cuker v. Mikalauskas*, July Term, 1993, No. 3470 (C.P.Phila.). The *Cuker* complaint, filed in July, 1993, made the same allegations as those in the Katzman demand, with extensive references to the Ernst & Young audit report. The *Cuker* complaint was filed before the special litigation committee had begun its substantive work of investigating and evaluating the Katzman demand, so the committee's work encompassed both the Katzman and Cuker matters. Only the twelve nondefendant members of the PECO board acted to create the special committee, which consisted of three outside directors who had never been employed by PECO and who were not named in the Katzman demand or the *Cuker* complaint.

The work of the special committee was aided by the law firm of Dilworth, Paxson, Kalish & Kauffman, as well as PECO's regular outside auditor, Coopers & Lybrand, selected to assist in accounting matters because Coopers was knowledgeable about the utility industry and was familiar with PECO's accounting practices. The special committee conducted an extensive investigation over many months while maintaining a separate existence from PECO and its board of directors and keeping its deliberations confidential. The special committee held its final meeting on January 26, 1994, whereupon it reached its conclusions and prepared its report.

The report of the special committee concluded that there was no evidence of bad faith, self-dealing, concealment, or other breaches of the duty of loyalty by any of the defendant officers. It also concluded that the defendant officers "exercised sound business judgment in managing the affairs of the company" and that their actions "were reasonably calculated to further the best interests of the company." The three-hundred-page report identified numerous factors underlying the conclusions of the special committee. Significant considerations included the utility's efforts before the PUC to raise electricity rates in consequence of the expense of new nuclear generating plants. Other factors were the impact of PUC regulations limiting wintertime termination of residential service and other limitations on the use of collection techniques such as terminations of overdue customers, particularly with a large population of poverty level users among PECO's customer base. These considerations were supported by PUC documents which criticized PECO for aggressive and excessive terminations in recent years. The report of the special litigation committee also described how PECO's management had been attentive to the credit and collection function, with constant efforts to improve performance in that area. According to the report, limiting the use of terminations as a collection technique was a sound business judgment, reducing antagonism between the PUC and PECO and resulting in rate increases which produced revenue far in excess of the losses attributed to nonaggressive collection tactics. The report concluded that proceeding with a derivative suit based largely on findings of the Ernst & Young audit would not be in the best interests of PECO.

When it received the report of the special litigation committee with appendices containing the documents and interviews underlying the report, the board debated the recommendations at two meetings early in 1994. The twelve nondefendant members of the PECO board voted unanimously on March 14, 1994 to reject the Katzman demand and to terminate the *Cuker* action.

In the *Cuker* action, the court of common pleas rejected PECO's motion for summary judgment. The court stated that "the 'business judgment rule' [has been] adopted in some states but never previously employed in Pennsylvania." The court held that as a matter of Pennsylvania public policy, a corporation lacks power to terminate pending derivative litigation. . . .

When the PECO board, following the recommendation of the special litigation committee, rejected the Katzman demand, the Katzman claimants filed a shareholder derivative action. *Katzman v. Mikalauskas*, August Term 1995, No. 1278 (C.P.Phila.). After the Superior Court denied interlocutory review of *Cuker*, the two cases were consolidated by the court of common pleas on February 20, 1996.

PECO then filed a petition to terminate the consolidated actions which raised issues of fact regarding the independence of the special committee and the adequacy of its investigation. The plaintiffs responded that the court of common pleas could not resolve the factual issues because of the earlier decision in the same court that a Pennsylvania corporation lacks the power to terminate pending derivative litigation. . . .

... PECO sought extraordinary relief in this court under our King's Bench powers, which we granted.

The issue is whether the business judgment rule permits the board of directors of a Pennsylvania corporation to terminate derivative lawsuits brought by minority shareholders. The business judgment rule insulates an officer or director of a corporation from liability for a business decision made in good faith if he is not interested in the subject of the business judgment, is informed with respect to the subject of the business judgment to the extent he reasonably believes to be appropriate under the circumstances, and rationally believes that the business judgment is in the best interests of the corporation. 1 ALI, *Principles of Corporate Governance: Analysis and Recommendations*, (1994) ("*ALI Principles*") § 4.01(c)....

... [I]f a court makes a preliminary determination that a business decision was made under proper circumstances, however that concept is currently defined, then the business judgment rule prohibits the court from going further and examining the merits of the underlying business decision.

Decisions regarding litigation by or on behalf of a corporation, including shareholder derivative actions, are business decisions as much as any other financial decisions. As such, they are within the province of the board of directors.... Such business decisions of a board of directors are, unless taken in violation of a common law or statutory duty, within the scope of the business judgment rule. It follows that the court of common pleas erred when it held that the business judgment rule is not the law of Pennsylvania....

... [T]he practical effect of this holding needs elaboration. Assuming that an independent board of directors may terminate shareholder derivative actions, what is needed is a procedural mechanism for implementation and judicial review of the board's decision. Without considering the merits of the action, a court should determine the validity of the board's decision to terminate the litigation; if that decision was made in accordance with the appropriate standards, then the court should dismiss the derivative action prior to litigation on the merits.

The business judgment rule should insulate officers and directors from judicial intervention in the absence of fraud or self-dealing, if challenged decisions were within the scope of the directors' authority, if they exercised reasonable diligence, and if they honestly and rationally believed their decisions were in the best interests of the company. It is obvious that a court must examine the circumstances surrounding the decisions in order to determine if the conditions warrant application of the business judgment rule. If they do, the court will never proceed to an examination of the merits of the challenged decisions, for that is precisely what the business judgment rule prohibits. In order to make the business judgment rule meaningful, the preliminary examination should be limited and precise so as to minimize judicial involvement when application of the business judgment rule is warranted.

To achieve these goals, a court might stay the derivative action while it determines the propriety of the board's decision. The court might order limited discovery or an evidentiary hearing to resolve issues respecting the board's decision. Factors bearing on the board's decision will include whether the board or its special litigation committee was disinterested, whether it was assisted by counsel, whether it prepared a written report, whether it was independent, whether it conducted an adequate investigation, and whether it rationally believed its decision was in the best interests of the corporation (i.e., acted in good faith). If all of these criteria are satisfied,[2] the business judgment rule applies and the court should dismiss the action.

These considerations and procedures are all encompassed in Part VII, chapter 1 of the *ALI Principles* (relating to the derivative action), which provides a comprehensive mechanism to address shareholder derivative actions. A number of its provisions are implicated in the action at bar. Sections 7.02 (standing), 7.03 (the demand rule), 7.04 (procedure in derivative action), 7.05 (board authority in derivative action), 7.06 (judicial stay of derivative action), 7.07, 7.08, and 7.09 (dismissal of derivative action), 7.10 (standard of judicial review), and 7.13 (judicial procedures) are specifically applicable to this case.[3] These sections set forth guidance which is consistent with Pennsylvania law and precedent, which furthers the policies inherent in the business judgment rule, and which provides an appropriate degree of specificity to guide the trial court in controlling the proceedings in this litigation.

We specifically adopt §§ 7.02–7.10, and § 7.13 of the *ALI Principles*.[4,5] In doing so we have weighed many considerations.

2. It should be noted that respondents contest all of these criteria, representing that the special litigation committee was not disinterested or independent, counsel was not disinterested or independent, the investigation was inadequate, and that directors breached their fiduciary duties. Until factual determinations are made in regard to these disputed issues, a trial court cannot conclude whether or not the business judgment rule requires dismissal of the action.

3. *ALI Principles* §§ 4.01, 4.02, and 4.03 (duties of directors and officers; the business judgment rule; reliance on committees and other persons) are similar but not identical to the statutory standards found in 15 Pa.C.S. §§ 512, 513, 515, 1712, 1713, and 1715. The statutory standards, of course, control the duties of directors and the appli-

cation of the business judgment rule in Pennsylvania.

4. The full text of these sections is set forth in the appendix to this opinion.

5. Our adoption of these sections is not a rejection of other sections not cited. We have identified and studied the sections which apply to this case and have adopted those which appear most relevant.

The entire publication, all seven parts, is a comprehensive, cohesive work more than a decade in preparation. Additional sections of the publication, particularly procedural ones due to their interlocking character, may be adopted in the future. Issues in future cases or, perhaps, further proceedings in this case might implicate additional sections of the *ALI Principles*. Courts of the Commonwealth are free to consider other

First, the opinion of the trial court, the questions certified to the Superior Court, and the inability of PECO to obtain a definitive ruling from the lower courts all demonstrate the need for specific guidance from this court on how such litigation should be managed; the ALI principles provide such guidance in specific terms which will simplify this litigation. Second, we have often found ALI guidance helpful in the past, most frequently in adopting or citing sections of various Restatements; the scholarship reflected in work of the American Law Institute has been consistently reliable and useful. Third, the principles set forth by the ALI are generally consistent with Pennsylvania precedent. Fourth, although the *ALI Principles* incorporate much of the law of New York and Delaware, other states with extensive corporate jurisprudence, the ALI Principles better serve the needs of Pennsylvania. Although New York law parallels Pennsylvania law in many respects, it does not set forth any procedures to govern the review of corporate decisions relating to derivative litigation, and this omission would fail to satisfy the needs evident in this case. Delaware law permits a court in some cases ("demand excused" cases) to apply its own business judgment in the review process when deciding to honor the directors' decision to terminate derivative litigation. In our view, this is a defect which could eviscerate the business judgment rule and contradict a long line of Pennsylvania precedents. Delaware law also fails to provide a procedural framework for judicial review of corporate decisions under the business judgment rule.

Accordingly, we adopt the specified sections of the *ALI Principles*, reverse the orders of the court of common pleas, and remand the matter for further proceedings consistent with this opinion.

Orders reversed and case remanded.

[In an Appendix to its opinion, the court set out Principles of Corporate Governance sections 7.02-7.10 and 7.13 in full.]

———

On remand, the trial court found that the litigation committee and its counsel were independent and disinterested, the committee's investigation was adequate, and the committee acted rationally and with a good faith belief that its decision was in the best interest of PECO, and concluded that the derivative actions should be dismissed.

———

parts of the work and utilize them if they are helpful and appear to be consistent with Pennsylvania law.

SECTION 8. PLAINTIFF'S COUNSEL FEES

Insert the following Note at p. 1087 of the Unabridged Edition, after the Report of the Third Circuit Task Force:

GOODRICH v. E.F. HUTTON GROUP, 681 A.2d 1039 (Del. Supr.1996). The court here summarized current federal law as follows: "In the 1970s, courts began to use the 'lodestar' approach to calculate fee awards in common fund cases. *Lindy Bros. Builders, Inc. of Phila. v. American Radiator & Standard Sanitary Corp.,* 487 F.2d 161, 167–68 (3d Cir.1973). *See* Report of the Third Circuit Task Force, *Court Awarded Attorney Fees,* 108 F.R.D. 237, 242 (1985). That method requires a court to calculate the product of an attorney's reasonable hours expended on the litigation and reasonable hourly rate to arrive at the 'lodestar.' *Swedish Hosp. Corp. v. Shalala,* 1 F.3d at 1266. That lodestar calculation can then be adjusted, through application of a 'multiplier' or fee enhancer, to account for additional factors, *e.g.,* the contingent nature of the case and the quality of an attorney's work. *Lindy Bros. Builders, Inc. of Phila. v. American Radiator & Standard Sanitary Corp.,* 540 F.2d 102, 112 (3d Cir.1976); *Swedish Hosp. Corp. v. Shalala,* 1 F.3d at 1266. During the 1970s, the 'lodestar/multiplier' method of awarding fees was frequently invoked in common fund cases, instead of determining a reasonable percentage of recovery from the fund, based upon a multifactor analysis. *Johnson v. Georgia Highway Express, Inc.,* 488 F.2d 714, 716–19 (5th Cir.1974) ('Johnson' factors); *Lindy Bros. Builders, Inc. v. American Radiator & Standard Sanitary Corp.,* 487 F.2d at 164–69 ('Lindy' factors).

"In the 1980s, however, two events led to a reconsideration of the lodestar method of calculating common fund fee awards. First, in 1984, the Supreme Court distinguished the calculation of awards under fee-shifting statutes from the calculation of attorney's fees under the common fund doctrine. In doing so, the Supreme Court suggested that an award in a common fund case should be based upon a percentage of the fund:

> Unlike the calculation of attorney's fees under the 'common fund doctrine,' where a reasonable fee is based on a percentage of the fund bestowed on the class, a reasonable fee under [42 U.S.C.] § 1988 reflects the amount of attorney time reasonably expended on the litigation.

Blum v. Stenson, 465 U.S. 886, 900 n. 16, 104 S.Ct. 1541, 1550 n. 16, 79 L.Ed.2d 891 (1984). Footnote 16 in *Blum* has been cited for the proposition that the Supreme Court's approval of the lodestar method in the fee-shifting context was not intended to overrule decisions which had approved percentage of the fund awards of attorney's fees in common fund cases. *Swedish Hosp.,* 1 F.3d at

1268. *See, e.g., Sprague v. Ticonic National Bank*, 307 U.S. 161, 59 S.Ct. 777, 83 L.Ed. 1184 (1939); *Central Railroad & Banking Co. v. Pettus*, 113 U.S. 116, 5 S.Ct. 387, 28 L.Ed. 915 (1885). That interpretation of *Blum* did not change when the Supreme Court held that the lodestar should not be enhanced through the use of a multiplier in statutory fee-shifting cases. *City of Burlington v. Dague*, 505 U.S. 557, 565–67, 112 S.Ct. 2638, 2642–44, 120 L.Ed.2d 449 (1992).

"The second significant event in the 1980s was the report issued in 1985 by a Task Force the Third Circuit had appointed to evaluate the practical effectiveness of the lodestar method in making attorney fee awards. *See* Report of the Third Circuit Task Force, *Court Awarded Attorney Fees*, 108 F.R.D. 237 (1985). The Task Force recommended continued use of the lodestar technique in statutory fee-shifting cases. *Id. See also City of Burlington v. Dague*, 505 U.S. at 562, 112 S.Ct. at 2641 (acknowledging, in the statutory fee-shifting context, 'a strong presumption that the lodestar represents the reasonable fee'). The Task Force concluded, however, that all attorney fee awards in common fund cases should be structured as a percentage of the fund. Report of the Third Circuit Task Force, *Court Awarded Attorney Fees*, 108 F.R.D. at 255.

"At the present time, the majority of federal courts use a reasonable percentage of the fund method when making attorney fee awards in common fund cases. *See Swedish Hosp. Corp. v. Shalala*, 1 F.3d at 1266 (chronicling history of the methodologies). *See also* FEDERAL JUDICIAL CENTER, AWARDING ATTORNEYS' FEES AND MANAGING FEE LITIGATION 63–64 (1994) (canvassing case law.)[9] The Third Circuit has recently held that the percentage of the fund is generally the preferable method for awarding fees in common fund cases, but noted that a lodestar analysis might be used to cross check the propriety of the award (a 'hybrid' approach). *See In re General Motors Corp. Pick–Up Truck Fuel Tank Products Liability Litigation*, 55 F.3d at 821. Ultimately, however, the Third Circuit permits

---

9. The D.C. Circuit and the Eleventh Circuit require the use of the percentage method in common fund cases. *See Swedish Hospital Corp. v. Shalala*, 1 F.3d 1261, 1271 (D.C.Cir.1993); *Camden I Condominium Assoc., Inc. v. Dunkle*, 946 F.2d 768, 774 (11th Cir.1991). At least five other circuits leave it to the trial court's discretion to choose between the lodestar and percentage methods in common fund cases. *See In re Thirteen Appeals Arising out of the San Juan DuPont Plaza Hotel Fire Litigation*, 56 F.3d 295, 306–308 (1st Cir.1995); *In re Washington Public Power Supply System Securities Litigation*, 19 F.3d 1291, 1295 (9th Cir.1994); *Rawlings v. Prudential–Bache Properties, Inc.*, 9 F.3d 513, 516 (6th Cir.1993); *Florin v. Nationsbank of Georgia, N.A.*, 34 F.3d 560 (7th Cir.1994);

Brown v. Phillips Petroleum Co., 838 F.2d 451, 454 (10th Cir.), *cert. denied*, 488 U.S. 822, 109 S.Ct. 66, 102 L.Ed.2d 43 (1988). *But see In re Continental Illinois Securities Litigation*, 962 F.2d 566, 572–73 (7th Cir. 1992) (leaving method of calculation discretionary but expressing a preference for percentage method). Although the Sixth Circuit has acknowledged the methodologies used in the other circuits, it "require[s] only that awards of attorney's fees ... in common fund cases be reasonable under the circumstances." *Rawlings v. Prudential–Bache Properties, Inc.*, 9 F.3d at 516. Accordingly, the Sixth Circuit leaves it to the trial court's discretion to choose the method or variation and combination of methods that best account for the exigencies of the particular case before it.

the trial court to exercise its discretion in choosing *either* the percentage method *or* the lodestar method, *or* some combination or hybrid, as the circumstances warrant, in making common fund fee awards. *Id.*"

SECTION 10. INDEMNIFICATION AND INSURANCE

Add the following Note and case at p. 1103 of the Unabridged Edition, after the Note on Plate v. Sun–Diamond Growers, and p. 736 of the Concise Edition, after Heffernan v. Pacific Dunlop GNB Corp.:

IN RE LANDMARK LAND CO., 76 F.3d 553 (4th Cir.1996). Gerald Barton and William Vaughan were directors and officers in various corporations in a group consisting of Landmark Land Co.; Landmark's wholly owned subsidiary, Oak Tree Savings Bank; the Bank's wholly owned subsidiary, Clock Tower; and various wholly owned real-estate subsidiaries of Clock Tower, which were financed by the Bank. An investigation by the federal Office of Thrift Supervision (OTS) revealed that the Bank was undercapitalized and had a pattern of consistent losses. On July 15, 1991, the Bank's directors signed a Consent Agreement with the OTS in which they agreed that the Bank's subsidiaries would not enter into any material transaction without the OTS's prior approval.

In violation of the Consent Agreement, the Bank's subsidiaries filed for bankruptcy, apparently for the purpose of keeping OTS from taking control of the subsidiaries. The OTS then took possession of the Bank and filed civil administrative changes against Barton, Vaughan, and certain other directors in the Landmark group. The OTS claimed that the directors had violated the terms of the Consent Agreement; had mishandled certain large loans; and had breached their fiduciary duty to the Bank because they knew that the bankruptcy filings would have a substantially adverse effect on the Bank's ability to collect its loans to the subsidiaries.

Clock Tower's board voted to indemnify Barton and Vaughan for the fees and costs of defending themselves against the OTS charges. Barton and Vaughan did not participate in the vote. The relevant indemnification statute (California Corp. Code 317(e)) provided for permissive indemnification of directors and officers if a corporation, acting through a majority vote of a quorum of directors who were not parties, or in other specified ways, made a determination that the directors or officers to be indemnified "acted in good faith and in a manner the person reasonably believed to be in the best interests of the corporation." Clock Tower's board had essentially made such a determination. Held, Barton and Vaughan could not be indemnified:

> ... At first glance, § 317(e) suggests that the corporation's finding of good faith settles the matter, and that the court's role is limited to ensuring that the corporation made its finding of good faith by proper procedures.

> We do not agree that the court's role is so narrow. Although a corporation has to find that the agent acted in good faith before authorizing indemnification, nothing in § 317(e) restricts a court's authority under § 317(b) to make an independent assessment of the agent's good faith. Section 317(b) allows permissive indemnification where the agent has acted in good faith, not where the corporation finds that the agent has acted in good faith. Reading § 317(b) together with § 317(e), we conclude that the issue of an agent's good faith is a question for the courts to decide. . . .

> ... [T]he Directors' action to file for bankruptcy was a deliberate attempt to circumvent the regulatory authority that Congress had clearly given to the OTS. . . .

> By placing the Debtors in bankruptcy, the Directors intended to prevent the OTS from enforcing the minimum capitalization requirement against the Bank. According to the OTS charges, the OTS investigated the Bank on June 4, 1990 and found that the Bank was inadequately capitalized and had demonstrated a pattern of repeated losses. The OTS directed the Bank to infuse sufficient capital to meet the minimum capitalization requirement, but the Bank did not submit an acceptable plan. Because of the Bank's inability to meet the requirement, the OTS forced the Bank directors to sign a Consent Agreement on January 15, 1991, signalling to the Directors that an OTS takeover was imminent. Instead of working with the OTS to correct the Bank's capitalization problem, the Directors filed the bankruptcy petitions to prevent the OTS from exercising control of the Bank's subsidiaries.

> We cannot conclude that the Directors' action was taken in good faith. If the OTS charges are accurate, the Director's action to place the Debtors in bankruptcy was a deliberate attempt to prevent the OTS from exercising control over the Bank's assets, thus hindering the OTS's ability to deal effectively with a failing savings and loan. ... [T]he Bank could not comply with the minimum capitalization requirement, and the OTS therefore had a statutory duty to force the Bank's management to comply with the capitalization requirement. The Directors acknowledged the OTS's regulatory authority when they signed the Consent Agreement and agreed that the Bank's subsidiaries would not enter into any material transaction with-

out prior approval from the OTS. When the OTS threatened to take control of the Bank, however, the Directors' used the bankruptcy code to stymie the OTS, even though their action breached the Consent Agreement with the OTS and violated their fiduciary duties to the Bank. We cannot condone the Directors' blatant attempt to circumvent the OTS's regulatory authority by holding that they acted in good faith.

Even if the bankruptcy filings benefitted the Debtors, we still could not conclude that the Directors acted in good faith. An agent who has intentionally participated in illegal activity or wrongful conduct against third persons cannot be said to have acted in good faith, even if the conduct benefits the corporation. *Plate [v. Sun–Diamond Growers], 275 Cal.Rptr. at 672.* "For example, corporate executives who participate in a deliberate price-fixing conspiracy with competing firms could not be found to have acted in good faith, even though they may have reasonably believed that a deliberate flouting of the antitrust laws would increase the profits of the corporation." 1 Harold Marsh, Jr. and R. Roy Finkle, Marsh's California Corporation Law (3d ed.) § 10.43, at 751; see *Plate, 275 Cal.Rptr. at 672* (citing same language from second edition). We recognize that the Directors did not break any law by filing the bankruptcy petitions, and that the OTS has not filed criminal charges against the Directors. Nonetheless, we find that a deliberate attempt to undermine the regulatory authority of a government agency cannot constitute good faith conduct, even if such actions benefit the corporation.

The Directors intentionally breached their fiduciary duties to the Bank and their Consent Agreement with the OTS in order to prevent the OTS from exercising the powers granted to it . . . .   The Directors knew the impropriety of their actions . . . .   We therefore conclude that the Directors did not act in good faith when they placed the Debtors in bankruptcy.

————

WALTUCH v. CONTICOMMODITY SERVICES, INC.

United States Court of Appeals, Second Circuit, 1996.
88 F.3d 87.

Before: VAN GRAAFEILAND, JACOBS and PARKER, Circuit Judges.

JACOBS, Circuit Judge:

Famed silver trader Norton Waltuch spent $2.2 million in unreimbursed legal fees to defend himself against numerous civil lawsuits and an enforcement proceeding brought by the Commodity Futures Trading Commission (CFTC). In this action under Delaware law, Waltuch seeks indemnification of his legal expenses from his former employer. The district court denied any indemnity, and Waltuch appeals.

As vice-president and chief metals trader for Conticommodity Services, Inc., Waltuch traded silver for the firm's clients, as well as for his own account. In late 1979 and early 1980, the silver price spiked upward as the then-billionaire Hunt brothers and several of Waltuch's foreign clients bought huge quantities of silver futures contracts. Just as rapidly, the price fell until (on a day remembered in trading circles as "Silver Thursday") the silver market crashed. Between 1981 and 1985, angry silver speculators filed numerous lawsuits against Waltuch and Conticommodity, alleging fraud, market manipulation, and antitrust violations. All of the suits eventually settled and were dismissed with prejudice, pursuant to settlements in which Conticommodity paid over $35 million to the various suitors. Waltuch himself was dismissed from the suits with no settlement contribution. His unreimbursed legal expenses in these actions total approximately $1.2 million.

Waltuch was also the subject of an enforcement proceeding brought by the CFTC, charging him with fraud and market manipulation. The proceeding was settled, with Waltuch agreeing to a penalty that included a $100,000 fine and a six-month ban on buying or selling futures contracts from any exchange floor. Waltuch spent $1 million in unreimbursed legal fees in the CFTC proceeding.[1]

Waltuch brought suit in the United States District Court for the Southern District of New York (Lasker, J.) against Conticommodity and its parent company, Continental Grain Co. (together "Conti"), for indemnification of his unreimbursed expenses.[2] Only two of Waltuch's claims reach us on appeal.

Waltuch first claims that Article Ninth of Conticommodity's articles of incorporation requires Conti to indemnify him for his expenses in both the private and CFTC actions. Conti responds that this claim is barred by subsection (a) of § 145 of Delaware's General Corporation Law, which permits indemnification only if the corporate officer acted "in good faith," something that Waltuch has not established. Waltuch counters that subsection (f) of the same statute permits a corporation to grant indemnification rights outside the limits of subsection (a), and that Conticommodity did so with Article Ninth (which has no stated good-faith limitation). The district court held that, notwithstanding § 145(f), Waltuch could

1. The parties have stipulated that Waltuch's "reasonable attorney's fees and costs" for the private lawsuits totaled $1,228,586.67, and that the comparable expenses for the CFTC proceeding are an even $1 million.

2. Conticommodity and Continental Grain are incorporated in Delaware and have their principal places of business in New York; Waltuch is a New Jersey citizen. We therefore have diversity jurisdiction under 28 U.S.C. § 1332. All parties agree that Delaware law governs.

recover under Article Ninth only if Waltuch met the "good faith" requirement of § 145(a).[3] 833 F.Supp. 302, 308–09 (S.D.N.Y.1993). On the factual issue of whether Waltuch had acted "in good faith," the court denied Conti's summary judgment motion and cleared the way for trial. Id. at 313. The parties then stipulated that they would forgo trial on the issue of Waltuch's "good faith," agree to an entry of final judgment against Waltuch on his claim under Article Ninth and § 145(f), and allow Waltuch to take an immediate appeal of the judgment to this Court. Thus, as to Waltuch's first claim, the only question left is how to interpret §§ 145(a) and 145(f), assuming Waltuch acted with less than "good faith." As we explain in part I below, we affirm the district court's judgment as to this claim and hold that § 145(f) does not permit a corporation to bypass the "good faith" requirement of § 145(a).

Waltuch's second claim is that subsection (c) of § 145 requires Conti to indemnify him because he was "successful on the merits or otherwise" in the private lawsuits.[4] The district court ruled for Conti on this claim as well. The court explained that, even though all the suits against Waltuch were dismissed without his making any payment, he was not "successful on the merits or otherwise," because Conti's settlement payments to the plaintiffs were partially on Waltuch's behalf. Id. at 311. For the reasons stated in part II below, we reverse this portion of the district court's ruling, and hold that Conti must indemnify Waltuch under § 145(c) for the $1.2 million in unreimbursed legal fees he spent in defending the private lawsuits.

I

Article Ninth, on which Waltuch bases his first claim, is categorical and contains no requirement of "good faith":

> The Corporation shall indemnify and hold harmless each of its incumbent or former directors, officers, employees and agents . . . against expenses actually and necessarily incurred by him in connection with the defense of any action, suit or proceeding threatened, pending or completed, in which he is made a party, by reason of his serving in or having held such position or capacity, except in relation to matters as to which he shall be

---

3. A Special Committee of Continental Grain Co.'s Board of Directors reached the same conclusion in November 1991. Waltuch filed his complaint two months later. In the district court, Conti argued that under the business judgment rule, the Special Committee's decision was immune from challenge, an argument the district court rejected. 833 F.Supp. at 305. Although the parties signed a stipulation preserving Conti's right to contest the district court's ruling on this issue, Conti has abandoned its business judgment rule argument on appeal.

4. The district court held that Waltuch was not successful "on the merits or otherwise" in the CFTC proceeding. 833 F.Supp. at 311. Waltuch does not appeal this aspect of the court's ruling.

adjudged in such action, suit or proceeding to be liable for negligence or misconduct in the performance of duty.[5]

Conti argues that § 145(a) of Delaware's General Corporation Law, which does contain a "good faith" requirement, fixes the outer limits of a corporation's power to indemnify; Article Ninth is thus invalid under Delaware law, says Conti, to the extent that it requires indemnification of officers who have acted in bad faith. The affirmative grant of power in § 145(a) is as follows:

> *A corporation shall have power to indemnify* any person who was or is a party or is threatened to be made a party to any threatened, pending or completed action, suit or proceeding, whether civil, criminal, administrative or investigative (other than an action by or in the right of the corporation) by reason of the fact that he is or was a director, officer, employee or agent of the corporation, or is or was serving at the request of the corporation as a director, officer, employee or agent of another corporation, partnership, joint venture, trust or other enterprise, against expenses (including attorneys' fees), judgments, fines and amounts paid in settlement actually and reasonably incurred by him in connection with such action, suit or proceeding *if he acted in good faith and in a manner he reasonably believed to be in or not opposed to the best interests of the corporation,* and, with respect to any criminal action or proceeding, had no reasonable cause to believe his conduct was unlawful.

56 Del.Laws 50, § 1 at 170–71 (1967) (emphasis added) (rewriting Delaware's General Corporation Law, title 8, chapter 1 of the Delaware Code), *codified at* 8 Del.Code Ann. tit. 8, § 145(a) (Michie 1991). Key language in the Delaware Code Annotated's version of this subsection is in error, as explained in the margin.[6]

---

5. Because the private suits and the CFTC proceeding were settled, it is undisputed that Waltuch was not "adjudged ... to be liable for negligence or misconduct in the performance of duty."

6. There is some confusion about whether this subsection begins, "A corporation *shall have power* to indemnify ..." or "A corporation *may* indemnify ...". As originally enacted, § 145(a) contained the phrase "shall have power". 56 Del.Laws 50, § 1 at 170 (1967). According to the annotations in the *Delaware Code Annotated* (and confirmed by a review of the legislative records since 1967), § 145(a) has never been amended. *See* 8 Del.Code Ann. tit. 8, § 145(a) (1991 & 1995 Supp.).

Nevertheless, the *Delaware Code Annotated*, a private compilation by the Michie Company of all Delaware legislative acts, at some point began using the phrase "may"

in place of "shall have power". *See* 8 Del. Code Ann. tit. 8, § 145(a) (1974). We have not been able to explain this non-legislative change in statutory language. The *Delaware Corporation Law Annotated,* published by the Corporation Trust Company, continues to use the phrase "shall have power". Del.Corp.L.Ann. § 145(a) (20th ed. Corp. Trust Co.1991).

One treatise uses the phrase "shall have power", *see* Ernest L. Folk, III, et al., *Folk on the Delaware General Corporation Law* at 145:1 (3d ed. 1994), while another uses "may". *See* 5 R. Franklin Balotti & Jesse A. Finkelstein, *The Delaware Law of Corporations and Business Organizations* at 100 (1990 & 1993 Supp.) ("Balotti & Finkelstein"). The parties to this appeal perpetuate the confusion: their joint appendix contains a version of § 145(a) that says "shall have power", but one of the briefs quotes a version that says "may".

In order to escape the "good faith" clause of § 145(a), Waltuch argues that § 145(a) is not an *exclusive* grant of indemnification power, because § 145(f) expressly allows corporations to indemnify officers in a manner broader than that set out in § 145(a). The "nonexclusivity" language of § 145(f) provides:

> The indemnification and advancement of expenses provided by, or granted pursuant to, the other subsections of this section *shall not be deemed exclusive of any other rights* to which those seeking indemnification or advancement of expenses may be entitled under any bylaw, agreement, vote of stockholders or disinterested directors or otherwise, both as to action in his official capacity and as to action in another capacity while holding such office.

56 Del.Laws 50, § 1 at 172 (emphasis added), *as amended and codified* at 8 Del.Code Ann. tit. 8, § 145(f). Waltuch contends that the "nonexclusivity" language in § 145(f) is a separate grant of indemnification power, not limited by the good faith clause that governs the power granted in § 145(a). Conti on the other hand contends that § 145(f) must be limited by "public policies," one of which is that a corporation may indemnify its officers only if they act in "good faith."

In a thorough and scholarly opinion, Judge Lasker agreed with Conti's reading of § 145(f), writing that "it has been generally agreed that there are public policy limits on indemnification under Section 145(f)," although it was "difficult ... to define precisely what limitations on indemnification public policy imposes." 833 F.Supp. at 307, 308. After reviewing cases from Delaware and elsewhere and finding that they provided no authoritative guidance, Judge Lasker surveyed the numerous commentators on this issue and found that they generally agreed with Conti's position. *Id.* at 308–09. He also found that Waltuch's reading of § 145(f) failed to make sense of the statute as a whole:

> [T]here would be no point to the carefully crafted provisions of Section 145 spelling out the permissible scope of indemnification under Delaware law if subsection (f) allowed indemnification in additional circumstances without regard to these limits. The exception would swallow the rule.

Id. at 309. The fact that § 145(f) was limited by § 145(a) did not make § 145(f) meaningless, wrote Judge Lasker, because § 145(f) "still 'may authorize the adoption of various procedures and presumptions to make the process of indemnification more favorable to

---

When there is a conflict between an original enactment of the Delaware Legislature and the codification of the law, the original enactment controls. *Elliott v. Blue Cross & Blue Shield,* 407 A.2d 524, 528 (Del.1979); *Kimmey v. Farmers Bank,* 373 A.2d 569, 570 (Del.1977). We therefore employ the Legislature's version of § 145(a), which says "shall have power".

We are indebted to Lesley Lawrence and the staff at the Third Circuit library in Wilmington for their assistance on this issue.

the indemnitee without violating the statute.' " *Id.* at 309 (quoting 1 Balotti & Finkelstein § 4.16 at 4–321). As will be evident from the discussion below, we adopt much of Judge Lasker's analysis.

A. *Delaware Cases*

No Delaware court has decided the very issue presented here; but the applicable cases tend to support the proposition that a corporation's grant of indemnification rights cannot be *inconsistent* with the substantive statutory provisions of § 145, notwithstanding § 145(f). We draw this rule of "consistency" primarily from our reading of the Delaware Supreme Court's opinion in *Hibbert v. Hollywood Park, Inc.,* 457 A.2d 339 (Del.1983). In that case, Hibbert and certain other directors sued the corporation and the remaining directors, and then demanded indemnification for their expenses and fees related to the litigation. The company refused indemnification on the ground that directors were entitled to indemnification only as *defendants* in legal proceedings. The court reversed the trial court and held that Hibbert was entitled to indemnification under the plain terms of a company bylaw that did not draw an express distinction between plaintiff directors and defendant directors. *Id.* at 343. The court then proceeded to test the bylaw for consistency with § 145(a):

> Furthermore, *indemnification here is consistent with current Delaware law.* Under 8 Del.C. § 145(a) . . ., "a corporation may indemnify any person who was or is a party or is threatened to be made a party to any threatened, pending or completed" derivative or third-party action. By this language, indemnity is *not limited to* only those who stand as a defendant in the main action. The corporation can also grant indemnification rights beyond those provided by statute. 8 Del.C. § 145(f).

Id. at 344 (emphasis added and citations omitted). *See supra* note 6 (explaining the error in the *Delaware Code Annotated*'s use of the phrase "may indemnify" in § 145(a)). This passage contains two complementary propositions. Under § 145(f), a corporation may provide indemnification rights that go "beyond" the rights provided by § 145(a) and the other substantive subsections of § 145. At the same time, any such indemnification rights provided by a corporation must be "consistent with" the substantive provisions of § 145, including § 145(a). In *Hibbert,* the corporate bylaw was "consistent with" § 145(a), because this subsection was "not limited to" suits in which directors were defendants. *Hibbert*'s holding may support an inverse corollary that illuminates our case: if § 145(a) had been expressly limited to directors who were named as defendants, the bylaw could not have stood, regardless of § 145(f), because the bylaw would not have been "consistent with" the substantive statutory provision.[7]

A more recent opinion of the Delaware Supreme Court, analyzing a different provision of § 145, also supports the view that the express limits in § 145's substantive provisions are not subordinated to § 145(f). In *Citadel Holding Corp. v. Roven,* 603 A.2d 818, 823 (Del.1992), a corporation's bylaws provided indemnification "to the full extent permitted by the General Corporation Law of Delaware." The corporation entered into an indemnification agreement with one of its directors, reciting the parties' intent to afford enhanced protection in some unspecified way. The director contended that the agreement was intended to afford mandatory advancement of expenses, and that this feature (when compared with the merely permissive advancement provision of § 145(e)) was the enhancement intended by the parties. The corporation, seeking to avoid advancement of expenses, argued instead that the agreement enhanced the director's protection only in the sense that the precontract indemnification rights were subject to statute, whereas his rights under the contract could not be diminished without his consent. *Id.*

In rejecting that argument, the court explained that indemnification rights provided by contract could not exceed the "scope" of a corporation's indemnification powers as set out by the statute:

> If the General Assembly were to amend Delaware's director indemnification statute with the effect of curtailing the scope of indemnification a corporation may grant a director, the fact that [the director's] rights were also secured by contract would be of little use to him. Private parties may not circumvent the legislative will simply by agreeing to do so.

Id. Citadel thus confirms the dual propositions stated in *Hibbert:* indemnification rights may be broader than those set out in the statute, but they cannot be inconsistent with the "scope" of the corporation's power to indemnify, as delineated in the statute's substantive provisions. *See also Shearin v. E.F. Hutton Group, Inc.,* 652 A.2d 578, 593–94 & n. 19 (Del.Ch.1994) (Allen, Ch.) (bylaw that

---

7. The *Hibbert* court cites to a 1978 article by Samuel Arsht, chairman of the committee of experts that drafted Delaware's General Corporation Law in 1967, *id.,* which supports our conclusion that indemnification rights permitted under § 145(f) must be consistent with the other substantive provisions of § 145. At the pages cited by the court, Arsht writes:

> The question most frequently asked by practicing lawyers is what subsection (f), the nonexclusive clause, means.... The question which subsection (f) invariably raises is whether a corporation can adopt a by-law or make a contract with its directors providing that they will be in-

demnified for whatever they may have to pay if they are sued and lose or settle. The answer to this question is "no." Subsection (f) ... permits additional rights to be created, but *it is not a blanket authorization to indemnify directors* against all expenses, fines, or settlements of whatever nature and *regardless of the directors' conduct.* The statutory language is circumscribed by limits of public policy....

S. Samuel Arsht, *Indemnification Under Section 145 of Delaware General Corporation Law,* 3 Del.J.Corp.L. 176, 176–77 (1978) (emphasis added).

provided indemnification "to the full extent permissible under Section 145" must be interpreted in way that is consistent with substantive provisions of § 145(a); nonexclusivity provision of § 145(f) not mentioned by the court); *Merritt–Chapman & Scott Corp. v. Wolfson,* 321 A.2d 138, 142 (Del.Super.Ct.1974) (bylaw provided for mandatory entitlement to indemnification unless officer was "derelict in the performance of his duty"; although the court considered this entitlement to be "independent of any right under the statute," it did not hold that the bylaw was inconsistent with the "good faith" standard of § 145(a)).

B. *Statutory Reading*

The "consistency" rule suggested by these Delaware cases is reinforced by our reading of § 145 as a whole. Subsections (a) (indemnification for third-party actions) and (b) (similar indemnification for derivative suits) expressly grant a corporation the power to indemnify directors, officers, and others, if they "acted in good faith and in a manner reasonably believed to be in or not opposed to the best interest of the corporation." These provisions thus limit the scope of the power that they confer. They are permissive in the sense that a corporation may exercise less than its full power to grant the indemnification rights set out in these provisions.[8] *See Essential Enter. Corp. v. Dorsey Corp.,* 182 A.2d 647, 653 (Del.Ch. 1962). By the same token, subsection (f) permits the corporation to grant additional rights: the rights provided in the rest of § 145 "shall not be deemed exclusive of any other rights to which those seeking indemnification may be entitled." But crucially, subsection (f) merely acknowledges that one seeking indemnification may be entitled to "other rights" (of indemnification or otherwise); it does not speak in terms of corporate power, and therefore cannot be read to free a corporation from the "good faith" limit explicitly imposed in subsections (a) and (b).

An alternative construction of these provisions would effectively force us to ignore certain explicit terms of the statute. Section 145(a) gives Conti the power to indemnify Waltuch "*if* he acted in good faith and in a manner reasonably believed to be in or not opposed to the best interest of the corporation." 56 Del.Laws 50, § 1 at 171 (emphasis added). This statutory limit must mean that there is *no power* to indemnify Waltuch if he did not act in good faith. Otherwise, as Judge Lasker pointed out, § 145(a)—and its good faith clause—would have no meaning: a corporation could indemnify whomever and however it wished regardless of the good

---

8. We therefore disagree with *PepsiCo, Inc. v. Continental Casualty Co.,* 640 F.Supp. 656, 661 (S.D.N.Y.1986), which characterizes subsections (a) and (b) as " 'backstop' provisions." A leading treatise on Delaware corporate law casts doubt on *PepsiCo,* finding it "questionable whether a Delaware court would be quite this sweeping in its language in a case properly presented to it involving the outer limits of the authority provided in Section 145(f)." 1 Balotti & Finkelstein, § 4.16 at 4–319.

faith clause or anything else the Delaware Legislature wrote into § 145(a).

When the Legislature intended a subsection of § 145 to augment the powers limited in subsection (a), it set out the additional powers expressly. Thus subsection (g) explicitly allows a corporation to circumvent the "good faith" clause of subsection (a) by purchasing a directors and officers liability insurance policy. Significantly, that subsection is framed as a grant of corporate power:

> A corporation shall have power to purchase and maintain insurance on behalf of any person who is or was a director, officer, employee or agent of the corporation ... against any liability asserted against him and incurred by him in any such capacity, or arising out of his status as such, *whether or not the corporation would have the power to indemnify him against such liability under this section.*

56 Del.Laws 50, § 1 at 172 (1967) (emphasis added), *codified at* 8 Del.Code Ann. tit. 8, § 145(g) (Michie 1991). The italicized passage reflects the principle that corporations have the power under § 145 to indemnify in some situations and not in others. Since § 145(f) is neither a grant of corporate power nor a limitation on such power, subsection (g) must be referring to the limitations set out in § 145(a) and the other provisions of § 145 that describe corporate power. If § 145 (through subsection (f) or another part of the statute) gave corporations unlimited power to indemnify directors and officers, then the final clause of subsection (g) would be unnecessary: that is, its grant of "power to purchase and maintain insurance" (exercisable regardless of whether the corporation itself would have the power to indemnify the loss directly) is meaningful only because, in some insurable situations, the corporation simply lacks the power to indemnify its directors and officers directly.

A contemporaneous account from the principal drafter of Delaware's General Corporation Law confirms what an integral reading of § 145 demonstrates: the statute's affirmative grants of power also impose limitations on the corporation's power to indemnify. Specifically, the good faith clause (unchanged since the Law's original enactment in 1967) was included in subsections (a) and (b) as a carefully calculated improvement on the prior indemnification provision and as an explicit limit on a corporation's power to indemnify:

> During the three years of the Revision Committee's study, no subject was more discussed among members of the corporate bar than the subject of indemnification of officers and directors. As far as Delaware law was concerned, the existing statutory provision on the subject had been found inadequate. Numerous by-laws and charter provisions had been adopted clarifying and extending its terms, but *uncertainty existed in many instances as to whether such provisions transgressed the*

limits which the courts had indicated they would establish based on public policy.

. . .

It was ... apparent that revision was appropriate with respect to *the limitations which must necessarily be placed on the power to indemnify* in order to prevent the statute from undermining the substantive provisions of the criminal law and corporation law....

[There was a] need for a ... provision to protect the corporation law's requirement of loyalty to the corporation.... Ultimately, it was decided that *the power to indemnify should not be granted unless* it appeared that the person seeking indemnification had "acted in good faith and in a manner reasonably believed to be in or not opposed to the best interest of the corporation."

S. Samuel Arsht & Walter K. Stapleton, *Delaware's New General Corporation Law: Substantive Changes*, 23 Bus.Law. 75, 77–78 (1967).[9] This passage supports *Hibbert*'s rule of "consistency" and makes clear that a corporation has no power to transgress the indemnification limits set out in the substantive provisions of § 145.

Waltuch argues at length that reading § 145(a) to bar the indemnification of officers who acted in bad faith would render § 145(f) meaningless. This argument misreads § 145(f). That subsection refers to "any other rights to which those seeking indemnification or advancement of expenses may be entitled." Delaware commentators have identified various indemnification rights that are "beyond those provided by statute," *Hibbert*, 457 A.2d at 344, and that are at the same time consistent with the statute:

[S]ubsection (f) provides general authorization for the adoption of various procedures and presumptions making the process of indemnification more favorable to the indemnitee. For example, indemnification agreements or by-laws could provide for: (i) mandatory indemnification unless prohibited by statute; (ii) mandatory advancement of expenses, which the indemnitee can, in many instances, obtain on demand; (iii) accelerated procedures for the "determination" required by section 145(d) to be made in the "specific case"; (iv) litigation "appeal" rights of the indemnitee in the event of an unfavorable determination; (v) procedures under which a favorable determination will be deemed to have been made under circumstances where the

9. Delaware commentators consider this article to be part of (if not all of) "[t]he legislative history of Section 145." A. Gilchrist Sparks, III, et al., *Indemnification, Directors and Officers Liability Insurance* *and Limitations of Director Liability Pursuant to Statutory Authorization: The Legal Framework Under Delaware Law*, 696 PLI/ Corp. 941 (1990) (at page 10 out of 123 on WESTLAW). ...

board fails or refuses to act; [and] (vi) reasonable funding mechanisms.

E. Norman Veasey, et al., *Delaware Supports Directors With a Three–Legged Stool of Limited Liability, Indemnification, and Insurance,* 42 Bus.Law. 399, 415 (1987).[10] Moreover, subsection (f) may reference nonindemnification rights, such as advancement rights or rights to other payments from the corporation that do not qualify as indemnification.

We need not decide in this case the precise scope of those "other rights" adverted to in § 145(f). We simply conclude that § 145(f) is not rendered meaningless or inoperative by the conclusion that a Delaware corporation lacks power to indemnify an officer or director "unless [he] 'acted in good faith and in a manner reasonably believed to be in or not opposed to the best interest of the corporation.'" *See* Arsht & Stapleton, 23 Bus.Law. at 78. As a result, we hold that Conti's Article Ninth, which would require indemnification of Waltuch even if he acted in bad faith, is inconsistent with § 145(a) and thus exceeds the scope of a Delaware corporation's power to indemnify. Since Waltuch has agreed to forgo his opportunity to prove at trial that he acted in good faith, he is not entitled to indemnification under Article Ninth for the $2.2 million he spent in connection with the private lawsuits and the CFTC proceeding. We therefore affirm the district court on this issue.

II

Unlike § 145(a), which grants a discretionary indemnification power, § 145(c) affirmatively *requires* corporations to indemnify its officers and directors for the "successful" defense of certain claims:

> To the extent that a director, officer, employee or agent of a corporation has been successful on the merits or otherwise in defense of any action, suit or proceeding referred to in subsections (a) and (b) of this section, or in defense of any claim, issue or matter therein, he shall be indemnified against expenses (including attorneys' fees) actually and reasonably incurred by him in connection therewith.

56 Del.Laws 50, § 1 at 171 (1967), *codified at* 8 Del.Code Ann. tit. 8, § 145(c) (Michie 1991). Waltuch argues that he was "successful on the merits or otherwise" in the private lawsuits, because they were dismissed with prejudice without any payment or assumption of liability by him. Conti argues that the claims against Waltuch were dismissed only because of Conti's $35 million settlement

---

10. Veasey is now Chief Justice of the Delaware Supreme Court. *See also* 1 Balotti & Finkelstein § 4.16 at 4–321, which makes the same suggestions. Other suggestions are made in Joseph F. Johnston, Jr., *Corporate Indemnification and Liability Insurance for Directors and Officers,* 33 Bus.Law. 1993, 1996, 2009–10 (1978).

payments, and that this payment was contributed, in part, "on behalf of Waltuch." [11]

The district court agreed with Conti that "the successful settlements cannot be credited to Waltuch but are attributable solely to Conti's settlement payments. It was not Waltuch who was successful, but Conti who was successful for him." 833 F.Supp. at 311. The district court held that § 145(c) mandates indemnification when the director or officer "is vindicated," but that there was no vindication here:

> Vindication is also ordinarily associated with a dismissal with prejudice without any payment. However, a director or officer is not vindicated when the reason he did not have to make a settlement payment is because someone else assumed that liability. Being bailed out is not the same thing as being vindicated.

Id. We believe that this understanding and application of the "vindication" concept is overly broad and is inconsistent with a proper interpretation of § 145(c).

No Delaware court has applied § 145(c) in the context of indemnification stemming from the settlement of civil litigation. One lower court, however, has applied that subsection to an analogous case in the criminal context, and has illuminated the link between "vindication" and the statutory phrase, "successful on the merits or otherwise." In *Merritt–Chapman & Scott Corp. v. Wolfson,* 321 A.2d 138 (Del.Super.Ct.1974), the corporation's agents were charged with several counts of criminal conduct. A jury found them guilty on some counts, but deadlocked on the others. The agents entered into a "settlement" with the prosecutor's office by pleading nolo contendere to one of the counts in exchange for the dropping of the rest. *Id.* at 140. The agents claimed entitlement to mandatory indemnification under § 145(c) as to the counts that were dismissed. In opposition, the corporation raised an argument similar to the argument raised by Conti:

> [The corporation] argues that the statute and sound public policy require indemnification only where there has been vindication by a finding or concession of innocence. *It contends that the charges against [the agents] were dropped for practical reasons,* not because of their innocence....

> The statute requires indemnification to the extent that the claimant "has been successful on the merits or otherwise." *Success is vindication.* In a criminal action, any result other than conviction must be considered success. *Going behind the result,* as [the corporation] attempts, is neither authorized by

---

11. Although this is not essential to our holding, we note that Conti points to no evidence in support of its contention that the plaintiffs would have continued to pursue their suits as to Waltuch if Conti had paid some lesser amount.

subsection (c) nor consistent with the presumption of innocence.

Id. at 141 (emphasis added).

Although the underlying proceeding in *Merritt* was criminal, the court's analysis is instructive here. The agents in *Merritt* rendered consideration—their guilty plea on one count—to achieve the dismissal of the other counts. The court considered these dismissals both "success" and (therefore) "vindication," and refused to "go[ ] behind the result" or to appraise the reason for the success. In equating "success" with "vindication," the court thus rejected the more expansive view of vindication urged by the corporation. Under *Merritt*'s holding, then, vindication, when used as a synonym for "success" under § 145(c), does not mean moral exoneration. Escape from an adverse judgment or other detriment, for whatever reason, is determinative. According to *Merritt*, the only question a court may ask is what the result was, not why it was.[12]

Conti's contention that, because of its $35 million settlement payments, Waltuch's settlement without payment should not really count as settlement without payment, is inconsistent with the rule in *Merritt*. Here, Waltuch was sued, and the suit was dismissed without his having paid a settlement. Under the approach taken in *Merritt*, it is not our business to ask why this result was reached. Once Waltuch achieved his settlement gratis, he achieved success "on the merits or otherwise." And, as we know from *Merritt*, success is sufficient to constitute vindication (at least for the purposes of § 145(c)). Waltuch's settlement thus vindicated him.

The concept of "vindication" pressed by Conti is also inconsistent with the fact that a director or officer who is able to defeat an adversary's claim by asserting a technical defense is entitled to indemnification under § 145(c). *See* 1 Balotti & Finkelstein, § 4.13 at 4–302. In such cases, the indemnitee has been "successful" in the palpable sense that he has won, and the suit has been dismissed, whether or not the victory is deserved in merits terms. If a

---

12. Our adoption of *Merritt*'s interpretation of the statutory term "successful" does not necessarily signal our endorsement of the result in that case. The *Merritt* court sliced the case into individual counts, with indemnification pegged to each count independently of the others. We are not faced with a case in which the corporate officer claims to have been "successful" on some parts of the case but was clearly "unsuccessful" on others, and therefore take no position on this feature of the *Merritt* holding.

We also do not mean our discussion of *Merritt* to suggest that the line between success and failure in a criminal case may be drawn in the same way in the civil context. In a criminal case, conviction on a particular count is obvious failure, and dismissal of the charge is obvious success. In a civil suit for damages, however, there is a monetary continuum between complete success (dismissal of the suit without any payment) and complete failure (payment of the full amount of damages requested by the plaintiff). Because Waltuch made no payment in connection with the dismissal of the suits against him, we need not decide whether a defendant's settlement payment automatically renders that defendant "unsuccessful" under § 145(c).

technical defense is deemed "vindication" under Delaware law, it cannot matter why Waltuch emerged unscathed, or whether Conti "bailed [him] out", or whether his success was deserved. Under § 145(c), mere success is vindication enough.

This conclusion comports with the reality that civil judgments and settlements are ordinarily expressed in terms of cash rather than moral victory. No doubt, it would make sense for Conti to buy the dismissal of the claims against Waltuch along with its own discharge from the case, perhaps to avoid further expense or participation as a non-party, potential cross-claims, or negative publicity. But Waltuch apparently did not accede to that arrangement, and Delaware law cannot allow an indemnifying corporation to escape the mandatory indemnification of subsection (c) by paying a sum in settlement on behalf of an unwilling indemnitee.

We note that two non-Delaware precedents (one from this Court) support our conclusion. In *Wisener v. Air Express Int'l Corp.*, 583 F.2d 579 (2d Cir.1978), we construed an Illinois indemnification statute that was intentionally enacted as a copy of Delaware's § 145. *See id.* at 582 n. 3; 1 Balotti & Finkelstein, § 4.12 at 4–296 n. 1048 (§ 145 was the "prototype" for Illinois's indemnification statute). Our holding in that case is perfectly applicable here:

> It is contended that [the director] was not "successful" in the litigation, since the third-party claims against him never proceeded to trial. The statute, however, refers to success "on the merits or otherwise," which surely is broad enough to cover a termination of claims by agreement without any payment or assumption of liability.

583 F.2d at 583. It is undisputed that the private lawsuits against Conti and Waltuch were dismissed with prejudice, "without any payment of assumption of liability" by Waltuch. Applying the analysis of *Wisener*, Conti must indemnify Waltuch for his expenses in connection with the private lawsuits.

The second case, from the Eastern District of Pennsylvania, is almost on point. In *B & B Investment Club v. Kleinert's, Inc.*, 472 F.Supp. 787 (E.D.Pa.1979), suit had been brought against a corporation and two of its officers. The corporation settled the suit against it (on unspecified terms). One of the officers (Stephens) settled by paying $35,000, and the other (Brubaker) settled without paying anything. Brubaker claimed indemnification under a Pennsylvania statute that was virtually identical to § 145(c), *id.* at 789 n. 3, as the court noted, *id.* at 791 n. 5. The corporation argued that Brubaker was not "successful on the merits or otherwise," because his settlement was achieved only as a result of Stephens's $35,000 payment. The court rejected this argument, explaining that "[Brubaker] is entitled to indemnification because *he* made no monetary payment and the case was dismissed with prejudice *as to him*." *Id.* at 790 (emphasis added). Even though there was evidence that the plaintiffs dismissed their claims against Brubaker only because of Stephens's payment, this payment was irrelevant to the determination of "success":

> That the class plaintiffs at one point in the negotiations sought a cash payment from Brubaker but later settled with him for no monetary consideration does not render Brubaker any less successful than the plaintiff in *Wisener.* Nor is the extent of Brubaker's success affected by Stephens' having paid sufficient consideration to enable Brubaker to negotiate a dismissal with prejudice without making any payment. In short, Brubaker was "successful on the merits or otherwise"....

Id. at 791. The same logic applies to our case. "[T]he extent of [Waltuch's] success" is not lessened by Conti's payments, even if it is true (as it stands to reason) that his success was achieved because Conti was willing to pay. Whatever the impetus for the plaintiffs' dismissal of their claims against Waltuch, he still walked away without liability and without making a payment. This constitutes a success that is untarnished by the process that achieved it.

For all of these reasons, we agree with Waltuch that he is entitled to indemnification under § 145(c) for his expenses pertaining to the private lawsuits.

III

The judgment of the district court is affirmed in part and reversed in part. This case is remanded to the district court so that judgment may be entered in favor of Waltuch on his claim for $1,228,586.67, representing the unreimbursed expenses from the private lawsuits. *See supra* note 1.

Chapter XI

STRUCTURAL CHANGES: COMBINATIONS AND TENDER OFFERS

SECTION 2. TENDER OFFERS

Insert the following Note at p. 1254 of the Unabridged Edition, following Revlon, Inc. v. MacAndrews & Forbes Holdings, Inc., and p. 822 of the Concise Edition, following the Note on Revlon:

BARKAN v. AMSTED INDUSTRIES, INC., 567 A.2d 1279 (Del. Supr.1989). "There is some dispute among the parties as to the meaning of *Revlon*, as well as its relevance to the outcome of this case. We believe that the general principles announced in *Revlon*, in *Unocal Corp. v. Mesa Petroleum Co.*, 493 A.2d 946 (Del. Supr.1985), and in *Moran v. Household International, Inc.*,, 500 A.2d 1346 (Del.Supr.1985) govern this case and every case in which a fundamental change of corporate control occurs or is contemplated. However, the basic teaching of these precedents is simply that the directors must act in accordance with their fundamental duties of care and loyalty. *Unocal*, 493 A.2d at 954–55; *Revlon*, 506 A.2d at 180. It is true that a court evaluating the propriety of a change of control or a takeover defense must be mindful of 'the omnipresent specter that a board may be acting primarily in its own interests, rather than those of the corporation and its shareholders.' *Unocal*, 493 A.2d at 954. Nevertheless, there is no single blueprint that a board must follow to fulfill its duties. A stereotypical approach to the sale and acquisition of corporate control is not to be expected in the face of the evolving techniques and financing devices employed in today's corporate environment. *Mills Acquisition Co. v. Macmillan, Inc.*, 559 A.2d 1261, 1286–88 (Del.Supr.1989). Rather, a board's actions must be evaluated in light of relevant circumstances to determine if they were undertaken with due diligence and in good faith. If no breach of duty is found, the board's actions are entitled to the protections of the business judgment rule. *Id.* at 954–55.

"This Court has found that certain fact patterns demand certain responses from the directors. Notably, in *Revlon* we held that when several suitors are actively bidding for control of a corpora-

253

tion, the directors may not use defensive tactics that destroy the auction process. *Revlon,* 506 A.2d at 182–85. When it becomes clear that the auction will result in a change of corporate control, the board must act in a neutral manner to encourage the highest possible price for shareholders. *Id.* However, *Revlon* does not demand that every change in the control of a Delaware corporation be preceded by a heated bidding contest. *Revlon* is merely one of an unbroken line of cases that seek to prevent the conflicts of interest that arise in the field of mergers and acquisitions by demanding that directors act with scrupulous concern for fairness to shareholders. When multiple bidders are competing for control, this concern for fairness forbids directors from using defensive mechanisms to thwart an auction or to favor one bidder over another. *Id.* When the board is considering a single offer and has no reliable grounds upon which to judge its adequacy, this concern for fairness demands a canvas of the market to determine if higher bids may be elicited. *In re Fort Howard Corp. Shareholders Litig.,* C.A. No. 9991, 1988 WL 83147 (Del.Ch.1988). When, however, the directors possess a body of reliable evidence with which to evaluate the fairness of a transaction, they may approve that transaction without conducting an active survey of the market. As the Chancellor recognized, the circumstances in which this passive approach is acceptable are limited. 'A decent respect for reality forces one to admit that . . . advice [of an investment banker] is frequently a pale substitute for the dependable information that a canvas of the relevant market can provide.' *In re Amsted Indus. Litig.,* letter op. at 19–20. The need for adequate information is central to the enlightened evaluation of a transaction that a board must make. Nevertheless, there is no single method that a board must employ to acquire such information. Here, the Chancellor found that the advice of the Special Committee's investment bankers, when coupled with the special circumstances surrounding the negotiation and consummation of the MBO, supported a finding that Amsted's directors had acted in good faith to arrange the best possible transaction for shareholders. Our own review of the record leads us to rule that the Chancellor's finding was well within the scope of his discretion."

―――――――

Add the following cross-reference at p. 1299 of the Unabridged Edition, after the Note on Unitrin, Inc. v. American General Corp.

WILLIAMS v. GEIER

[p. 29, supra]

―――――――

Add the following case at p. 1299 of the Unabridged Edition, after the Note on Unitrin, Inc. v. American General Corp.:

QUICKTURN DESIGN SYSTEMS, INC. v. SHAPIRO

Supreme Court of Delaware, 1998.
721 A.2d 1281.

Before WALSH, HOLLAND and HARTNETT, Justices.

HOLLAND, Justice:

This is an expedited appeal from a final judgment entered by the Court of Chancery. The dispute arises out of an ongoing effort by Mentor Graphics Corporation ("Mentor"), a hostile bidder, to acquire Quickturn Design Systems, Inc. ("Quickturn"), the target company. The plaintiffs-appellees are Mentor[1] and an unaffiliated stockholder of Quickturn. The named defendants-appellants are Quickturn and its directors.

In response to Mentor's tender offer and proxy contest to replace the Quickturn board of directors, as part of Mentor's effort to acquire Quickturn, the Quickturn board enacted two defensive measures. First, it amended the Quickturn shareholder rights plan ("Rights Plan") by adopting a "no hand" feature of limited duration (the "Delayed Redemption Provision" or "DRP"). Second, the Quickturn board amended the corporation's by-laws to delay the holding of any special stockholders meeting requested by stockholders for 90 to 100 days after the validity of the request is determined (the "Amendment" or "By–Law Amendment").

Mentor filed actions for declaratory and injunctive relief in the Court of Chancery challenging the legality of both defensive responses by Quickturn's board. The Court of Chancery conducted a trial on the merits. It determined that the By–Law Amendment is valid. It also concluded, however, that the DRP is invalid on fiduciary duty grounds.

In this appeal, Quickturn argues that the Court of Chancery erred in finding that Quickturn's directors breached their fiduciary duty by adopting the Delayed Redemption Provision. We have concluded that, as a matter of Delaware law, the Delayed Redemption Provision was invalid. Therefore, on that alternative basis, the judgment of the Court of Chancery is affirmed.

STATEMENT OF FACTS
The Parties

Mentor (the hostile bidder) is an Oregon corporation, headquartered in Wilsonville, Oregon, whose shares are publicly traded

---

1. Mentor and MGZ Corp., a wholly owned Mentor subsidiary specially created as a vehicle to acquire Quickturn, are referred to collectively as "Mentor." Unless otherwise indicated, Mentor and Howard Shapiro, the shareholder plaintiff in Court of Chancery Civil Action No. 16588, are referred to collectively as "Mentor."

on the NASDAQ national market system. Mentor manufactures, markets, and supports electronic design automation ("EDA") software and hardware. It also provides related services that enable engineers to design, analyze, simulate, model, implement, and verify the components of electronic systems. Mentor markets its products primarily for large firms in the communications, computer, semiconductor, consumer electronics, aerospace, and transportation industries.

Quickturn, the target company, is a Delaware corporation, headquartered in San Jose, California. Quickturn has 17,922,518 outstanding shares of common stock[3] that are publicly traded on the NASDAQ national market system. Quickturn invented, and was the first company to successfully market, logic emulation technology, which is used to verify the design of complex silicon chips and electronics systems. Quickturn is currently the market leader in the emulation business, controlling an estimated 60% of the worldwide emulation market and an even higher percentage of the United States market. Quickturn maintains the largest intellectual property portfolio in the industry, which includes approximately twenty-nine logic emulation patents issued in the United States, and numerous other patents issued in foreign jurisdictions. Quickturn's customers include the world's leading technology companies, among them Intel, IBM, Sun Microsystems, Texas Instruments, Hitachi, Fujitsu, Siemens, and NEC.

Quickturn's board of directors consists of eight members, all but one of whom are outside, independent directors.[4] All have distinguished careers and significant technological experience. Collectively, the board has more than 30 years of experience in the EDA industry and owns one million shares (about 5%) of Quickturn's common stock.

Since 1989, Quickturn has historically been a growth company, having experienced increases in earnings and revenues during the past seven years. Those favorable trends were reflected in Quick-

---

3. As of July 30, 1998.

4. The Quickturn board includes Messrs. Glen Antle (President and Chairman of Quickturn's board of directors); Michael D'Amour (Quickturn's founding CEO and chairman through 1993, and Executive Vice President for research and development and head of international sales until he left Quickturn management in 1995); Dean William A. Hasler (a former Vice Chairman and partner of KPMG Peat Marwick; a former Dean of the Haas Graduate School of Business at the University of California, Berkeley, a position he held until 1998; and currently a technology and business advisor); Keith Lobo (Quickturn's President and CEO); Charles D. Kissner (currently CEO and Chairman of the Board of Digital Microwave Corporation, a telecommunications company, and a former

President, CEO, and director for Aristacom International, Inc.; also a former AT & T executive); Richard Alberding (a management consultant for high technology companies; and who currently serves on the board of directors of several technology companies); Dr. David Lam (former Vice President at Wyse Technology, former President and CEO of Expert Edge, Inc., and currently a technology and business advisor in the semiconductor equipment industry and Chairman of the David Lam Group); Dr. Yen–Son (Paul) Huang (a co-founder and President of PiE and, following PiE's merger with Quickturn in 1993, Executive Vice President of Quickturn until June 1997. Since then, Dr. Huang has served Quickturn only as a director).

turn's stock prices, which reached a high of $15.75 during the first quarter of 1998, and generally traded in the $15.875 to $21.25 range during the year preceding Mentor's hostile bid.

Since the spring of 1998, Quickturn's earnings, revenue growth, and stock price levels have declined, largely because of the downturn in the semiconductor industry and more specifically in the Asian semiconductor market. Historically, 30%–35% of Quickturn's annual sales (approximately $35 million) had come from Asia, but in 1998, Quickturn's Asian sales declined dramatically with the downturn of the Asian market.[5] Management has projected that the negative impact of the Asian market upon Quickturn's sales should begin reversing itself sometime between the second half of 1998 and early 1999.

Quickturn–Mentor Patent Litigation

Since 1996, Mentor and Quickturn have been engaged in patent litigation that has resulted in Mentor being barred from competing in the United States emulation market. Because its products have been adjudicated to infringe upon Quickturn's patents, Mentor currently stands enjoined from selling, manufacturing, or marketing its emulation products in the United States. Thus, Mentor is excluded from an unquestionably significant market for emulation products.

The origin of the patent controversy was Mentor's sale of its hardware emulation assets, including its patents, to Quickturn in 1992. Later, Mentor reentered the emulation business when it acquired a French company called Meta Systems ("Meta") and began to market Meta's products in the United States in December 1995. Quickturn reacted by commencing a proceeding before the International Trade Commission ("ITC") claiming that Meta and Mentor were infringing Quickturn's patents. In August 1996, the ITC issued an order prohibiting Mentor from importing, selling, distributing, advertising, or soliciting in the United States, any products manufactured by Meta. That preliminary order was affirmed by the Federal Circuit Court of Appeals in August 1997. In December 1997, the ITC issued a Permanent Exclusion Order prohibiting Mentor from importing, selling, marketing, advertising, or soliciting in the United States, until at least April 28, 2009, any of the emulation products manufactured by Meta outside the United States.

At present, the only remaining patent litigation is pending in the Oregon Federal District Court. Quickturn is asserting a patent infringement damage claim that, Quickturn contends, is worth

---

5. By the summer of 1998, Quickturn's stock price had declined to $6 per share. On August 11, 1998, the closing price was $8.00 It was in this "trough" period that Mentor, which had designs upon Quickturn since the fall of 1997, saw an opportunity to acquire Quickturn for an advantageous price.

approximately $225 million. Mentor contends that Quickturn's claim is worth only $5.2 million or even less.

Mentor's Interest in Acquiring Quickturn

Mentor began exploring the possibility of acquiring Quickturn. If Mentor owned Quickturn, it would also own the patents, and would be in a position to "unenforce" them by seeking to vacate Quickturn's injunctive orders against Mentor in the patent litigation. The exploration process began when Mr. Bernd Braune, a Mentor senior executive, retained Arthur Andersen ("Andersen") to advise Mentor how it could successfully compete in the emulation market. The result was a report Andersen issued in October 1997, entitled "PROJECT VELOCITY" and "Strategic Alternatives Analysis." The Andersen report identified several advantages and benefits Mentor would enjoy if it acquired Quickturn.[10]

In December 1997, Mentor retained Salomon Smith Barney ("Salomon") to act as its financial advisor in connection with a possible acquisition of Quickturn. Salomon prepared an extensive study which it reviewed with Mentor's senior executives in early 1998. The Salomon study concluded that although a Quickturn acquisition could provide substantial value for Mentor, Mentor could not afford to acquire Quickturn at the then-prevailing market price levels. Ultimately, Mentor decided not to attempt an acquisition of Quickturn during the first half of 1998.

After Quickturn's stock price began to decline in May 1998, however, Gregory Hinckley, Mentor's Executive Vice President, told Dr. Walden Rhines, Mentor's Chairman, that "the market outlook being very weak due to the Asian crisis made it a good opportunity" to try acquiring Quickturn for a cheap price. Mr. Hinckley then assembled Mentor's financial and legal advisors, proxy solicitors, and others, and began a three month process that culminated in Mentor's August 12, 1998 tender offer.

Mentor Tender Offer and Proxy Contest

On August 12, 1998, Mentor announced an unsolicited cash tender offer for all outstanding common shares of Quickturn at $12.125 per share, a price representing an approximate 50% premium over Quickturn's immediate pre-offer price, and a 20% discount from Quickturn's February 1998 stock price levels. Mentor's tender offer, once consummated, would be followed by a second step merger in which Quickturn's nontendering stockholders would receive, in cash, the same $12.125 per share tender offer price.

---

10. These included: (i) eliminating the time and expense associated with litigation; (ii) creating synergy from combining two companies with complementary core competencies; (iii) reducing customer confusion over product availability, which in turn would accelerate sales; and (iv) eliminating the threat of a large competitor moving into the emulation market. Mentor has utilized these reasons in public statements in which it attempted to explain why its bid made sense.

Mentor also announced its intent to solicit proxies to replace the board at a special meeting. Relying upon Quickturn's then-applicable by-law provision governing the call of special stockholders meetings, Mentor began soliciting agent designations from Quickturn stockholders to satisfy the by-law's stock ownership requirements to call such a meeting.[11]

Quickturn Board Meetings

Under the Williams Act, Quickturn was required to inform its shareholders of its response to Mentor's offer no later than ten business days after the offer was commenced. During that ten day period, the Quickturn board met three times, on August 13, 17, and 21, 1998. During each of those meetings, it considered Mentor's offer and ultimately decided how to respond.

The Quickturn board first met on August 13, 1998, the day after Mentor publicly announced its bid. All board members attended the meeting, for the purpose of evaluating Mentor's tender offer. The meeting lasted for several hours. Before or during the meeting, each board member received a package that included (i) Mentor's press release announcing the unsolicited offer; (ii) Quickturn's press release announcing its board's review of Mentor's offer; (iii) Dr. Rhines's August 11 letter to Mr. Antle [Quickturn's president]; (iv) ... complaints filed by Mentor against Quickturn and its directors; and (v) copies of Quickturn's then-current Rights Plan and by-laws.

The Quickturn board first discussed retaining a team of financial advisors to assist it in evaluating Mentor's offer and the company's strategic alternatives. The board discussed the importance of selecting a qualified investment bank, and considered several investment banking firms. Aside from Hambrecht & Quist ("H & Q"), Quickturn's long-time investment banker, other firms that the board considered included Goldman Sachs & Co. and Morgan Stanley Dean Witter. Ultimately, the board selected H & Q, because the board believed that H & Q had the most experience with the EDA industry in general and with Quickturn in particular.[12]

During the balance of the meeting, the board discussed for approximately one or two hours (a) the status, terms, and conditions of Mentor's offer; (b) the status of Quickturn's patent litigation with Mentor; (c) the applicable rules and regulations that would

11. The applicable by-law (Article II, § 2.3) authorized a call of a special stockholders meeting by shareholders holding at least 10% of Quickturn's shares. In their agent solicitation, Mentor informed Quickturn stockholders that Mentor intended to call a special meeting approximately 45 days after it received sufficient agent designations to satisfy the 10% requirement under the original by-law. The solicitation also disclosed Mentor's intent to set the date for the special meeting, and to set the record date and give formal notice of that meeting.

12. Apparently, the board had already decided to retain Quickturn's outside counsel, Wilson, Sonsini, Goodrich & Rosati, as its legal advisors. Larry Sonsini, Esquire, a senior partner of that firm, is shown on the minutes of all three board meetings as "Secretary of the Meeting," and appears to have authored those minutes in that capacity.

govern the board's response to the offer required by the Securities Exchange Act of 1934 (the "34 Act"); (d) the board's fiduciary duties to Quickturn and its shareholders in a tender offer context; (e) the scope of defensive measures available to the corporation if the board decided that the offer was not in the best interests of the company or its stockholders; (f) Quickturn's then-current Rights Plan and special stockholders meeting by-law provisions; (g) the need for a federal antitrust filing; and (h) the potential effect of Mentor's offer on Quickturn's employees. The board also instructed management and H & Q to prepare analyses to assist the directors in evaluating Mentor's offer, and scheduled two board meetings, August 17, and August 21, 1998.

The Quickturn board next met on August 17, 1998. That meeting centered around financial presentations by management and by H & Q. Mr. Keith Lobo, Quickturn's President and CEO, presented a Medium Term Strategic Plan, which was a "top down" estimate detailing the economic outlook and the company's future sales, income prospects and future plans (the "Medium Term Plan"). The Medium Term Plan contained an optimistic (30%) revenue growth projection for the period 1998–2000.[13] After management made its presentation, H & Q supplied its valuation of Quickturn, which relied upon a "base case" that assumed management's 30% revenue growth projection. On that basis, H & Q presented various "standalone" valuations based on various techniques, including a discounted cash flow ("DCF") analysis. Finally, the directors discussed possible defensive measures, but took no action at that time.

The Quickturn board held its third and final meeting in response to Mentor's offer on August 21, 1998. Again, the directors received extensive materials and a further detailed analysis performed by H & Q. The focal point of that analysis was a chart entitled "Summary of Implied Valuation." That chart compared Mentor's tender offer price to the Quickturn valuation ranges generated by H & Q's application of five different methodologies.[14] The chart showed that Quickturn's value under all but one of those methodologies was higher than Mentor's $12.125 tender offer price.

Quickturn's Board Rejects Mentor's Offer as Inadequate

After hearing the presentations, the Quickturn board concluded that Mentor's offer was inadequate, and decided to recommend that Quickturn shareholders reject Mentor's offer. The directors based

---

13. The Court of Chancery concluded that the Quickturn board had grounds to anticipate that the company could "turn around" in a year and perform at the projected revenue levels.

14. The five methodologies and the respective price ranges were: Historical Trad-

ing Range ($6.13–$21.63); Comparable Public Companies ($2.55–$15.61); Comparable M & A Transactions ($6.00–$31.36); Comparable Premiums Paid ($9.54–$10.72); and Discounted Cash Flow Analysis ($11.88–$57.87).

their decision upon: (a) H & Q's report; (b) the fact that Quickturn was experiencing a temporary trough in its business, which was reflected in its stock price; (c) the company's leadership in technology and patents and resulting market share; (d) the likely growth in Quickturn's markets (most notably, the Asian market) and the strength of Quickturn's new products (specifically, its Mercury product); (e) the potential value of the patent litigation with Mentor; and (f) the problems for Quickturn's customers, employees, and technology if the two companies were combined as the result of a hostile takeover.

Quickturn's Defensive Measures

At the August 21 board meeting, the Quickturn board adopted two defensive measures in response to Mentor's hostile takeover bid. First, the board amended Article II, § 2.3 of Quickturn's by-laws, which permitted stockholders holding 10% or more of Quickturn's stock to call a special stockholders meeting. The By–Law Amendment provides that if any such special meeting is requested by shareholders, the corporation (Quickturn) would fix the record date for, and determine the time and place of, that special meeting, which must take place not less than 90 days nor more than 100 days after the receipt and determination of the validity of the shareholders' request.

Second, the board amended Quickturn's shareholder Rights Plan by eliminating its "dead hand" feature and replacing it with the Deferred Redemption Provision, under which no newly elected board could redeem the Rights Plan for six months after taking office, if the purpose or effect of the redemption would be to facilitate a transaction with an "Interested Person" (one who proposed, nominated or financially supported the election of the new directors to the board).[15] Mentor would be an Interested Person.

The effect of the By–Law Amendment would be to delay a shareholder-called special meeting for at least three months. The effect of the DRP would be to delay the ability of a newly-elected, Mentor-nominated board to redeem the Rights Plan or "poison pill" for six months, in any transaction with an Interested Person. Thus, the combined effect of the two defensive measures would be to

---

15. The amended Rights Plan pertinently provides that: "[I]n the event that a majority of the Board of Directors of the Company is elected by stockholder action at an annual or special meeting of stockholders, then until the 180th day following the effectiveness of such election (including any postponement or adjournment thereof), the Rights shall not be redeemed if such redemption is reasonably likely to have the purpose or effect of facilitating a Transaction with an Interested Person."

An "Interested Person" is defined under the amended Rights Plan as "any Person who (i) is or will become an Acquiring Person if such Transaction were to be consummated or an Affiliate or Associate of such a Person, and (ii) is, or directly or indirectly proposed, nominated or financially supported, a director of [Quickturn] in office at the time of consideration of such Transaction who was elected at an annual or special meeting of stockholders."

delay any acquisition of Quickturn by Mentor for at least nine months.

PROCEDURAL HISTORY

Mentor filed this action in the Court of Chancery on August 12, 1998, seeking a declaratory judgment that Quickturn's newly adopted takeover defenses are invalid and an injunction requiring the Quickturn board to dismantle those defenses. After expedited briefing and oral argument, the Court of Chancery denied Quickturn's case dispositive pre-trial motion on October 9, 1998. A trial was held on October 19, 20, 23, 26 and 28, 1998. Thereafter, the parties submitted post-trial briefs on an expedited schedule.

During the course of the litigation in the Court of Chancery, the Quickturn board, relying upon the By–Law Amendment, noticed the special meeting requested by Mentor for January 8, 1999—71 days after the October 1, 1998 meeting date originally noticed by Mentor.[17] After the trial, Mentor announced in Amendments to its Schedule 14A–1 that were filed with the Securities and Exchange Commission, that it had received tenders of Quickturn shares which, together with the shares that Mentor already owned, represented over 51% of Quickturn's outstanding stock.

QUICKTURN BY–LAW AMENDMENT

At the time Mentor commenced its tender offer and proxy contest, Quickturn's by-laws authorized shareholders holding at least 10% of Quickturn's voting stock to call a special meeting of stockholders. The then-applicable by-law, Article II, § 2.3, read thusly:

> A special meeting of the stockholders may be called at any time by (i) the board of directors, (ii) the chairman of the board, (iii) the president, (iv) the chief executive officer or (v) one or more shareholders holding shares in the aggregate entitled to cast not less than ten percent (10%) of the votes at that meeting.

At the August 21, 1998 board meeting, the Quickturn board amended § 2.3 in response to the Mentor bid, to read as follows:

> A special meeting of the stockholders may be called at any time by (i) the board of directors, (ii) the chairman of the board, (iii) the president, (iv) the chief executive officer or (v) subject to the procedures set forth in this Section 2.3, one or more stockholders holding shares in the aggregate entitled to cast not less than ten percent (10%) of the votes at that meeting.

---

17. Mentor later renoticed the special meeting date to November 24, 1998, anticipating that the Court of Chancery would issue its decision before that time. After the Court of Chancery informed the parties that it would be unable to issue a decision by November 24, Mentor agreed that its meeting would be convened and then immediately adjourned to a later date.

Upon request in writing sent by registered mail to the president or chief executive officer by any stockholder or stockholders entitled to call a special meeting of stockholders pursuant to this Section 2.3, the board of directors shall determine a place and time for such meeting, which time shall be not less than ninety (90) nor more than one hundred (100) days after the receipt and determination of the validity of such request, and a record date for the determination of stockholders entitled to vote at such meeting in the manner set forth in Section 2.12 hereof. Following such receipt and determination, it shall be the duty of the secretary to cause notice to be given to the stockholders entitled to vote at such meeting, in the manner set forth in Section 2.4 hereof, that a meeting will be held at the time and place so determined.

The Court of Chancery found that the Quickturn board amended the By–Law because (i) the original § 2.3 was incomplete: it did not explicitly state who would be responsible for determining the time, place, and record date for the meeting and (ii) the original by-law language arguably would have allowed a hostile bidder holding the requisite percentage of shares to call a special stockholders meeting on minimal notice and stampede the shareholders into making a decision without time to become adequately informed.

The Court of Chancery concluded that the By–Law Amendment responded to those concerns by explicitly making the Quickturn board responsible for fixing the time, place, record date and notice of the special meeting and by mandating a 90 to 100 day period of delay for holding the meeting after the validity of the shareholder's meeting request is determined. That specific delay period was chosen to make § 2.3 parallel to, and congruent with, Quickturn's "advance notice" by-law, which contained a similar 90 to 100 day minimum advance notice period.

The only By–Law Amendment-related issue that the Court of Chancery decided was whether the Amendment, standing alone, fell outside any range of potentially reasonable responses and, therefore, constituted a disproportionate response to the threat posed by the Mentor tender offer and proxy contest. Among the factors the Court of Chancery considered were whether the challenged defensive response "is a statutorily authorized form of business decision that a board of directors may routinely make in a non-takeover context,"[18] and whether the response "was limited and corresponded in degree or magnitude to the degree or magnitude of the threat."[19]

---

18. Unitrin, Inc. v. American General Corp., Del.Supr., 651 A.2d 1361, 1389 (1995); Unocal Corp. v. Mesa Petroleum Co., Del.Supr., 493 A.2d 946, 958 (1985); Cheff v. Mathes, Del.Supr., 199 A.2d 548, 554 (1964).

19. Unitrin, Inc. v. American General Corp., 651 A.2d at 1389.

The Court of Chancery concluded that the Quickturn board's adoption of the By-Law Amendment did not violate the fiduciary principles embodied in Unocal and its progeny. Although the Delayed Redemption Provision and the By-Law Amendment were enacted as a concerted defensive response to Mentor's hostile takeover efforts, Mentor did not file a cross-appeal challenging the Court of Chancery's decision upholding the validity of Quickturn's amendment to its by-laws. Consequently, the Court of Chancery's ruling on the By-Law Amendment is not at issue in this appeal and has become final.

QUICKTURN'S DELAYED REDEMPTION PROVISION

At the time Mentor commenced its bid, Quickturn had in place a Rights Plan that contained a so-called "dead hand" provision. That provision had a limited "continuing director" feature that became operative only if an insurgent that owned more than 15% of Quickturn's common stock successfully waged a proxy contest to replace a majority of the board. In that event, only the "continuing directors" (those directors in office at the time the poison pill was adopted) could redeem the rights.

During the same August 21, 1998 meeting at which it amended the special meeting by-law, the Quickturn board also amended the Rights Plan to eliminate its "continuing director" feature, and to substitute a "no hand" or "delayed redemption provision" into its Rights Plan. The Delayed Redemption Provision provides that, if a majority of the directors are replaced by stockholder action, the newly elected board cannot redeem the rights for six months if the purpose or effect of the redemption would be to facilitate a transaction with an "Interested Person."[21]

It is undisputed that the DRP would prevent Mentor's slate, if elected as the new board majority, from redeeming the Rights Plan for six months following their election, because a redemption would be "reasonably likely to have the purpose or effect of facilitating a Transaction" with Mentor, a party that "directly or indirectly proposed, nominated or financially supported" the election of the new board. Consequently, by adopting the DRP, the Quickturn board built into the process a six month delay period in addition to the 90 to 100 day delay mandated by the By-Law Amendment.

---

21. The "no hand" or Delayed Redemption Provision is found in a new Section 23(b) of the Rights Plan, which states: (b) Notwithstanding the provisions of Section 23(a), in the event that a majority of the Board of Directors of the Company is elected by stockholder action at an annual or special meeting of stockholders, then until the 180th day following the effectiveness of such election (including any postponement or adjournment thereof), the Rights shall not be redeemed if such redemption is reasonably likely to have the purpose or effect of facilitating a Transaction with an Interested Person.

Substantially similar provisions were added to Sections 24 ("Exchange") and 27 ("Supplements and Amendments") of the Rights Plan.

COURT OF CHANCERY INVALIDATES DELAYED
REDEMPTION PROVISION

When the board of a Delaware corporation takes action to resist a hostile bid for control, the board of directors' defensive actions are subjected to "enhanced" judicial scrutiny.[22] For a target board's actions to be entitled to business judgment rule protection, the target board must first establish that it had reasonable grounds to believe that the hostile bid constituted a threat to corporate policy and effectiveness; and second, that the defensive measures adopted were "proportionate," that is, reasonable in relation to the threat that the board reasonably perceived. The Delayed Redemption Provision was reviewed by the Court of Chancery pursuant to that standard.

The Court of Chancery found: "the evidence, viewed as a whole, shows that the perceived threat that led the Quickturn board to adopt the DRP, was the concern that Quickturn shareholders might mistakenly, in ignorance of Quickturn's true value, accept Mentor's inadequate offer, and elect a new board that would prematurely sell the company before the new board could adequately inform itself of Quickturn's fair value and before the shareholders could consider other options." The Court of Chancery concluded that Mentor's combined tender offer and proxy contest amounted to substantive coercion.[25] Having concluded that the Quickturn board reasonably perceived a cognizable threat, the Court of Chancery then examined whether the board's response—the Delayed Redemption Provision—was proportionate in relation to that threat.

In assessing a challenge to defensive measures taken by a target board in response to an attempted hostile takeover, enhanced judicial scrutiny requires an evaluation of the board's justification for each contested defensive measure and its concomitant results. The Court of Chancery found that the Quickturn board's "justification or rationale for adopting the Delayed Redemption Provision was to force any newly elected board to take sufficient time to become familiar with Quickturn and its value, and to provide shareholders the opportunity to consider alternatives, before selling Quickturn to any acquiror." The Court of Chancery concluded that the Delayed Redemption Provision could not pass the proportionality test. Therefore, the Court of Chancery held that "the DRP cannot survive scrutiny under Unocal and must be declared invalid."

DELAYED REDEMPTION PROVISION VIOLATES
FUNDAMENTAL DELAWARE LAW

In this appeal, Mentor argues that the judgment of the Court of Chancery should be affirmed because the Delayed Redemption Provision is invalid as a matter of Delaware law. According to

22. Unocal Corp. v. Mesa Petroleum Co., Del.Supr., 493 A.2d 946, 955 (1985).

25. Unitrin, Inc. v. American General Corp., 651 A.2d at 1387.

Mentor, the Delayed Redemption Provision, like the "dead hand" feature in the Rights Plan that was held to be invalid in *Toll Brothers*,[29] will impermissibly deprive any newly elected board of both its statutory authority to manage the corporation under 8 Del.C. § 141(a) and its concomitant fiduciary duty pursuant to that statutory mandate. We agree.

Our analysis of the Delayed Redemption Provision in the Quickturn Rights Plan is guided by the prior precedents of this Court with regard to a board of directors authority to adopt a Rights Plan or "poison pill." In *Moran*, this Court held that the "inherent powers of the Board conferred by 8 Del.C. § 141(a) concerning the management of the corporation's 'business and affairs' provides the Board additional authority upon which to enact the Rights Plan."[30] Consequently, this Court upheld the adoption of the Rights Plan in *Moran* as a legitimate exercise of business judgment by the board of directors. In doing so, however, this Court also held "the rights plan is not absolute":

In *Moran*, this Court held that the "ultimate response to an actual takeover bid must be judged by the Directors' actions at the time and nothing we say relieves them of their fundamental duties to the corporation and its shareholders." Consequently, we concluded that the use of the Rights Plan would be evaluated when and if the issue arises.

One of the most basic tenets of Delaware corporate law is that the board of directors has the ultimate responsibility for managing the business and affairs of a corporation.[36] Section 141(a) requires that any limitation on the board's authority be set out in the certificate of incorporation.[37] The Quickturn certificate of incorpo-

---

29. Carmody v. Toll Brothers, Inc., Del. Ch., C.A. No. 15983, Jacobs, V.C., 1998 WL 418896 (July 24, 1998) ("Toll Brothers"). See Bank of New York Co., Inc. v. Irving Bank Corp., N.Y.Sup.Ct., 139 Misc.2d 665, 528 N.Y.S.2d 482 (1988). See also Shawn C. Lese, Note: Preventing Control From the Grave: A Proposal for Judicial Treatment of Dead Hand Provisions in Poison Pills, 96 Colum.L.Rev. 2175 (1996); Jeffrey N. Gordon, "Just Say Never?" Poison Pills, Dead Hand Pills, and Shareholder Adopted By-Laws: An Essay for Warren Buffett, 19 Cardozo L.Rev. 511 (1997). Cf. Invacare Corp. v. Healthdyne Technologies, Inc., N.D.Ga., 968 F.Supp. 1578 (1997) (applying Georgia law).

30. Moran v. Household International, Inc., Del.Supr., 500 A.2d 1346, 1353 (1985), citing Unocal Corp. v. Mesa Petroleum Co., Del.Supr., 493 A.2d 946, 953 (1985).

When the Household Board of Directors is faced with a tender offer and a request to redeem the Rights [Plan], they will not be able to arbitrarily reject the offer. They will be held to the same fiduciary standards any other board of directors would be held to in deciding to adopt a defensive mechanism, the same standards as they were held to in originally approving the Rights Plan.

36. 8 Del.C. § 141(a). See Mills Acquisition Co. v. Macmillan, Inc., Del.Supr., 559 A.2d 1261, 1280 (1989).

37. 8 Del.C. § 141(a) states: "The business and affairs of every corporation organized under this chapter shall be managed by or under the direction of a board of directors, except as may be otherwise provided in this chapter or in its certificate of incorporation. If any such provision is made in the certificate of incorporation, the powers and duties conferred or imposed upon the board of directors by this chapter shall be exercised or performed to such extent and by such person or persons as shall be provided in the certificate of incorporation."

ration contains no provision purporting to limit the authority of the board in any way. The Delayed Redemption Provision, however, would prevent a newly elected board of directors from completely discharging its fundamental management duties to the corporation and its stockholders for six months. While the Delayed Redemption Provision limits the board of directors' authority in only one respect, the suspension of the Rights Plan, it nonetheless restricts the board's power in an area of fundamental importance to the shareholders—negotiating a possible sale of the corporation. Therefore, we hold that the Delayed Redemption Provision is invalid under Section 141(a), which confers upon any newly elected board of directors full power to manage and direct the business and affairs of a Delaware corporation.

In discharging the statutory mandate of Section 141(a), the directors have a fiduciary duty to the corporation and its shareholders. This unremitting obligation extends equally to board conduct in a contest for corporate control. The Delayed Redemption Provision prevents a newly elected board of directors from completely discharging its fiduciary duties to protect fully the interests of Quickturn and its stockholders.[41]

This Court has recently observed that "although the fiduciary duty of a Delaware director is unremitting, the exact course of conduct that must be charted to properly discharge that responsibility will change in the specific context of the action the director is taking with regard to either the corporation or its shareholders."[42] This Court has held "[t]o the extent that a contract, or a provision thereof, purports to require a board to act or not act in such a fashion as to limit the exercise of fiduciary duties, it is invalid and unenforceable."[43] The Delayed Redemption Provision "tends to limit in a substantial way the freedom of [newly elected] directors' decisions on matters of management policy."[44] Therefore, "it violates the duty of each [newly elected] director to exercise his own best judgment on matters coming before the board."[45]

In this case, the Quickturn board was confronted by a determined bidder that sought to acquire the company at a price the Quickturn board concluded was inadequate. Such situations are

41. See Moran v. Household International, Inc., 500 A.2d at 1354.

42. Malone v. Brincat, Del.Supr., 722 A.2d 5 (1998).

43. See Paramount Communications, Inc. v. QVC Network, Inc., 637 A.2d at 51 (emphasis added). See, e.g., Mills Acquisition Co. v. Macmillan, Inc., 559 A.2d at 1281 (holding that a "board of directors . . . may not avoid its active and direct duty of oversight in a matter as significant as the sale of corporate control"); Grimes v. Donald, Del.Ch., C.A. No. 13358, slip op. at 17,

Allen, C., 1995 WL 54441 (Jan. 11, 1995, revised Jan. 19, 1995), aff'd, Del.Supr., 673 A.2d 1207 (1996) ("[t]he board may not either formally or effectively abdicate its statutory power and its fiduciary duty to manage or direct the management of the business and affairs of this corporation").

44. Abercrombie v. Davies, Del.Ch., 123 A.2d 893, 899 (1956), rev'd on other grounds, Del.Supr., 130 A.2d 338 (1957).

45. Id.

common in corporate takeover efforts.[46] In Revlon, this Court held that no defensive measure can be sustained when it represents a breach of the directors' fiduciary duty. A fortiori, no defensive measure can be sustained which would require a new board of directors to breach its fiduciary duty. In that regard, we note Mentor has properly acknowledged that in the event its slate of directors are elected, those newly elected directors will be required to discharge their unremitting fiduciary duty to manage the corporation for the benefit of Quickturn and its stockholders.[47]

Conclusion

The Delayed Redemption Provision would prevent a new Quickturn board of directors from managing the corporation by redeeming the Rights Plan to facilitate a transaction that would serve the stockholders' best interests, even under circumstances where the board would be required to do so because of its fiduciary duty to the Quickturn stockholders. Because the Delayed Redemption Provision impermissibly circumscribes the board's statutory power under Section 141(a) and the directors' ability to fulfill their concomitant fiduciary duties, we hold that the Delayed Redemption Provision is invalid. On that alternative basis, the judgment of the Court of Chancery is AFFIRMED.

---

46. Revlon, Inc. v. MacAndrews & Forbes Holdings, Inc., 506 A.2d at 185.

47. Malone v. Brincat, Del.Supr., 722 A.2d 5 (1998).

Chapter XII

LEGAL CAPITAL AND DISTRIBUTIONS

SECTION 2. DIVIDENDS

Add the following case at p. 1357 of the Unabridged Edition, and p. 891 of the Concise Edition, at the end of Section 2(d):

KLANG v. SMITH'S FOOD & DRUG CENTERS, INC.

Supreme Court of Delaware, 1997.
702 A.2d 150.

Before VEASEY, C.J., WALSH, HOLLAND, HARTNETT and BERGER, JJ., constituting the Court en Banc.

VEASEY, Chief Justice:

This appeal calls into question the actions of a corporate board in carrying out a merger and self-tender offer. Plaintiff in this purported class action alleges that a corporation's repurchase of shares violated the statutory prohibition against the impairment of capital....

No corporation may repurchase or redeem its own shares except out of "surplus," as statutorily defined, or except as expressly authorized by provisions of the statute not relevant here. Balance sheets are not, however, conclusive indicators of surplus or a lack thereof. Corporations may revalue assets to show surplus, but perfection in that process is not required. Directors have reasonable latitude to depart from the balance sheet to calculate surplus, so long as they evaluate assets and liabilities in good faith, on the basis of acceptable data, by methods that they reasonably believe reflect present values, and arrive at a determination of the surplus that is not so far off the mark as to constitute actual or constructive fraud.

We hold that, on this record, the Court of Chancery was correct in finding that there was no impairment of capital and there were no disclosure violations. Accordingly, we affirm.

Facts

Smith's Food & Drug Centers, Inc. ("SFD") is a Delaware corporation that owns and operates a chain of supermarkets in the Southwestern United States. Slightly more than three years ago,

Jeffrey P. Smith, SFD's Chief Executive Officer, began to entertain suitors with an interest in acquiring SFD. At the time, and until the transactions at issue, Mr. Smith and his family held common and preferred stock constituting 62.1% voting control of SFD. Plaintiff and the class he purports to represent are holders of common stock in SFD.

On January 29, 1996, SFD entered into an agreement with The Yucaipa Companies ("Yucaipa"), a California partnership also active in the supermarket industry. Under the agreement, the following would take place:

> (1) Smitty's Supermarkets, Inc. ("Smitty's"), a wholly-owned subsidiary of Yucaipa that operated a supermarket chain in Arizona, was to merge into Cactus Acquisition, Inc. ("Cactus"), a subsidiary of SFD, in exchange for which SFD would deliver to Yucaipa slightly over 3 million newly-issued shares of SFD common stock;

> (2) SFD was to undertake a recapitalization, in the course of which SFD would assume a sizable amount of new debt, retire old debt, and offer to repurchase up to fifty percent of its outstanding shares (other than those issued to Yucaipa) for $36 per share; and

> (3) SFD was to repurchase 3 million shares of preferred stock from Jeffrey Smith and his family.

SFD hired the investment firm of Houlihan Lokey Howard & Zukin ("Houlihan") to examine the transactions and render a solvency opinion. Houlihan eventually issued a report to the SFD Board replete with assurances that the transactions would not endanger SFD's solvency, and would not impair SFD's capital in violation of 8 *Del.C.* § 160. On May 17, 1996, in reliance on the Houlihan opinion, SFD's Board determined that there existed sufficient surplus to consummate the transactions, and enacted a resolution proclaiming as much. On May 23, 1996, SFD's stockholders voted to approve the transactions, which closed on that day. The self-tender offer was over-subscribed, so SFD repurchased fully fifty percent of its shares at the offering price of $36 per share.

Disposition in the Court of Chancery

This appeal came to us after an odd sequence of events in the Court of Chancery. On May 22, 1996, the day before the transactions closed, plaintiff Larry F. Klang filed a purported class action in the Court of Chancery against Jeffrey Smith and his family, various members of the SFD Board, Yucaipa, Yucaipa's managing general partner Ronald W. Burkle, Smitty's and Cactus. On May 30, 1996, plaintiff filed an amended complaint as well as a motion to have the transactions voided or rescinded, advancing a variety of claims, only two of which are before us on appeal. First, he contended that the stock repurchases violated 8 *Del.C.* § 160[1] by impairing SFD's capital. Second, he alleged that SFD's directors violated their fiduciary duties by failing to disclose material facts relating to the transactions prior to obtaining stockholder approval.

After defendants answered the amended complaint, plaintiff took full discovery. The Court of Chancery heard plaintiff's motion to have the transactions rescinded, and released a Memorandum Opinion dismissing plaintiff's claims in full.

Plaintiff's Capital–Impairment Claim

A corporation may not repurchase its shares if, in so doing, it would cause an impairment of capital, unless expressly authorized by Section 160. A repurchase impairs capital if the funds used in the repurchase exceed the amount of the corporation's "surplus," defined by 8 *Del.C.* § 154 to mean the excess of net assets over the par value of the corporation's issued stock.[5]

Plaintiff asked the Court of Chancery to rescind the transactions in question as violative of Section 160. As we understand it, plaintiff's position breaks down into two analytically distinct arguments. First, he contends that SFD's balance sheets constitute conclusive evidence of capital impairment. He argues that the negative net worth that appeared on SFD's books following the repurchase compels us to find a violation of Section 160. Second, he suggests that even allowing the Board to "go behind the balance sheet" to calculate surplus does not save the transactions from violating Section 160. In connection with this claim, he attacks the SFD Board's off-balance-sheet method of calculating surplus on the theory that it does not adequately take into account all of SFD's assets and liabilities. Moreover, he argues that the May 17, 1996 resolution of the SFD Board conclusively refutes the Board's claim that revaluing the corporation's assets gives rise to the required surplus. We hold that each of these claims is without merit.

1. Section 160(a) provides:

(a) Every corporation may purchase, redeem, receive, take or otherwise acquire, own and hold, sell, lend exchange, transfer or otherwise dispose of, pledge, use and otherwise deal in and with its own shares; provided, however, that no corporation shall:

(1) Purchase or redeem its own shares of capital stock for cash or other property when the capital of the corporation is impaired or when such purchase or redemption would cause any impairment of the capital of the corporation, except that a corporation may purchase or redeem out of capital any of its own shares which are entitled upon any distribution of its assets, whether by dividend or in liquidation, to a preference over another class or series of its stock, or, if no shares entitled to such a preference are outstanding, any of its own shares, if such shares will be retired upon their acquisition and the capital of the corporation reduced in accordance with §§ 243 and 244 of this title.

5. Section 154 provides, "Any corporation may, by resolution of its board of directors, determine that only a part of the consideration ... received by the corporation for ... its capital stock ... shall be capital.... The excess ... of the net assets of the corporation over the amount so determined to be capital shall be surplus. Net assets means the amount by which total assets exceed total liabilities. Capital and surplus are not liabilities for this purpose."

SFD's balance sheets do not establish
a violation of 8 *Del.C.* § 160

In an April 25, 1996 proxy statement, the SFD Board released a pro forma balance sheet showing that the merger and self-tender offer would result in a deficit to surplus on SFD's books of more than $100 million. A balance sheet the SFD Board issued shortly after the transactions confirmed this result. Plaintiff asks us to adopt an interpretation of 8 *Del.C.* § 160 whereby balance-sheet net worth is controlling for purposes of determining compliance with the statute.[6] Defendants do not dispute that SFD's books showed a negative net worth in the wake of its transactions with Yucaipa, but argue that corporations should have the presumptive right to revalue assets and liabilities to comply with Section 160.

Plaintiff advances an erroneous interpretation of Section 160. We understand that the books of a corporation do not necessarily reflect the current values of its assets and liabilities. Among other factors, unrealized appreciation or depreciation can render book numbers inaccurate. It is unrealistic to hold that a corporation is bound by its balance sheets for purposes of determining compliance with Section 160. Accordingly, we adhere to the principles of *Morris v. Standard Gas & Electric Co.*[7] allowing corporations to revalue properly its assets and liabilities to show a surplus and thus conform to the statute.

It is helpful to recall the purpose behind Section 160. The General Assembly enacted the statute to prevent boards from draining corporations of assets to the detriment of creditors and the long-term health of the corporation.[8] That a corporation has not yet realized or reflected on its balance sheet the appreciation of assets is irrelevant to this concern. Regardless of what a balance sheet that has not been updated may show, an actual, though unrealized, appreciation reflects real economic value that the corporation may borrow against or that creditors may claim or levy upon. Allowing corporations to revalue assets and liabilities to reflect current realities complies with the statute and serves well the policies behind this statute.

The SFD Board appropriately revalued corporate
assets to comply with 8 *Del.C.* § 160.

Plaintiff contends that SFD's repurchase of shares violated Section 160 even without regard to the corporation's balance sheets. Plaintiff claims that the SFD Board was not entitled to rely on the solvency opinion of Houlihan, which showed that the transactions would not impair SFD's capital given a revaluation of

---

6. *See, e.g., Wright v. Heizer Corp.,* N.D.Ill., 503 F.Supp. 802, 810 (1980); *In re Kettle of Fried Chicken of America, Inc.,* 513 F.2d 807, 811 (6th Cir.1975).

7. *Morris v. Standard Gas & Electric Co.,* Del.Ch., 63 A.2d 577 (1949).

8. *See Pasotti v. United States Guardian Corp.,* 156 A. 255, at 257 (Del.Ch.1931).

corporate assets. The argument is that the methods that underlay the solvency opinion were inappropriate as a matter of law because they failed to take into account all of SFD's assets and liabilities. In addition, plaintiff suggests that the SFD Board's resolution of May 17, 1996 itself shows that the transactions impaired SFD's capital, and that therefore we must find a violation of 8 *Del.C.* § 160. We disagree, and hold that the SFD Board revalued the corporate assets under appropriate methods. Therefore the self-tender offer complied with Section 160, notwithstanding errors that took place in the drafting of the resolution.

On May 17, 1996, Houlihan released its solvency opinion to the SFD Board, expressing its judgment that the merger and self-tender offer would not impair SFD's capital. Houlihan reached this conclusion by comparing SFD's "Total Invested Capital" of $1.8 billion—a figure Houlihan arrived at by valuing SFD's assets under the "market multiple" approach—with SFD's long-term debt of $1.46 billion. This comparison yielded an approximation of SFD's "concluded equity value" equal to $346 million, a figure clearly in excess of the outstanding par value of SFD's stock. Thus, Houlihan concluded, the transactions would not violate 8 *Del.C.* § 160.

Plaintiff contends that Houlihan's analysis relied on inappropriate methods to mask a violation of Section 160. Noting that 8 *Del.C.* § 154 defines "net assets" as "the amount by which total assets exceeds total liabilities," plaintiff argues that Houlihan's analysis is erroneous as a matter of law because of its failure to calculate "total assets" and "total liabilities" as separate variables. In a related argument, plaintiff claims that the analysis failed to take into account all of SFD's liabilities, *i.e.*, that Houlihan neglected to consider current liabilities in its comparison of SFD's "Total Invested Capital" and long-term debt. Plaintiff contends that the SFD Board's resolution proves that adding current liabilities into the mix shows a violation of Section 160. The resolution declared the value of SFD's assets to be $1.8 billion, and stated that its "total liabilities" would not exceed $1.46 billion after the transactions with Yucaipa. As noted, the $1.46 billion figure described only the value of SFD's long-term debt. Adding in SFD's $372 million in current liabilities, plaintiff argues, shows that the transactions impaired SFD's capital.

We believe that plaintiff reads too much into Section 154. The statute simply defines "net assets" in the course of defining "surplus." It does not mandate a "facts and figures balancing of assets and liabilities" to determine by what amount, if any, total assets exceeds total liabilities.[9] The statute is merely definitional. It does not require any particular method of calculating surplus, but simply prescribes factors that any such calculation must include. Although courts may not determine compliance with Section 160 except by methods that fully take into account the assets and liabilities of the

---

9. *See Farland v. Wills*, Del.Ch., 1 Del. J.Corp.L. 467, 475 (1975).

corporation, Houlihan's methods were not erroneous as a matter of law simply because they used Total Invested Capital and long-term debt as analytical categories rather than "total assets" and "total liabilities."

We are satisfied that the Houlihan opinion adequately took into account all of SFD's assets and liabilities. Plaintiff points out that the $1.46 billion figure that approximated SFD's long-term debt failed to include $372 million in current liabilities, and argues that including the latter in the calculations dissipates the surplus. In fact, plaintiff has misunderstood Houlihan's methods. The record shows that Houlihan's calculation of SFD's Total Invested Capital is already net of current liabilities. Thus, subtracting long-term debt from Total Invested Capital does, in fact, yield an accurate measure of a corporation's net assets.

The record contains, in the form of the Houlihan opinion, substantial evidence that the transactions complied with Section 160. Plaintiff has provided no reason to distrust Houlihan's analysis. In cases alleging impairment of capital under Section 160, the trial court may defer to the board's measurement of surplus unless a plaintiff can show that the directors "failed to fulfill their duty to evaluate the assets on the basis of acceptable data and by standards which they are entitled to believe reasonably reflect present values."[10] In the absence of bad faith or fraud on the part of the board, courts will not "substitute [our] concepts of wisdom for that of the directors."[11] Here, plaintiff does not argue that the SFD Board acted in bad faith. Nor has he met his burden of showing that the methods and data that underlay the board's analysis are unreliable or that its determination of surplus is so far off the mark as to constitute actual or constructive fraud.[12] Therefore, we defer to the board's determination of surplus, and hold that SFD's self-tender offer did not violate 8 *Del.C.* § 160.

On a final note, we hold that the SFD Board's resolution of May 17, 1996 has no bearing on whether the transactions conformed to Section 160. The record shows that the SFD Board committed a serious error in drafting the resolution: the resolution states that, following the transactions, SFD's "total liabilities" would be no more than $1.46 billion. In fact, that figure reflects only the value of SFD's long-term debt. Although the SFD Board was guilty of sloppy work, and did not follow good corporate practices, it does not follow that Section 160 was violated. The statute requires only that there exist a surplus after a repurchase, not that the board memori-

---

10. *Morris*, 63 A.2d at 582.

11. *Id.* at 583.

12. We interpret 8 *Del.C.* § 172 to entitle boards to rely on experts such as Houlihan to determine compliance with 8 *Del.C.* § 160. Plaintiff has not alleged that the SFD Board failed to exercise reasonable

care in selecting Houlihan, nor that rendering a solvency opinion is outside Houlihan's realm of competence. Compare 8 *Del.C.* § 141(e) (providing that directors may rely in good faith on records, reports, experts, etc.).

alize the surplus in a resolution. The statute carves out a class of transactions that directors have no authority to execute, but does not, in fact, require any affirmative act on the part of the board. The SFD repurchase would be valid in the absence of any board resolution. A mistake in documenting the surplus will not negate the substance of the action, which complies with the statutory scheme . . . .

The judgment of the Court of Chancery is affirmed.

†